T0297798

C++ GEMS

SIGS Reference Library

Donald G. Firesmith
Editor-in-Chief

1. Object Methodology Overview, CD-ROM, *Doug Rosenberg*

2. Directory of Object Technology, *edited by Dale J. Gaumer*

3. Dictionary of Object Technology: The Definitive Desk Reference, *Donald G. Firesmith and Edward M. Eykholt*

4. Next Generation Computing: Distributed Objects for Business, *edited by Peter Fingar, Dennis Read, and Jim Stikeleather*

5. C++ Gems, *edited by Stanley B. Lippman*

6. OMT Insights: Perspectives on Modeling from the Journal of Object-Oriented Programming, *James Rumbaugh*

7. Best of Booch: Designing Strategies for Object Technology, *Grady Booch (Edited by Ed Eykholt)*

8. Wisdom of the Gurus: A Vision for Object Technology, *selected and edited by Charles F. Bowman*

9. Open Modeling Language (OML) Reference Manual, *Donald G. Firesmith, Brian Henderson-Sellers, and Ian Graham*

10. Java™ Gems: Jewels from *Java™ Report, collected and introduced by Dwight Deugo, Ph.D.*

11. The Netscape Programmer's Guide: Using OLE to Build Componentware™ Apps, *Richard B. Lam*

12. Advanced Object-Oriented Analysis and Design Using UML, *James J. Odell*

13. The Patterns Handbook: Techniques, Strategies, and Applications, *selected and edited by Linda Rising*

Additional Volumes in Preparation

C++ Gems

EDITED BY

STANLEY B. LIPPMAN

PUBLISHED BY THE PRESS SYNDICATE OF THE UNIVERSITY OF CAMBRIDGE
The Pitt Building, Trumpington Street, Cambridge, United Kingdom

CAMBRIDGE UNIVERSITY PRESS
The Edinburgh Building, Cambridge CB2 2RU, UK www.cup.cam.ac.uk
40 West 20th Street, New York, NY 10011-4211, USA www.cup.org
10 Stamford Road, Oakleigh, Melbourne 3166, Australia
Ruiz de Alarcón 13, 28014 Madrid, Spain

Published in association with SIG Books and Multimedia

First published by SIGS Books and Multimedia1996
First published by Cambridge University Press 1998
Reprinted 1999

Design and companion by Kevin Callahan
Cover design by Yin Moy

Typeset in Adobe Garamond

A catalog record for this book is available from the British Library

Library of Congress Cataloging in Publication Data is available

ISBN 0 13 570581 9 paperback

Transferred to digital printing 2003

About the Editor

Stanley B. Lippman currently is a Principal Software Engineer in the development technology group of Walt Disney Feature Animation. Prior to that, he spent over 10 years at Bell Laboratories. He began working with C++ back in 1985 and led the Laboratory's C++ cfront Release 3.0 and Release 2.1 compiler development teams. He was also a member of the Bell Laboratories Foundation Project under Bjarne Stroustrup and was responsible for the Object Model component of a research C++ programming environment.

Lippman is the author of two highly successful editions of *C++ Primer* and of the recently released *Inside the C++ Object Model,* both published by Addison-Wesley. He has spoken on and taught C++ worldwide.

Lippman recently "retired" as editor of *C++ Report,* which he edited for nearly four years.

FOREWORD

FOREWORDS FOR TECHNICAL BOOKS ARE TYPICALLY WRITTEN TO IMPRESS the potential reader with the technical expertise and skills of the author(s). In this case, the task is pointless: The authors whose work appears here represent a cross-section of the most widely known and respected C++ experts. Their technical skills are beyond question. But technical skills are only part of the equation. The *C++ Report* has been successful in getting topnotch technical people to write articles that are not only technically impressive but actually interesting and useful. There are several reasons for this:

- The authors really use this stuff. When we started the *C++ Report* in late 1989, we decided to target the people who wrote C++ code for a living. High-level management overviews were left to the competition. After all, we reasoned, there are more C++ programmers in the world than there are C++ managers. To write articles for programmers, we needed to find authors who were programmers.
- The editors really use this stuff. All the editors have been C++ programmers first and editors second. We have tended to choose articles that we personally found interesting. We were also able to spot (and reject) submissions that were polished but technically flawed.
- The articles are short. Ostensibly, this was to ensure that readers would get a condensed digest of the most critical material without having to invest a great deal of time. Short articles had other advantages for us. We had a competitor (now long since defunct) that was trying to be a forum for long articles. We were happy to concede this niche, because we thought that 20-page articles were the province of academic journals (who wants to

compete with CACM?). There was also the matter of perceived effort. Nobody was going to get rich at the rates we paid, so we were essentially asking people to write for the good of their careers and for the language in general. We figured we could get more authors if we asked them to write short articles.

- Technical content was more important than artistic beauty. As Stan Lippman comments in his introduction to this book, the first issue of the *C++ Report* had a far from polished appearance. This was deliberate; we even decided not to print it on glossy paper despite the fact that the cost was the same. We wanted to look like a newsletter, not a magazine. Obviously, today's *C++ Report* pays much more attention to appearances than we did in 1990, but unlike certain men's magazines, people really do look at the *Report* for the articles, not for the pictures.

Now that I've left AT&T Bell Labs and become a management type at Quantitative Data Systems, I've noticed one more interesting thing. The *C++ Report* has become a useful management tool, in large part because it does not try to cater to managers. Though I no longer read every line of code in the examples, I still learn a lot about C++ from reading the *Report.* Good ideas and good practices in this business tend to percolate from the bottom up. I trust the opinions and judgments of people who are doing actual work.

Stan has assembled a truly remarkable collection, valuable not just for its historical interest but also for its technical merit. The time spent reading these articles will be a valuable investment for anyone who uses C++.

Robert Murray
Irvine, California
January 1996

Introduction: The C++ Report—So Far

Stan Lippman

The C++ Report published its first issue in January 1989. Rob Murray, the founding editor, had agreed to take on the task back in October 1988. At the time, cfront release 2.0 was still in beta and would not be released for another nine months (we still had to add `const` and `static` member functions, abstract base classes, and support for pure virtual functions, apart from any debugging that remained). Bjarne [Stroustrup] estimates at the time there were approximately 15,000 C++ users[1]—enough perhaps to fill the Royal Albert Hall, but support a magazine devoted to covering C++? Nobody was sure. As Rick Friedman, the founder and publisher of SIGS Publications, writes[2]:

> Just between you and me, I must confess I was worried. There I was, traveling back on the train from Liberty Corner, New Jersey, having just convinced AT&T Bell Labs' Rob Murray that he should edit a start-up publication on C++. "We only need 1,000 subscribers to make it all go," I told him confidently. Returning to my office, I looked dazedly out the window at the passing countryside, my head buzzing with strategies on how and where to find the critical mass of readers.
>
> You see, this was back in October 1988 . . . and it was unclear which, if any, OOP language would emerge as winner. Several software pundits, including Bertrand Meyer, OOP's notorious enfant terrible, vociferously predicted doom for C++. But all the very early signs indicated to me that C++ would eventually gain popularity. It would then need an open forum, I postulated. So I rolled the dice.

Or, as Barbara Moo, my supervisor at Bell Laboratories for many years used to say, "Everybody into the pool." Let's try to remember the C++ landscape back then.

October 1988: Borland would not provide its C++ compiler until May, 1990. Microsoft, after a false start, lurched across the compiler line, led by Martin O'Riordan, in March 1992. (Martin and Jon Carolan were the first to port cfront to the PC back in 1986 under Carolan's Glockinspiel company. Greg Comeau also provided an early cfront port to the PC.) Who else was out there back then? Michael Tiemann provided his g++ GNU compiler, version 1.13, in December 1987. Michael Ball and Steve Clamage delivered TauMetric's commercial compiler to Oregon Software in January 1988. Walter Bright's PC compiler was brought to the market in June 1988 through Zortech (now owned by Symantec). The full set of available books on C++ was less than a fistful. My book, for example, *C++ Primer,* was still under development, as was the Dewhurst and Stark book; Coplien hadn't even begun his yet.

The first issue of the *C++ Report* in fact proved to be a (relatively) smashing success: a first printing of 2,000 copies sold out; a second printing of 2,000 also sold out. Were you to look at the first issue now, honestly, I think you'd feel more than a tad disappointed. There's nothing glossy or hi-tech about it: it reminds me of the early cfront releases. No fancy color, but a lot of content. The first issue is 16 pages, except the back page isn't a page at all: it has a subscription form and a blank bottom half that looks like a hotel postcard you get free if you poke around the middle drawer of the hotel room desk. Bjarne begins the first issue of the first page with an article on the soon-to-begin C++ standards work. There are five advertisements: three for C++ compilers (Oregon Software, Oasys, and Apollo Computers—back then, anyway, AT&T not only didn't take out any ads for cfront but didn't have a full-time marketing representative), and two for training (Semaphore and something called the Institute for Zero Defect Software, which, not surprisingly with a mandate like that, no longer seems to be in operation). No libraries, no programming support environments, no GUI builders: C++ was still in Lewis and Clark territory.

The *Report* published 10 issues per year for its first three years, at 16 pages in 1989, 24 pages in 1990, and 32 pages in 1991. 1991 was an important watershed for C++: we (that is, Bell Laboratories) had finally nudged cfront release 2.0—then the de facto language standard, and the first to provide multiple inheritance, class instance operators `new` and `delete`, `const` and static member functions, etc.—out the door. More important, perhaps, the *Annotated C++ Reference Manual* (a.k.a. the ARM) by Bjarne and Peggy Ellis had been published,* as well as Bjarne's second edition of his classic *The C++ Programming*

* This is important for three reasons: (1) the obvious reason, of course, is that it provided a (reasonably) concise and complete (well, perhaps templates were a necessary exception!) definition of the language, (2) it provided detailed commentary on implementation strategy, and (3) the most significant reason is that it had undergone an industry-wide review incorporating criticisms/comments from companies such as Microsoft, Apple, IBM, Thinking Machines, etc.

Language (more than doubling in size).† C++ users were estimated to have reached near to ½ million,[2] and 1992 promised the first C++ compilers from Microsoft and IBM. Clearly, C++ was no longer a niche language. Rick's roll of the dice had come up a winner.

In 1992, beginning with the combined March/April issue, *The C++ Report* transformed itself from a sort of newsletter caterpillar into a full-blown magazine butterfly: 72 to 80 glossy, full-color pages, with imaginative cover art and feature illustrations. Wow. As Rob planned the transition from newsletter to magazine, he also worked out the editorial transition that saw me succeed him as editor. As Rob wrote back then:

> With this issue, I am stepping down as editor of *The C++ Report.* It has been both exhilarating and exhausting to manage the transition from newsletter to magazine. . . . However, there are only so many hours in a day, and while editing the *Report* has been a blast, my primary interests are in compiler and tools development, not the publishing business. The growth of *The C++ Report* (from a 16-page newsletter to an 80-page magazine) has reached the point where something has to give. Besides, it's been three-and-a-half years (35 issues!), and it's time for me to move on.

As Rob moved on, I moved in. At the time, I was hip-deep in release 3.0. Rob was just down the hall, of course, and so the amount of work required to push out an issue was blatantly obvious with each scowl and slump of the shoulder as Rob would rush by.‡ Barbara Moo, my manager, was more than a little dubious about the wisdom of taking on an obviously impossible task on top of the already seemingly impossible task of nailing down templates and getting virtual base classes right! Rick Friedman, of course, concerned over the retirement of Rob just at the time the magazine most needed a steady hand (after all, it had just more than doubled in size and cost of production), was also somewhat dubious: was I serious about the position and committed to seeing it through? Of course, I didn't let on to either exactly how dubious the whole thing seemed to me as well. As Barbara had so often said, "Everybody into the pool!"

---

† Bjarne was abundantly engaged during this period, in fact: through Release 2.0, Bjarne was the primary implementor of cfront, plus pushing the evolution of the language and serving as arbitrator and chief spokesperson in articles (not a few of which appeared in the C++ Report), on the internet (particularly comp.lang.c++), and at conferences.

‡ Of course, this is more than slightly exaggerated for poetic effect!

What I wrote back then was the following:

> This is actually the second time I've followed in Rob's footsteps. The first time was back in May 1986 when I volunteered to work on getting Release 1.1 of the then barely known AT&T C++ Translator out the door. Rob had been responsible for the 1.0 release, and had it not been for his extraordinary patience and help, I might now be writing about, oh, perhaps the proposed object-oriented extensions to COBOL or something as similarly *not* C++.
>
> But that was then. This is now. Only it's been deja vu all over again, at least with regard to Rob's extraordinary patience and help in getting me up to speed as editor. As to the actual outcome, well, happily, there is a very able SIGS support staff and a great set of writers to help me steer clear of the shoals.

Being editor involves a number of simultaneous tasks, and one has to nurse each issue into print: read the material as it is submitted, check the proofs, then give the issue one final read-through prior to publication. For a while, I was even let in on the artwork, design, pull quotes, and "decks." This means that usually two issues are being juggled at one time: the issue going to press and the next issue, which is beginning production. At the same time, one is beating the bushes for authors, nudging this or that reluctant colleague to finally sit down and write the article he or she had been talking about for—oh, my, has it really been over a year now? Additionally, there are product reviews to schedule and get the logistics right on, and—oh, yeah—all those pesty phone calls. It gets even worse if you're preposterous enough to think of writing for each issue as well. Add to that, of course, your full-time day job (which spills over into the night more often than not), and you get the idea of why, traditionally (that is, at least, for both Rob and myself), an editor's stint is limited to 3.5 years.

The *C++ Report* was and remains a unique magazine due to its unprecedented active support by the pioneers of the language. Bjarne has had two or three articles in the magazine in each of its first seven years: the run-time type identification paper proposal, for example, was first published here (the combined March/April, 1992 issue). More important than a single voice, however, is the voice of the community itself: Jerry Schwarz, inventor of the iostream library and of the Schwarz counter idiom for handling the initialization of static variables, for example, first wrote of the technique here (it was the feature story of the second issue). Michael Tiemann, Doug Lea, Andy Koenig, myself, Tom Cargill, Stephen Dewhurst, Michael Ball, Jim Coplien, Jim Waldo, Martin Carroll, Mike Vilot, and Grady Booch—nearly all the original C++ pioneers found a home here at *The C++ Report* thanks to Rob. And as a new generation of C++ expertise evolved, those individuals, too, were sought out, and many found a voice at the *Report*: Scott Meyers, Josée Lajoie, John Vlissides, Pete Becker, Doug Schmidt, Steve Vinoski, Lee Nackman, and John Barton, to name just a few. Moreover, *The C++ Report* has been, traditionally, not a magazine of professional writers but of professional programmers—and of programmers with busy schedules. This has been true of its editors as well.

As had Rob, I remained editor for three-and-a-half years, from June 1992 through December 1995. Finally, I was overwhelmed by having hauled my family and career both physically across the American continent and mentally across the continent that separates Bell Laboratories from Walt Disney Feature Animation. Beginning with the January 1996 issue, Doug Schmidt assumed the editorship of *The C++ Report* (presumably until June 1998 :-).[§] Doug is "different" from both Rob and myself—he's tall, for one thing :-). More significantly, he is outside the gang within Bell Labs that originally brought you C++. As Doug writes in his first editorial:

> This month's *C++ Report* . . . marks the first issue where the editor wasn't a member of the original group of cfront developers at AT&T Bell Labs. Both Stan and founding editor Rob Murray . . . were "producers" of the first C++ compiler (cfront). In contrast, I'm a "consumer" of C++, who develops reusable communication frameworks. . . .
>
> Early generations of the *C++ Report* focused extensively on C++ as a programming language. . . . As the ANSI/ISO C++ standard nears completion, however, the challenges and opportunities for C++ over the next few years are increasingly in the frameworks and applications we build and use, rather than in the language itself. In recent years, Stan has been broadening the magazine to cover a range of application-related topics. I plan to continue in this direction. . . .
>
> The world of programming has changed significantly since the mid-1980s. Personal computers have become the norm, the standard mode of interacting with these computers are graphical user interfaces, the Internet has become wildly popular, and object-oriented techniques are now firmly in the mainstream. So, to compete successfully in today's marketplace, C++ programmers must become adept at much more than just programming language features. . . . I'm excited to have an opportunity to help shepherd the *C++ Report* into its third generation.

[§] Informally, we speak of this as the "Murray precedent."

As Doug begins sheparding the *C++ Report* into its third generation, it seems appropriate to look back over the first two generations. This collection covers the first seven years of the *C++ Report*, from January 1989 through December 1995. The most difficult aspect of putting this collection together has not been in finding sufficient material but in having to prune, then prune back, then prune back even further. What were the criteria for selection, apart from general excellence (which in itself did not prove to be a sufficient exclusion policy)?

- ***Relevancy for today's programmer.*** I decided not to include any piece (with the possible exception of Bjarne's two pages of reflection at the start of the C++ standardization effort) whose interest was primarily historical. So, for example, I chose not to run the RTTI article by Lenkov and Stroustrup, the article "As Close to C as Possible but No Closer" by Koenig and Stroustrup, or the controversy on multiple inheritance carried out in these pages through articles by Cargill, Schwarz, and Carroll. I believe that every article included in this collection offers insights into C++ for today's programmers.
- ***Not otherwise readily available.*** Scott Meyers (his column: "Using C++ Effectively") Martin Carroll and Peggy Ellis (their column: "C++ Trade-Offs"), myself (my column: "C++ Primer"), and Grady Booch and Mike Vilot (their column: "Object-Oriented Analysis and Design") have all written columns of great excellence in the *C++ Report* (well, I'll leave the characterization of my column to others). These columns, however, are all generally available in book form—many of the columns marked the first appearance of material that later made up leading texts on C++ and object-oriented design.
- ***Exclude tutorial material on the language itself.*** Although we have carried some of the best introductory pieces on the language, the pieces by themselves strike me as disjointed and inappropriate in a collection serving the intermediate and experienced C++ programmer.

The collection is bookended by two assessments by Bjarne of the process of C++ standardization. It begins at the beginning: the first article (on the first page) of the very first issue (Volume 1, Number 1) of *The C++ Report:* "Standardizing C++." In the first sentence of that article, Bjarne writes:

> When I was first asked, "Are you standardizing C++?" I'm afraid I laughed.

The collection ends with, if I may, Bjarne's last laugh: in Volume 7 (each volume, of course, represents a year), Number 8, Bjarne provides "A Perspective on ISO C++" following completion of the public review period for the draft working paper of the standard. His conclusion?

> C++ and its standard library are better than many considered possible and better than many are willing to believe. Now we "just" have to use it and support it better.

Sandwiched in between these two articles by Bjarne are, I believe, a collection of articles that will help the C++ programmer do just that! The collection is organized around four general topics: design, programming idioms, applications, and language.

Prefacing these four sections is a language retrospective on C++ by Tom Cargill in which he looks back on 10 years of programming in C++. My first exposure to C++ was through a talk Tom gave back in 1984 describing the architecture of his Pi (process inspector) debugger. As it happens, that program was the first use Tom had made of C++. When I left Bell Laboratories in 1994, it was still my debugger of choice.

The Design section is broken into two subsections, Library Design in C++ and Software Design/Patterns in C++. The subsection on library design is a set of four pieces I commissioned for the June 1994 issue. I asked the providers of prominent foundation class libraries (Doug Lea on the GNU C++ Library, Tom Keffer of Rogue Wave Software, Martin Carroll on the Standard Component Library, and Grady Booch and Mike Vilot on the Booch Components) to discuss the architecture of their libraries. In addition, I asked Bjarne if he would write a general introduction to library design under C++ (he later incorporated portions of this article into his book *Design and Evolution of C++*). It was my favorite issue that I put together as editor, and I am pleased to be able to present four-fifths of it here.[||]

The software design/patterns subsection contains one piece each on patterns by James Coplien and John Vlissides, two extraordinary pioneers in the field who, while poles apart in their approach, together form what I think of as a fearful

---

[||] Unfortunately, we were not able to secure permission to reprint Martin Carroll's excellent article. I would still heartily recommend it, particularly as a counterpoint to the excellent Booch/Vilot article.

symmetry—getting the two as alternating columnists is something I consider close to my crowning editorial achievement. The other two selections are excellent general design pieces, one by Doug Schmidt, which happens to be one of my favorite pieces in the collection, and a second by Steve Dewhurst, who in fact taught me most of what I first learned about C++ while we worked on competing C++ compilers within Bell Labs' Summit Facility, which would later be spun off into UNIX Software Labs, and then subsequently sold off to Novell.

The section on C++ Programming idioms begins with a typically witty and insightful selection by Andy Koenig from his C++ Traps and Pitfalls column with the provocative title, "How to Write Buggy Code." This is followed by a selection from Tom Cargill's C++ Gadfly column in which he shows just how easy it is to unintentionally write buggy code when trying to provide for dynamic arrays. Avoiding problems when programming with threads under exception handling is the focus of Pete Becker's article. (Doug Schmidt's earlier article in the software design section also discusses thread syncronization.) Under the category of sheer programming zest, Steve Teale, in his article "Transplanting a Tree-Recursive LISP Algorithm in C++," first provides a correct implementation, then a progressively more efficient ones, in the process moving from a LISP to C++ state of mind.

Three common C++ programming idioms still difficult to get right are the simulation of virtual constructors (I've made a bookend of Dave Jordan's original article defining the idiom with an article by Tom Cargill in which he illustrates how the idiom can go wrong), static variable initialization (I've included Jerry Schwarz's original article describing the problem and presenting his solution within his implementation of the iostream library. I had hoped to bookend that with a piece¶ by Martin Carroll and Peggy Ellis reviewing current thinking about static initialization, but unfortunately we could not work out the reprint permissions), and returning a class object by value (another two article bookending: Michael Tiemann's original short article, and a more extensive recent article by myself**).

The third section, A Focus on Applications, presents three case studies of using C++ in the "real world"—an early and quite influential paper by Jim Waldo on the benefits on converting an application from Pascal to C++ for the Apollo workstation (since purchased by Hewlett-Packard), a description of the use of C++ in the financial markets within Goldman, Sachs, and Company by Tasos Kontogiorgos and Michael Kim, and a discussion of work to provide an

---

¶ "Dealing with Static Initialization in C++," *The C++ Report,* Volume 7, Number 5.

** This piece has been reworked in my book, *Inside the C++ Object Model.*

object-oriented framework for I/O support within the AS/400 operating system at the IBM Rochester Laboratory by Bill Berg and Ed Rowlance. The section ends with an outstanding three-piece introduction to distributed object computing in C++ coauthored by Doug Schmidt and Steve Vinoski.

Templates, exception handling, and memory management through operators `new` and `delete` are the focus of the final section, A Focus on Language. C++ programming styles and idioms have been profoundly transformed since the introduction (within cfront, release 3.0, in 1991) and continued experience with templates. Originally viewed as a support for container classes such as Lists and Arrays, templates now serve as the foundation for, among a growing list of uses:

- Generic programming (the Standard Template Library [STL]: I've included a tutorial overview of STL by Mike Vilot and an article by Bjarne on his assessement of STL).
- As an idiom for attribute mix-in where, for example, memory allocation strategies (see the Booch/Vilot article in the section on library design) are parameterized.
- As a technique for template metaprograms, in which class expression templates are evaluated at compile-time rather than run-time, providing significant performance improvements ("Using C++ Template Metaprograms" by Todd Veldhuizen).
- As an idiom for "traits," a useful idiom for associating related types, values, and functions with a template parameter type without requiring that they be defined as members of the type ("A New and Useful Template Technique: Traits" by Nathan Myers).
- As an idiom for "expression templates," an idiom in which logical and algebraic expressions can be passed to functions as arguments and inlined directly within function bodies ("Expression Templates" by Todd Veldhuizen).
- As a method of callback support ("Callbacks in C++ Using Template Functors" by Richard Hickey)

John Barton and Lee Nackman, in the final two articles in this section, "What's That Template Argument About" and "Algebra for C++ Operators," use the construction of, respectively, a family of multidimensional array class templates and a system of class templates to define a consistent and complete set of arithmetic operators, to explore advance template design techniques.

Nathan Myers' article on *Memory Management in C++* points out a potential weakness in class specific memory management and proposes the alternative solution of a global memory manager—one that eventually became part of the Rogue Wave product offering as Heap.h++.

Speaking of heaps, if you "do windows," Pete Becker's article, "Memory Management, DLLs and C++," is about a particularly tricky area of memory management under Windows. Not to worry if you don't, for, as Pete writes, "This article really isn't about Windows, it's about memory management and multiple heaps. If that's a subject that interests you, read on." You can't lose.

Steve Clamage, who currently chairs the C++ Standards committee, alternated with Mike Ball on a column that had the agreed-upon title of "A Can of Worms," but which, despite my best efforts, each issue was titled "Implementing C++." Steve's article "Implementing `new` and `delete`" is the best of an excellent series that came to a premature end with the ending of their company, TauMetric. Mike and Steve are currently both at Sun.

Although I've worked on relatively high-end UNIX workstations both within Bell Laboratories (Sun Sparc) and Disney Feature Animation (SGI Indigo2), and done all my professional sofware development for the last 10 years in C++, I've never yet had access to a C++ compiler that supported exception handling. In addition, it is the only major C++ language feature that I've never had an opportunity to implement. Josee Lajoie's "Exception Handling: Behind the Scenes" is a fine tutorial both on the language facility and its implementation. "Exceptions and Windowing Systems" by Pete Becker looks at the problems of handling exceptions in event-driven windowing systems. Tom Cargill's article, "Exception Handling: A False Sense of Security," looks at the problems of handling exceptions in our programs in general. As Tom shows, exception handling can prove exceptionally hard to get right. Luckily for me, I suppose, I've not as yet even had a chance to try.

Whenever something exceptional occurs—in the program of one's life, I mean—such as accepting or passing on this or that job, for example, in which one's life is changed forever, but which, on reflection, seems overwhelmingly arbitrary and knotted by happenstance, for a brief moment the staggering multiplicity of "what if" and "as it happened" that pave the apparent inevitability of our present is revealed. The success of *The C++ Report,* of course, was never guaranteed; it truly was a roll of the dice back then, and at any number of different points, things could have gone very differently. That they went well is a testament to, on the one hand, the commitment of the publisher, and, on the other hand, the hard work of the editors—but, more than either, it is a testament to the extraordinary quality and breadth of the writers that combined to give voice to each issue. Finally, this collection, then, is intended as a celebration of that voice.

REFERENCES

1. Stroustrup, B. *The Design and Evolution of C++*, Addison-Wesley Publishing Company, Reading, MA 1994.
2. Friedman, R. "Creating creating," *The C++ Report,* 5(4), May, 1993.
3. Murray, R., and S. Lippman. "Editor's Corner," *The C++ Report,* 4(5), June, 1992.
4. Schmidt, D. "Editor's Corner," *The C++ Report,* 8(1), January, 1996.

Contents

Section Two • A Focus on Programming Idioms

C++ Programming

Special Programming Idioms

Section Three • A Focus on Applications

Experience Case Studies

Distributing Object Computing in C++

Section Four · A Focus on Language

Operators New and Delete

Exception Handling

Templates

Standard Template Library

Last Thoughts

First Thoughts

STANDARDIZING C++

BJARNE STROUSTRUP

WHEN I WAS FIRST ASKED "ARE YOU STANDARDIZING C++?" I'M AFRAID I laughed. That was at OOPSLA'87, and I explained that although C++ was growing fast we had a single manual, a single—and therefore standard—implementation, and that everybody working on new implementations was talking together. No, standards problems were for older languages where commercial rivalries and bad communications within a large fragmented user community were causing confusion, not for us. I was wrong, and I apologized to her the next time we met. I was wrong for several reasons; all are related to the astounding speed with which the C++ community is growing.

Consider C. Five years went by from the publication of K&R in 1978 until formal standardization began in 1983 and if all goes well we will have ANSI and ISO standards in 1989. For C++ to follow this path we should begin standardizing in 1990 or 1991. This way we would also be ready with a good standards document by the time the ANSI C standard expires in 1994. However, C++ is already in use on almost the same variety of machines as C is and the projects attempted with C++ are certainly no less ambitious than those being tackled using C. Consequently, the demands for portability of C++ programs and for a precise specification of the language and its assorted libraries are already approaching those of C. This is so even though C++ is about 10 years younger than C, even though C++ contains features that are more advanced than commonly seen in nonexperimental languages, and even though C++ is still being completed by the addition of essential features.

It follows that, because we *as users* want to port our C++ programs from machine to machine and from C++ compiler to C++ compiler, we must somehow ensure that we *as compilers and tool builders* agree on a standard language and achieve a minimum of order in the difficult area of libraries and execution environments. To give a concrete example, it is nice that you can buy three different C++ compilers for a Sun 3, but it is absurd that each has its own organization of the "standard" header files. This is unsatisfactory to suppliers of implementations and unacceptable to users.

On the other hand, standardizing a language isn't easy, and formal standardization of a relatively new—but heavily used—language is likely to be even harder. To complicate matters further, C++ is also quite new to most of its users, new uses of the language are being found daily, many C++ implementors have little or no C++ experience, and major language extensions—such as parameterized types and exception handling—are still only planned or experimental. Most issues of standard libraries and programming and execution environments are speculative or experimental.

So what do we do? The C+ + reference manual[1] clearly needs revision. The C++ reference manual and the assorted papers and documentation that have appeared since *The C++ Programming Language* are not a bad description of C++, but they are a bit dated and not sufficiently precise or comprehensive enough to serve the needs of a very diverse and only loosely connected group of users and implementors.

Three kinds of improvements are needed:

1. Making the manual clearer, more detailed, and more comprehensive.

2. Describing features added since 1985.

3. Revising the manual in the light of the forthcoming ANSl and ISO C standard.

Furthermore, this needs to be done *now.* We cannot afford to wait for several years. I have for some time now been working on a revision of the reference manual. In addition, Margaret Ellis and I are working on a book containing that manual as well as some background information, explanation of design choices, program fragments to illustrate language rules, information about implementation techniques, and elaboration on details—it will not be a tutorial. It should be complete in the summer of 1989.

Thoughts of a reference manual revision will send shivers down the spines of seasoned programmers. Language revisions inevitably cause changes that inconvenience users and create work for implementors. Clearly, a major task here is to avoid "random" incompatible changes. Some incompatible changes are necessary to avoid gratuitous incompatibilities with ANSI C, but most of those are of a nature that will make them a greater nuisance to C++ compiler writers than to C++ users. Almost all of the rest are pure extensions and simple resolutions of issues that were left obscure by the original manual. Many of those have been resolved over the years and some were documented in papers[2,4,6] and in the release notes of the AT&T C++ translator.[7]

For the manual revision, I rely on a significant section of the C++ user community for support. In particular, a draft of the new reference manual is being submitted for review and comment to dozens of individuals and groups—most outside AT&T. Naturally, I also draw heavily on the work of the C++ groups within AT&T.

I would also like to take this opportunity to remind you that C++ isn't silly putty; there are things that neither I nor anyone else could do to C++ even if we wanted to. The only extensions to C++ that we are likely to see are those that can be added in an upwardly compatible manner—notably parameterized types[5] and exception handling.[3]

When this revision is done, and assuming that it is done well, will that solve our problems? Of course not; but it will solve many problems for many people for some years to come. These years we can use to gather experience with C++ and eventually to go through the elaborate and slow process of formal standardization.

In the shorter term, the greatest benefit to C++ users would be if the C++ suppliers would sit down with some of the experienced users to agree on a standard set of header files. In particular, it is extremely important to the users that this standard set of header files minimize the differences between operating systems including BSD, UNIX System V, and MS/DOS. It looks to me as if we are making progress toward this goal.

In the slightly longer term, execution environment problems will have to be faced. Naturally, we will have standardized (ANSI) C libraries and a very small number of genuine C++ standard libraries available, but we can go much further than that. There is an enormous amount of work that could be done to help programmers avoid reinventing the wheel. In particular, somebody ought to try to coordinate efforts to provide high-quality C++ toolkits for the variety of emerging windowing environments. I don't know of anyone who has taken this difficult task upon themselves. Maybe a standing technical committee under the auspices of one of the technical societies could provide a semi-permanent forum for people to discuss these issues and recommend topics and directions for standards as the technologies mature?

Does this mean that you should avoid C++ for a year or so? Or that you should wait for five years for ISO C++? Or that you must conclude that C++ is undefined or unstable? Not at all. C++ is as well defined as C was for the first 15 years of its life and the new documentation should improve significantly over that. You might have to review the code and the tools you build this year after the new manual and the compilers that support it start to appear next year, but that ought to be a minor effort measured in hours (not days) per 25,000 lines of C++.

REFERENCES

1. Stroustrup, B., *The C++ Programming Language,* Addison-Wesley, Reading, MA 1985.
2. Stroustrup, B. The Evolution of C++: 1985-1987, Proc. USENIX C++ workshop, Santa Fe, Nov. 1987.
3. Stroustrup, B. Possible Directions for C++, Proc. USENIX C++ workshop, Santa Fe, Nov. 1987.
4. Stroustrup, B. Type-Safe Linkage for C++, Proc. USENIX C++ conference, Denver, Oct. 1988.
5. Stroustrup, B. Parameterized types for C++, Proc. USENIX C++ conference, Denver, Oct. 1988.
6. Lippman, S., and B. Stroustrup. Pointers to Class Members in C++, Proc. USENIX C++ conference, Denver, Oct. 1988.
7. UNIX System V, AT&T C++ Translator Release Notes 2.0 (preliminary).

Retrospective

Tom Cargill
cargill@csn.org
71574,1374@compuserve.com

As I try to concentrate on the topic that I had originally chosen for this column in December 1993, my thoughts keep returning to December 1983. Ten years ago this month, my first C++ program (written at Bell Labs, Murray Hill, NJ) had progressed to the point that I could offer it to friendly users for alpha testing. Versions of that code have now been in daily use for a decade. Moreover, the code has been modified and extended by several projects within AT&T to meet diverse needs. With respect to that program, C++ and object technology delivered the goods: a decade later the code is robust, maintainable, and reusable. In this column, I would like to reflect on why I think the code succeeded.

When I started using C++ in 1983, most of my programming in the previous decade had been in B, C, and other languages from the BCPL family. As a competent programmer, I could write working code in these languages. During development and for a short period thereafter, I considered each program I wrote to be an elegant masterpiece. However, after a year or so of maintenance, most programs were in a state that made me wince at the thought of touching them.

My reaction to my own software changed radically when I started programming in C++. Over a relatively short period, I found myself producing better programs. I don't attribute this change to any sudden expansion of my intellect. I attribute the change to using a better tool: when I program in C++, I am a better programmer. I write better code in C++ because the language imposes a discipline on my thinking. C++ makes me think harder about what I am trying to accomplish.

That first C++ program I wrote was a debugger called Pi, for "process inspector." I had written debuggers on and off since 1970—I was a "domain expert." I knew why debuggers were hard to create, port, and maintain: details from so many related hardware and software systems converge in a debugger. A debugger has to deal with the properties of an operating system, a processor, and a compiler (both code generation and symbol-table representation). A typical code fragment from a debugger written in C from that era would extract some information from a symbol table file, combine it with the contents of an obscure machine register, and use the result to navigate through raw operating system data structures. This kind of code (of which I wrote my fair share) is just too brittle to maintain effectively for any length of time. Therefore, a major goal of the Pi design was to bring some order to this chaos, that is, to find some way to separate the debugger's concerns into independent components.

In retrospect, encapsulation of various parts of the debugger would have been sufficient reason to move to C++. However, my real motivation was the user interface that I wanted to offer with Pi. I had observed that programmers using debuggers on classical "glass teletypes" wasted a lot of time copying information from the screen to a notepad, only to feed the same information back into the debugger a few seconds later through the keyboard. I had also been using and programming an early multiwindow bitmap graphics terminal (the Blit). I thought that a browser-like interface would work well for a debugger. I could imagine using an interface where, for example, the programmer could select and operate on an entry in a callstack backtrace in one window to highlight the corresponding line of source text in another, scroll through the source, operate on a statement to set a breakpoint, and so forth. I could imagine using such an interface, but I didn't know how to build it in C.

The descriptions of C++ that I had heard from Bjarne Stroustrup and a little that I knew about how user interfaces were built in Smalltalk suggested that I could build my user interface if every significant image on the screen mapped to a corresponding object within the debugger. The debugger would carry thousands of related but autonomous objects, any one of which might be the recipient of the next stimulus from the user. The only hope I saw for managing this architecture was to use objects, and C++ had just appeared as a viable tool. (In 1983, C++ was viable for use in a research environment.)

Driven by its user interface, Pi's object architecture spread throughout the rest of the code. As my understanding of object-oriented techniques improved, I found that objects simplified many difficult problems. For example, for various reasons, a debugger needs to read information from the address space of its target process. Interpreting the contents of memory correctly depends on the alignment and byte-order properties of the target processor. In Pi's architecture, the responsibility for fetching from the address space of the target process lies with an object that encapsulates the interface to the operating system. However, the fetch operation does not deliver raw memory. Instead, the fetch delivers an object that can later be interrogated to yield various interpretations of that piece of memory, such as char, short, int, float, and so on. Using one object to hide the operating system and another object to defer the decision about the interpretation of memory was a significant simplification, especially in the debugger's expression evaluator.

A debugger must extract symbol table information from whatever representation the compiler chooses to leave it in. Over the years, I had suffered enough in handling format changes from compilers and in moving debuggers between compilers that I chose to insulate most of Pi from the compiler's format. I developed a symbol table abstraction for Pi that reflected program syntax rather than any particular compiler's format. Pi's symbol table is a collection of classes that captures abstractions like statements, variables, types, and so forth. From the perspective of the rest of the debugger, the symbol table is a network of such objects. For example, a function object may be interrogated to deliver the set of statement objects within it, each of which maps to a location that can carry a breakpoint. The symbol table abstraction made other parts of Pi dramatically simpler than they would have been if a conventional approach had been used. Moreover, inheritance simplified the symbol table itself, because the common properties of all symbol classes were captured in a base class.

The symbol table abstraction was fine. However, its performance characteristics in the first implementation were awful. There was neither the time nor the space to build a complete network of symbol objects for any but the smallest programs. The correction was straightforward: keep the abstraction, but change the implementation. A critical observation is that most debugging sessions need only a handful of symbols. There is no need to build the complete network. The second implementation used a "lazy" strategy, in which a symbol object was created only when another part of the debugger needed it. For example, until the user scrolls a source text window to display a function, there is no need to create the statement objects from within that function. The mechanism is transparent to the remainder of the program. If asked for a statement object that had not yet been created, the function object asks a symbol table server to build that part of the network so that the statement object can be delivered. Theoretically, there is nothing to prevent the use of this technique in any language, but without an encapsulation mechanism, I don't believe that it would be sufficiently robust to survive for any length of time. I would not have tried anything like it in C. In C++ it was straightforward and reliable.

As I became more comfortable with objects, I found myself using them naturally, even when the benefits were not manifest. Initially, I intended Pi to be a single process debugger, that is, a debugger that manages just one target process. I didn't want to contemplate the complexities of controlling multiple errant processes. Programmers who needed to debug multiple processes would have to run multiple copies of the debugger. However, I did decide to gather all the state and all the code for managing the single process into a class called `Process`, even though there would be only one instance. The decision felt right because the class captured a fundamental, coherent abstraction. After all, Pi is a "process inspector"—the abstraction of a process is central to its job.

It struck me later that the `Process` class made it trivial to create a multiprocess debugger. Indeed, it only took a couple of days to add a window from which the user could choose an arbitrary set of target processes. An instance of class `Process` was created for each target process that user chose to examine. I was amazed at how well the object architecture responded to this change. The work would have been weeks or months of gruesome coding and debugging had the program been written in C. Over those few days I was remarkably productive, but only because I had taken the time earlier to cultivate a key abstraction.

A conscious goal in separating Pi's platform-specific components into classes was to make it easier to port the debugger to new compilers, processors, and operating systems. Significant components, such as expression evaluation, were written portably, completely free of platform-specific code. Initially, I assumed that the way to port Pi was to build a new program by replacing the implementation of each platform-specific class. However, when faced with the first port, I decided to be more ambitious. My experience with inheritance suggested that it might be possible to turn each platform-specific class into a hierarchy in which the general abstraction was captured in a base class, with each derived class providing an implementation corresponding to a facet of a specific platform.

Building the class hierarchies was not a trivial change. As is commonly observed, good inheritance hierarchies in C++ take some forethought, and retrofitting a generalization can be painful. In the end, though, the results were striking. A single copy of Pi can control multiple processes distributed across multiple heterogeneous processors running different operating systems.

Once the multiplatform architecture was in place, maintenance of the code produced a phenomenon that surprised me repeatedly, until it eventually became commonplace. When adding new functionality that had platform-independent semantics (like step-out-of-the-current-function), I found that once the code ran correctly on one platform, it almost invariably worked on others. This may be as it should, but it was beyond my expectations, given all my experience with other "portable" debuggers of that era. I found myself working in a new environment, where I started to demand more from my software.

Over the years, versions of Pi have been developed for a variety of hardware and software platforms, mostly for time-sharing systems and workstations, though also for distributed, real-time, multiprocessor, and embedded systems. I participated in some of this work, but often I discovered only after the fact that a Pi had migrated to another machine. Gradually, Pi became what today would be dubbed an "application framework" for debuggers, that is, a set of classes that provide the basic components for assembling a debugger.

My final observation is subjective but perhaps telling: I continued to actively enjoy working on Pi until I left AT&T in 1989. The code was six years old, but I still didn't wince when I picked it up to fix a bug or add a feature. This was a novelty, so unlike my experience with any previous code. I believe my mellow relationship with the code was the result of the persistent support that C++ gives to the maintenance programmer. The programmer is gently encouraged to find cleaner ways to solve problems. For example, when correcting for missing logic, code must be added, and the programmer must decide where it should go. On the one hand, in a typical C program, there is no guidance; the code probably ends up in the first place the programmer can find that solves the current problem. On the other hand, when modifying a C++ program, the architecture of the program implicitly asks the programmer "What are you doing to me? Does this code really belong here?" A modification may work, but what is its impact on the cohesion of the class? Maybe the code belongs somewhere else. Maybe two smaller separate modifications would be better. The programmer is more likely to stop and think. The pause may mean that each individual change takes a little longer, but the reward emerges the next time a programmer has to look at the affected code, because its integrity is retained. The architecture is manifest in the code; the programmer minimizes damage to the architecture; the architecture survives.

If the benefits of C++ come from the preservation of an architecture, how do we build an architecture worth preserving? I believe the answer lies in the quality of the abstractions captured in the C++ classes. In the case of Pi, I was a novice with respect to object-oriented programming, but I had a good feel for the problem domain and knew where to look for the essential objects. C++ can help in the concrete expression and preservation of a conceptual framework in software, thereby delivering the benefits of object technology. To derive the benefits, the original programmers must put the necessary effort into the discovery and capture of good abstractions, which maintenance programmers should then respect.

Section One

A Focus on Programming Design

Library Design Using C++

Bjarne Stroustrup

A Fortran library is a collection of subroutines, a C library is a collection of functions with some associated data structures, and a Smalltalk library is a hierarchy rooted somewhere in the standard Smalltalk class hierarchy. What is a C++ library? Clearly, a C++ library can be very much like a Fortran, C, or Smalltalk library. It might also be a set of abstract types with several implementations, a set of templates, or a hybrid. You can imagine further alternatives. That is, the designer of a C++ library has several choices for the basic structure of a library and can even provide more than one interface style for a single library. For example, a library organized as a set of abstract types might be presented as a set of functions to a C program, and a library organized as a hierarchy might be presented to clients as a set of handles.

We are obviously faced with an opportunity, but can we manage the resulting diversity? Must diversity lead to chaos? I don't think it has to. The diversity reflects the diversity of needs in the C++ community. A library supporting high-performance scientific computation has different constraints from a library supporting interactive graphics, and both have different needs from a library supplying low-level data structures to builders of other libraries.

C++ evolved to enable this diversity of library architectures and some of the newer C++ features are designed to ease the coexistence of libraries. Other articles in this issue provide concrete examples of libraries and design techniques. Consequently, I will focus on generalities and language support for library building.

Library Design Trade-Offs

Early C++ libraries often show a tendency to mimic design styles found in other languages. For example, my original task library[1,2] (the very first C++ library) provided facilities similar to the the Simula67 mechanisms for simulation, the complex arithmetic library[3] provided functions like those found for floating point arithmetic in the C math library, and Keith Gorlen's *NIH* library[4] provides a C++ analog to the Smalltalk library. New "early C++" libraries still appear as programmers migrate from other languages and produce libraries before they have fully absorbed C++ design techniques and appreciate the design trade-offs possible in C++.

What trade-offs are there? When answering that question people often focus on language features: Should I use inline functions, virtual functions, multiple inheritance, single-rooted hierarchies, abstract classes, overloaded operators, etc. That is the wrong focus. These language features exist to support more fundamental trade-offs: Should the design

- Emphasize runtime efficiency?
- Minimize recompilation after a change?
- Maximize portability across platforms?
- Enable users to extend the basic library?
- Allow use without source code available?
- Blend in with existing notations and styles?
- Be usable from code not written in C++?
- Be usable by novices?

Given answers to these kinds of questions the answers to the language-level questions will follow.

Concrete Types

For example, consider the trade-off between runtime speed and cost of recompilation after a change. The original complex number library emphasized runtime efficiency and compactness of representation. This led to a design where the representation was visible (yet private so users can't access it directly), key operations were provided by inline functions, and the basic mathematical operations were granted direct access to the implementation:

```
class complex {
 double re, im;
public:
 complex(double r = 0, double i = 0) { re=r; im=i; }
```

```
    friend double abs(complex);                            //inlined
    friend double norm(complex);                           //inlined
    friend double arg(complex);                            //inlined
    friend complex conj(complex);
    friend complex cos(complex);
    friend complex cosh(complex);
    friend complex exp(complex);
    friend double imag(complex);                           //inlined
    friend complex log(complex);
    friend complex pow(double, complex);
    friend complex pow(complex, int);

    friend complex pow(complex, double);
    friend complex pow(complex, complex);
    friend complex polar(double, double = 0);
    friend double real(complex);                           //inlined
    friend complex sin(complex);
    friend complex sinh(complex);
    friend complex sqrt(complex);

    friend complex operator+(complex, complex);    //inlined
    friend complex operator-(complex);             //inlined
    friend complex operator-(complex, complex);    //inlined
    friend complex operator*(complex, complex);
    friend complex operator/(complex, complex);
    friend int   operator==(complex, complex);     //inlined
    friend int   operator!=(complex, complex);     //inlined

    void operator+=(complex);                      //inlined
    void operator-=(complex);                      //inlined
    void operator*=(complex);
    void operator/=(complex);
};
```

Was this overblown? Maybe. Modern taste dictates a reduction of the number of friends (given inline access functions we don't need to grant access to all of those mathematical functions). However, the basic requirements—runtime and space efficiency, and the provision of the traditional C match functions—were met without compromise. As desired, usage looks entirely conventional:

```
complex silly_fct(complex a, complex b)
{
 if (a == b) {
   complex z = sqrt(a)+cos(b);
   z *= 22/7;
   return z + a;
 }
 else
   return pow(a/b,2);
}
```

Abstract Types

If we change the requirements, the basic structure of the solution typically changes as a consequence. What if the requirement had been that user code needn't be recompiled if we changed the representation? This would be a reasonable choice in many contexts (if not for a complex number type, then for many other types). We have two ways of meeting this requirement: The interface is an abstract class and the users operate on objects through pointers and references only, or the interface is a handle (containing just enough information to find, access, and manage the real object.[5] In either case, we make an explicit physical separation between the interface and the implementation instead of the merely logical one implied by the public/private mechanism. For example, borrowing and slightly updating an example from the Choices operating system[6]:

```
class MemoryObject {
public:
 virtual int read(int page, char* buff) = 0; // into buff
 virtual int write(int page, const char* buff) = 0;
 // from buff
 virtual int size() = 0;
 virtual int copyFrom(const MemoryObject*) = 0;

 virtual ~MemoryObject();
};
```

We clearly have some memory that we can read, write, and copy. We can do that knowing class `MemoryObject` and nothing further. Equally, we have no idea what the representation of a memory object is—that information is supplied later for each individual kind of `MemoryObject`. For example:

```
class MemoryObjectView : public MemoryObject {
 MemoryObject* viewedObject;
 virtual int logicalToPhysical(int blkNum);
public:
 int read(int page, char* buff);
 int write(int page, const char* buff);
};
```

and

```
class ContiguousObjectView : public MemoryObjectView {
 int start, length;
 virtual int logicalToPhysical(int blkNum);
public:
 int read(int page,  char*  buff);
 int write(int page,  const char* buff);
};
```

A user of the interface specified by `MemoryObject` can be completely oblivious to the existence of the `MemoryObjectView` and `ContiguousObjectView` classes that are used through that interface:

```
void print_mem(ostream& s, const MemoryObject* p)
{
 char buffer[PAGESIZE];
 for (int i = 0; i<p->size(); i++) {
  p->read(i,buffer);
  // print buffer to stream "s"
 }
}
```

This usage allows the derived classes to be redefined or even replaced with other classes without the client code using `MemoryObject` having to be recompiled.

The cost of this convenience is minimal for this class, though it would have been unacceptable for the complex class: Objects are created on the free store and accessed exclusively through virtual functions. The (fixed) overhead for virtual function calls is small when compared to ordinary function calls, though large compared to an add instruction. That's why the complex class must use a more efficient and less flexible solution than the memory object class.

USING C LIBRARIES FROM OTHER LANGUAGES

What if a C or Fortran program wanted to use these classes? In general, an alternative that matches the semantic level of the user language must be provided. For example:

```
/* C interface to MemoryObject: */

struct MemoryObject;

Memory_read(struct MemoryObject *, int, char*);
Memory_write(struct MemoryObject *, int, const char*);
Memory_size(struct MemoryObject *);
Memory_copyFrom(struct MemoryObject *,
                const struct MemoryObject*);
void Memory_delete(struct MemoryObject *);
```

The interface is trivial, and so is its implementation:

```
// C++ implementation of C interface to MemoryObject:

extern "C" int Memory_read(MemoryObject * p, int i,
    const char* pc)
{
 return p->read(i,pc);
}
```

The basic techniques are easy; the important point is for both library purveyors and library users to realize that libraries can be designed to meet diverse criteria and that interfaces can be created to suit users. The point of the exercise isn't to use the most advanced language features or to follow the latest fad most closely. The aim must be for the provider and user to find the closest match to the user's real needs that is technically feasible. There is no one right way to organize a library; rather, C++ offers a variety of features and techniques to meet diverse needs. This follows from the view that a programming language is a tool for expressing solutions, not a solution in itself.

Language Features

So, what facilities does C++ offer to library builders and users?

The C++ class concept and type system is the primary focus for all C++ library design. The strengths and weaknesses determine the shape of C++ libraries. My main recommendation to library builders and users is simple: Don't fight the type system. Against the basic mechanisms of a language a user can win Pyrrhic victories only. Elegance, ease of use, and efficiency can only be achieved within the basic framework of a language. If that framework isn't viable for what you want to do it is time to consider another programming language.

The basic structure of C++ encourages a strongly typed style of programming. In C++, a class is a type and the rules of inheritance, the abstract class mechanism, and the template mechanism all combine to encourage users to manipulate objects strictly in accordance to the interfaces they present to their users. To put it more crudely: Don't break the type system with casts. Casts are necessary for many low-level activities and occasionally for mapping from higher-level to lower-level interfaces, but a library that requires its end users to do extensive casting is imposing an undue and usually unnecessary burden on them. C's `printf` family of functions, `void*` pointers, and other low-level features are best kept out of library interfaces because they imply holes in the library's type system.

Compile-Time Checking

This view of C++ and its type system is sometimes misunderstood: But we can't do that! We won't accept that! Are you trying to turn C++ into one of those "discipline and bondage" languages? Not at all: casts, `void*`, etc., have an essential part in C++ programming. What I'm arguing is that many uses familiar to people coming from a weaker-typed language such as C or from a dynamically typed language such as Smalltalk are unnecessary, error-prone, and ultimately self-defeating in C++.

Consider a simple container class implemented using a low-level list of `void*` pointers for efficiency and compactness:

```
template<class T> class Queue : private List<void*> {
public: //code
 void put(T* p) { append(p); }
  T* get() { return (T*) get(); }
};
```

```
void f(Container<Ship>* c)
{
 while (Ship* ps = c->get()) {
  // use ship
 }
}
```

Here, a template is used to achieve type safety. The (implicit) conversion to `void*` in `put()` and the explicit cast back from from `void*` to `T*` in `get()` are—within the implementation of `Queue`—used to cross the abstraction barrier between the strongly typed user level and the weakly typed implementation level. Since every object placed on the list by `put()` is a `T*`, the cast to `T*` in `get()` is perfectly safe. In other words, the cast is actually used to ensure that the object is manipulated according to its true type rather than to violate the type system.

Runtime Checking

To contrast, consider a library built on the notion of a "universal" base class and runtime type inquiries:

```
class Object {
 // ...
 virtual int isA(Object&);
 // ...
};

class Container : public Object {
 // ...
public:
 void put(Object*);
 Object* get();
 // ...
};

class Ship : public Object { /* ... */ };

void f(Container* c)
{
 while (Object* po = c->get()) {
   if (po->isA(ShipObj) {
```

```
        Ship* ps = (Ship*) po;
        // use ship
      }
      else {
        // Oops, do something else
    }
  }
```

This, too, is perfectly legal C++, but organized in such a way as to take no advantage of the type system. This puts the burden of ensuring type safety on the library user: the user must apply tests and explicitly cast based on those tests. The result is more elaborate and expensive. Usually, that is neither necessary nor desirable.

Runtime Type Information

However, not all checking can be done at compile time. Trying to do so is a good design and implementation strategy, but if taken to excess it can lead to inflexibility and inconvenience. In recognition of that, a mechanism for using runtime type information has been voted into C++ by the ANSI/ISO C++ standards committee. The primary language mechanism is a cast that is checked at run time. Naturally, it should be used with care and, like other casts, its main purpose is to allow abstraction barriers to be crossed. Unlike other casts, it has built-in mechanisms to achieve this with relative safety. Consider:

```
class dialog_box : public window { // library class
  // ...
public:
  virtual int ask();
  // ...
};

class dbox_w_str : public dialog_box { // my class
  // ...
public:
  int ask();
  virtual char* get_string();
  // ...
};
```

Assume that a library supplies class dialog_box and that its interfaces are expressed in terms of dialog_boxes. I however, use both dialog_boxes and my own dbox_w_strs. So, when the system/library hands me a pointer to a dialog_box how can I know whether it is one of my dbox_w_strs?

Note that I can't modify the library to understand about my dbox_w_strs. Even if I could, I wouldn't because then I would have to worry about dbox_w_strs in new versions of the library and about errors I might have introduced into the "standard" library.

The solution is to use a dynamic cast:

```
void my_fct(dialog_box* bp)
{
 if (dbox_w_str* dbp = dynamic_cast<dbox_w_str*>(bp))
{
   // here we can use dbox_w_str::get_string()
  }
 else {
   // `plain' dialog box
  }
}
```

The dynamic_cast<dbox_w_str*>(bp) operator converts its operand bp to the desired type dbox_w_str* if *pb really is a dbox_w_str or something derived from dbox_w_str; otherwise, the value of dynamic_cast-<dbox_w_str*>(bp) is 0.

Was this facility added to encourage the use of runtime type checking? No! On the contrary, it was included to reduce the need for scaffolding—such as "universal" base classes—in cases where runtime checking is genuinely needed, to standardize what is already widespread practice, and to provide a better defined and more thoroughly checked alternative to the runtime type checking mechanisms that abound in major C++ libraries. The basic rule is as ever: Use static (compile-time checked) mechanisms wherever possible—such mechanisms are feasible and superior to the runtime mechanisms in more cases than most programmers are aware of.

Managing Library Diversity

You can't just take two libraries and expect them to work together. Many do, but, in general, quite a few concerns must be addressed for successful joint use.

Some issues must be addressed by the programmer, some by the library builder, and a few fall to the language designer.

For years, C++ has been evolving toward a situation where the language provided sufficient facilities to cope with the basic problems that arise when a user tries to use two independently designed libraries. To complement, library providers are beginning consider multiple library use when they design libraries.

Name Clashes

Often, the first problem a programmer finds when trying to use two libraries that weren't designed to work together is that both have used the same global name, say `String`, `put`, `read`, `open`, or `Bool`. It doesn't matter much whether the names were used for the same thing or for something different. The results range from the obvious nuisance to the subtle and hard-to-find disaster. For example, a user may have to remove one of two identical definitions of a `Bool` type. It is much harder to find and correct the problems caused by a locally defined `read` function being linked in and unexpectedly used by functions that assume the semantics of the standard `read()`.

Traditional solutions abound. One popular defense is for the library designer to add a prefix to all names. Instead of writing:

```
// library XX header:

class String { /* ... */ };
ostream& open(String);
enum Bool { false, true }
```

we write

```
// library XX header:

class XX_String { /* ... */ };
ostream& open(XX_String);
enum XX_Bool { XX_false, XX_true };
```

This solves the problem, but leads to ugly programs. It also leads to inflexibility by forcing the user to either write application code in terms of a specific `String` or introduce yet another name, say `myString` that is then mapped to the library function by a macro or something. Another problem is that there are ony a few hundred two-letter prefixes and already hundreds of C++ libraries. This is one of the oldest problems in the book. Old-time C programmers will be reminded of the time where struct member names were given one or two letter suffixes to avoid clashes with members of other structs.

The ANSI/ISO C++ standards committee is currently discussing a proposal to add namespaces to C++ to solve this problem.[8] Basically, this would allow names that would otherwise have been global to be wrapped in a scope so they won't interfere with other names:

```
// XX library:

namespace Xcorp_Xwindows {
 class String { /* ... */ };
 ostream& open(String);
 enum Bool { false, true };
}
```

People can use such names by explicitly qualifying uses:

```
Xcorp_Xwindows::String s = "asdf";
Xcorp_Xwindows::Bool b = Xcorp_Xwindows::true;
```

Alternatively, we can explicitly make the names from a specific library available for use without qualification:

```
using namespace Xcorp_Xwindows;
  // make names from Xcorp_Xwindows available

String s = "asdf";
Bool b = true;
```

Naturally, there are more details, but the proposal can be explained in ten minutes and was implemented in five days, so the complexity isn't great. To encourage longer namespace names to minimize namespace name clashes the user can define shorter aliases:

```
namespace XX = Xcorp_Xwindows;

XX::String s = "asdf";
XX::Bool b = XX::true;
```

This allows the library provider to choose long and meaningful names without imposing a notational burden on users. It also makes it much easier to switch from one library to another.

"Universal" Base Classes

Once the basic problem of resolving name clashes to get two libraries to compile together has been solved, the more subtle problems start to be discovered. Smalltalk-inspired libraries often rely on a single "universal" root class. If you have two of those you could be out of luck, but if the libraries were written for distinct application domains the simplest form of multiple inheritance sometimes helps:

```
class GDB_root : public GraphicsObject,
                 public DataBaseObject { };
```

A problem that cannot be solved that easily is when the two universal base classes both provide some basic service. For example, both may provide a runtime type identification mechanism and an object I/O mechanism. Some such problems are best solved by factoring out the common facility into a standard library or a language feature. That is what is being done for runtime type identification. Others can be handled by providing functionality in the new common root. However, merging "universal" libraries will never be easy. The best solution is for library providers to realize that they don't own the whole world and never will, and that it is in their interest to design their libraries accordingly.

Memory Management

The general solution to memory management problems is garbage collection. Unfortunately, that solution is not universally affordable and, therefore, cannot in general be assumed available to a library provider or library user.

This implies that a library designer must present the user with a clean and comprehensible model of how memory is allocated and deallocated. One such policy is "whoever created an object must also destroy it." This pushed an obligation of record keeping onto the library user. Another policy is "if you give an object to the library, the library is responsible for it, if you get an object from the library, you become responsible for it." Both policies are manageable for many applications. However, writing an application using one library using the one policy and another library with the other will often not be manageable. Consequently, library providers will probably be wise to look carefully at other libraries that their users might like to use and adopt a strategy that will mesh.

Initialization and Cleanup

Who initializes an object? Who cleans up after it when it is destroyed? From the outset C++ provided constructors and destructors as the answer to these questions. By and large it has been a satisfactory answer.

The related question of how to guarantee initialization of a larger unit, such as a complete library, is still being discussed. C++ provides sufficient mechanisms to ensure that a library is initialized before use and cleaned up after use.[9] To guarantee that a library is "initialized" before it is used simply place a class definition containing the initialization code in the header file for the library.

```
class Lib_counter { // Lib initialization and cleanup
 static count;
public:
 Lib_counter()
 {
   if (count++ == 0) {
     // first user initializes Lib
   }
 }

 ~Lib_counter()
 {
   if (--count == 0) {
     //last user cleans up Lib
   }
 }
};

static Lib_counter Lib_ctr;
```

However, this solution isn't perfectly elegant and can be unpleasantly expensive in a virtual memory system if this initialization code is scattered throughout the address space of a process.[10]

Error Handling

There are many styles of error handling and a library must chose one. For example, a C library often reports errors through the global variable errno, some library requires the user to define a set of error handling functions with specific names, others rely on signals, yet others on `setjmp/longjmp`, and some have adopted primitive exception handling mechanisms. Using two libraries with different error-handling strategies is difficult and error-prone.

Exception handling was introduced into C++ to provide a common framework for error handling.[11] A library that wants to report an error throws an exception and a user that is interested in an exception provides a handler for it. For example:

```
template<class T> T& Array<T>::operator[](int i)
{
 if (0<=i && i<sz) return p[i];
 throw Range(i);
}
```

A user can catch that exception and possibly recover:

```
void f( /* arguments */ )
{
 // ...
 try {
   Array<double> a(200);
   // use array
 }
 catch (Array<double>::Range& r)
 {
   if (r.val <MAXR) {
     a.resize(val);
     // retry algorithm
   }
   else {
     // give up
   }
 }
}
```

The exception handling mechanism is designed to work correctly with the view that constructors do initialization and destructors do cleanup. Thus, there is language support for errors involving uninitialized objects, initialized objects, and partly initialized objects.

C++ implementations that support exception handling are now just becoming available.

TRANSITION PROBLEMS

A library must serve its users over a period of time. It will therefore be used on a variety of systems and compiled by a variety of compilers. Even if only a single system and a single compiler supplier is used, new versions of that system and that compiler will appear. In particular, the C++ compiler will change to accommodate new language features as the standards process converges. This can be a real nuisance to both library users and suppliers. It is also an opportunity, though, and it is typically preferable to sticking with an outdated compiler and language version or changing to another language.

To manage, both users and library implementors must program in a way that eases the necessary transition. How? That depends on the future feature one wants to anticipate or the older version of C++ one wants also to support/use. The general technique is as always to encapsulate, isolate, localize, etc. the feature that might change or be missing on some platform. Consider runtime type information. There is to my knowledge no compiler shipping today that can handle the `dynamic_cast` example. However, every C++ compiler shipped (even 1.0) supplies the basic features to build a scaffold to achieve its functionality when one is willing to put in a bit of work. Maybe your library already has the scaffolding in place? Otherwise, section 13.5 of Reference 5 shows one way to build it. Once in place, a simple macro can be used to hide the actual mechanism and we can write:

```
void my_fct(dialog_box* bp)
{
 dbox_w_str* dbp = ptr_cast(dbox_w_str,bp);
 if (dbp) {

   // here we can use dbox_w_str::get_string()
 }
 else {
```

```
        // `plain' dialog box
    }
}
```

In a transition period where runtime type information is available somewhere, but not in all places, two versions of the `ptr_cast` macro can be supplied, and when—finally—the old systems die `ptr_cast` can be removed.

Similarly, templates can be simulated by macros and an unpleasant number of casts in the implementations. That was how I survived before templates became available to me.

Some Conclusions

We live in interesting times. The way to manage, both as a library provider and as a library user, is to focus on user requirements and general design constraints and trade-offs. When considering language features, try to work with the features and the type system of C++ rather than fighting it. Try to anticipate new language features and concepts as they become defined and available, but don't let language features or fads dominate your thinking. Be alert to transition and portability issues and design to minimize the impact of changes from such sources.

References

1. Stroustrup, B. A set of C classes for co-routine style programming. *Bell Laboratories Computer Science Technical Report CSTR*-90. Nov 1980.
2. Stroustrup, B.and J. Shopiro. A set of C classes for co-routine style programming. *Proceedings of the USENIX C++ Conference,* Santa Fe, NM, Nov 1987.
3. Rose, L.V. and B. Stroustrup. Complex arithmetic in C++, Internal *AT&T* Bell Labs Technical Memorandum, Jan 1984. Reprinted in *AT&T C++ Translator Release Notes,* Nov 1985.
4. Gorlen, K.E. An object-oriented class library for C++ Programs, *Proceedings of the USENIX C++ Conference,* Santa Fe, NM, Nov 1987.
5. Stroustrup, B. *The C++ Programming Language* (2d ed), Addison-Wesley, Reading, MA, 1991.
6. Johnson, R.E. The importance of being abstract. *C++ Report,* 1(3), 1989.
7. Stroustrup, B., and D. Lenkov. Runtime type identification for C++. *C++ Report* 4(3), 1992.

8. Stroustrup, B. Name space management in C++ (revised), Document x3j16/93-0055, WG21/N0262.
9. Ellis, M.A., and B. Stroustrup. *The Annotated C++ Reference Manual.* Addison-Wesley, Reading, MA, 1990.
10. Reiser, J.F. Static initializers: reducing the value-added tax on programs. *Proceedings of the USENIX C++ Conference.* Portland, OR, Aug 1992.
11. Koenig, A., and B. Stroustrup: Exception handling for C++ (revised), *Proceedings of the USENIX C++ Conference,* Apr 1990. Also in *Journal of Object Oriented Programming* 3(2): 16–33, 1990.

The GNU C++ Library

Doug Lea

The GNU C++ library (libg++) was one of the first widely available general-purpose C++ class libraries. Some classes were designed and implemented as early as 1985 (originally in support of other efforts). The library was made available in 1987. I was the primary original developer. Several others have contributed ideas and code. Contributors include Dirk Grunwald, Doug Schmidt, Kurt Baudendistel, Marc Shapiro, Eric Newton, Michael Tiemann, Richard Stallman, and Per Bothner. Cygnus Support currently maintains and distributes the library on behalf of the Free Software Foundation (FSF). Hundreds of users have also contributed improvements, fixes, suggestions, clarifications, and bug reports. While it has been ported to other platforms, libg++ is normally used on UNIX systems in conjunction with the GNU C++ (g++) compiler. It is available via anonymous ftp from prep.ai.mit.edu, among other sources.

The basic structure of libg++ remains almost unchanged from that described in a 1988 USENIX C++ conference paper. It contains the following:

1. Classes representing strings, numbers, and other black box values, along with similar abstract data type (ADT) classes representing sets, sequences, maps, etc.
2. IO streams and related support provided by any minimal C++ library
3. Storage allocation classes and utilities
4. "Lightweight" veneers organizing functionality commonly supported in C libraries
5. A few other uncategorizable classes and sample applications

Libg++ is mainly an "abstract data structure library." Most libg++ classes are somewhat different in design philosophy, design, and implementation than the classes you or I ordinarily construct for specific applications. The remainder of this article focuses mainly on these differences without otherwise going into much detail about particular components.

Abstract Data Types and Values

While both may be described as C++ classes, there is a big difference between, say, a complex number and, say, a `BankAccount`. For example, there is a large, well-established mathematical theory of complex numbers but essentially none for bank accounts. One consequence is that it is simply much easier to develop a `Complex` class containing features that you can be reasonably certain will make sense across a wide range of applications. This is not true of any `BankAccount` class one could construct.

A more important distinction underlies the resulting design differences. The theory of complex numbers revolves around the properties of complex values, not objects. Mathematical approaches typically abstract over the actual identities of objects possessing (Re, Im) attributes, and just deal with the values themselves. For example, the complex quantity (2.4, 17.17) remains the same regardless of which or how many objects report this quantity as `real()`, and `imag()` attribute functions. By design, many operations don't care about the objects, and just deal with the quantities, but that would be a losing attitude for a class like `BankAccount`. For example, even when we happen to both have the same bank balance, the fact that a particular identifiable `BankAccount` instance belongs to you and not me is an obvious but critical design issue.

These differences result in different styles, approaches, and plans of attack for designing the associated classes and utilities. For example, while it is perfectly sensible to write a "constructive" function that accepts two complex numbers and returns a third representing their sum, there is hardly ever a reason to create a function that accepts two bank accounts and returns a third representing (among other things) the sum of their balances. Instead, the `BankAccount` class contains methods such as `withdraw`, `transfer`, and so on that mutate the states of particular objects.

Libg++ contains substantially more components like `Complex` than those like `BankAccount`. Many classes maintain "value semantics," in a manner more similar to classic ADT approaches than to classic object-oriented approaches. There are some distinct advantages to ADT approaches in those cases where they are appropriate:

- Value properties are generally better behaved than object properties. Well-understood algebraic properties may be relied upon in the specification, design, testing, and use of associated classes.
- When users care only about values, not about object structure, it is often easier to hide clever representations and algorithms behind the scenes, and to develop interoperable versions of the same general functionality.
- The resulting semantics are familiar to most programmers. For example, a value-based Complex class acts pretty much just like the built-in value type float.

However, no one ever uses a straight ADT approach in designing classes. For example, a "purist" approach to a `Stack` ADT would define `push` to return a new stack state value, different than the original. So, if `Stack s` denoted a stack with a million items on it, `s.push(23)` would return something representing a million and one. Nobody wants this, partially just because of efficiency. Even with a lot of underlying cleverness, too much data copying is required to represent new values resulting from `push`es. However, it also represents the point at which object-oriented thinking rightfully creeps into ADT-based design. When clients push `17` onto `Stack s`, they essentially always wants `s` itself to change, not to construct a new, distinct representation. For this reason, object-oriented approaches to ADTs usually include mutative operations on objects that propel them into different states rather than, or in addition to, operations that construct new representations of new states and values. (Non–object-oriented ADT approaches often do this too, but usually describe them differently. For example, they might talk about the "symbol `s` being rebound to a new value" after a push.)

The twist in libg++ and other object-oriented libraries is to support some mixture of value-oriented and object-oriented usage, almost always within the very same classes. This is a natural practice, especially in C++, since the C base of C++ already does this. For example, unlike most procedural languages, C contains both the constructive value-oriented `+` operation for adding built-in number types, as well as the (vaguely) object-oriented `+=` "method" for mutating number objects.

Libg++ was originally a set of experiments in how to go about meeting the occasionally conflicting demands of the two approaches. The two approaches do indeed sometimes conflict, and lead to different trade-offs seen in different classes. Many of these, in turn, reflect trade-offs made in the language itself. Stroustrup has described C++ as a language supporting both data abstraction and object-oriented design. Crosses between ADT and object-oriented designs often find themselves at the very borders of both kinds of support, in ways that most other C++ designs do not.

Arguments, Results, and Copying

Generally, operations defined within a value-oriented approach rest on value-based arguments and results, while those from an object-oriented approach use pointers or references to new or existing objects. When applied to classes, value-passing relies on copy-construction, not reference propagation.

Designers of value-oriented classes often give in to the urge to minimize copying overhead while still conforming to value semantics. There are many techniques for doing this, for example, via internal pointers to underlying representations that are shared whenever the support procedures determine that this is possible. The original versions of many libg++ classes in fact contained reference counting and other ploys to maintain this effect. They were later removed. C++ already contains simple ways for people to obtain copy versus reference semantics. Programmers themselves are in a much better position to know when to make copies and when to use references. Hiding these matters often leads to less efficient and predictable behavior, especially for classes like `Strings`. In many applications, tricks like copy-on-write add more overhead than they save. In many others, explicit use by programmers of pointers to shared `Strings` only when desirable and possible is more effective than any automated policy. Thus, except in a few cases where copy-prevention strategies are transparent and algorithmically superior, libg++ classes maintain the convention that a copy-constructor actually makes a copy. Similar remarks hold for assignment and other operations.

Storage Management

Such decisions reflect the idea that a basic support library should provide mechanism not policy. Most libg++ classes are designed so that users who want to implement their own policies are provided with all the tools to do so. Libg++ contains several classes and utilities that facilitate development of specialized allocation and management. For example, an `Obstack` class supports "mark/release" allocation and deallocation. The `MPlex` class helps manage sparse tables. An optionally included version of `malloc` (underlying operator `new`) has been shown to provide superior performance than most other versions for typical C++ (and C) programs. Other classes provide mechanisms useful for very special allocation needs.

However, this stance is probably the least defensible overall design decision in all of libg++. Effective, correct, and efficient storage management in C++ is sufficiently difficult and fragile to demand a better alternative. The only general solution is to rely on automated storage management (garbage collection). If attempts to provide full, transparent garbage collection in C++ succeed, the library (or a version thereof) should be redesigned to exploit it.

INHERITANCE AND OVERLOADING

Value approaches traditionally lie in the world of overloading and parameterization, while object-oriented approaches obtain generality via inheritance. The two do not always mix well in C++, and the resulting "edge effects" lead to some pervasive design trade-offs.

For example, suppose you define a `String` class, along with a value-oriented `operator +` method or function that returns a new `String` representing the concatenation of its arguments. Now define subclass `RString` that adds an in-place reverse method to `String`. Without evasive action, this leads to a problem in user code such as:

```
RString t, u; //...
RString s = t + u;
```

Depending on other class details, users may obtain either a type error or unexpected behavior, due to the fact that the expression `t + u` returns a new `String`, not an `RString`. There are workarounds to this, but none of them are very satisfying or general. For example, if `+` were a non-class operation, then overloading another special version for `RStrings` would work here, but not when `s`, `t`, and `u` were passed to:

```
void app(String& a, String& b, String& c) {a = b + c;}
```

Here, the `String` version would be called instead, leading to undesired behavior. Similar snags result from other strategies.

The net result of these considerations is that value-oriented classes are not readily subclassable in C++. The best two solutions are the most extreme: Either give up on value semantics (at least for troublesome operations) or give up on subclassability for classes with extensive reliance on constructive functions.

Most "lightweight" classes (e.g., strings, multiple precision numbers, bit sets) take the latter option. In consequence:

- Class interfaces are very extensive. The base classes provide functionality that, although rarely needed, is otherwise difficult to support without subclassing.
- No operations are virtual, and many are inlinable.

These consequences are not all bad. However, in classes like `String`, these issues along with the additional need to interconvert with other representations (`char`, `char*`, `RegExp`), lead to an embarassing number of methods and related functions.

If I were redesigning them today, I would surely take the first option, and not provide an extensive value-based support interface. This would place the structural design of such classes closer to that of the kinds of OO applications classes people ordinarily write, enable better separation of interfaces and implementation, simplify some algorithmics, avoid nasty C++ issues such as redundant copy construction and the deletion of temporaries, and allow the use of inheritance to express commmonalities among classes. However, it is also very likely that users would complain about inconveniences stemming from the lack of simple value-based operations such as constructive string concatenation. The code would probably also be a bit slower because of virtuals and lack of inlinability. In classes like `String`, obtaining efficiency close to that of raw `char*`'s was an important design decision early on in C++ and C++ libraries. Making `Strings` simultaneously better and (often enough) faster than raw C character manipulation made the transition from C to C++ far easier for many programmers.

Containers

The first option (not supporting many constructive operations) was indeed taken for libg++ container classes including sets, maps, lists, and queues. These classes mainly support standard "object semantics." For example, there is a `Set::operator |=(Set b)` to union all of the elements of `b` into the receiver, but not a `Set operator |(Set a, Set b)` to construct a new `Set` by unioning two others. There were a number of reasons for this decision. The simplest is that mutative operations are most typically needed in applications using such classes.

There is also a technical reason. It is a common (if not always defensible) policy to tie the interfaces of classes like `String` and `Complex` to particular representations. However, classes like `Set` really must be abstract base classes<. They provide interfaces without providing implementations. There are countless ways of implementing `Sets` (lists, arrays, trees, tables, and so on). It is a terrible idea to settle on any one particular strategy. The many libg++ classes that implement this functionality in particular ways are defined as subclasses. But one cannot construct (direct) instances of abstract base classes. Thus, it is impossible to declare a constructive version of `operator |()` that covers all cases in the first place, regardless of whether other overloading versus inheritance issues could be settled. (A workaround would be to define this operator to return a pointer or reference, but this interferes with value semantics and leads to storage management responsibility problems.)

Inheritance and Parameterization

Container classes may be used in two slightly different roles:

- ***Collections.*** Classes that keep track of groups of objects that are all related in some way or are all to be manipulated in a certain fashion.
- ***Repositories.*** Classes that "house" groups of objects while also providing structured access.

The basic implementation difference is that collections hold pointers to objects that "live" elsewhere, while repositories hold and internally manage the objects themselves. Luckily, the low-level mechanics do not vary so much that these two forms cannot be combined via the convention that any object used as an element in a repository must support a copy constructor, an assignment operator, and, in some classes, a default constructor, an equality function, and/or a magnitude comparison function.

There are two reasonable approaches to designing and using pointer-based collections. For example, for Stacks, one may either define a single class that holds pointers to *any* object, or design a special class for each different element type. In the latter case, parameterization mechanisms avoid the need to write so many special classes that differ only with respect to element pointer type information. Libg++ does not provide policy about this issue, only mechanism. One may define a Stack that holds pointers to anything as*:

* Libg++ containers were designed long before C++ templates were defined and implemented. They still rely on the use of a manual expansion tool rather than template mechanisms. As support for parameterized types in C++ improves, the distributed versions are being modified accordingly. Dependence on simple manual tools resulted in other minor trade-offs as well. For example, even though desirable, different collection classes are not linked to, say, a Collection superclass or other intervening abstract classes. The two-level abstract/concrete organization was hard enough to use as it was. This, in turn, led to unnecessary code duplication within the library.

```
typedef void* AnyPtr;
AnyPtrSLStack mystack;
```

These declarations define a stack that may hold instances of any kind of class whatsoever. This is OK for putting things into a stack, but sometimes less so when they are pulled out. Unless it somehow happens to have additional information, a client looking at the top element does not know anything at all about its capabilities. As far as type information is concerned, it could be anything.

On the other hand, if a client has a `WindowPtrStack` (i.e., a stack holding pointers to objects of class `Window`), it knows that all elements are `Windows`. The objects might still be of any subclass of `Window`; perhaps `BorderedWindow`, `ScrollableWindow`, or whatever. But they are surely at least `Windows`. This guarantees that clients can perform window-based operations on all of the objects without having to bother with type tests, downcasting, or error-handling details.

Parameterized collection classes are thus generally safer than unrestricted classes and lead to simpler use by clients. However, because this is a matter of relative safety, there is much room for judgment and disagreement about designs. For example, in a particular application operation, one may really require that all objects are in fact `BorderedWindows`, in which case type testing, etc. would still be warranted whether stacks of `Any` or `Window` were accepted as arguments. Given this, along with the fact that parameterization can generate wasteful multiple versions of the same code but with different type contraints, a library must provide both options.

Moreover, only the parameterization option is viable in the case of repositories. Even though the high-level source code is identicial, each version of a parameterized class maintains storage space, arranges construction, etc., specialized for a particular element type. Thus, both types and executable code are different for each kind of element. In fact, while very useful, the resulting code is slightly dangerous. For example, the type information in a repository set, s, of Windows does not indicate that if `s.add(b)` for a `BorderedWindow b`, then only a "sliced copy" of `b` is actually held in `s` (i.e., the internally held copy of `b` will act only as a `Window` on access).

PERFORMANCE

It is not very hard to come up with a basic data structures library. Programming techniques for implementing most components are familiar to most programmers. It is another matter to design and implement a library containing among the *best* data structures and algorithms known for supporting common applications. Libg++ includes both elementary structures such as the obvious implementations of lists, complex numbers, etc., as well as fancy ones such as balanced trees, self-adjusting arrays, and sophisticated random number generators. Nearly all of these are implemented in a completely interoperable fashion. For example, programmers may switch from a simple array-based implementation of `Sets` to one based on `SplayTrees` with very little effort, without caring at all about *why* splay trees happen to speed up their applications. Of course, it might be that simple arrays are faster. One reason for including so many different implementations is that general-purpose library classes are used in a much broader range of contexts than are application-specific classes. The library writer has no idea of the expected execution profile and possible trade-offs. The best that can be done is to supply enough versions so that the likelihood of acceptable performance is high enough for the library to be considered useful.

Specification and Testing

In part because most of them are based on ADTs, libg++ classes and utilities include some fairly effective specification and testing constructs.

Most classes themselves include an internal invariant check method `OK()`. Whenever invoked, this function checks a collection of runtime-evaluatable constraints that must hold internally for the object to be in a consistent state (not necessarily the "right" state, just a legal one). For example, the `OK()` method in a binary search tree checks that the tree is actually ordered, and `OK()` in the multiple-precision integer class checks that the internal representation describes a legal integer. There are limits on these kinds of checks. For example, they cannot usually diagnose contamination or other errors surrounding dynamically allocated storage. However, they serve effectively as internal and external guides to correctness—every public method must respect listed invariants.

The libg++ distribution also includes a number of *trace tests* that propel objects through states for which known properties should hold. This is where the wealth of knowledge about ADTs comes in handy. For a simple example, a stack should come back to its original state when a push; pop sequence is applied. The test suites place objects through a large number of such exercises. Of course, these measures cannot themselves guarantee total correctness. Implementation errors stemming from nonportable constructions, insufficient testing, and incompatibilities across different versions of classes do still occur.

Conclusions

Libg++ and other libraries (e.g., NIHCL) designed relatively early in the evolution of C++ have served as examples and counter-examples for the development of many others of their general form. The language, compilers, users, and typical applications have all evolved since their original design. In addition to pseudo-templates, libg++ contains other designs and code that are almost anachronistic design assumptions that no longer hold. (For example, a few existing marginal efficiency measures may actually slightly degrade performance on some RISC platforms.) Still, many of the design issues and solutions remain useful guides in the development of reusable C++ components of any kind

The Design and Architecture of Tools.h++

Thomas Keffer
keffer@roguewave.com

Rogue Wave Software's Tools.h++ has its roots in the Data Analysis and Interactive Modeling Software (DAIMS) project at the University of Washington. The objective of the project was to develop reusable mathematical modeling tools for use in fluid dynamics. Bruce Eckel and I evaluated a lot of languages and, in 1987, settled on C++, then in its infancy. We wrote a set of foundation classes that later diverged into two distinct libraries. The more mathematically oriented structures became Math.h++, the first commercially offered C++ library. The fundamental data structures, after feedback from various compiler manufacturers and the growing C++ community, became Tools.h++. One of the older C++ class libraries around, it is now in its sixth version and consists of about 40,000 lines of code (not counting test suites).

Design Philosophy

The C++ language has several design goals that set it apart from most other object-oriented languages. First and foremost is efficiency: It is possible to write production-quality code that is every bit as efficient and small as code that has been written in C yet more maintainable. A second is a "less is more" philosophy: No feature has been included in the language that will make those who don't use it suffer. For example, you will not find built-in garbage collection. The result is a lean and mean language (as far as object-oriented languages go) that compiles fast and results in small and efficient code.

Successful libraries play to the strengths of the language they are written in and do not try to mask them. It follows that the fundamental design goal of a library written in C++ should be run-time efficiency. This was the fundamental goal of Tools.h++. We did not want to write a prototyping tool that would be fun to play with but got pushed aside when the "real" coding began. Tools.h++ was written with an eye toward production-quality code.

In general, it has no features that will slow things down for anyone who doesn't use them. As many decisions as possible are made at compile-time, consistent with the C++ philosophy of static type checking. In most cases, Tools.h++ offers a choice between classes with extreme simplicity but little generality and classes that are a little more complex but more general. We have chosen not to require all classes to inherit a secular base class (such as the class `Object` used by Smalltalk and the NIH classes), which would require large amounts of unused code to be dragged in.

Another design goal was to adhere to the "Principle of Least Astonishment" for predictability and ease of learning. Many new users of C++ become so giddy with the power of being able to overload esoteric operators like `"&="` that they forget about tried-and-true function calls and start redefining everything in sight. Tools.h++ tries to avoid all this. All of the familiar operators work just as you might expect—there are no surprises. We also wanted to write an API that would protect the programmer from large classes of mistakes by taking advantage of C++'s strong type checking.

Various language tricks were kept to a minimum. The goal was fairly generic code that would compile reliably and uneventfully on a wide variety of platforms. Exotic language features such as virtual base classes, with their unreliable implementations, were not used.

Organization

What does the library look like?

Tools.h++ provides implementation, not policy. It consists mostly of a large and rich set of concrete classes that are usable in isolation and do not depend on other classes for their implementation or semantics: They can be pulled out and used one or two at a time. The concrete classes consist of a set of simple classes (such as dates, times, strings, etc.) and three different families of collection classes:

- A set of collection classes based on templates
- A set of collection classes that use the preprocessor `<generic.h>` facilities
- A set of "Smalltalk-like" classes for heterogeneous collections

Regardless of their implementation, all collection classes generally follow the Smalltalk abstractions for collection classes—`SortedCollection`, `Diction-`

aries, Bags, Sets, etc.—and use similar interfaces, allowing for them to be interchanged easily.

The library also includes a set of abstract data types (ADTs) and corresponding specializing classes that provide a framework for persistence, localization, and other issues, although this is not the central focus of the library. It has been our experience that extensive use of ADTs requires a commitment on the part of the programmer to follow their conventions from the beginning, thus intruding on the overall design.

In the following sections, we discuss the various concrete classes offered by Tools.h++ and its various abstraction facilities. This is followed by a look at various implementation issues including implementation conventions, error handling, and dynamic link libraries.

Simple Classes

Tools.h++ provides a rich set of lightweight simple classes. By "lightweight" we mean classes with low-cost initializers and copy constructors. Examples include RWDate (dates, following the Gregorian calendar), RWTime (times, including support for various time zones and locales), RWCString (single- and multi-byte strings), RWWString (wide character strings), and RWCRegexp (regular expressions). Most of these classes are four bytes or less, with very simple copy constructors (usually just a bit copy) and no virtual functions.

It is worth looking at the string classes in more detail to see how the design objectives were achieved. The goal is to be fast enough that the programmer would not be tempted to go back to strcpy() and the like. We also wanted very simple value semantics that would be easy to understand. Both goals were achieved by using copy-on-write and reference counting. Here's a schematic look at class RWCString, used for single and multi-byte strings (omitting many details critical for performance and robustness in multithreaded environments):

```
class RWCStringRef
{
  // All constructors are private:
  RWCStringRef(const char* cstr);
  // NB: deep copy:
  RWCStringRef(const RWCStringRef&);
  ~RWCStringRef;
  void append(const char*);          // Append to self
```

```
    .
    . // etc.
    .

    unsigned short refs_;        // Reference count
    unsignednchars_;             // String length
    unsignednpts_;               // Length of array_
    char* array_;                // Array of data

  friend class RWCString;
  };

  class RWCString
  {
  public:
    RWCString();   // Null string

    RWCString(const char * a)
    { pref_ = new RWCStringRef(a); }

    RWCString(const RWCString& S)
    { pref_ = S.pref_; ++pref_->refs_; }

    ~RWCString()
    { if (--pref_->refs_ == 0) delete pref_; }

    RWCString& append(const char* cstr)
    { cow();
      pref_->append(cstr);
      return *this; }

    .
    . // etc.
    .

  protected:

    void cow()
    { if (pref_->refs_ > 1) clone(); }
```

```
    void clone()
    { // NB: Deep copy of representation:
      RWCStringRef* temp = new RWCStringRef(*pref_);
      if (--pref_->refs_ == 0) delete pref_;
      pref_ = temp; }
  private:
    RWCStringRef* pref_;
  };
```

The copy constructor of `RWCString` merely increments a reference count rather than making a whole new copy of the string data. This makes read-only copies very inexpensive. A true copy is made only just before an object is to be modified. This also allows all null strings to share the same data, making initialization of arrays of `RWCStrings` fast and efficient:

```
// Global null string representation, shared by
// all strings:
RWCStringRef* nullStringRef = 0;

// Default constructor becomes inexpensive, with
// no memory allocations:
RWCString::RWCString()
{
  if (nullStringRef==0) nullStringRef =
       new RWCStringRef("");
  pref_ = nullStringRef;
  pref_->refs_++;
}
```

Version 6 also includes a wide character-string class with facilities for converting to and from multibyte character strings:

```
class RWWString
{
public:

  enum widenFrom {ascii, multiByte};
```

```
    RWWString(const wchar_t * a);
    RWWString(const char* s,   widenFrom codeset);
    RWWString(const RWCString& s, widenFrom codeset);

    RWBoolean isAscii() const;        // Nothing but ASCII?

    RWCString toAscii() const;        // strip high bytes
    RWCString toMultiByte() const;    // use wcstombs()
    .
    .
    .
};
```

Ordinarily, conversion from multibyte to wide character string is performed using `mbstowcs()`. The reverse conversion is performed using `wcstombs()`. If through other information the character string is known to be ASCII (i.e., no multibyte characters and no characters with their high-order bit set) then optimizations may be possible by using the enum "`widenFrom`" and function `toAscii()`.

TEMPLATES

Three different kinds of template-based collection classes are included in Tools.h++:

- ***Intrusive lists.*** These are lists in which the type `T` inherits directly from the link type itself. The results are optimal in space and time but require the user to honor the inheritance hierarchy.
- ***Value-based collections.*** Value-based collections copy the object in and out of the collection. The results are very robust and easy to understand, but they are not terribly efficient for large objects with nontrivial copy constructors.
- ***Pointer-based collections.*** Pointer-based collections hold a reference to inserted objects, rather than the objects themselves. Because all pointers are of the same size, a given collection type (say, a vector) need only be written for generic `void*` pointers, then the template becomes an interface class that adjusts the type of the pointer to `T*`. The results can be very efficient in space and time, but memory management requires extra care on the part of the user.

All collection classes have a corresponding iterator. Multiple iterators can be active on the same collection at the same time.

Using the template-based collection classes can result in a big performance win because so much is known at compile-time. For example, sorted collection classes can do a binary sort with direct comparison of objects without function calls:

```
template <class T> int
RWTValSortedVector<T>::bsearch(const T& key) const
{
  if (entries())
  {
    int top = entries() - 1, bottom = 0, idx;

    while (top>=bottom)
    {
      idx = (top+bottom) >> 1;
      // Direct, possibly inlined, comparison
      if (key == (*this)(idx))
        return idx;
      else if (key < (*this)(idx))
        top    = idx - 1;
      else
        bottom = idx + 1;
    }
  }
  // Not found:
  return -1;
}
```

This can result in extremely fast searches. It is worth mentioning that the original version of this code used an external class to define the comparison semantics. This resulted in much slower code because current compilers cannot optimize out the thicket of inline functions. Hence we decided to use direct object comparisons. As compilers become better at optimizing, this decision will be revisited. This is an example of our preference for the pragmatic, if theoretically less elegant, in the search for good run-time performance.

GENERIC COLLECTION CLASSES

Generic collection classes are very similar to templates in concept, except that they use the C++ preprocessor and the header file `<generic.h>` as their instantiation mechanism. While they are definitely crude, they do have certain advantages until the widespread adoption of templates. For example, they have the same type safe interface:

```
// Ordered collection of strings
declare(RWGOrderedVector,RWCString)
implement(RWGOrderedVector,RWCString)

RWGOrderedVector(RWCString) vec;
RWCString a("a");

vec.insert(a);            // OK
vec.insert("b");          // Type conversion occurs

RWDate today;
vec.insert(today);        // Rejected!
```

Because their interface and properties are very similar to templates, generic collection classes can be an important porting tool to support compilers and platforms that may not have templates.

SMALLTALK CLASSES

Tools.h++ also includes a comprehensive set of Smalltalk-like collection classes (e.g., `Bag`, `Set`, `OrderedCollection`, etc.), by which we mean classes that are rooted in a single class, in this case `RWCollectable`. Because `RWCollectable` classes can make use of the isomorphic persistence machinery of Tools.h++, all Smalltalk-like classes are fully persistent (see following).

With the widespread adoption of templates by many compilers, these classes will undoubtedly become less important in the future. Nevertheless, they will still offer a number of advantages over templates. For example, heterogeneous Smalltalk-like collections can take advantage of code reuse through polymorphism.

PERSISTENCE

The previous sections offered an overview of the concrete classes in Tools.h++. In this section, we begin discussing some of the abstractions offered by the library.

All objects that inherit from RWCollectable can enjoy isomorphic persistence, that is, the ability to save and restore not only objects but also their interrelationships, including multiple references to the same object.

Persistence is done to and from virtual streams RWvostream (for output) and RWvistream (for input), abstract data types that define an interface for storing primitives and vectors of primitives:

```
class RWvostream
{
public:
virtual RWvostream&     operator<<(char)=0;
virtual RWvostream&     operator<<(double)=0;
virtual RWvostream&     put(const char* p, unsigned N)=0;
virtual RWvostream&     put(const double* p, unsigned N)=0;
// etc. ...
};

class RWvistream
{
virtual RWvistream&     operator>>(char&) = 0;;
virtual RWvistream&     operator>>(double&) = 0;
virtual RWvistream&     get(char*, unsigned N) = 0;
virtual RWvistream&     get(double*, unsigned N) = 0;
// etc. ...
};
```

Clients are freed from concern for not only the source and sink of bytes but the formatting they will use. Two types of specializing virtual streams are supplied: classes RWpostream and RWpistream (formatting in a portable ASCII format), and RWbostream and RWbistream (binary formatting). ASCII formatting offers the advantage of portability between operating systems while binary formatting is typically slightly more efficient in space and time. Users can easily develop other specializing classes. For example, SunPro has developed versions of RWvostream and RWvistream for XDR formatting.

The actual source and sink of bytes is set by a streambuf, such as filebuf or strstream, which is normally supplied by the compiler manufacturer. Tools.h++ also includes two specializing streambufs for Microsoft Windows users: RWCLIPstreambuf for persisting to the Windows Clipboard, and RWDDEstreambuf for persisting between applications using DDE (Dynamic

Data Exchange). The latter can also be used to implement Object Linking and Embedding (OLE) features.

Internationalization

Version 6 of Tools.h++ introduces very powerful facilities for internationalization and localization. Central to these is the `RWLocale` class, which is an abstract base class with an interface designed for formatting and parsing things such as numbers, dates, and times:

```
class RWLocale {
public:
  virtual RWCString asString(long) const = 0;
  virtual RWCString asString(struct tm* tmbuf,
   char format, const RWZone& = RWZone::local())
   const = 0;

  virtual RWBoolean stringToNum (const RWCString&,
   long*) const = 0;
  virtual RWBoolean stringToDate(const RWCString&,
   struct tm*) const = 0;
  virtual RWBoolean stringToTime(const RWCString&,
   struct tm*) const = 0;

  // returns [1..12] (1 for January), 0 for error
  virtual int monthIndex(const RWCString&) const = 0;
  // returns 1 for Monday equivalent, 7 for Sunday,
  // 0 for error.
  virtual int weekdayIndex(const RWCString&) const = 0;

  // the default locale for most functions:
  static const RWLocale& global();
  // A function to set it:
  static const RWLocale* global(const RWLocale*);

  // etc. ...
};
```

Two specializing versions of `RWLocale` are supplied: a lightweight "default" version with English names and `strftime()` formatting conventions, and a version that queries the Standard C locale facilities. The user can easily add other specializing versions that, for example, consult a database.

The RWLocale abstract interface is used by the various concrete classes to format information:

```
class RWDate {

public:

  // 3/12/93 style formatting
  RWCString asString(char format = 'x',
                     const RWLocale& locale =
                       RWLocale::global()) const
  {
   struct tm tmbuf;
   extract(&tmbuf); // Convert date to struct tm
   return locale.asString(&tmbuf, format);
  }
  .
  .
  .
};
```

Here, the member function asString() converts a date into a string, using the formatting information supplied by the locale argument. The global "default locale" is used by binary operators such as the l-shift operator:

```
ostream& operator<<(ostream& s, const RWDate& d)
{
  s << d.asString();
  return s;
}
```

Design and Implementation Conventions

Tools.h++ uses a number of design and implementation conventions that make it easier for the user to understand the library.

Information is generally thought of as flowing into a function via its arguments and then back out via its return value. Functions generally do not change their arguments and so all formal parameters are either passed by value or as a constant reference.

There are two important exceptions. The first is a collection class or other class that must maintain a relationship with another object. In this case, a pointer—but never a reference—to the other object is passed. This is to remind the user that an interrelationship has been established. Hence:

```
RWTPtrOrderedVector<T>::insert(T*);
RWModel::addDependent(RWModelClient* client);
```

and not:

```
RWTPtrOrderedVector<T>::insert(T&);
RWModel::addDependent(RWModelClient&);
```

In the latter example, it is all too easy to think that the argument is being passed in by value, forgetting that a reference to the argument will be retained. Passing in pointers also discourages passing in a stack-based argument because the address of the argument would have to be taken:

```
RWTPtrOrderedVector<RWCString> collect;

// Insert stack-based variable:
RWCString s("a string");
collect.insert(&s); // Looks weird; should ring bells

// Proper idiom:
collect.insert(new RWCString("a string"));
```

The second exception is objects that require initialization with another object in order to work. In C++, a reference represents a real object. It cannot be nil. Hence, it can be useful in the constructor of an object that requires a "partner" object to function. Iterators are an example:

```
RWOrderedIterator(RWOrdered& ord);
```

NAMING CONVENTIONS

Tools.h++ takes great care not to pollute the global name space. All global class, variable, and macro names are prefixed with the letters `RW`. This makes it easy to work with other libraries, including such libraries as the X Window System, which use generic names such as `Object` or `Boolean`.

All function names start with a lowercase letter, but subsequent words are capitalized. Generally, abbreviations are not used.

Where appropriate, all classes use the same member function name. For example, the number of items in a collection class is always returned by member function `entries()`.

ERRORS

Errors are all too common in coding, yet little attention has been paid to them in the literature. Tools.h++ uses an error model that divides errors into one of four different categories:

- Coding errors
- Run-time errors
- Range errors
- Acts of God (or, failures of abstraction)

CODING ERRORS

The distinguishing characteristic of coding errors is that their cost of detection exceeds the cost of the operation contemplated. A good example is bounds errors: The cost of checking to make sure an index is in range can exceed the cost of the array access itself. Hence, good performance demands that the library, at least in a production version, not check indices for validity. This will require some minimal level of correction on the part of the user's program. Anything that falls short is a coding error.

Obviously, to be so classified, such errors must be straightforward, easy to detect, and occur at a relatively low level. Otherwise, it will be extremely difficult for the user to achieve the goal of eliminating all coding errors.

With Tools.h++, coding errors are discovered and eliminated by compiling the library in a "debug" version, which typically activates a set of precondition and postcondition clauses.[2] For example, the debug version includes bounds checking on all array accesses. If the debug version of the library discovers an error, it typically aborts the program.

RUN-TIME ERRORS

The distinguishing characteristic of run-time errors is that they cannot reasonably be predicted in advance. An example is using a bad date (e.g., 31 June 1992) to initialize a date object.

The line between a coding error and a run-time error can sometimes be fuzzy. Attempting to set a date object to an invalid date could be regarded as a violated precondition, but this would result in a less than useful library as the date object is probably in a better position to make this judgment than the user.

The response to a run-time error is either to throw an exception or to provide a test for object validity. The program is never aborted.

RANGE ERRORS

Range errors are similar to run-time errors, but the distinguishing characteristic is that they involve a unary or binary operator where there is no opportunity to return a "status value." An example is an arithmetic overflow from legal arguments. Because a "status value" is not possible, the response is always to throw an exception. No range errors are possible in Tools.h++ (they are primarily an issue in Rogue Wave's math libraries).

ACTS OF GOD

These are more formally known as failures in abstraction. Two examples are:

- Stream write error
- Out-of-memory

These sorts of errors always occur at a highly abstract level and cannot reasonably be predicted in advance. The response is always to throw an exception.

DYNAMICALLY LINKED LIBRARY

Tools.h++, for example, it can be built as a Microsoft Windows Dynamically Linked Library (DLL), which allows it to be shared by multiple applications, reducing both disk and memory usage.

Allowing a library to be compiled as a DLL is not particularly difficult, but it does require attention to detail. By far the most difficult task is dealing with any global data: A Windows DLL has only one data segment, and it is shared between all applications. This means that if one application were to change the global data, all other tasks would see the change. The first defense is to eliminate any global data and, indeed, Tools.h++ has only minimal such data. The remaining data must be managed by an "instance manager" with the job of retrieving the correct piece of global data depending on which application is active, using the task ID as a key. If no data exists for a task, then the manager initializes a new instance.

The only problem comes when the task exits: The DLL should reclaim any instance data and return it to the operating system. This requires patching into the Windows exit procedure code to detect when the task exits.

All of this is handled by a small auxiliary DLL called `RWTSD` (Task Specific Data). This DLL is available to the programmer to implement other DLLs and can be used independently of Tools.h++.

In Closing

This article has focused on the design and architecture of Tools.h++. There is a danger of thinking that this is what library design is all about. Less sexy, but just as important, is what goes on behind the scenes: test suites, porting, installation scripts, dealing with compiler bugs and quirky operating systems, etc. All of these issues, and many more, must be addressed to deliver a robust, versatile, and portable library.

References

1. Stroustrup, B. *The C++ Programming Language.* Addison-Wesley, Reading, MA, 1991.
2. Meyer, B. *Object-Oriented Software Construction.* Prentice Hall, Englewood Cliffs, NJ, 1988.

Simplifying the Booch Components

Grady Booch
Mike Vilot

An often-cited benefit of object-oriented development is the degree of reuse that can be achieved in well-engineered systems. A high degree of software component reuse means that far less code must be written for each new application and, consequently, that there is far less code to maintain. But the idea is not new. In 1968, Doug McIlroy described an industry of such components, and software development has been reusing software in many forms in the 25 years since.[1] Nevertheless, the widespread adoption of software components as commercial products did not take place until recently. Why did it take so long to get to this point, and why are the overwhelming majority of these products written in C++?

We claim that the concepts of object-oriented design (OOD), together with effcient implementation of these concepts in a commercially viable language such as C++, were the key ingredients to making software components available on the scale they are today. Previous design techniques and languages simply made it impractical to offer components with adequate flexibility, ease of use, and performance needed in industrial-strength software development.

Reusing individual lines of code is the simplest form of reuse (what programmer has not used an editor to copy the implementation of some algorithm and paste it into another application?), but it offers the fewest benefits (because the code must be replicated across applications). We can do far better when using object-oriented programming languages by specializing classes through inheritance. We can achieve even greater leverage by reusing whole groups of classes. We call such a collaboration of classes a *class library.*

Our experience with the Booch Components libraries supports the claim that earlier approaches and languages were impractical for developing industrial-strength components. The current version of the library is a second-generation product, and customers have been embedding these components into applications as diverse as telephone communications applications and CASE-like C++ development environments. The original Ada version of the library, developed between 1984 and 1987, required over 150,000 source code lines (approximately 125,000 noncomment source lines, or NCSL). The initial delivery of the C++ version, developed in 1990, required less than 17,000 NCSL, while the current release (version 1.4.7) contains less than 15,000 NCSL. An upcoming release (version 2.0) contains about 10,000 NCSL and offers *additional* capabilities over the earlier versions.

What factors contributed to making the C++ Booch Components into "the incredible shrinking library"? In this article, we'll examine how the concepts of OOD and the features of C++ helped to organize and simplify the library. First, we'll provide a brief overview of the library, showing its contents and organization, and then we'll explore how inheritance and parameterization helped to streamline and simplify the library. The article concludes with a summary of how much each design change contributed to the overall size reduction. These insights may be helpful to other C++ developers, even if they are not currently designing reusable component library products.

Library Overview

The Booch Components are a carefully designed collection of domain-independent data structures and algorithms. Such general-purpose components are also known as *foundation classes* because they raise the level of abstraction of the underlying programming language, forming a more abstract foundation for programming.

The original design of these components was based on a domain analysis of the kinds of data structures and algorithms actually used in industrial software development. Based on that analysis, the library was organized around a framework for classifying components into structures, tools, and subsystems (Figure 1).[2]

The design of any genuinely useful class library demands the delicate balance of competing and often conflicting technical and social requirements. In a general sense, the Booch Components are simply one solution in the design space of constructing a set of domain-independent foundation classes. The design of this particular library was guided by the principles described in *Object-Oriented Design with Applications*,[3] together with a set of pragmatic design rules we have derived through our participation in the development of several very large C++ applications.

These rules contribute to the clear and consistent organization of the C++ Booch Components and thus are of immediate relevance to any user of this library. Additionally, the style employed in the construction of this library has general applicability to other software projects, and so may be of value to

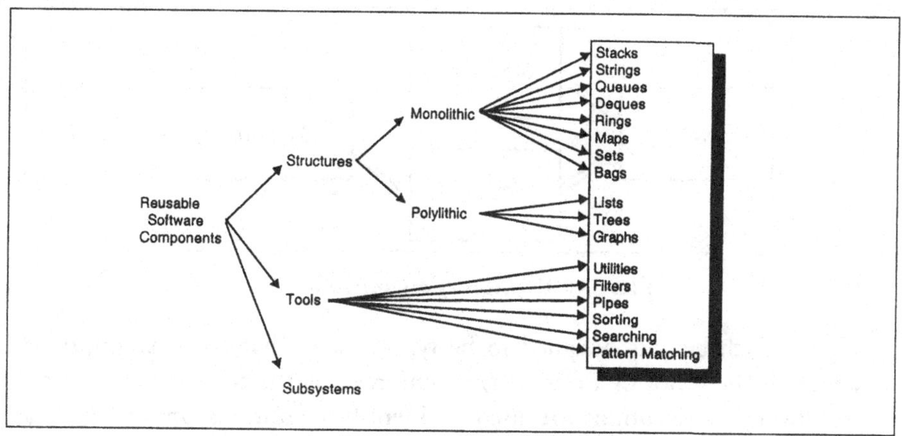

FIGURE 1. *Structures, tools, and subsystems.*

developers in other application domains. This library is carefully organized and precisely defined; as a result, there is an opportunity to formally specify the behavior of all classes in the library.

As discussed elsewhere,[4] a key design goal for this library was to use the full expressive power of the C++ language to make the resulting components reliable, effcient, flexible, and easy to use. We designed the library to meet several specific goals:

- *Completeness.* The library provides classes for many of the basic data structures and algorithms required in production-quality software. Additionally, for each kind of structure, the library offers a family of classes, united by a shared interface, but each employing a different representation, so that a developer can select the one with the time and space semantics most appropriate to a given application.
- *Adaptability.* The library's environment-specific aspects are clearly identified and isolated using template arguments so that local substitutions may be made; in particular, a developer has control over the storage management policy used by each structure as well as the semantics of process synchronization for those forms of a class designed for use in the presence of more than one thread of control.
- *Efficiency.* Our goal was to provide easily assembled components (effcient in compilation resources) that impose minimal runtime and memory overhead (effcient in execution resources) and that are more reliable than hand-built mechanisms (effcient in developer resources).

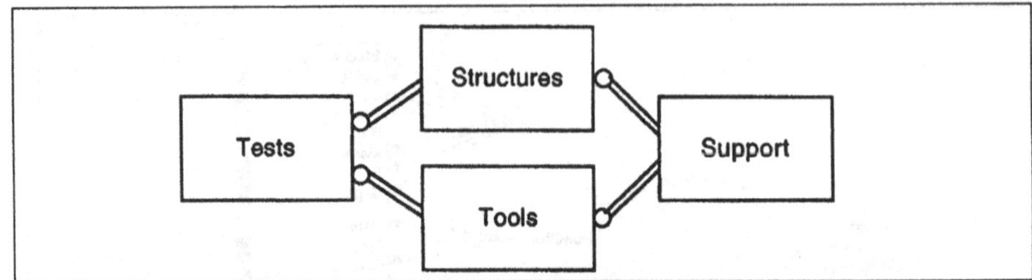

Figure 2. *Library organization.*

- *Safety.* Each class is designed to be type-safe, so that static assumptions about the behavior of a class may be enforced by the compilation system. Additionally, exceptions are used to identify conditions under which a class's dynamic semantics are violated but without corrupting the state of the object that threw the exception.
- *Ease of use.* A clear and consistent organization makes it easy to identify and select appropriate forms of each structure and tool.
- *Extensibility.* It is possible for developers to independently add new data structures and algorithms while preserving the design integrity of the library.

The resulting library design meets these goals. The rest of this section describes how the features of C++ helped realize the overall design.

Library Contents and Structure

The C++ Booch Components are contained in four class categories, as the class diagram in Figure 2 illustrates.*

All of the data structures are placed in the category labeled *Structures*, and all of the algorithms are placed in the category labeled *Tools*. As Figure 2 indicates, all of the data structures and algorithms in the library are constructed from more primitive classes, found in the category named *Support*. Additionally, there exists a *Test* category, which contains comprehensive tests of all of the structures and tools, and which is included as part of software distribution.

The Structures category is further divided into the following categories:

- *Bags.* A collection of items from some domain that may contain duplicates.

* For more information on the OOD notation, including class categories, see References 3, 12, and 13.

- ***Deques.*** A sequence to which items may be added and removed from either end.
- ***Maps.*** A collection forming a dictionary of domain/range pairs.
- ***Queues.*** A sequence to which items may be added from one end and removed from the opposite end.
- ***Rings.*** A sequence in which items may be added and removed from the top of a circular structure.
- ***Sets.*** A collection of items from some domain; may not contain duplicates.
- ***Stacks.*** A sequence in which items may be added to and removed from the same end.
- ***Strings.*** A sequence of zero or more items.
- ***Graphs.*** An unrooted collection of nodes and arcs that may contain cycles and cross-references; structural sharing is permitted.
- ***Lists.*** A sequence of zero or more items; structural sharing is permitted.
- ***Trees.*** A rooted collection of nodes and arcs that cannot contain cycles or cross-references; structural sharing is permitted.

Each of these categories stands alone: There are no dependencies among any categories at this level. The Deques, Queues, Graphs, Lists, and Trees categories are all further divided, and each subcategory represents a family of classes that specializes the more general abstraction (such as in `Priority_Queues` and `Directed_Graphs`).

The first eight categories represent each of the monolithic structures. A *monolithic* structure is one that is always treated as a single unit: There are no identifiable, distinct components, and thus referential integrity is guaranteed. Alternatively, a *polylithic* structure is one in which structural sharing is permitted. For example, we may have objects that denote a sublist of a longer list, a branch of a larger tree, or individual vertices and arcs of a graph. The fundamental distinction between monolithic and polylithic structures is that, in monolithic structures the semantics of copying, assignment, and equality are deep, whereas in polylithic structures copying, assignment, and equality are all shallow (meaning that aliases may share a reference to a part of a larger structure).

The Tools category is further divided into the following subcategories:

- *Filters.* Input, output, and process transformations.
- *Pattern matching.* Vector multi-item searching operations.
- *Searching.* Graph, list, tree, and vector single-item searching operations.
- *Sorting.* Graph and vector ordering operations.
- *Utilities.* Primitive class operations.

Each of these categories also stands alone: There are no dependencies among any categories at this level, although many of these tools operate upon objects that are instances of certain structural classes.

The Support category provides several distinct groups of abstractions:

- *Bound.* Elementary stack-based lists.
- *Except.* Definitions of exceptional conditions.
- *Free.* Facilities for free list management.
- *Heap.* Facilities for stack-based heap management.
- *Node.* Elementary containers.
- *Shared.* Primitive counting abstractions.
- *Synch.* Facilities for process management.
- *Unbound.* Elementary free list-based lists.
- *Vector.* Elementary stack-based vectors.

As Figure 2 suggests, the C++ Booch Components are organized as a forest of classes, rather than as a tree—there is no single base class. The use of class categories is currently only a design convention: They are not represented through inheritance. This design represents a compromise between two other popular alternatives.

The Ada version of the library used no explicit organization in the code. It relied on naming convention only, resulting in a loose collection of 501 packages and subprograms. This alternative was unsatisfactory for two reasons. First, the library was large and unstructured, making it diffcult to locate and select an appropriate component. Second, it increased the overall size of the library because the independence of the components caused too much code duplication.

Other C++ libraries that imitate the form of the Smalltalk library organize their components into a single tree.[5] We considered such a design inappropriate for two reasons. First, these libraries tend to overuse inheritance when type parameterization is more appropriate—such designs often abandon static typing, decreasing the components' reliability. Second, the metaclass mechanisms and other support added to the root class (typically named `Object`) add significant time and space performance overheads. While possibly acceptable in application frameworks or other user interface–intensive code, we felt the overhead was unacceptably high for foundation class components.

Use of C++ Language Features

We found the following language features helpful in realizing the design of the C++ Booch Components:

- Abstract classes
- Inheritance and multiple inheritance
- Templates
- Exceptions

C++ features such as class-specific operators `new` and `delete`, constructors, and destructors were also helpful in making key simplifications to the library.

Abstract Classes and Inheritance

A principle central to the design of this library is the concept of building families of classes related by lines of inheritance. For each kind of structure, the library provides several different classes that are united by a shared interface (such as the abstract base class `Queue`), but which have several concrete subclasses, each with a slightly different representation and thus different time and space semantics. In this manner, a developer can select the one concrete class that has the time and space semantics that best fit the needs of a given application and still be confident that no matter which concrete class is selected, it will behave functionally the same as any other concrete class in the family. Because of this intentional and clear separation of concerns between an abstract class and its concrete classes, it is possible for a developer to initially select one concrete class and later, as the application is being tuned, replace it with a sibling concrete class with minimal effort. The developer can be confident that the application will still work, because all sibling concrete classes share the same interface and the same basic behavior. Another implication of this organization is that it is possible to copy, assign, or test for equality among objects of the same family of classes, even if each object has a radically different representation.

We call these time/space variations the *forms* of an abstraction. In our experience, there are two fundamental forms that any developer must consider when building a serious application. The first of these is the form of representation, which establishes the concrete implementation of an abstract base class. Ultimately, there are only two meaningful choices for in-memory structures. We call these variations the *unbounded* and *bounded* forms of an abstraction, respectively:

- ***Unbounded.*** The structure is stored in the heap and, thus, may grow to the limits of available memory.
- ***Bounded.*** The structure is stored on the stack or in static storage and, thus, has a static size. Clients must specify the structure's size at the time of template instantiation.

Because the unbounded and bounded forms of an abstraction share a common interface (as well as some common state), we choose to make them direct subclasses of the abstract base class for each structure.

Unbounded forms are applicable in cases where the ultimate size of the structure cannot be predicted, and where allocating and deallocating storage from the heap is neither too costly nor unsafe (as it may be in certain time-critical applications). Alternatively, bounded forms are better suited to smaller structures, whose average and maximum sizes are predictable, and where heap usage is deemed insecure. Because both concrete representations of a structure share the same interface and behavior, a developer can choose one representation or the other, with minimal impact to the semantics of the application. Additionally, because of the manner in which copying, assignment, and equality are implemented, it is possible to perform these operations among objects that share the same abstract base class, yet are of different representational subclasses.

The second important variation concerns process synchronization. Many useful applications involve only a single process: We call them *sequential* systems because they involve only a single thread of control. Certain applications, especially those involving real-time control, may require the synchronization of several simultaneous threads of control within the same system. We call such systems *concurrent.*

The synchronization of multiple threads of control is important, because of the issues of mutual exclusion. Simply stated, it is improper to allow two or more threads of control to directly act upon the same object at the same time because they may interfere with the state of the object, and ultimately corrupt its state. For example, consider two active agents that both try to add an item to the same `Queue` object.** The first agent might start to add the new item, be preempted, and so leave the object in an inconsistent state for the second agent.

Basically, three design alternatives are possible, requiring different degrees of cooperation among the agents that interact with a shared object:

- ***Sequential.*** The semantics of the structure are guaranteed only in the presence of a single thread of control.
- ***Guarded.*** The semantics of the structure are guaranteed in the presence of multiple threads of control. Client processes must cooperate in the use of a shared semaphore. Clients must specify the guard class at the time of template instantiation.
- ***Synchronized.*** The semantics of the structure are guaranteed in the presence of multiple threads of control. Each operation is considered atomic, and no explicit collaboration among client processes is required. Clients must specify the monitor class at the time of template instantiation.

The simplest of these three variations is the sequential form, which is equivalent to the behavior of the unbounded and bounded forms described earlier. Because the guarded and synchronized forms of an abstraction share a common interface (as well as some common state) with each corresponding concrete representation class, we chose to make the guarded and synchronized forms direct subclasses of the unbounded and bounded concrete classes.

Bringing these concepts together, the interactions among the abstract base class, the representation forms, and the synchronization forms yield the family of classes for every structure in the library shown in Figure 3.

As this figure illustrates, the cardinality of the base class Queue is zero,† indicating that it is an abstract class and so may have no direct instances. The cardinality of all other classes is unspecified, indicating that (once instantiated) these classes may have any number of instances.

Templates

Except for a few cases, the classes provided in this library are actually templates for classes, using the type parameterization facility described in *The Annotated C++ Reference Manual,*[6] and now an official part of the ANSI/ISO standard

---

** An active agent embodies its own thread of control, and thus may operate autonomously.

† In this article, we will use the Queue class to illustrate our style; its semantics are described in complete detail in Chapter 2 of Reference 14.

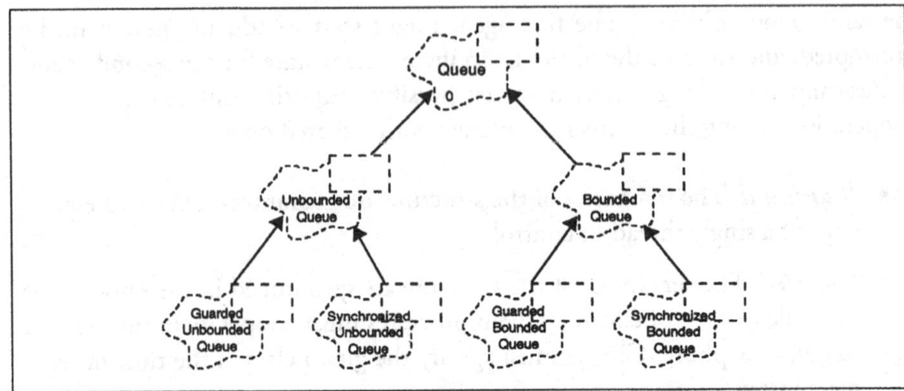

FIGURE 3. *Fundamental forms.*

C++ language. This kind of type parameterization is a fundamental mechanism for combining building blocks and creating the individual classes needed for the application at hand, while preserving a measure of type safety. In this library, templates are used to parameterize each structure with the kind of item it contains. Thus we can devise a `Queue` class whose instances behave the same way, regardless of whether these objects hold primitive items such as integers and pointers or user-defined items such as windows and inventory records. For the abstract base class `Queue`, we may indicate that it is parameterized according to the kind of the Item held in each queue object, as follows:

```
template<class Item>
class Queue...
```

Thus to denote a queue of integers, we may write `Queue<int>` or `Queue<Window>` for a queue of windows.

For example, given the following incomplete declarations:

```
template<class Item, unsigned int Size>
class Bounded_Queue...

class Window {
public:

  unsigned order() const; // the stacking order
                          // of the window
};
```

we may declare a bounded queue object as follows:

```
Bounded_Queue<Window, 36> window_directory;
```

Since the actual instantiated class is anonymous (that is, it has no simple name), we have provided a name for it in brackets as shown in Figure 3.

C++ templates are deliberately underspecified, which leaves a degree of flexibility (and responsibility) in the hands of developers who instantiate templates. It also creates opportunities for optimization, such as sharing definitions of member functions and not instantiating unnecessary member functions, which otherwise would lead to large amounts of code being generated.

In this library, the primary use of templates is to parameterize each structure with the kind of item it contains; this is why such structures are often called *container classes.* As the preceding example illustrates, templates may also be used to provide certain implementation information to a class. In fact, all bounded classes (such as `Bounded_Queue` in the example) require that an instantiator provide an unsigned integer representing the static size of its objects. The library also uses this same approach to import the kind of container used by each unbounded structure, and to import agents responsible for process synchronization.

Exceptions

Whereas we may use the C++ language itself to enforce most static assumptions about an abstraction, we must have some means of reporting any dynamic violations, such as trying to add an item to an already full queue or removing an item from an empty queue. In this library, we apply the exception facility as described in *The Annotated C++ Reference Manual,* now an official part of standard C++. The library provides a base Exception class and derived classes to describe exceptional conditions.

A partial declaration of the base class `Exception` appears as follows:

```
class Exception {
public:

  Exception(const char* name, const char* who, const
            char* what);
  virtual ~Exception();

  virtual void display(ostream&) const;
```

```
    const char* name() const;
    const char* who() const;
    const char* what() const;

  };
```

For every exception, we may attach its name, who threw it, and why it was thrown. Additionally, we provide a means for displaying an exception on an output stream.

Member functions in library classes only *throw* exceptions; they neither try nor catch exceptions. For example, consider the implementation of the member function pop in the abstract base class Queue:

```
template<class Item>
Queue<Item>& Queue<Item>::pop()
{
  if (rep_length == 0)
    throw(Underflow("Queue<Item>::pop()", _EMPTY));
  --rep_length;
  return *this;
}
```

Underflow is a subclass of the base class Exception. In the above function, if the queue object is already empty, we throw the exception. Our convention is to provide the name of the member function that threw the exception together with some meaningful phrase explaining the reason. Using Exception as a base class, clients can derive new kinds of exceptions. The library already provides several such useful subclasses.

One very important aspect of our use of exceptions is that they are guaranteed not to corrupt the state of any object that throws an exception, except in the case of out-of-memory conditions. Member functions always throw an exception before any changes to the state of the object are made. For example, in the implementation of the member function pop above, we first check that all preconditions to the function are satisfied, and only then do we alter the state of the object. This is a style that has been carefully followed, and should be preserved by any subclasses derived from this library.

Library Simplification

As described in the first section, the design of the Booch Components library revolves around four key facets:

- Representation
- Storage management
- Synchronization
- Iteration

Reexamining these from an OOD perspective was the key to simplifying the C++ version of the library. As it turns out, we were able to combine several popular C++ class design idioms.[7,8]

We found the following design idioms helpful to each of the simplifications that led to substantial decreases in the overall size of the library:

- Abstract data types (ADTs)
- Concrete data types (CDTs)
- Iterators as friends
- Virtual constructors
- Resource acquisition as initialization

The following subsections describe how we used these idioms. First, we'll explore how we supplemented the basic ADT idiom used in the Structures category with CDTs drawn from the Support class category. Next, we'll discuss how making iterator classes as friends of the abstract base classes reduced the size of the library, yet allowed us to offer an additional kind of iteration. Then we'll explain how virtual constructors[9,10] and class-specific operators `new` and `delete` simplified the design of storage management options. Next, we'll show how constructors and destructors improved both reliability and performance of the concurrent forms, even in the presence of exceptions.[11] Finally, we'll explain how using template parameters for things other than types helped increase the flexibility and customizability of the library.

The ADT and CDT Idioms

In the "pure" *ADT* idiom, an abstract base class defines an interface, and derived classes provide implementations. We extended this idiom to use *CDTs* for efficient implementations and multiple inheritance to simplify the combination.

In a very simple sense, an abstract base class thus serves to capture all of the relevant public design decisions about the abstraction. Another use of abstract base classes in this library is to cache state that might otherwise be expensive to compute. This can convert an `O(n)` computation to an `O(1)` retrieval. The cost of this style is the required cooperation between the abstract base class and its derived classes, to keep the cached result up to date.

One fundamental design decision in this library was the concept of separating policy from implementation. In a sense, any of the structures in this library are merely abstractions that enforce a certain protocol or policy upon a list or a vector. For example, the policy of a `Stack` object permits adding and removing items only from the top the policy of a `Queue` object permits adding from one end and removing from the other. More complicated classes, such as the class `Ring`, are no different: The policy of a `Ring` permits adding and removing from one point in a list that wraps back around on itself.

A domain analysis of all the structures in this library reveals that by separating policy from implementation, we can extract a significant amount of redundancy among the classes, ultimately resulting in a smaller, more versatile library. This discovery led us to create three low-level classes, upon which all structures are layered. In general, the typical developer using this library need never be concerned with these low-level abstractions, although knowledge of them will help in understanding the time/space trade-offs they represent.

These three lower-level classes include:

- `Simple_List`. A singly linked list, whose nodes are stored on the heap
- `Simple_Bounded_List`. A singly linked list, whose nodes are stored on the stack
- `Simple_Vector`. A simple sequence, whose nodes are stored on the stack

Lists and vectors represent fundamentally different abstractions. A list offers an abstraction that permits the efficient and arbitrary manipulation of linked nodes. Vectors, on the other hand, provide the abstraction of a well-ordered sequence, whose items may be indexed by some ordinal number. Both kinds of classes have a representation optimized to these abstractions. In lists, manipulating nodes is very fast, but finding a particular item is slow (on the order of `O(n)`). In vectors, manipulating items is slow (the worst case is only `O(n/2)`, however), whereas finding an item is very fast (on the order of `O(1)`).

We apply a mixin style of multiple inheritance, to construct both the unbounded and bounded concrete classes. As Figure 4 shows, our style involves using public inheritance to share interfaces and private inheritance to share implementation. Private derivation nheritance;public vs. private ensures that the implicit conversion rules (i.e., using a derived object as a base object) do not apply. Notice

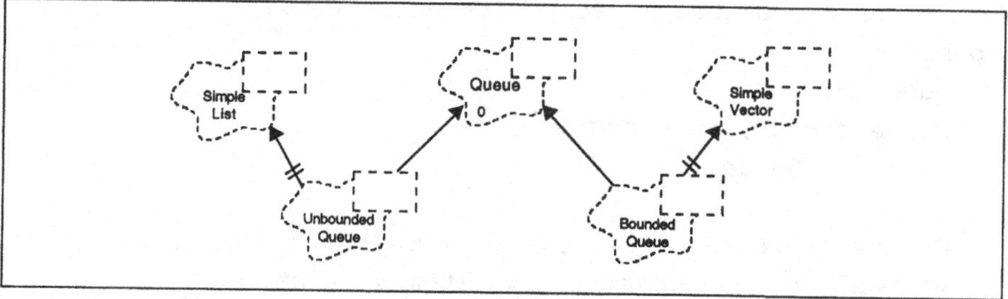

FIGURE 4. *Layering abstractions.*

that we use the class `Simple_Vector` rather than `Simple_Bounded_List` in the bounded forms. We do so because the `Simple_Vector` class is much more space-efficient (as a bounded form should be): the `Simple_Bounded_List` requires storage for an additional unsigned integer for every item. However, this added complexity of the `Simple_Bounded_List` is required for the class `Map` and all of the polylithic structures.

Using this design approach, we were able to factor out much of the duplicated code from the components in the Structures category. We estimate that this saved 20 to 30% of the NCSL count when going from the Ada version to the C++ version of the library.

Polymorphic Iterators

In the Ada version of the library, each component provided two trivially different forms: those with an iterator, and those without. In C++, the ability to introduce an iterator class as a friend of a component led to an important simplification—the notion of iteration was distinct from the semantics of each component. The resulting design was not only simpler, but more flexible. For example, the library offers two different styles of iteration, which we term active and passive. An *active iterator* yields a pointer to successive items in the component, remembering the state of the iteration. A *passive iterator* applies a supplied function to all the items within a component in one logical step:

```
template<class Item> class Queue_Active_Iterator;
template<class Item> class Queue_Passive_Iterator;

// Queue abstract base class

template<class Item>
class Queue {
  friend class Queue_Active_Iterator<Item>;
```

```
    friend class Queue_Passive_Iterator<Item>;
  public:
    Queue();
    Queue(const Queue<Item>&);
    virtual ~Queue();

    Queue<Item>& operator=(Queue<Item>&);
    virtual int operator==(Queue<Item>&) const;
    virtual int operator!=(Queue<Item>&) const;

    virtual Queue<Item>& clear();
    virtual Queue<Item>& add(const Item&);
    virtual Queue<Item>& pop();

    virtual unsigned length() const;
    virtual int is_empty() const;
    virtual Item& front() const = 0;
    ...
  };

  // Queue iterators

  template <class Item>
  class Queue_Active_Iterator {
  public:
    Queue_Active_Iterator(const Queue<Item>&);
    virtual ~Queue_Active_Iterator();

    virtual void reset();
    virtual int next();

    virtual int is_done();
    virtual Item* item();
    ...
  };

  template <class Item>
  class Queue_Passive_Iterator {
  public:
```

```
    Queue_Passive_Iterator(const Queue<Item>&);
    virtual ~Queue_Passive_Iterator();
    virtual int apply(int (*)(Item*));
    ...
};
```

Each component in this library is designed so that a client may copy, assign, and test for equality among objects of the same abstract base class that have different representations. We achieve this capability through an elegant use of iterators and helper functions. This style allows us, in the abstract base class, to traverse any structure in a representation-independent manner.

We estimate that designing iterators as friends saved 50% of the NCSL in the C++ version over the Ada version, since each component did not need the trivial variants.

Virtual Constructors

The major implication of separating policy from implementation in this manner is that each concrete representation form becomes almost trivial. For example, the implementation of the member function pop for the `Unbounded_Queue` is as follows:[††]

```
template<class Item, class Container>
Queue<Item>& Unbounded_Queue<Item, Container>::pop()
{
  Queue<Item>::pop();
  Simple_List<Item>::remove();
  return *this;
}
```

Because the protocols of the list and vector low-level classes are somewhat the same, the implementation of the bounded forms of structures parallels the unbounded forms fairly closely.

Unbounded forms raise the issues of storage management: One must choose a policy whereby nodes are allocated and deallocated from the heap. Our design is to place this policy decision in the hands of the developer, not the library, thus offering many more degrees of freedom in tuning the library for serious

[††] We introduce a `typedef` only for the purpose of readability.

applications. We achieve this design by constructing the `Simple_List` so that it manipulates containers of the class `Node` or its subclasses. Therefore, the template signature of every unbounded form is roughly the same, since each must provide an argument for the instantiator to supply a particular kind of container. The `Unbounded_Queue` is a typical example of this style:

```
template<class Item, class Container>
class Unbounded_Queue : private Simple_List<Item>,
                        public Queue<Item>...
```

Notice our use of public and private inheritance. To instantiate this class, an instantiator must provide an item and a container for that item, as follows:[§]

```
typedef Node<char> Char_Node;
Unbounded_Queue<char, Char_Node> char_queue_1;
```

Bounded forms are different, in that items are stored directly within the component, and so do not require any containers for storage management. However, an instantiator is responsible for specifying the size of a structure at the point of instantiation, and so the template signature of every bounded form appears similar to the following example:

```
template<class Item,  unsigned int Size>
class Bounded_Queue : private Simple_Vector<Item, Size>,
                      public Queue<Item>...
```

To instantiate this class, an instantiator must provide an item and a size, as follows:

```
Bounded_Queue<char, 100U> char_queue_2;
```

All bounded forms provide the member function available, which allows a client to query how much space is available in the structure.

Storage management is an issue for all unbounded forms, because the library designer must consider their policies for allocating and deallocating nodes from the heap. A naive approach will simply use the global `new` and `delete` functions for each item, but this strategy can have very poor runtime performance. With a little more work, a library can be constructed with a much more robust facility.

The low-level class `Simple_List` is defined to work upon containers of the

---

[§] We introduce a `typedef` only for the purpose of readability.

class `Node` and its subclasses. A basic node is the most primitive of all containers, and consists of an item value and a pointer to the next node. This structure is sufficient for many structures, but not expressive enough for structures such as the classes `Bag`, `Map`, and `Ring`.

A domain analysis reveals that six kinds of nodes are sufficient for all the monolithic structures in this library:

- `Node`. The most primitive container, consisting of an item value and a pointer to the next node
- `Double_Node`. A kind of `Node`, with the addition of a pointer to the previous node
- `Tree_Node`. A kind of `Double_Node`, with the addition of a pointer to a parent node
- `Graph_Node`. A kind of `Tree_Node`, with the addition of a pointer to a connected node
- `Counting_Node`. A kind of `Node`, with the addition of a counter
- `Association_Node`. A kind of `Node`, with the addition of a second value

Polylithic structures offer a greater challenge. Because C++ does not directly provide any mechanisms for automatic garbage collection, clients must be very particular about storage management in objects that allow structural sharing. Otherwise, large amounts of garbage will be generated, and the application will quickly run out of usable heap space. Our style in this library was to design all such components so that storage leaks were eliminated.‡

For example, when manipulating a list, we would like all relevant nodes to be reclaimed, once that list or any parts of that list could no longer be reached. We achieve this behavior through the interaction of two techniques. First, the interfaces of all polylithic classes are carefully designed to export only those operations that are guaranteed not to produce any memory leaks, unless grossly misused. Specifically, most polylithic operations generally do not create new objects, but rather, alias existing ones. Second, we use simple reference counting on nodes, which we get inexpensively by mixing in the class `Shared` (a reference counting class) to each of the six basic node classes above.

The mixin class `Shared` is quite simple: It provides a counter, which a polylithic structure uses to keep track of how many references there are to the node. When a modifier function causes this count to drop to zero, then the structure can safely reclaim the node.

---

‡ Except in the case of intentional abuses by the client, which no library can defend against.

A client of `Simple_List` (such as any unbounded structure) is responsible for allocating the kind of node appropriate to that structure, and placing it in the list in its proper place. We have designed every unbounded structure, so that allocation is isolated in exactly one member function, thus simplifying the task of any developer who wishes to specialize an existing concrete unbounded class. `Simple_List` then relies upon the polymorphic behavior of nodes, especially with regard to their constructors, destructors, and copying operations, so that the behavior of the given node subclass is correctly performed.

Stopping our design at this point yields the naive solution to storage management described above. This is not necessarily a terrible solution; it may be sufficient for simple applications. However, this solution can have some distressing runtime characteristics. Specifically, when nodes are allocated and deallocated at arbitrary times and interleaved with the allocation and deallocation of other items on the heap, the heap can become very fragmented and, ultimately, the application can run out of usable heap space. Additionally, for certain time-critical applications where microseconds count, the cost of allocating nodes at critical moments may actually be prohibitive.

In light of these circumstances, we may employ at least three meaningful storage management policies. This library provides predefined mechanisms for all of them, plus the facilities that allow library developers to create their own policies. Figure 5 illustrates how these three policies are organized in the library.

Unmanaged

We call the first storage management policy *unmanaged* because it involves doing nothing. Under this policy, allocation, and deallocation rely upon the behavior of the global functions `new` and `delete`, respectively.

Managed

The second policy is called *managed.* Under this policy, nodes are allocated and deallocated from a free list managed by an instance of the class `Storage_Manager`. Unused nodes of any kind are reclaimed to this free list, and allocation takes nodes from the free list unless it is empty, in which case new nodes of an appropriate size are allocated from the heap. This policy has the advantage of minimizing new allocation from the heap and localizing references to often-used nodes, but has the disadvantage that when structures grow very large and then shrink to a small size in the steady state, the free list becomes filled with storage that is unusable outside all clients of the storage manager. To mitigate this problem, we do make it possible for a client to purge the free list.

The library achieves the managed policy through the collaboration of the

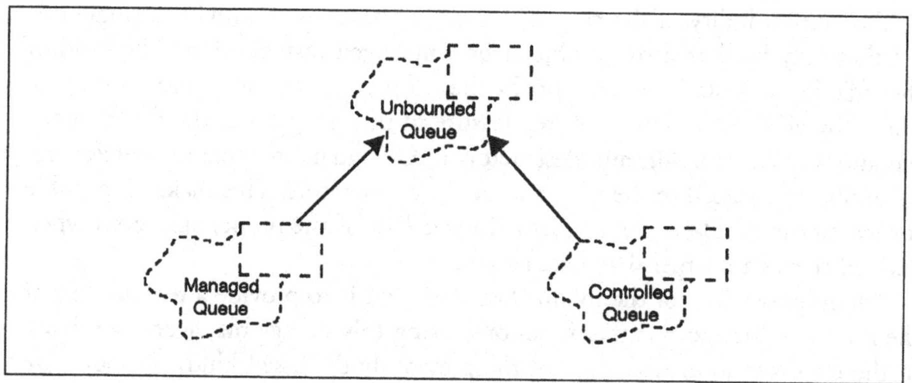

FIGURE 5. *Storage management.*

concrete class `Storage_Manager`, the mixin class `Managed`, and the various node classes. This collaboration is encapsulated in the `allocate()` member functions of the `Unbounded` and `Controlled` forms:

```
template<class Item, class Container>
class Unbounded_Queue : private Simple_List<Item>,
                        public Queue<Item> {
public:

  Unbounded_Queue();
  Unbounded_Queue(const Unbounded_Queue<Item,
    Container>&);
  virtual ~Unbounded_Queue();

  Unbounded_Queue<Item, Container>& operator=
    (Unbounded_Queue<Item, Container>&);
  virtual int operator==(Queue<Item>&) const;
  virtual int operator!=(Queue<Item>&) const;

  virtual Queue<Item>& clear();
  virtual Queue<Item>& add(const Item&);
  virtual Queue<Item>& pop();

  virtual unsigned length() const;
  virtual Item& front() const;

protected:
  virtual Node<Item>* allocate(const Item&);
...
};
```

The responsibility of the class `Storage_Manager` is to provide a single free list that may be shared by all objects of a managed instantiation. The head of this free list is a static declaration in the `Storage_Manager`, and so may be shared by all of its instances. A key feature of this design uses the fact that the semantics of constructors and destructors in C++ guarantee that the correct size of an object is passed to the `new` and `delete` operators. This makes it possible for the `Storage_Manager` to maintain free lists of the proper size, even when derived classes are larger than base classes.

The responsibility of the mixin class `Managed` is to provide a redefinition of the `new` and `delete` member functions, using this storage manager. By mixing in the class `Managed` with each of the previously discussed kinds of nodes, we produce a new family of nodes that uses the free list. In this manner, the interaction between all unbounded forms and managed storage management is indirect: the essential link is through the specialized behavior of all the managed kinds of nodes. Because each kind of managed node object knows how to copy itself and respond to the operators `new` and `delete` (inherited from the `Managed` mixin), no other member functions have to be redefined. This style not only reduces the overall size of the library, but contributes to its reliability and maintainability.

Controlled

The third policy is called *controlled* and is required in certain circumstances because of the semantics of process synchronization. For all sequential applications, the simpler unmanaged and managed policies are generally sufficient. For some multithreaded applications, these policies may indeed still apply. As we will discuss in the next section, we make the assumption that for every object of a guarded or synchronized form, there may be more than one active agent that manipulates it. By implementing these forms so that their member functions are treated as atomic actions, we can guarantee that there is mutual exclusion over any actions that manipulate the free list, and so are safe in the presence of multiple threads of control. However, there is one hybrid situation that must be considered. Suppose we can guarantee that exactly one active agent will manipulate an object at one time. Under these circumstances, we do not need the complexity of the guarded or concurrent forms, because there are no problems of mutual exclusion within an object. Specifically, no one object may have its state manipulated by more than one thread of control at a time. However, there are problems of mutual exclusion within the class. Although individual objects are not shared by active agents, any free list is common to all such objects, and so must be given mutual exclusion. This leads us to to create the mixin class

`Controlled`. `Controlled` is exactly like the class `Managed`, except that allocation and deallocation are guaranteed to be atomic actions. In this manner, we achieve mutual exclusion over the free list, without having to use the more complex guarded or synchronized forms.

Introducing virtual constructors saved about 50% of the NCSL in the C++ version over the Ada version of the library. However, the richer storage management and `Node` components offset some of this savings.

Concurrency as Incremental Extension

An important feature of this library is its support for concurrent uses of the structures. A purely sequential version of the library could be made to work in a concurrent environment (e.g., with client applications that manually guarded every call to any library operation). However, besides being tedious and error-prone, such an approach can be inefficient. Certain operations (especially in complex components) can be made more effective when implemented at the finer granularity available to the library's implementor.

The design of this library makes the following assumption: Developers who care about concurrency will have ported or implemented at least a `Semaphore` class for synchronizing light-weight processes, such as found in the *AT&T* task library. Other clients won't care and won't miss not having the guarded or synchronized forms of structures (and will appreciate not having to pay the overhead). The guarded and synchronized forms are an independent, layered part of the library, and rely upon local implementations of concurrency mechanisms. The library's only dependencies upon the local implementation are intentionally isolated in the implementation of the class `Semaphore`.

This library provides two predefined process synchronization policies:

- ***Single.*** Guarantees the semantics of a structure in the presence of multiple threads of control, with a single reader or writer
- ***Multiple.*** Guarantees the semantics of a structure in the presence of multiple threads of control, with multiple simultaneous readers or a single writer

A *writer* is an agent that alters the state of an object. Writers invoke modifier member functions. A *reader* is an agent that operates upon an object, yet preserves its state; readers are objects that only invoke selector functions. The multiple form therefore provides the greatest amount of parallelism possible.

These two policies are implemented via the predefined monitors `Single_Read_Write_Monitor` and `Multiple_Read_Write_Monitor`, respectively.

These classes are both subclasses of the base class `Read_Write_Monitor` and are layered on top of the class `Semaphore`.

Monitors collaborate with the predefined classes `Read_Lock` and `Write_Lock` to achieve exclusive invocation of each individual member function. A lock contains a semaphore or a monitor as the agent responsible for process synchronization, and the lock is responsible for seizing this agent upon construction and releasing it upon destruction. The class `Write_Lock` has a very simple declaration, as follows:

```
class Write_Lock {
public:

  Write_Lock (const Read_Write_Monitor&);

  Write_Lock ();
...
};
```

By separating the abstractions of the lock and its monitor, our design permits a client to attach a different policy to the mechanism of locking.

The definition of the class `Read_Lock` is equally simple. When used with the class `Multiple_Read_Write_Monitor`, a read lock object permits multiple simultaneous readers, but when used with the class `Single_Read_Write_Monitor`, a read lock object treats readers and writers the same.

The definition of each member function in a synchronized form uses locks to wrap around the corresponding operation inherited from its superclass:

```
template<class Item, class Container, class Monitor>
Queue<Item>&
  Synchronized_Unbounded_Queue<Item, Container,
     Monitor>::pop()
{
  Write_Lock _x(rep_monitor);
  return Unbounded_Queue<Item, Container>::pop();
}
```

Here, we employ a write lock, because we are guarding a modifier. The simple elegance of this design is that it guarantees that every member function represents an atomic action, even in the face of exceptions and without any explicit action on the part of a reader or writer.

In a similar fashion, we employ a read lock object to guard selectors:

```
template<class Item, class Container, class Monitor>
unsigned
  Synchronized_Unbounded_Queue<Item, Container,
     Monitor>::length() const
{
  Read_Lock _x(rep_monitor);
  return Queue<Item>::length();
}
```

Given the predefined monitors, an instantiator may declare the following:

```
typedef Node<char> Char_Node;
Synchronized_Unbounded_Queue
  <char, Char_Node, Multiple_Read_Write_Monitor>
     concurrent_queue;
```

Clients who use synchronized objects need not follow any special protocol, because the mechanism of process synchronization is handled implicitly and is therefore less prone to the deadlocks and livelocks that may result from incorrect usage of guarded forms. A developer should choose a guarded form instead of a synchronized form, however, if it is necessary to invoke several member functions together as one atomic transaction, the synchronized form only guarantees that individual member functions are atomic.

Our design renders synchronized forms relatively free of circumstances that might lead to a deadly embrace. For example, assigning an object to itself or testing an object for equality with itself is potentially dangerous because, in concept, it requires locking the left and right elements of such expressions, which in these cases is the same object. Once constucted, an object cannot change its identity so these tests for self-identify are performed first, before either object is locked.

Even then, member functions that have instances of the class itself as arguments must be carefully designed to ensure that such arguments are properly locked. Our solution relies upon the polymorphic behavior of two helper functions, `lock_argument` and `unlock_argument`, defined in every abstract base class. Each abstract base class provides a default implementation of these two functions that does nothing; synchronized forms provide an implementation that seizes and releases the argument. As shown in an earlier example, member functions such as `operator=` use this technique.

We estimate that the use of Lock classes saved about 50% of the NCSL when moving from Ada to C++. The Guarded, Concurrent, and Multiple forms accounted for 75% of the packages in the Ada versions of the library. Each such package was larger and slower than its sequential counterparts, due to the need to explicitly handle each exception and release any locks.

Parameterizing Concurrency and Storage Managers

Templates may also be used to provide certain implementation information to a class. To make this library more adaptable, we give the instantiator control over which storage management policy is used, on a class-by-class basis. This places some small additional demands upon the instantiator, but yields the much greater benefit of giving us a library that can be tuned for serious applications.

Similar to the mechanism of storage management, the template signature of guarded forms imports the guard rather than making it an immutable feature. This makes it possible for library developers to introduce new process synchronization policies. Using the predefined class `Semaphore` as a guard, the library's default policy is to give every object of the class its own semaphore. This policy is acceptable only up to the point where the total number of processes reaches some practical limit set by the local implementation.

An alternate policy involves having several guarded objects share the same semaphore. A developer need only produce a new guard class that provides the same protocol as `Semaphore` (but is not necessarily a subclass of `Semaphore`). This new guard might then contain a `Semaphore` as a static member object, meaning that the semaphore is shared by all its instances. By instantiating a guarded form with this new guard, the library developer introduces a different policy whereby all objects of that instantiated class share the same guard, rather than having one guard per object. The power of this policy comes about when the new guard class is used to instantiate other structures: All such objects ultimately share the same guard. The policy shift is subtle, but very powerful: Not only does it reduce the number of processes in the application, but it permits a client to globally lock a group of otherwise unrelated objects. Seizing one such object blocks all other objects that share this new guard, even if those objects are entirely different types.

Guarded

A guarded class is a direct subclass of its concrete representation class. A guarded class contains a guard as a member object. All guarded classes introduce the member functions seize and release, which allow an active agent to gain exclusive access to the object.

For example, consider the class `Guarded_Unbounded_Queue`, which is a kind of `Unbounded_Queue`:

```
template<class Item, class Container, class Guard>
class Guarded_Unbounded_Queue : public
Unbounded_Queue<Item, Container> {
public:

  Guarded_Unbounded_Queue();
  Guarded_Unbounded_Queue
    (const Guarded_Unbounded_Queue<Item, Container,
       Guard>&);
  virtual ~Guarded_Unbounded_Queue();

  Guarded_Unbounded_Queue<Item, Container, Guard>&
    operator=(Guarded_Unbounded_Queue<Item,
      Container, Guard>&);

  virtual Queue<Item>& seize();
  virtual Queue<Item>& release();

protected:

    Guard rep_guard;

};
```

This library provides the interface of one predefined guard: the class `Semaphore`. Users of this library must complete the implementation of this class, according to the needs of the local definition of light-weight processes.

Given this predefined guard, an instantiator may declare the following:

```
typedef Node<char> Char_Node;
Guarded_Unbounded_Queue<char, Char_Node, Semaphore>
  guarded_queue;
```

Clients who use guarded objects must follow the simple protocol of first seizing the object, operating upon it, and then releasing it (especially in the face of any exceptions thrown). To do otherwise is considered socially inappropriate, because aberrant behavior on the part of one agent denies the fair use by other agents. Seizing a guarded object and then failing to release it blocks the object indefinitely; releasing an object never first seized by the agent is subversive. Lastly, ignoring the seize/release protocol is simply irresponsible.

The primary benefit offered by the guarded form is its simplicity, although it does require the fair collective action of all agents that manipulate the same object. Another key feature of the guarded form is that it permits agents to form critical regions, in which several operations performed upon the same object are guaranteed to be treated as an atomic transaction.

Synchronized

A synchronized class is also a direct subclass of its concrete representation class. It contains a monitor as a member object. Synchronized classes do not introduce any new member functions, but, rather, redefine every virtual member function inherited from their base class. The semantics added by a synchronized class cause every member function to be treated as an atomic transaction. Whereas clients of guarded forms must explicitly seize and release an object to achieve exclusive access, synchronized forms provide this exclusivity, without requiring any special action on the part of their clients. For example, consider the class `Synchronized_Unbounded_Queue`, which is a kind of `Unbounded_Queue`:

```
template<class Item, class Container, class Monitor>
class Synchronized_Unbounded_Queue :
  public Unbounded_Queue<Item, Container> {
public:

  Synchronized_Unbounded_Queue();
  Synchronized_Unbounded_Queue
    (const Synchronized_Unbounded_Queue<Item,
       Container, Monitor>&);

  virtual ~Synchronized_Unbounded_Queue();

  Synchronized_Unbounded_Queue<Item, Container,
    Monitor>&
    operator=(Synchronized_Unbounded_Queue<Item,
       Container, Monitor>&);
  virtual int operator==(Queue<Item>&) const;
```

```
    virtual Queue<Item>& clear();
    virtual Queue<Item>& add(Item&);
    virtual Queue<Item>& pop();

    virtual unsigned length() const;
    virtual int is_empty() const;
    virtual Item& front() const;

protected:

    Monitor rep_monitor;

    virtual void lock_argument();
    virtual void unlock_argument();

};
```

We estimate that parameterizing by storage and concurrency managers saved another 25% of the NCSL count. Using parameterization instead of inheritance allowed us to remove the Unmanaged, Controlled, and Multiple forms as explicit components, instead allowing clients to re-create them through instantiation.

Conclusions

Object-oriented development provides a strong basis for designing flexible, reliable, and efficient reusable software components. However, a language offering direct support for the concepts of OOD (specifically, abstraction, inheritance, and parameterization) makes it much easier to realize the designs. The C++ language, with its efficient implementation of these concepts and increasing adoption among commercial software developers, is a key contribution toward the development of a reusable software components industry.

We feel that our experience with the Ada and C++ versions of the Booch Components library supports this claim. Table 1 summarizes the factors leading to substantial NCSL reductions in the C++ Booch Components. As with all such tables, the figures should not be taken too seriously, nor should they be extrapolated to apply to all C++ development projects around the world.

Table 1 indicates how each of the design topics discussed earlier contributed to the reduction. Each percentage factor reduced the previous NCSL total, resulting in a new estimated total. For example, factoring out support classes saved about 25%, reducing the NCSL count from about 125,000 to about 94,000. Having iterators as friends saved another 50% of that, reducing the 94,000 to about 47,000, and so on.

Table 1. *Factors leading to substantial NCSL reductions in the C++ Booch Components.*

	Factor	NCSL (total)
Original Ada version		125,000
Factoring support	25%	94,000
Polymorphic iterators	50%	47,000
Virtual constructors	50%	23,500
Layered concurrency	50%	12,000
Parameterizing managers	25%	10,000

These figures are somewhat conservative, because we actually added features and components in the C++ version that have no counterpart in the Ada version. We also expect that future versions of the library will be larger as we extend it with new capabilities. For example, release 2.0 features `Hash_Table` support as a third form of representation for each component.

As the ANSI/ISO standard definition of C++ emerges, we also contemplate taking advantage of its features. For example, the library could rely on support from iostreams in the standard library to provide input/output support across all components. The proposed namespace management mechanism would allow this library to reflect class categories directly. We also expect to add components and features requested by the growing number of C++ Booch Components customers around the world.

References

1. McIlroy, M.D. Mass-produced software components, *Proceedings of the NATO Conference on Software Engineering,* 1969.
2. Booch, G. *Software Components with Ada,* Benjamin/Cummings, Menlo Park, CA, 1987.
3. Booch, G. *Object-Oriented Design with Applications,* Benjamin/Cummings, Redwood City, CA, 1991.
4. Booch, G. and M.J. Vilot. The Design of the C++ Booch Components, *OOPSLA/ECOOP Conference,* Ottawa, Canada, Oct, 1990.
5. Goldberg, A. and D. Robson. *Smalltalk80: The Language and its Implementation,* Addison-Wesley, Reading, MA, 1983.
6. Ellis, M.A. and B.Stroustrup. *The Annotated C++ Reference Manual,* Addison-Wesley, Reading, MA, 1990.

7. Coplien, J.O. *Advanced C++ Programming Styles and Idioms*, Addison-Wesley, Reading, MA, 1992.
8. Stroustrup, B. *The C++ Programming Language, 2d ed.*, Addison-Wesley, Reading, MA, 1991.
9. Carroll, M.D., and M.A. Ellis. Simulating virtual constructors in C++, *The C++ Journal* 1(3): 3134.
10. Jordan, D. Class derivation and emulation of virtual constructors, *C++ Report* 1(8): 1–5.
11. Koenig, A., and B. Stroustup. Exception handling for C++, *C++ at Work*, Tyngsboro MA, Nov 68, 1989, pp. 93120.
12. Booch, G. The Booch method: notation, *Computer Language*, Aug 1992.
13. Martin, R.C. *Designing C++ Applications Using the Booch Notation*, Prentice Hall, Englewood Cliffs, NJ, 1993.
14. Vilot, M.J., *C++ Programming PowerPack*, SAMS Publishing, Carmel, IN, 1993.

Design Generalization in the C++ Standard Library

Michael J. Vilot
603.429.3808
mjv@objects.mv.com

One of the advantages of a standard library is that C++ developers can count on its availability across all (standard-conforming) implementations. Whether they actually use it depends on how effectively the library's facilities meet their needs.

In developing the C++ Standard Library, we worked to achieve this effectiveness by balancing some competing concerns. In particular, we wanted to respect the architectural advantages that characterize the C++ language itself, including efficiency, generality, and extensibility.

The resulting library meets these goals. In doing so, it applies some consistent design ideas (design *patterns*, if you will) that may be useful to C++ developers facing similar requirements in their own class library designs.

Introduction

Few library proposals submitted for standardization survived the design review process unscathed. Even the *STL*, with its clear and consistent design, required some important changes to be general enough for a library as (eventually) ubiquitous as the C++ Standard Library.

In this article, we'll focus on the design ideas that help make the library's components more general, and also more adaptable to a C++ developer's needs. The following sections review how various library components generalize key aspects of their design, including:

- Generalizing character type
- Generalizing numeric type

- Generalizing "characteristics"
- Generalizing storage

Generalizing Character Type

Text processing is fundamental to many C++ applications.[1] A string class is a fundamental part of many C++ class libraries. Indeed, the existence of so many varieties of string classes is one impediment to combining libraries in today's C++ applications—and therefore an ideal candidate for standardization.

The essential abstraction of a string is a sequence of "characters." The C++ Standard Library inherits the C library's functions for manipulating null-terminated sequences of char types. It also inherits the parallel set of functions (defined in Amendment 1 to the *ISO* C standard) for manipulating sequences of `wchar_t types`.

At one point, the C++ Standard Library had a similar redundancy—two independent classes (named `string` and `wstring`) for handling the two types of strings. They were identical in all respects (storage semantics, public operations, member names, etc.), except for the type of character they contained and manipulated. As such, they represented little more than a slight syntactic improvement over the C library. Obviously, we could improve upon this design in C++.

A key goal of this design improvement was a more direct representation of the fundamental commonality of text strings. An obvious solution, from an object-oriented design perspective, was a class hierarchy. With this design approach, the base class would define the common operations, while the derived classes would provide specializations for each character type.

That design approach proved infeasible, for two reasons. First, even the modest overhead of C++'s virtual functions would be too expensive for a significant number of performance-critical, text-handling, C++ programs. Second, the character type is a fundamental part of each class' interface—supporting both `char` and `wchar_t` led to a base class with a "fat interface."[2] Such a solution was more unwieldy than the problem it was trying to solve.

An alternative design was to use the C++ template mechanism to generalize strings by the type of character they contain. The class template `basic_string` defines the common interface for text strings:

```
template<class charT> class basic_string { /* ... */ };
```

Classes `string` and `wstring` are specializations of this template (see Figure 1, where the dashed lines denote the instantiation relationship):

```
typedef basic_string<char> string;
```

```
typedef basic_string<wchar_t> wstring;
```

This achieves the desired goal of specifying string handling semantics once, in the `basic_string` definition.

METAFILEPICT

It is important to note that an implementation is not constrained to implementing these `typedefs` as compiler-generated instantiations of the template. In particular, they can be defined as template specializations[3]:

```
class basic_string<char> { /* ... */ };
class basic_string<wchar_t> { /* ... */ };
```

In this way, the implementation of text-handling can take advantage of any platform-dependent optimizations. For example, an implementation on a CISC platform can exploit character-handling machine instructions. Thus, the C++ Standard Library's text-handling facilities will be at least as efficient as those of the C library. Indeed, with the additional state information available to a class, the C++ version is likely to be more efficient.

One obvious optimization would exploit the observation that the vast majority of text strings are read-only copies of one another (a reference-counting implementation can avoid many expensive storage allocation and string copying operations). Another observation is that most strings are shorter than a typical size (an implementation that directly contains short strings avoids dynamic storage allocation for them).

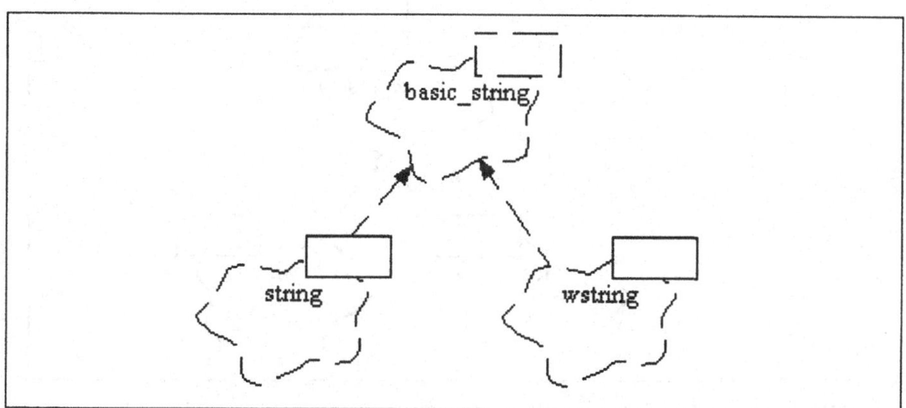

FIGURE 1. `string` *and* `wstring` *as template instances.*

The iostreams library is also parameterized by character type, with some additional considerations. In the original iostreams library developed at *AT&T*, the base class `ios` contained the state information for a stream. It also served as the base class for the derived classes `istream`, `ostream`, `fstream`, `strstream`, and others.

This design had an important advantage: C++ code designed to operate polymorphically on class `ios` (that is, operating on types `ios&` or `ios*`) was able to work equally well on any kind of stream. One example of this kind of design is the iostream manipulators, such as `endl`, `hex`, and `setw`.

Parameterizing class `ios` into the class template `basic_ios` destroyed this kind of extensibility—each instance of `basic_ios` is a distinct type. The solution to this problem was to derived the parameterized class from a nonparameterized base class, `ios_base`, as illustrated in Figure 2.

This design retains the advantages of both polymorphism and parameterization: state-manipulation operations (such as manipulators) can be applied to all types of streams, and new stream types can be added for new kinds of "characters."

Generalizing Numeric Type

The same basic idea can be applied to other types, as well. At one point, the C++ Standard Library contained the three independent classes `float_complex`,

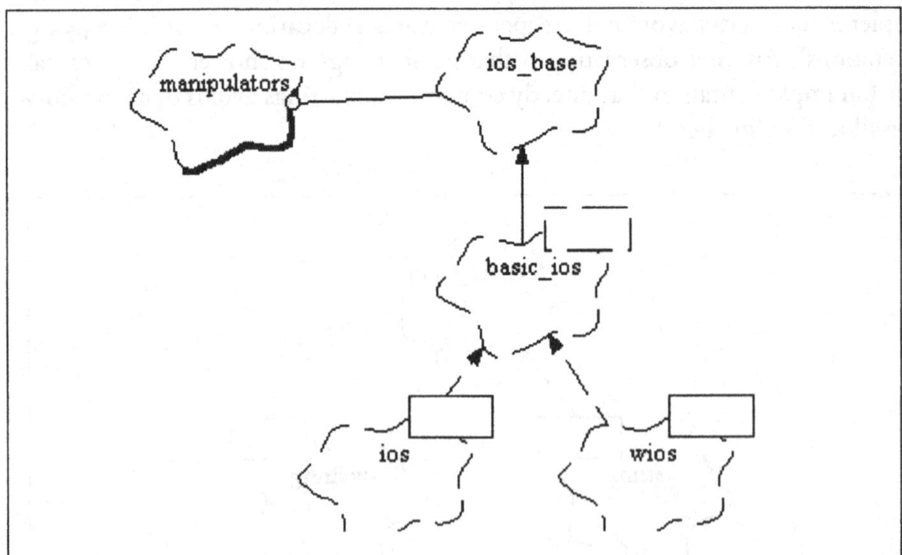

Figure 2. *Iostreams combine polymorphism and parameterization.*

`double_complex`, and `long_double_complex`. Parameterizing them by their numeric type yields the class template complex, as illustrated in Figure 3.

This design had one interesting wrinkle, due to implicit conversions. For the predefined floating point types, both C and C++ define automatic promotions from float to double, and from double to long double. An effective design for numeric classes (such as complex) provides similar conversions. However, there isn't a reasonable way to specify this in a general template.

The solution to this problem was template specialization. The class template complex defines the operations common to all complex number types, while the specializations `complex<float>`, `complex<double>`, and `complex<long double>` add the necessary conversion operators.

Generalizing "Characteristics"

As a general rule, the C++ Standard avoids prescribing specific implementation details. However, the semantics of components such as strings and iostreams depend on certain implementation-dependent properties, such as the definition for an end-of-file marker. The Standard C library addressed this problem with `#defined` constants, such as EOF and WEOF.

However, the designs for both `basic_string` and `basic_ios` are inherently extensible, and a closed set of constants would be an inadequate solution. So, their design had to provide a way to describe implementation-dependent properties of characters, without causing the standard to specify implementation details.

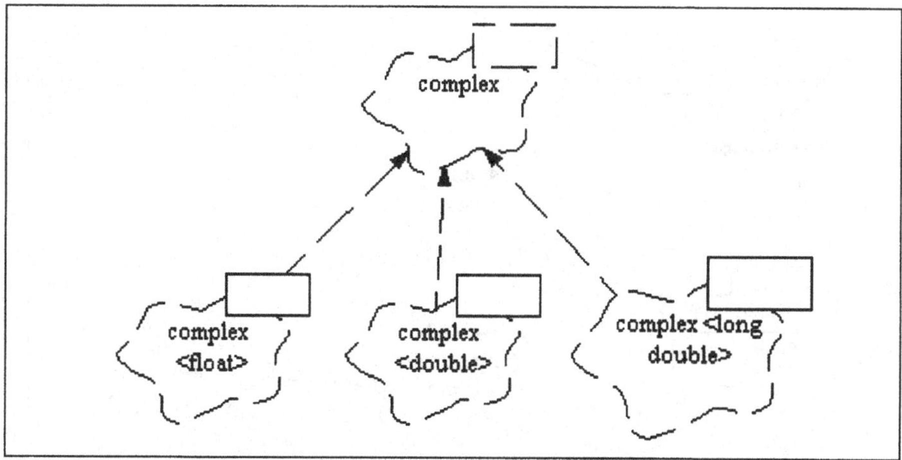

FIGURE 3. *Parameterizing complex numbers.*

The solution to this problem was to extend the parameterization of `basic_string` and `basic_ios`, to include parameters describing character properties (see Figure 4).

For convenience, their definitions rely on default arguments for their template parameters:

```
template <class charT, class traits =
string_char_traits<charT> >
   class basic_string { /* ... */ };
template <class charT, class traits =
ios_char_traits<charT> >
   class basic_ios : public ios_base { /* ... */ };
```

Thus, the instantiations `basic_string<char>` and `basic_ios<char>` do the right thing and use the library-provided instantiations `string_char_traits<char>` and `ios_char_traits<char>`, respectively. The C++ Standard Library's `numeric_limits` class template provides a similar description for numeric types.

This design is both customizable for existing types and extensible to new types:

```
class my_string_properties { /* ... */ };
basic_string<char, my_string_properties> My_String;
```

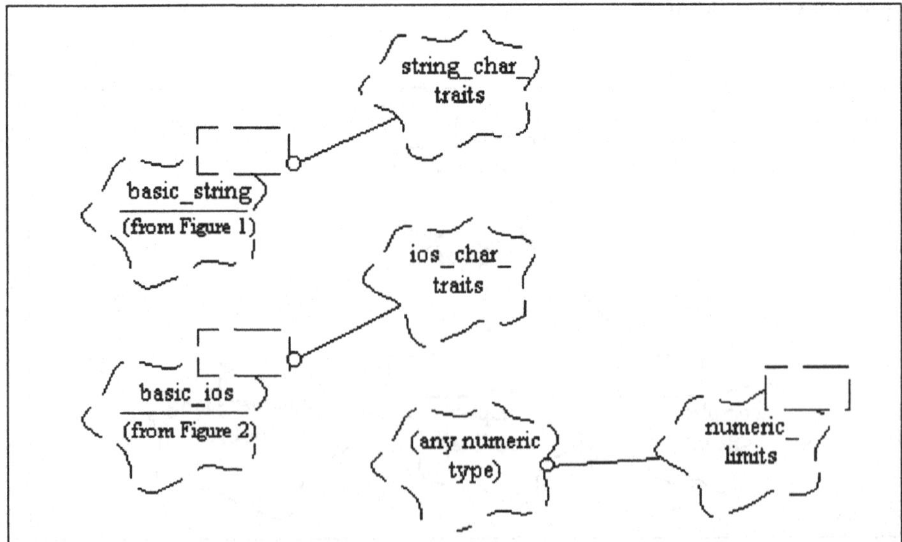

Figure 4. *Parameterizing parameter characteristics.*

```
class Unicode_Char { /* ... */ };
class ios_char_traits<Unicode_Char> { /* ... */ };
basic_ios<Unicode_Char> Unicode_ios;
```

Generalizing Storage

As originally designed, the *STL* components assumed that the types `size_t` and `ptrdiff_t`, together with the global operators `new` and `delete`, were adequate descriptions of dynamic storage management. However, this made it difficult to use the components with custom storage management schemes (such as shared memory or persistent storage managers), and therefore would make the C++ Standard Library less effective.

The solution to this problem was to parameterize the data structure components (and strings) with a storage allocator, as illustrated in Figure 5.

For convenience, these components default to the C++ Standard Library's allocator component, which provides access to the dynamic storage managed by operator `new()` and operator `delete()`:

```
template<class T, class Allocator = allocator>
class vector { /* ... */ };
```

With this design, it is possible to create data structures that use various storage management policies:

```
class vector<MyClass> v;                          // default
class SharedMemoryAllocator { /* ... */ };
// custom
class vector<MyClass,SharedMemoryAllocator> v2;

// persistent
class ODMGAllocator { /* ... */ };
class vector<MyClass,ODMGAllocator> v3;
```

Summary

The components in the C++ Standard Library provide some interesting examples in class design. This library, a fundamental part of every standard-conforming C++ implementation, has been designed to be general, customizable, extensible, and yet efficient.

Interestingly, the library achieves these goals without the extensive use of inheritance and polymorphism found in many object-oriented designs. Instead,

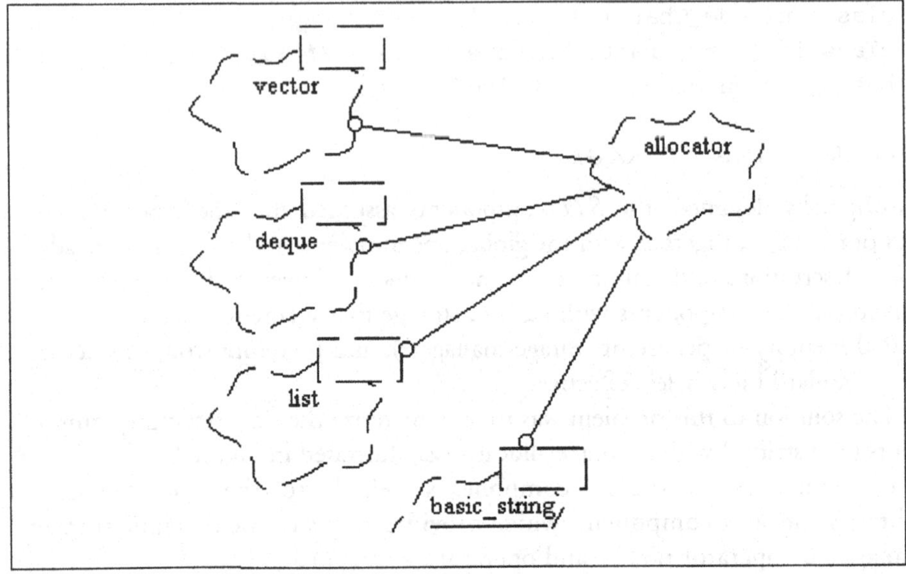

FIGURE 5. *Parameterizing storage allocation.*

the C++ Standard Library uses parameterization for most of its components.

Indeed, combining the two techniques can result in dramatic simplifications in a C++ class library's design.ß The C++ Standard Library provides, within a relatively compact and concise design, an extremely flexible set of general-purpose components. C++ developers should find them to be an effective foundation for their own work, and the design ideas a valuable addition to their design pattern collection.

REFERENCES

1. Vilot, M. The C++ Standard Library, *Dr. Dobb's Journal,* Aug. 1995.
2. Booch, G. Object-Oriented Analysis and Design. Benjamin-Cummings, 1994.
3. Stroustrup, B. The C++ Programming Language, second ed., Addison-Wesley, Reading, MA, 1993.
4. Ellis, M., and B. Stroustrup. The Annotated C++ Reference Manual. Addison-Wesley, Reading, MA, 1991.
5. Vilot, M., and G. Booch. Simplifying the C++ Booch components, *C++ Report,* 5(5), 1993.

A Case Study of C++ Design Evolution

Douglas C. Schmidt

Many useful C++ classes have evolved incrementally by generalizing from solutions to practical problems that arise during system development. After the interface and implementation of a class have stabilized, however, this iterative process of class generalization is often deemphasized. That is unfortunate since two major barriers to entry for newcomers to object-oriented design and C++ are (1) learning and internalizing the process of how to identify and describe classes and objects, and (2) understanding when and how to apply (or not apply) C++ features such as templates, inheritance, dynamic binding, and overloading to simplify and generalize their programs.

In an effort to capture the dynamics of C++ class design evolution, the following article illustrates the process by which object-oriented techniques and C++ idioms were incrementally applied to solve a relatively small, yet surprisingly subtle problem. This problem arose during the development of a family of concurrent> distributed applications that execute efficiently on uniprocessor and multiprocessor platforms. This article focuses on the steps involved in generalizing from existing code by using templates and overloading to transparently parameterize synchronization mechanisms into a concurrent application. Some of the infrastructure code is based on components in the freely available ADAPTIVE Service eXecutive (ASX) framework.[1-5]

Motivation

The following C++ code illustrates part of the main event-loop of a typical distributed application (such as a CORBA location broker or a file server):

Example 1

```
typedef unsigned long COUNTER;
COUNTER request_count; // At file scope

void*
run_svc (void *)
{
  MessageBlock *mb;

  while (get_next_request (mb) > 0) {
  // Keep track of number of requests
  request_count++;

  // Identify request and
  // perform service processing here...
  }
}
```

This code waits for messages to arrive from client, dequeues the messages from a message queue using `get_next_request`, and performs some type of processing (e.g., database query, file update, etc.) depending on the type of message that is received.

This code works fine as long as `run_svc` runs in a single thread of control. However, incorrect results will occur on many multiprocessor platforms when `run_svc` is executed simultaneously by multiple threads of control running on different CPUs. The problem here is that the auto-increment operation on the global variable `request_count` contains a race condition where different threads may increment obsolete versions of the `request_count` variable stored in their per-CPU data caches.

The remainder of this section illustrates this phenomenon by executing the following C++ code example on a shared memory multiprocessor running the SunOS 5.x operating system. SunOS 5.x a version of UNIX that allows multiple threads of control to execute in parallel on a shared memory multiprocessor.[6] This code is a greatly simplified version of the original distributed application:

```
//Manage a group of threads atomically
Thr_Manager thr_manager;
```

```
typedef unsigned long COUNTER;
COUNTER request_count; // At file scope
void*
run_svc (int iterations)
{
  Thr_Cntl t (&thr_manager);

  for (int i = 0; i < iterations; i++)
      request_count++; // Count # of requests

  return t.exit ((void *) i);
}

int
main (int argc, char *argv[])
{
  int n_threads =
      argc > 1 ? atoi (argv[1]) : 4;
  int n_iterations =
      argc> 2 ? atoi (argv[2]) : 1000000;

  //Divide iterations evenly among threads
  int iterations = n_iterations / n_threads;

  // Spawn off N threads to run in parallel
  thr_manager.spawn_n (n_threads, &run_svc,
    (void *) iterations,
    THR_BOUND | THR_SUSPENDED);

  // Start executing all the threads together
  thr_manager.resume_all ();

  // Wait for all the threads to exit
  thr_manager.wait ();

  cout << n_iterations << " = iterations\n"
      << request_count << "= request_count"
      << endl;
  return 0;
}
```

Thr_Manager is a class from the ASX framework. It contains a set of mechanisms for managing groups of threads that collaborate to implement collective actions (such as a pool of threads that render different portions of a large image in parallel). The Thr_Manager::spawn_n member function creates n new threads of control. In the SunOS implementation of Thr_Manager, the spawn_n member function calls the thr_create thread library routine to create a new thread. In this example, each newly created thread will execute the function run_svc, which iterates n_iterafions/n_threads times. Each thread is spawned using the THR_BOUND and THR_SUSPENDED flags. THR_BOUND indicates to the SunOS thread runtime library that each thread may run in parallel on a separate CPU in a multiprocessor system. The THR_SUSPENDED flag creates each thread in the "suspended" state, which ensures that all threads are completely initialized before starting the tests with Thr_Manager::resume_all.

The Thr_Manager::wait member function blocks the execution of the main thread until all the threads that are running run_svc have exited. When all the other threads have exited, the main thread prints out the total number of iterations and the final value of request_count.

Compiling this code into an executable a.out file and running it on 1 thread for 10,000,000 iterations produces the following:

```
% a.out 1 10000000
10000000 iterations
10000000 request_count
```

However, when executed on four threads for 10,000,000 iterations on a four CPU machine, the program prints:

```
% a.out 4 10000000
10000000 iterations
5000000 request_count
```

Clearly, something is wrong since the value of the global variable request_count is only one half the total number of iterations! The problem here is that auto-increments to request_count are not on variable being serialized properly. In particular, run_svc will produce incorrect results when executed in parallel on shared memory multiprocessor platforms that do not provide *strong sequential order* cache consistency models. To enhance performance, many shared memory multiprocessors employ "weakly ordered" cache consistency semantics. For example, the SPARC V.8 and V.9 multiprocessor family provides both *total store order* and *partial store order* memory cache consistency semantics. With total store order semantics, reading a variable that is being accessed by threads on different CPUs may not be serialized with simultaneous writes to the same variable by threads on other CPUs. Likewise, with partial store order semantics, writes may also not be serialized with other writes. In either case, expressions that require more than a single load and store of a memory location (such as `foo++ or i = i - 10`) may produce inconsistent results due to cache latencies across CPUs. To ensure that reads and writes of variables shared between threads are updated correctly, programmers must manually enforce the order that changes to these variables become globally visible.

A common technique for enforcing a strong sequential order on a *total store order* or *partial store order* shared memory multiprocessor is to protect the increment of the `request_count` variable by using some type of synchronization mechanism, such as a *mutex* (short for "mutual exclusion").[7] A mutex is used to protect the integrity of a shared resource that may be accessed concurrently by multiple threads of control. A mutex serializes the execution of multiple threads by defining a critical section where only one thread executes its code at a time.

One of the simplest and most efficient types of mutual exclusion mechanisms is a nonrecursive mutex (this and other types of mutexes that are discussed in a later section). SunOS 5.x implements nonrecursive mutexes via the `mutex_t` data type and its corresponding `mutex_lock` and `mutex_unlock` functions. On SunOS 5.x, a thread may enter a critical section by invoking the `mutex_lock` function on a `mutex_t` variable. A call to this function will block until the thread that currently owns the lock has left the critical section. To leave a critical section, a thread invokes the `mutex_unlock` function on the same `mutex_t variable`. Calling `mutex_unlock` enables another thread that is blocked on the mutex to enter the critical section.

On SunOS 5.x, operations on mutex variables are implemented via adaptive spin-locks that ensure mutual exclusion by using an atomic hardware instruction. An adaptive spin-lock operates by polling a designated memory location using the atomic hardware instruction until 1) the value at this location is changed by the thread that currently owns the lock (signifying that the lock has been released by the previous owner and may now be acquired) or 2) the thread that is holding the lock goes to sleep (at which point the thread that is spinning also goes to sleep to avoid needless polling). On a multiprocessor, the system overhead incurred by a spin-lock is relatively minor since polling affects only the local CPU cache of the thread that is spinning. A spin-lock is a simple and efficient synchronization mechanism for certain types of short-lived resource contention such as auto-incrementing the global `request_count` variable illustrated in the previous example.

The code in Example 2 illustrates how SunOS mutex variables may be used to solve the auto-increment serialization problem we observed earlier with `request_count`.

Example 2

```
typedef unsigned long COUNTER;
COUNTER request_count; // At file scope
mutex_t m; // mutex protecting request_count
          // initialized to zero...

void*
run_svc (void *)
{
  Thr_Cntl t (&thr_manager);

  for (int i = 0; i < iterations; i++) {
    mutex_lock (&m);
    request_count++; // Count # of requests
    mutex_unlock (&m);
  }

  return t.exit ((void *) i);
}
```

Although it solves the original synchronization problem, this approach is somewhat inelegant and error-prone since it mixes C functions with C++ objects, it leaves open the possibility that the programmer will forget to initialize the mutex `variable`*, or forget to call `mutex_unlock`, and it requires obtrusive changes to the code (in a larger system, managing these types of changes becomes a serious maintenance headache . . .).

C++ Solutions

C++ offers a number of language features that may be employed to solve the serialization problem more elegantly. This section illustrates a progression of C++ solutions, each one building upon insights from prior design iterations.

---

* In SunOS 5.x, a zeroed `mutex_t` variable is considered to be inplicitly initialized, but other systems (such as Windows NT) do not make these guarantees, and all synchronization objects must be initialized explicitly.

An initial C++ solution

A somewhat more elegant solution to the original problem is to encapsulate the existing SunOS `mutex_t` operations with a C++ wrapper, as follows:

```
class Mutex
{
public:
  Mutex (void) {
      mutex_init (&this->lock, USYNC_THREA0, 0);
  }
  ~Mutex (void) {
      mutex_destroy (&this->lock);
  }
  int acquire (void) {
      mutex_lock (&this->lock);
  }
  int release (void) {
      mutex_untock (&this->lock);
  }

private:
  // SunOS 5.x serialization mechanism
  mutex_t lock;
};
```

One advantage of defining a C++ wrapper interface to mutual exclusion mechanisms is that our code now becomes more portable across OS platforms. For example, the following code is an implementation of the Mutex class interface based on mechanisms in the Windows NT WIN32 API8:

```
class Mutex
{
public:
  Mutex (void) {
      InitializeCriticalSection (&this->lock);
  }
  ~Mutex (void) {
      DeleteCriticalSection (&this->lock);
  }
```

```
    int acquire (void) {
        EnterCriticalSection (&this->lock);
        return 0;
    }
    int release (void) {
        LeaveCriticalSection (&this->lock);
        return 0;
    }

private:
    // Win32 serialization mechanism
    CRITICAL_SECTION lock;
};
```

The use of the `Mutex` C++ wrapper class cleans up the original code somewhat and ensures that initialization occurs automatically when a `Mutex` object is defined, as shown in the code fragment in Example 3.

Example 3

```
typedef unsigned long COUNTER;
COUNTER request_count; // At file scope
Mutex m; // mutex protecting request_count

void *
run_svc (void *)
{
  Thr_Cntl t (&thr_manager);

  for (int i = 0; i < iterations; i++) {
    m.acquire ();
    request_count++; // Count # of requests
    m.release ();
  }

  return t.exit ((void *) i);
}
```

However, the C++ wrapper approach does not solve the problem of forgetting to release the `mutex` (which still requires manual intervention by programmers), and it still requires obtrusive changes to the original source code.

Another C++ Solution

A straightforward way to ensure the lock will be released is to leverage off the semantics of C++ class constructors and destructors to automate the acquisition and release of a `mutex` by supplying the following helper class for class `Mutex`:

```
class Mutex_Block
{
public:
  Mutex_Block (Mutex &m): lock (m) {
    this->lock.acquire ();
  }
  ~Mutex_Block (void) {
    this->lock.release ();
  }
private:
  Mutex &lock;
}
```

The `Mutex_Block` class defines a "block" of code over which a `Mutex` is acquired and then automatically released when the block is exited. It employs a C++ idiom[9] that uses the constructor of a `Mutex_Block` class to acquire the lock on the `Mutex` object automatically when an object of the class is created. Likewise, the `Mutex_Block` class destructor automatically unlocks the `Mutex` object when the object goes out of scope. By defining the lock data member as a reference to a `Mutex` object, we avoid the overhead of creating and destroying an underlying SunOS `mutex_t` variable every time the constructor and destructor of a `Mutex_Block` are executed.

By making a slight change to the code, we now guarantee that a `Mutex` is automatically acquired and released.

Example 4

```
void *
run_svc (void *)
{
  Thr_Cntl t (&thr_manager);

  for (int i = 0; i < iterations; i++) {
    {
       // Automatically acquire the mutex
```

```
        Mutex_Block monitor (m);
        request_count++;
        // Automatically release the mutex
      }
    }
  }
```

However, this solution still has not fixed the problem with obtrusive changes to the code. Moreover, adding the extra curly brace delimiters `{}` around the `Mutex_Block` is inelegant and error-prone since a maintenance programmer might misunderstand the importance of the curly braces and remove them, yielding the following erroneous code:

```
for (int i = 0; i < iterations; i++) {
  Mutex_Block monitor (m);
  request_count++;
}
```

Unfortunately, this "curly-brace elision" has the side-effect of eliminating all concurrent execution within the system by serializing the main event-loop!

YET ANOTHER C++ SOLUTION

To solve the remaining problems in a transparent, unobtrusive, and efficient manner requires the use of two additional C++ features: parameterized types and operator overloading. We may use these features to provide a template class called `Atomic_Op`, a portion of which is shown as follows:

```
template <class TYPE>
class Atomic_Op
{
public:
  Atomic_Op (void) { this->count = 0; }
  Atomic_Op (TYPE c) { this->count = c; }
  TYPE operator++ (void) {
    Mutex_Block m (this->lock);
    return ++this->count;
  }
  TYPE operator== (const TYPE i) {
    Mutex_Block m (this->lock);
    return this->count == i
  }
```

```
    void operator = (const Atomic_Op &ao) {
      // Check for identify to avoid deadlock!
      if (this!  &ao) {
          Mutex_Block m (this->lock);
          this->count = ao.count;
        }
    }
        operator TYPE () {
        Mutex_Block m (this->lock);
        return this->count;
        }
        // Other arithmetic operations omitted...

  private:
    Mutex lock;
    TYPE count;
  };
```

The Atomic_Op class transparently redefines the normal arithmetic operations (such as ++, - -, +=, etc.) on built-in data types to make these operations work atomically. In general, any class that defines the basic arithmetic operators will work with the Atomic_Op class due to the "deferred instantiation" semantics of C++ templates.

Since the Atomic_Op class uses the mutual exclusion features of the Mutex class, arithmetic operations on objects of instantiated Atomic_Op classes now work correctly on a multiprocessor. Moreover, C++ features such as templates and operator overloading allow this technique to work *transparently* on a multiprocessor. In addition, all the member function operations in Atomic_Op are defined as inline functions. Therefore, a highly optimizing C++ compiler should be able to generate code that ensures the runtime performance of this approach is no greater than using the mutex_lock and mutex_unlock function calls directly.

Using the Atomic_Op class, we can now write the following code, which is almost identical to the original non–thread-safe code (in fact, only the typedef of COUNTER has changed).

Example 5

```
typedef AtomicOp <unsigned long> COUNTER;
COUNTER request_count; // At file scope
```

```
void *
run_svc (void *)
{
  Thr_Cntl t (&thr_manager);

  for (int i = 0; i < iterations; i++) {
    // Actually calls Atomic_Op: :operator++()
    request_count++;
  }
}
```

By combining the C++ constructor/destructor idiom for acquiring and releasing the `Mutex` automatically together with the use of templates and overloading, we have produced a simple yet expressive parameterized class abstraction that operates correctly and atomically on an infinite family of types that require atomic operations. For example, to provide the same thread-safe functionality for other arithmetic types we simply instantiate new objects of the `Atomic_Op` template class as follows:

```
Atomic_Op <double> atomic_double;
Atomic_Op <Complex> atomic_complex;
```

Extending `Atomic_Op` by Parameterizing the Type of Mutual Exclusion Mechanism

Although the design of the `Atomic_Op` and `Mutex_Block` classes described previously yielded correct and transparently thread-safe programs, there is still room for improvement. In particular, note that the type of the `Mutex` data member is hard-coded into the `Atomic_Op` class. Since templates are available in C++, this design decision represents an unnecessary restriction that is easily overcome by parameterizing `Mutex_Block` and adding another type parameter-to the template class `Atomic_Op`, as follows:

```
template <class MUTEX>
class Mutex_Block
{
// Basically the same as before...

private:
  MUTEX &lock; // new data member change
};
```

```
template <class MUTEX, class TYPE>
class Atomic_Op
{
  TYPE operator++ (void) {
    Mutex_Block<MUTEX> m (this->lock);
    return ++this->count;
  }
  // . . .

private:
  TYPE count;
  MUTEX lock; // new data member
};
```

Using this new class, we can make the following simple change at the beginning of the file:

```
typedef Atomic_Op <Mutex, unsigned long> COUNTER;
COUNTER request_count; // At file scope

// . . . same as before
```

Before making this change, however, it is worthwhile to analyze the reasons *why* using templates to parameterize the type of mutual exclusion mechanism used by a program is beneficial. After all, just because templates exist does not necessarily make them useful in all circumstances. In fact, parameterizing and generalizing the problem space via templates without clear and sufficient reasons may increase the difficulty of understanding and reusing a class.

One motivation for parameterizing the type of mutual exclusion mechanism is to increase portability across OS platforms. Templates decouple the formal paramater class name "`MUTEX`" from the actual name of the class used to provide mutual exclusion. This is useful for platforms that already use the symbol `Mutex` to denote an existing type or function. By using templates, the `Atomic_Op` class source code would not require any changes when porting to such platforms.

However, a more interesting motivation arises from the observation that there are actually several different flavors of `mutex` semantics one might want to use (either in the same program or across a family of related programs). Each of these mutual exclusion flavors share the same basic protocol (i.e., acquire/release), but they possess different serialization and performance properties. Five flavors of mutual exclusion mechanisms that I have found useful in practice are described as follows:

- *Nonrecursive mutexes* provide an efficient form of mutual exclusion. They define a critical section in which only a single thread may execute at a time. They are nonrecursive since the thread that currently owns a `mutex` may not reacquire it without releasing it first. Otherwise, deadlock will occur immediately. SunOS 5.x provides support for nonrecursive mutexes via its `mutex_t` type. The ASX framework provides the `Mutex` C++ wrapper shown previously to encapsulate the `mutex_t` semantics.
- *Readers/writer mutexes* help to improve performance for situations where an object protected by the `mutex` is read far more often than it is written. Multiple threads may acquire the `mutex` simultaneously for reading, but only one thread may acquire the mutex for writing. SunOS 5.x provides support for readers/writer mutexes via its `rwlock_t` type. The ASX framework provides a C++ wrapper called `RW_Mutex` that encapsulates the `rwlock_t` semantics.
- *Recursive mutexes* are a simple extension to nonrecursive `mutex`es. A recursive `mutex` allows calls to acquire to be nested as long as the thread that owns the `Mutex` is the one that re-acquires it. For example, if an `Atomic_Op` counter is called by multiple nested function calls within the same thread, a recursive `mutex` will prevent deadlock from occurring.

Recursive `mutex`es are particularly useful for callback-driven C++ frameworks,[3,4,10] where the framework event-loop performs a callback to arbitrary user-defined code. Since the user-defined code may subsequently reenter framework code via a member function entry point, recursive mutexes may be necessary to prevent deadlock from occurring on locks held within the framework during the callback. The mutual exclusion mechanisms in the Windows NT W1N32 subsystem provide recursive mutex semantics.

The following C++ template class implements recursive mutex semantics for SunOS 5.x, whose native mutex mechanisns do not provide recursive mutex semantics:

```
template <class MUTEX>
class Mutex_Rec
{
public:
  Mutex_Rec (void)
    : nesting (0), thr_id (0) { }
  int acquire (void) const {
    thread_t t_id = thr_self ();
```

```
    // Check if we already hold the lock
    if (t_id == this->thr_id){
    —this>nestinglevel;
    return 0;
    }
    else {
      int result = this>lock.acquire ();
      if (result == 0) {
        this->thr_id = t_id;
        —this->nesting = 0;
    }
        return result;
  }

  int release (void) const {
    if (this->nesting_level > 0)
      —this->nesting;
      return 0;
      }
    else {
      this->thr_id = 0
      return this->lock.release ();
    }
  }

  private:
    MUTEX lock;
    thread_t thr_id;
    mutable int nesting;
  };
```

Note that `Mutex_Rec` may be instantiated with any C++ mutex wrapper (e.g., `Mutex` or `RW_Mutex`) that conforms to the acquire/release protocol:

- ***Intraprocess versus interprocess mutexes.*** To optimize performance, many operating systems provide different mutex mechanisms for serializing threads that execute within the same process (i.e., intraprocess serialization) versus threads that execute in separate processes (i.e., interprocess serialization). For example, in Windows NT, the `CriticalSection` operations define a mutual exclusion mechanism that is optimized to serialize threads within a single process. In contrast, the Windows NT mutex operations (e.g., `CreateMutex`) define a more general, though less efficient, mechanism that allows threads in separate processes to serialize their actions. In SunOS 5.x, the `USYNC_THREAD` flag to the `mutex_init` function creates a mutex that is valid only within a single processes, whereas the `USYNC_PROCESS` flag creates a mutex that is valid in multiple processes. By combining C++ wrappers and templates, we can create a highly portable, platform-independent mutual exclusion class interface that does not impose arbitrary syntactic constraints on our use of different synchronization mechanisms.

- ***The null mutex.*** There are also cases where mutual exclusion is simply not needed (e.g., we may know that a particular program or service will *always* run in a single thread of control and/or will not contend with other threads for access to shared resources). In this case, it is useful to parameterize the `Atomic_Op` class with a `Null_Mutex`. The `Null_Mutex` class in the ASX framework implements the acquire and release member functions as "no-op" inline functions that may be removed completely by a compiler optimizer.

Often, selecting a mutual exclusion mechanism with the appropriate semantics depends on the context in which a class is being used. For instance, consider the following member functions in a C++ search structure container class that maps external identifiers (such as network port numbers) onto internal identifiers (such as pointers to control blocks):

```
template <class EX_ID, class IN_ID, class MUTEX>
class Map_Manager
{
public:
  int bind (EX_ID ex_d, INID &in_id) {
    Mutex_block<MUTEX> monitor (this->lock);
    // . . .
  }

  int unbind (EX_ID ex_id IN_ID &in_id) {
    Mutex_Block<MUTEX> monitor (this->lock);
    // . . .
  }

  int find (EX_ID ex_id, IN_ID &in_id) {
    Mutex_Block<MUTEX> monitor (this->lock);
```

```
        if (this->locate_entry (ex_id, in_id)
            /* ex_id is successfully located */
            return 0;
        else
            return -1;
    }

private:
    MUTEX lock;
    // . . .
};
```

One advantage to this approach is that the Mutex lock will be released regardless of which execution path exits a member function. For example, this->lock is released properly if either arm of the if/else statement returns from the find member function, In addition, this "constructor as resource acquisition" idiom also properly releases the lock if an exception is raised during processing in the definition of the locate_entry helper member function. The reason for this is that the C++ exception handling mechanism is designed to call all necessary destructors upon exit from a block in which an exception is thrown. Note that in the following had we written the definition of find using explicit calls to acquire and release the Mutex:

```
int find (EX_ID ex_id, IN_ID &in_id) {
  this->lock.acquire ();
  if (this->locate_entry (ex_id, in_id) {
  /* ex_id is successfully located */
    this->lock.release ();
    return 0;
  }
  else {
    this->lock.release ();
    return -1;
  }
}
```

that not only would the find member function logic have been more contorted, but there would be no guarantee that this->lock was released if an exception was thrown in the locate_entry member function.

The type of MUTEX that the Map_Manager template class is instantiated with depends upon the particular structure of parallelism in the program code when it is used. For example, in some situations it is useful to be able to declare:

```
typedef Map_Manager <Addr, TCB, Mutex>
  MAP_MANAGER;
```

and have all calls to find, bind, and unbind automatically serialized. In other situations, it is useful to turn off synchronization without touching any existing library code by using the `Null_Mutex` class:

```
typedef Map_Manager <Addr, TCB, Null_Mutex>
  MAP_MANAGER;
```

In yet another situation, it may be the case that calls to find are *far* more frequent than bind or unbind. In this case, it may make sense to use the `Readers/Writer Mutex`:

```
typedef Map_Manager <Addr, TCB, RW_Mutex>
  MAP_MANAGER;
```

By using templates to parameterize the type of locking, little or no application code must change to accommodate new synchronization semantics.

DISCUSSION

I frequently encounter several questions when discussing the use of templates in the `Atomic_Op` class. What is the runtime performance penalty for all the added abstraction? Aren't you obscuring the synchronization properties of the programs by using templates and overloading? Instead of templates, why not use inheritance and dynamic binding to emphasize uniform mutex interface and to share common code? Several of these questions are related, and I'll discuss my responses in this section.

The primary reason templates are used for the `Atomic_Op` class involve efficiency. Once expanded by an optimizing C++ compiler during template instantiation, the additional amount of runtime overhead is minimal. In contrast, inheritance and dynamic binding often incur more overhead at runtime to dispatch virtual member function calls.

Figure 1 illustrates the performance exhibited by the mutual exclusion techniques used in Examples 2 –5.[†] Figure 1 depicts the number of seconds required

[†] Example 1 is the original erroneous implementation that did not use any mutual exclusion operations. Although it operates extremely efficiently (approximately 0.09 sec to process 10,000,000 iterations), it produces completely incorrect results!

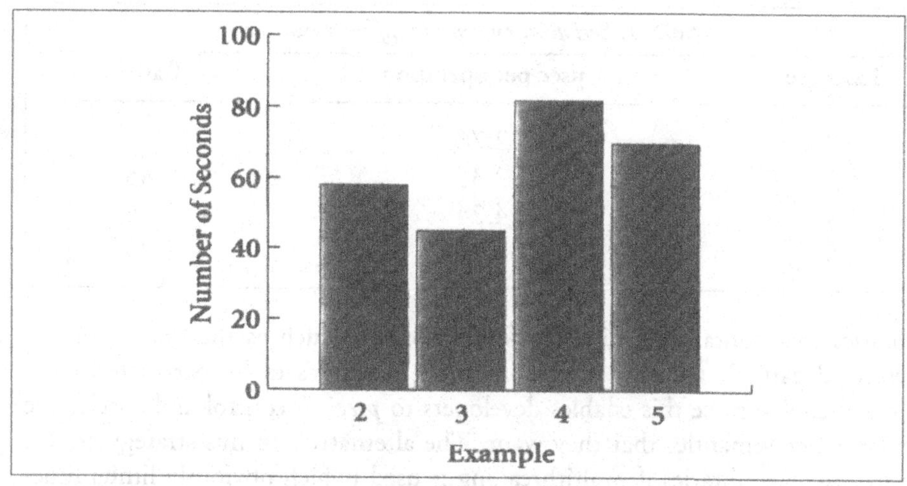

FIGURE 1. *Number of seconds required to process 10,000,000 iterations.*

to process 10 million iterations, divided into 2.5 million iterations per thread. The test examples were compiled using the -04 optimization level of the Sun C++ 3.0.1 compiler. Each test was executed 10 times on an otherwise idle 4 CPU Sun SPARCserver 690MP. The results were averaged to reduce the amount of spurious variation (which proved to be insignificant).

Example 2 uses the SunOS `mutex_t` functions directly. Example 3 uses the C++ `Mutex` class wrapper interface. Surprisingly, this implementation consistently performed better than Example 1, which used direct calls to the underlying SunOS mutex functions. Example 4 uses the `Mutex_Block` helper class inside of a nested curly brace block to ensure that the `Mutex` is automatically released. This version required the most time to execute. Finally, Example 5 uses the `Atomic_Op` template class, which is only slightly less efficient than using the SunOS mutex functions directly. More aggressively optimizing C++ compilers would likely reduce the amount of variation in the results.

Table 1 indicates the number of microseconds (µsec) incurred by each mutual exclusion operation for Examples 2–5. Recall that each iteration requires two mutex operations (i.e., one to acquire the lock and one to release the lock). Example 2 is used as the base-line value since it uses the underlying SunOS primitives directly. The third column of Examples 3–5 are normalized by dividing their values by Example 2.

An argument I have heard against using templates to parameterize synchronization is that it hides the mutual exclusion semantics of the programs. However, whether this is a problem or not depends on how one believes that concurrency and synchronization should be integrated into a program. For class

Table 1. *Serialization time for different examples.*		
Example	**µsec per operation**	**Ratio**
2	2.76	1
3	2.35	0.85
4	4.24	1.54
5	3.39	1.29

libraries that contain building-block components (such as the `Map_Manager` described earlier), allowing synchronization semantics to be parameterized is often desirable since this enables developers to *precisely* control and specify the concurrency semantics that they want. The alternatives to this strategy are (1) don't use class libraries if multithreading is used (which obviously limits functionality), (2) do all the locking outside the library (which may be inefficient or unsafe), or (3) hard-code the locking strategy into the library implementations (which is also inflexible and potentially inefficient). All these alternatives are antithetical to principles of reuse in object-oriented software systems.

An appropriate synchronization strategy for designing a class library depends on several factors. For example, certain library users may welcome simple interfaces that hide concurrency control mechanisms from view. In contrast, other library users may be willing to accept more complicated interfaces in return for additional control and increased efficiency. A layered approach to class library designs may be quite useful to satisfy both types of library users. In such an approach, the lowest layers of The class library would export most or all of the parameterized types as template arguments. The higher layers would provide reasonable default type values and provide an easier-to-use application developer's programming interface.

The new default template argument feature recently adopted by the ANSI C++ committee will facilitate the development of class libraries that satisfy both groups of library users. This feature allows library developers to specify reasonable default types as arguments to template class and function definitions. For example, the following modification to template class `Atomic_Op` provides it with typical default template arguments:

```
template <class MUTEX = Mutex,
  class TYPE = unsigned long>
class Atomic_Op
{
    // Same as before
};
```

```
// . . .

#if defined (MT_SAFE)
        // default is Mutex and unsigned long
        Atomic_Op request_count;
    #else /* don't serialize */
        Atomic_Op<Null_Mutex> request_count;
        #endif /* MT_SAFE */
```

Due to the complexity that arises from incorporating concurrency into applications, I've found the C++ template feature to be quite useful for reducing redundant development effort. However, as with any other language feature, it is possible to misuse templates and needlessly complicate a system's design and implementation. Currently, the heuristic I use to decide when to parameterize based on types is to keep track of when I'm about to duplicate existing code by only modifying the data types it uses. If I can think of another not-too-far-fetched scenario that would require me to make yet a third version that only differs according to the types involved, I typically generalize my original code to use templates.

Conclusion

The example described in this article was derived from a much larger distributed application that runs on a high-performance shared memory multiprocessor. The `Atomic_Op` class and `Mutex`-related classes are some of the components available in the ADAPTIVE Communication Environment (ACE), which is a freely available object-oriented toolkit designed to simplify the development of distributed applications on shared memory multiprocessor platforms.[11] ACE may be obtained via anonymous ftp from ics.uci.edu in the file `gnu/C++_wrappers.tar.Z` and `gnu/C++_wrappers_doc.tar.Z`. This distribution contains complete source code and documentation for the C++ components and examples described in this article. Components in ACE have been ported to both UNIX and Windows NT and are currently being used in a number of commercial products including the AT&T Q.port ATM signaling software product, the Ericsson EOS family of PBX monitoring applications, and the network management portion of the Motorola Iridium mobile communications system.

References

1. Schmidt, D.C. ASX: An object-oriented framework for developing distributed applications, *Proceedings of the 6th Usenix C++ Technical Conference,* Cambridge, MA, USENIX, April 1994.
2. Schmidt, D. C., and P. Stephenson, An object-oriented framework for developing network server daemons, Proceedings of the Second C++ World Conference, Dallas, TX, October 1993.
3. Schmidt, D. C. The reactor: An object-oriented interface for event-driven UNIX I/O multiplexing (Part 1 of 2), *C++ Report,* 5(2), 1993.
4. Schmidt, D. C. The object-oriented design and implementation of the reactor: A C++ wrapper for UNIX I/O multiplexing (Part 2 of 2), *C++ Report,* 5(8), 1993.
5. Schmidt, D. C. IPC_SAP: An object-oriented interface to interprocess communication services, *C++ Report,* 4(9), 1992.
6. Eykholt, J., S. Kleinman, S. Barton, R. Faulkner, A. Shivalingiah, M. Smith, D. Stein, J. Voll, M. Weeks, and D. Williams, Beyond Multiprocessing . . .Multithreading the SunOS Kernel, in Proceedings Summer Usenix Conference, San Antonio, TX, June 1992.
7. A. D. Birrell, An introduction to programming with threads, *Tech. Rep. SRC-035,* Digital Equipment Corporation, January 1989.
8. H. Custer, *Inside Windows NT,* Microsoft Press, Redmond, WA, 1993.
9. Booch, G., and M. Vilot. Simplifying the Booch components, *C++ Report,* vol. 5, June 1993.
10. M. A. Linton and P. R. Calder, The design and implementation of InterViews, in Proceedings USENIX C++ Workshop, November 1987.
11. Schmidt, D. C. The ADAPTIVE Communication Environment: Object-oriented network programming components for developing client/server applications, in Proceedings of the 15th Annual Sun Users Group Conference, San Jose, CA, SUG, December 1993, pp. 214–225.

Distributed Abstract Interfaces

Stephen C. Dewhurst

In C++, an abstract data type (ADT) and its class implementation are often viewed as equivalent. This is a useful simplification for many ADTs in those cases where the abstract operations of the type can be represented cleanly in the public (or public and protected) regions of a single class declaration. However, not all ADTs are so simple.

In this article, we shall see why it is often convenient to distribute the abstract interface of an ADT among a set of C++ classes. The usual one-to-one mapping of ADT to class can be viewed as a degenerate form of this more general case.

The discussion is motivated largely by the problems associated with performing (abstract) traversals of ADTs that have (abstract) structure. We therefore begin with an extended discussion of the techniques of control abstraction.

Abstract Data Types and Abstract Traversals

Consider a very simple ADT: a collection of members of a given type. For concreteness, we will fix the type to be `int`:

```
typedef int T;
class Collection {
    // Implementation details...
  public:
    Collection();
    virtual void insert( T );
    void apply( void (*)( T ) );
};
```

This type represents a simple idea and, therefore, has a simple interface: A constructor creates an empty `Collection`, and member functions allow one to insert a new element of type `T` into the collection and apply a function of a given type to each element of the collection. (Note that we have not specified the nature of the elements in the collection since this is not central to the topic under discussion. In particular, we do not know whether they are to be considered as objects or values of type `T`.) The simple interface provides a natural way to create and use unordered collections of `T`s:

```
extern void print( T );
extern int read( T & );
main() {
   Collection c;
   T t;
   while( read( t ) )
     c.insert( t );
   c.apply( print );
   return 0;
}
```

However, this interface is rather restrictive in that only functions that take a `T` argument and return void can be applied to the collection. Consider interfacing the `Collection` type with the standard C++ `streamio` library by writing an overloaded operator << that allows a `Collection` object to be written to an `ostream`.

```
static ostream *oarg;
static void
print( T t ) {
   *oarg << t << " ";
}
ostream &
operator <<( ostream &out, Collection &c ) {
   out << "{ ";
   oarg = &out; // hack!!!
   c.apply( print );
   out << "}";
   return out;
}
```

Our clever hack of dumping the output stream pointer into a static variable allows us to get around the deficiencies of the `Collection` class's interface.

However, we are reminded that "encountering the need for an outrageous hack during implementation is an indictment of our design concepts, not a challenge to our hacking skills."[3] (The reader may also like to speculate on the probable effect of such a hack in a program using multiple lightweight processes, or threads, and multiple output streams.) Seeking to avoid indictment, we realize that the apply member function is really a composition of two separate concepts: traversal of the data structure that holds the collection and application of a function to a member of the collection. By factoring apply into its components, we gain the flexibility needed to avoid the above hack:

```
class Collection {
      // ...
   public:
      Collection();
      virtual void insert( T );
      void reset();
      T *member();
};
```

The `member` member function returns a pointer to either some member of the collection that has not been accessed since the last reset or null if all members have been accessed since the last reset:

```
ostream &
operator <<( ostream &out, Collection &c ) {
   out << "{ ";
   c.reset();
   T *tp;
   while( tp = c.member() )
      out << *tp << " ";
   out << "}";
   return out;
}
```

This interface still has deficiencies. The major problem is that, while a `Collection` object may be accessed simultaneously by many processes or different parts of a program, a reset or member call will affect *all* users of the `Collection` object.

Control Abstraction and Traversal Objects

One way of dealing with such problems is through control abstraction. One might define control abstraction as the encapsulation of the traversal aspects of one ADT within another. Although the term *iterator* is probably more common, I prefer *control abstraction* because it allows one to be freer in conceptualizing other abstract traversals than does a simple, sequential unraveling of the internal structure of an abstract type. One can consider iterators as a subset of control abstractions. Let us return to our `Collection` type:

```
class Collection {
      // ...
   public:
      Collection();
      virtual void insert( T );
      friend class Ctl;
};
class Ctl {
      // ...
   public:
      Ctl( Collection & );
      void reset();
      T *member();
};
```

Here we have moved the reset and member functions to a separate type that has access to the private representation of the `Collection` type. The implementation of the operator << with a control abstraction is similar to the previous implementation, but there is now no danger of interference among different simultaneous traversals of the collection:

```
ostream &
operator <<( ostream &out, Collection &c ) {
   out << "{ ";
   T *tp;
   Ctl ctl = c;
   ctl.reset();
   while( tp = ctl.member() )
      out << *tp << " ";
   out << "}";
   return out;
}
```

As objects distinct from the objects for which they encapsulate traversal semantics, control objects can be passed as arguments, returned, and copied separately from the objects to which they refer. The control object maintains *within itself* the state of the traversal of the object to which it refers. Therefore, use of a given control object changes the state only of the traversal that object represents, and other control objects, representing other traversals, are unaffected.

Control Abstractions as Abstract Data Types

The two central ideas behind control abstraction are the same as those for data abstraction in general. First, the user of a control abstraction is unaffected by the details of its implementation. In addition to reducing the amount of knowledge that must be acquired before a user of a complex type can write a simple flow-of-control structure involving that type, this allows the implementor to change its implementation (and the implementations of its associated control abstractions) without affecting user code. Second, control abstraction brings the programming language closer to the control aspects of the problem in the same way that data abstraction does for the type aspects. This is especially valuable for types with complex implementations, in which the logic of control flow would otherwise be lost in the details of its implementation.

The distinction between abstract data types and control abstractions is conceptually convenient but artificial. Control abstractions are as much abstract data types as the types whose traversal aspects they encapsulate, and we can apply our techniques for data abstraction to control abstraction. For example, we can use inheritance to customize a control type:

```
class MyCtl : public Ctl {
  public:
    MyCtl( Collection &c )
      : Ctl(c) {}
    void apply( void (*)( T ) );
    T *member( int (*)( T ) );
    T *member()
      { return Ctl::member(); }
};

void
MyCtl::apply( void (*f)( T ) ) {
  reset();
  T *tp;
  while( tp = member() )
    f( *tp );
}
```

```
T *
MyCtl::member( int (*pred)( T ) ) {
  T *tp;
  while( (tp = member()) && !pred( *tp ) );
  return tp;
}
```

Here we have used the "atomic" operations supplied by the `Ctl` base class to reimplement the apply function and to implement a more selective member function that only returns members that satisfy an argument predicate.

Typically, a control type in C++ is related to its corresponding data type by friendship rather than inheritance. This leaves the control type relatively independent of changes to the inheritance hierarchy of the type to which it refers. Suppose we derive a sorted collection type from `Collection` in which the elements are fully ordered by some relation and are arranged in sorted order (or have the appearance of being so arranged):

```
class S_Collection : public Collection {
  public:
    void insert( T );
    friend class S_Ctl;
};
```

An `S_Collection` *is-a* `Collection` but with different insertion semantics. As the friend declaration indicates, a richer variety of traversals is possible if an ordering relationship exists between members:

```
class S_Ctl : public Ctl {
    // ...
  public:
    S_Ctl( S_Collection & );
    T *first();
    T *last();
    T *next();
    T *previous();
};
```

An `S_Ctl` *is-a* `Ctl` in the same way that an `S_Collection` *is-a* `Collection`. However, because of its richer set of traversals, an `S_Ctl` can refer only to a `Collection` that is also an `S_Collection`. This is indicated by the formal argument of the constructor, which allows an `S_Ctl` to be initialized only with an `S_Collection` or an object whose type is publicly derived from an `S_Collection`.

Note that the `Collection` and `Ctl` hierarchies are not parallel; the `Collection` hierarchy decomposes into progressively more specific types of collection, whereas the `Ctl` hierarchy is increasingly augmented in progressive derivations. This reflects one possible design strategy for providing customizable control abstractions. In this approach, a library would contain a hierarchy of abstract types and their associated control abstractions as indicated by the friendship relation. The control abstractions would provide control flow primitives from which users of the library would construct more sophisticated flow-of-control structures (cf., the `MyCtl` class).

Summary

At this point, we could attempt to summarize what we have learned through examination of the foregoing simple example by listing a set of rules for "proper" design of control abstractions:

- Provide atomic control flow operations.
- Separate structuring semantics from traversal semantics.
- Maintain the state of the traversal entirely within the control abstraction object.
- Remember that control abstractions are ADTs; treat them as such.
- Declare control abstraction types as friends of the corresponding ADT.

These rules will serve well in many circumstances, but their discovery was driven by our example. It is quite easy to imagine other situations in which, for instance, inheritance, rather than friendship, is the appropriate relationship between an abstract data type and its corresponding control abstractions or in which the state of the traversal might be shared between objects, and so on. The most important, and least restrictive, concept to be gleaned from the foregoing is that *the traversal aspects of one type can be encapsulated within another.*

The evolution of the abstract interface of the collection ADT was necessitated by its deficiencies in the context of the intended use of the collection. In the first instance, the apply operation lacked flexibility. The interface was changed to include the notion of an abstract traversal with the introduction of the reset and member operations. The second modification to `Collection`'s abstract interface arose in the face of its inability to perform multiple, simultaneous traversals.

Our approach was to conceive of a traversal as an entity separate from that which encapsulated the structuring properties of a collection. In effect, `Collection` *delegated* a portion of its abstract interface to another class, and the abstract interface to the collection ADT (as opposed to the `Collection` class) was distributed between the two classes.

A More Detailed Example

In the foregoing, we looked chiefly at the interfaces to control abstraction types, ignoring their implementations (as our data abstraction programming paradigm tells us is proper). Let us look at a slightly more complex example drawn from production code and see how examination of the implementation of a control type can affect our appreciation of the technique.

The data type of interest is an *n*-ary tree:

```
class Tree {
  protected:
    Node *root;
    int size;
  public:
    int count()
      { return size; }
    // ...
    friend Walk;
};
```

The tree is implemented as a fixed-size array of nodes arranged in preorder sequence. Each node has links to (potentially) three other nodes: its parent, its sibling, and its leftmost child. These links are recorded as relative indexes within the array:

```
typedef short Index;
class Node {
    Index parent;
    Index sibling;
    Index lchild;
    // other members...
    friend Access;
    friend Walk;
};
```

Since there may be simultaneous access to the *n*-ary tree from different threads of execution, we cannot easily embed traversal semantics as part of the `Tree` type. Therefore, we implement a control abstraction type for arbitrary traversal of the tree:

```
typedef int Bool;
class Walk {
  protected:
    Node *cur;
  public:
    Walk( Tree t )
      : cur( t.root ) {}
    inline Bool parent();
    inline Bool sibling();
    inline Bool lchild();
    inline Access get();
};
```

The traversal member functions `parent`, `sibling`, and `lchild` first check that the requested motion is possible. If it is, the motion is performed and success is returned. Otherwise, no motion is performed and failure is returned. The implementations of all three traversal functions are similar:

```
Bool
Walk::parent() {
  return cur->parent
    ? (cur += cur->parent, 1)
    : 0;
}
```

This control abstraction provides convenient, albeit low-level, traversal semantics over `Tree` objects. We can provide a higher-level preorder traversal by customizing the base `Walk` type:

```
class Preorder : public Walk {
  protected:
    Node *end;
  public:
    Preorder( Tree t )
      : Walk( t ),
        end( cur+t.count()-1 ) {}
    inline Bool next();
};
```

Since the array of Nodes that comprises the *n*-ary tree is in preorder, the implementation of the next function is trivial:

```
Bool
Preorder::next() {
    return cur == end
        ? 0
        : (cur++, 1);
}
```

Note that, by chance, the traversal member functions of the base class `Walk`, as well as assignment to and initialization of a `Walk` by a `Preorder`, may be used without harm by a `Preorder` object. If this were likely to change, these operations could be denied to users of the `Preorder` type by overriding them in a private section of the `Preorder` class declaration.

COROUTINES, EXECUTION SNAPSHOTS, AND CONTROL ABSTRACTION

A more involved situation presents itself in the creation of a postorder traversal type, in that recording the state of the traversal is more complex than for the case of the preorder traversal. (This disparity in complexity is, in a sense, artificial since it is related to a specific implementation of the `Tree` type.)

Let us look at the implementation of a postorder traversal. As a first step, we will transform a recursive postorder traversal:

```
postorder:
    save current position
    if( lchild )
        move to lchild
        postorder
        if( sibling )
            move to sibling
            postorder
        fi
    fi
        restore saved position
        visit
```

into a nonrecursive one:

```
postorder:
  loop
    if( lchild )
      move to lchild
    else
      visit – Ileaf node
      loop
        if( sibling )
          move to sibling
          exit loop
        else
          if( parent )
            move to parent
            visit – Iinternal node
          else
            return – Idone
          fi
        fi
      repeat
    fi
  repeat
```

Now, the goal of the postorder control abstraction is to move to the next node in the `postorder` sequence with each invocation, not to traverse through all the nodes at once. We would like the `postorder` routine to return at the point of each visit and take up just after that point on the next invocation. The `postorder` routine is, therefore, more properly implemented as a coroutine, with the visits in the above replaced by resumption of the calling routine. When the calling routine is ready to receive the next node in the sequence, the postorder routine is resumed. These semantics are easily accomplished with a slight extension of the control abstraction techniques applied earlier.

```
class Postorder : protected Walk {
  protected:
    enum {
      START,
      LEAF,
      INNER,
      DONE
    } pc;
  public:
```

```
        Postorder( Tree t )
          : Walk( t ), pc( START )
          { next(); }
        Bool next();
        Access get()
          { return Walk::get(); }
    };

    Bool
    Postorder::next() {
      switch( pc )
      case START:
      while( 1 )
        if( !lchild() ) {
          pc = LEAF;
          return 1;
      case LEAF: while( 1 )
              if( sibling() )
                break;
              else
                if( parent() ) {
                  pc = INNER;
                  return 1;
      case INNER: ;
                }
                else {
                  pc = DONE;
      case DONE: return 0;
                }
        }
    }
```

Here we have simulated coroutine semantics by moving information that would ordinarily be present in the coroutine's activation record (the current node and the program counter) to the data portion of the control abstraction object. In this case, the state of the traversal recorded in the control abstraction object includes not only an indication of the current position within the underlying data structure of the ADT being traversed, but also an indication of a location within the traversal function itself.

Note that we could also have based the implementation on the original recursive algorithm, but this approach would probably have required dynamic allocation of memory by the `Postorder` object to simulate the call stack.

This simple technique can be enormously useful. By simulating coroutines (or simple functions that may halt and later resume without "returning") with control objects, one gains the usual advantages of an abstract data type. Thus, our equivalent of an executing coroutine (or function) can be copied, duplicated, modified, backed up, skipped forward, restarted, etc. without having to resort to low-level or machine-specific programming.

Other Abstractions

For completeness, let us examine the `Access` type that is returned by `Walk::get`:

```
class Access {
  protected:
    Node *n;
  public:
    Access( Node *node ) : n( node ) {}
    friend operator ==( Access a, Access b )
      { return a.n == b.n; }
    friend operator !=( Access a, Access b )
      { return !(a == b); }
    // access routines...
};
```

This is an extraordinarily simple, but extraordinarily useful, type. First, if properly implemented its use will be as fast and as small as direct access to the Node with a pointer but with much greater safety. In addition, should the structure of a `Node` change, the implementation of `Access` can change along with it so that user code will be unaffected by the changes. This simple mechanism can accommodate, without change to user code, even dramatic changes in implementation such as lazy read-in of large trees from disk, persistent trees, or heterogeneous mixtures of different implementations of trees. Let us call this mechanism *access abstraction.*

The two central ideas behind access abstraction are the same as those for data abstraction in general. First, the user of an access abstraction is unaffected by the details of its implementation. In addition to reducing the amount of knowledge that must be acquired before a user of a complex type can perform simple access of that type, this allows the implementor to change its implementation (and the implementations of its associated access abstractions) without affecting user code. Second, access abstraction brings the programming language closer to the access aspects of the problem in the same way that data abstraction does for the type aspects.

The most important concept to be gleaned from the foregoing is that *the access aspects of one type can be encapsulated within another.*

DISTRIBUTED ABSTRACT INTERFACES

As the generic nature of the discussions of control and access abstraction indicate, there is really no formal difference between the two concepts; one could instantiate a similar discussion for any property of an abstract data type.

The most important concept to be gleaned from the foregoing is that *certain aspects of one type can be encapsulated within another.*

This brings us to the title of this article. Consider the *n*-ary tree type. Traversal and access semantics are part of the abstract semantics of this type, but their abstract interfaces do not belong in the `Tree` class. For the properties relegated to the `Walk` control abstraction, it was a case of traversals having a different lifetime and number than the tree being traversed. In C++, these differences imply that the corresponding properties are represented in a separate object at runtime and the abstract interface for traversal is encapsulated in a new, but related, class. For the properties relegated to the `Access` access abstraction, it was a case of aesthetics, safety, and flexibility. The approach in each case was to extend the implementation of the *n*-ary tree type to include a separate class that specified the abstract interface in question. The abstract interface to the *n*-ary tree type is distributed among several classes.

REFERENCES AND SUGGESTED READING

1. Coggins, J. Designing C++ libraries, *The C++ Journal* 1(1): 26, 1990.
2. Dewhurst, S. C. Abstracting data abstraction, *Proceedings of the Borland Languages Conference,* April 28–May 1, 1991.
3. Dewhurst, S. C. Control abstraction, *The C++ Journal* 1(2), 1990.

Curiously Recurring Template Patterns

James O. Coplien
cope@research.att.com

My previous columns have started with a discussion about patterns, followed by an exemplary pattern. This month, I'm weaving the two together to explore how we find and record patterns. This is a story of how I came to understand an interesting family of patterns that were independently invented by a telecommunications software designer at AT&T, by some scientific programmers at IBM, and by a computer linguist at Oregon State University. I'll use this pattern to explore the way we think about software and abstraction and to introduce multiparadigm design, a stepping-stone between object-oriented design and patterns. I feel like a cultural anthropologist who has discovered a grand unified theory of, well, something, and invite you to join me as I relive the quest for the underlying abstractions of this architectural construct.

The Genesis of an Idea

Four or five years ago, a good friend and coworker of mine, Lorraine Juhl, showed me a piece of code that has intrigued me to this day. The code combined templates and inheritance in a powerful pattern that I've seen at least three other people invent independently. What was remarkable about this pattern was that it used templates so powerfully so early after their introduction into the language. The code implemented a finite-state machine. FSMs are a big part of our business in telecommunications (I've often said that everyone discovers FSMs at least once during their career), so a robust FSM abstraction was a big deal. The programmers defined their contribution to the FSM like this:

```
class myFSM: public BaseFSM
  <myFSM,
  /*State=*/      char,
  /*Stimulus=*/   char> {
public:
  void x1(char);
  void x2(char);
  void init() {
    addState(1);
    addState(2);
    addTransition(EOF,1,2,&myFSM::x1);
    . . . .
  }
};
```

What's that again? The class `myFSM` is derived from a base class that is instantiated from a template, but the derived class is passed as a parameter to the template instantiation. Why? Let's look at the template used to build the base class:

```
template <class M, class State, class Stimulus>
class BaseFSM {
public:
  virtual void addState(State) = 0;
  virtual void addTransition(
    Stimulus, State, State,
    void (M::*)(Stimulus)) = 0;
  virtual void fire(Stimulus) = 0;
};
```

We'll talk more about the base class later; for now, think of it as an abstract base class in the conventional sense, one that provides an interface to a family of derived class state machines.

This framework is completed by a template that captures the FSM state and the common machinery for a state machine. The application programmer uses this template to create the FSM object:

```
template <class UserMachine, class State,
  class Stimulus>
class FSM: public UserMachine {
```

```
public:
  FSM() {  init(); }
  virtual void addState(State);
  virtual void addTransition(
    Stimulus, State from, State to,
    void (UserMachine::*)(Stimulus));
  virtual void fire(Stimulus);
private:
    State nstates,*states,currentState;
    Map<Stimulus,
        void(UserMachine::*)(Stimulus)>
        *transitionMap;
};

int main() {
      FSM<myFSM,/*State=*/char, /*Stimulus=*/char>
          myMachine;
        . . . .
}
```

The Pattern Resurfaces

It was several years later, and I had almost forgotten about this pattern, when Addison-Wesley asked me to review a book manuscript draft. The book was to become *Scientific and Engineering C++*, by John Barton and Lee Nackman of IBM.[1] It contained lots of code that looked like this:

```
template<class DerivedType>
class EquivalentCategory {
  friend Boolean operator==(
    const DerivedType &lhs,
    const DerivedType &rhs) {
    return lhs.equivalentTo(rhs);
  }
  friend Boolean operator!=(
    const DerivedType &lhs,
    const DerivedType &rhs) {
    return ! lhs.equivalentTo(rhs);
  }
};
```

```
class Apple:
  public EquivalentCategory<Apple> {
public:
  Apple(int n): a(n) { }
  virtual Boolean equivalentTo(
    const Apple &an_apple) const {
     return a == an_apple.a;
  }
private:
  int a;
};
```

Though it's not important for our purposes here, they go on to define a class `Orange` and, well, you can guess the rest. Sure enough, this was the same pattern that Lorraine had discovered a few years earlier. The Barton and Nackman manuscript raised the FSM trick to new heights by regularizing it and using it in many different ways. They had recognized a class of problems that called for this solution again and again.

Barton and Nackman are interested in scientific and engineering programming. They dwell on abstractions like numbers, vectors, matrices, groups, and other structure categories. They are also interested in efficiency, which is one reason the book leverages templates as much as it does (the term *template* takes a full column in the book's index, almost the same amount given to the term *type*). This pattern is important to them because common category properties (what we usually use inheritance for) and common code structure (what we usually use templates for) can be factored out of many of their designs. Used together, templates and inheritance support a design construct that we can capture as a pattern. The problem is factoring circular dependencies in code structure and behavior.

The context is a language that supports inheritance and templates, used with an object-oriented focus. The forces are interesting:

- We want a single base class that ties together the semantics of equality and inequality in the most general sense, so that one is guaranteed to be the logical negation of the other: in other words, the implementation should be type-restricted.
- Classes exhibiting the behaviors of an equivalence category should be derived from this class: in general, the derived class behaviors are derived from the base behaviors.

- The base class must know the derived class type, so it can dispatch the computation of equality to its derived class part: in other words, the implementation is type-dependent.
- The parameter list signature of the derived class must be compliant with that of the base class, so if the base class wants to call a derived class function through a base class virtual function interface, the function's interface must be invariant with respect to the derived type.
- The derived class member function that computes equality has a parameter list that is sensitive to the derived type.
- The derived classes of interest cover a broad range of otherwise unrelated types.

The type restriction of the equality equivalence class and type dependency in the derived class implementations leads to a circular dependency between the two. The solution:

- "To obtain both type-restricted and type-dependent functions, we combine the features of implementation and template categories. Specifically, we create an implementation base class, `EquivalentCategory <DerivedType>`, parameterized by the type of the derived class" (see p. 352 of Ref. 1).

That is, we encode the circular dependency directly using inheritance in one direction and templates in the other. The first time I saw the Barton and Nackman code, I told them that their compiler was broken and that this shouldn't compile: A compiler could never reduce the dependency of a base class on its derived class. They very politely cited the ARM chapter and verse to show where I was wrong. C++ allows such a dependency as long as the *structure* of the base class doesn't depend on a derived class type parameter.

Note that this is an outsider's view of the solution; I'm looking forward to an opportunity for the authors to set the record straight with me. I also defer to them the honor of naming this pattern.

Third Time's a Charm

Most recently, I attended Tim Budd's OOPSLA tutorial on multiparadigm programming. I had been looking forward to this tutorial for some time, as I've actively been researching how multiparadigm design techniques might be used to regularize hybrid designs. (Tim's book, *Multiparadigm Programming in Leda*, will soon be on the market). It turned out that Tim's talk didn't focus much on design, but it provided some fascinating lessons in programming language. He illustrated multiparadigm programming using the Leda language that he and his students have developed at Oregon State University. I looked through his extensive notes after the tutorial (his notes include generous excerpts from his forthcoming book) and found the following code snippets:

```
class ordered [T : ordered] of
  equality[T];
  . . . .
end;

class integer of ordered[integer];
  function asString ()->string
    begin . . . . end
  function equals (arg : integer)
    -> boolean;
    begin . . . . end;
end;

class string of ordered[string];
  function asString ()->string;
    begin return self; end;
  function equals (arg : integer) -> boolean;
    begin . . . . end;
end;
```

Deja vu all over again, and it's not even C++. What was particularly remarkable about this example is that it relates to equality tests, as does one of the earliest uses of this pattern in the Barton and Nackman book. By the time I discovered the third independently derived example of this style, I became convinced that this is a pattern, not just an isolated trick. Since then, I've encountered colleagues using this same pattern for finite state machines (Ralph Kolewe at Eridani in Ontario), and in a human–machine interface library (Paul Lucas at AT&T).

If this is a pattern, it must solve the same problem—at some level—in all these examples. It must derive from a single, common set of underlying forces. So what is going on here?

Let's look at the FSM example in Figure 1. Notice that this class diagram shows the same circular dependency we described for the Barton and Nackman

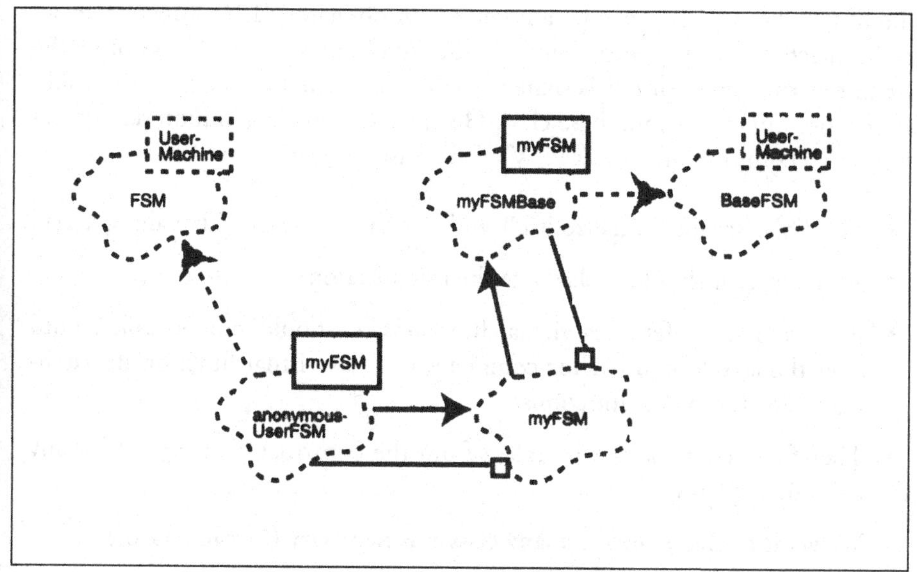

FIGURE 1. *Some abstractions that make a Finite State Machine.*

example. This pattern attempts to solve the following problem: Separate the common FSM mechanisms into a library of generic abstractions so the programmer need only write code for the FSM behaviors (or policies) that are of interest to the application.

(An exercise left to the reader: Compare this to the problem statement for the Barton and Nackman example.) Let's jump ahead to the rationale. We have broken the design into three parts. `BaseFSM` is a template that generates a family of abstract base class interfaces. More interestingly, class FSM contains all the state machine machinery: it is a generic state machine. What *is* a generic state machine? Its interface defines responsibilities for defining the semantics of a particular FSM: It can learn new states (`addState`) and new transition arcs between the states (`addTransition`). The fire member function causes the machine to cycle, processing the input provided as the member function argument. The FSM template also provides a generic implementation for all state machines: a state count, a current state, a vector of states, and a map from the current state to the transition function for the current state. (I have simplified the design for the sake of presentation; a production version would probably map a 2-tuple comprising the current state and an input, to a transition function.)

Programmers can develop their own classes like `myFSM` that capture the behavior of a state machine (its states and transitions) without worrying about the mechanics. The `BaseFSM` class provides a framework for the programmer to fill out: the class myFSM provides a home for an obligatory init function to set up the machine, as well as a home for the functions that do the work of the machine at run time. All FSMs share the same data structure; usually, we would factor those into a common base class. Here, we factor the common data structures into a common *derived* class! Why? Because:

- The FSM should initialize itself without the user explicitly calling init.
- A constructor should orchestrate the initialization.
- Because init references virtual functions, it should not be called until after the myFSM constructor completes (so that virtual function dispatching works for myFSM functions).
- Therefore, init cannot be called from the constructor for myFSM or any of its base classes.
- We want to create only as many classes as necessary (Occam's razor).

The solution is to call init from a derived class. The FSM template can generate a derived class that takes myFSM as a base class, with a constructor that calls myFSM::init. Capture the common data structure in the same class to avoid multiplying classes unnecessarily.

This is a pattern, at least in the sense that it documents the architect's rationale for this rather involved data structure. This pattern creates a new context where we face a new problem: We want the fire member function to be accessible through the base class interface.

However:

- Common member functions should be declared in the base class, usually as virtual functions.
- In this context (defined by the output of the previous pattern), the base class is the one provided by the user.
- Declaring fire in myFSM is make-work that a programmer might easily forget to do.

Therefore, we define a new base class, BaseFSM, that declares fire as a pure virtual function. Users are obligated to derive their state machines from BaseFSM. Calls to fire through a generic base class pointer will be dispatched around class myFSM to the derived class generated by the FSM template. Template type parameters tie the three classes together.

These patterns together form a small pattern language that documents this FSM framework. The framework code is hopelessly opaque by itself—as the author of the code, even I have trouble explaining the implementation from the code alone. The patterns organize my thoughts about the design so I can understand how to use the framework and perhaps teach others how to use it. I suspect we'll see a proliferation of patterns to document existing and emerging frameworks.

Pattern, Idiom, or Coincidence?

Is this trick with templates just a low-level idiom specific to C++? I suspect that a broader design pattern lurks here; we already have one non-C++ data point in Tim Budd's language. We will find this pattern only in languages that have both templates and inheritance. That is why we haven't seen the pattern in Ada, which lacks inheritance (I'll bet we see the pattern in Ada 9X); that's why we don't see it in Smalltalk, which lacks the compile-time binding semantics of templates. These language properties become a crucial component of the pattern context, but they don't limit the pattern to C++ alone.

The FSM pattern is a variant of the technique used by Barton, Nackman, and Budd. Do all these patterns belong in the same pattern language? Does the FSM pattern generalize as much as the Barton/Nackman/Budd technique, or does it just cover an obscure corner of design? Time will tell. As we gain experience with templates in practice, and as more people come up to speed with the Barton and Nackman material, we'll know better how to shape and assemble C++ template pattern languages.

We can broaden the question even further. Budd's code arose from a culture interested in multiparadigm design (though he doesn't count templates as a real paradigm). I, too, have been exploring multiparadigm design techniques for C++ (see my paper, "Multiparadigm design for C++" in the *Proceedings of the* 1994 SIGS OOP/*C++ World* in Munich, January 1994). My technique is based on commonality and variability analyses pioneered by my coworker David Weiss and his colleagues. Multiparadigm design has steps and notations that point the way to structures such as those discussed here. Curiously, we find that Barton and Nackman have made commonality and variability part of their vocabulary as they describe these designs. Might there be a way to regularize such designs and to provide a way of thinking about design that makes them more intuitive? If so, patterns might be overkill. Again, time will tell.

REFERENCE

1. Barton, J., and L. Nackman. *Scientific and Engineering C++*, Addison-Wesley, Reading, MA, 1994.

PATTERN HATCHING

JOHN VLISSIDES
vlis@watson.ibm.com

JIM COPLIEN HAS LAID THE GROUNDWORK FOR ALL SORTS OF DISCUSSIONS on software patterns in "The Column Without a Name." In this article, I'll offer another perspective on this emerging discipline, one that reflects my experience as a member of the "Gang of Four." I'm referring not to some group of malefactors (I think) but to Erich Gamma, Richard Helm, Ralph Johnson, and myself. Together, we authored *Design Patterns: Elements of Reusable Object-Oriented Software,* a book of 23 patterns distilled from numerous object-oriented software systems.[1]

In *Design Patterns,* we've tried to describe recurring snippets of object-oriented design that impart those elusive properties of good software: elegance, flexibility, extensibility, and reusability. We've recorded these snippets in a form that, although different from [Chris] Alexander's,[2] is nevertheless faithful to pattern ideals. More on our pattern form later.

The patterns in the book come from many application domains, including user interfaces, compilers, programming environments, operating systems, distributed systems, financial modeling, and computer-aided design. That's not to say design patterns are domain-specific. We were careful to include only proven designs we'd seen again and again across domains.

We call our patterns "design patterns" for at least a couple of reasons. Our work has its roots in Erich Gamma's doctoral dissertation, in which he coined the term.[3] He wanted to emphasize that he was capturing design expertise as opposed to other software development skills, such as domain analysis or implementation. Another reason is that *pattern* alone means different things to different people, even among pattern aficionados. Prepending *design* provides some needed qualification, but since I'll be talking mostly about design patterns in this column, I'll dispense with the *design* prefix whenever I can get away with it.

As for the title of this column, I chose "Pattern Hatching" initially for its similarity to a familiar concept in computer science. (Besides, all the good titles were taken.) But I've come around to thinking that it captures my intent for this column rather well. *Hatching* doesn't suggest that we are creating anything. It implies development from preexisting rudiments. That happens to be appropriate: *Design Patterns* is our incubator of eggs, as it were, from which much new life will hopefully emerge. (I trust we won't have opportunity to take this analogy too much further.)

The "Pattern Hatching" column will not merely echo the book. My aim is to build on what's in the book, to leverage its concepts so that we can learn from them and improve on them.

Design Patterns Versus Alexander's Patterns

Design patterns have a substantially different structure from Alexander's patterns. Basically, Alexander starts with a short statement describing the problem, followed by an example that explains and resolves the forces behind the problem and culminates in a succinct statement of the solution. Except for a few typographical embellishments, the pattern looks much like conventional prose. It invites reading through from start to finish. The down side is that this structure is rather coarse; there's no structure at a finer level, just narration. If, for example, you need detailed information about a particular "force" in the pattern, you have to scan through a lot of text.

Design patterns are more highly structured by comparison. They have to be. They contain more material than Alexander's patterns: the average design pattern is 10 pages, compared to four (smaller) pages for its Alexandrian counterpart. Design patterns also describe in detail how you might implement the pattern, including sample code and a discussion of implementation trade-offs. Alexander seldom deals with construction details on a comparable level.

We could have presented this material using a more Alexander-like structure, but we wanted to allow quick reference in the heat of design or implementation. Since we don't prescribe an order in which to apply the patterns (as would a true pattern language in the Alexandrian tradition), there's less to guide you to the right pattern. Even if you know which pattern you want, its size could make it hard to find the detail that interests you. We had to make it fast and easy for designers to find the patterns that are appropriate to their problems. That led us toward a finer-grained pattern structure.

Design Pattern Structure

A design pattern has the following 13 sections:

1. Name
2. Intent
3. Also Known As
4. Motivation
5. Applicability
6. Structure
7. Participants
8. Collaborations
9. Consequences
10. Implementation
11. Sample Code
12. Known Uses
13. Related Patterns

The first three sections identify the pattern. Section 4 approximates the content of an Alexandrian pattern: It gives a concrete example that illustrates the problem, its context, and its solution. Sections 5–9 define the pattern abstractly. Most people seem to understand things better when they're explained in concrete terms first, followed by more abstract terms. That's why a design pattern considers the problem and its solution concretely before describing them in the abstract. Section 10 gets concrete again, and section 11 is the most concrete of all. Section 12 is bibliographic, and section 13 provides cross references.

Building with Composites

Let's take the `Composite` pattern as an example. Its intent is twofold: Compose objects into tree structures to represent part-whole hierarchies, and give clients a uniform way of dealing with these objects whether they are internal nodes or leaves. To motivate the pattern, let's consider how we might design a hierarchical file system. For now, I'll focus on just two particularly important aspects of the design. I'll build on this example in subsequent columns as a way of showing you how other patterns address design issues.

From the user's perspective, the file system should handle file structures of arbitrary size and complexity. It shouldn't put arbitrary limits on how wide

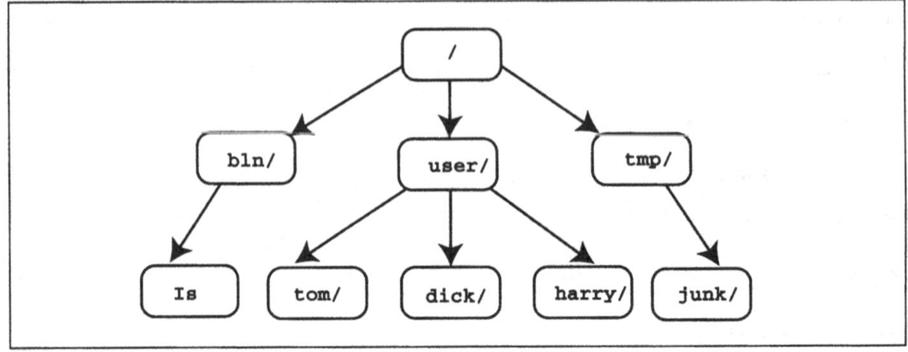

FIGURE 1.

or deep the file structure can get. From the implementor's perspective, the representation for the file structure should be easy to deal with and extend.

Suppose you are implementing a command that lists the files in a directory. The code you write to get the name of a directory shouldn't have to be different from the code you write to get the name of a file—the same code should work for both. In other words, you should be able to treat directories and files uniformly with respect to their names. The resulting code will be easier to write and maintain. You also want to accommodate new kinds of files (like symbolic links, for example) without reimplementing half the system.

It's clear that files and directories are key elements in our problem domain and that we need a way of introducing specialized versions of these elements after we've finalized the design. An obvious design approach would be to represent these elements as objects, as shown in Figure 1.

How do you implement such a structure? The fact that we have two kinds of objects suggests two classes, one for files and one for directories. We want to treat files and directories uniformly, which means they must have a common interface. In turn, that means the classes must be derived from a common (abstract) base class, which we'll call "Node." We also know that directories aggregate files. Together, these constraints essentially define the class hierarchy for us:

```
class Node {
public:
  // declare common interface here
protected:
  Node();
};
```

```
class File : public Node {

public:
  File();

  // redeclare common interface here
};

class Directory : public Node {
public:
  Directory();

  // redeclare common interface here
private:
  List<Node*> _nodes;
};
```

The next question to consider concerns the make-up of the common interface. What are the operations that apply equally to files and directories? Well, there are all sorts of attributes of interest, like name, size, protection, and so forth. Each attribute can have operations for accessing and modifying its value(s). Operations like these that have clear meaning for both files and directories are easy to treat uniformly. The tricky issues arise when the operations don't seem to apply as clearly to both.

For example, one of the most common things users do is ask for a list of the files in a directory. That means that `Directory` needs an interface for enumerating its children. Here's a simple one that returns the *n*th child:

```
virtual Node* GetChild(int n);
```

`GetChild` must return a `Node*`, because the directory may contain either `File` objects or `Directory` objects. The type of that return value has an important ramification: It forces us to define `GetChild` not just in the `Directory` class but in the `Node` class as well. Why? Because we want to be able to list the children of a subdirectory. In fact, the user will often want to descend the file system structure. We won't be able to do that unless we can call `GetChild` on the object `GetChild` returns. So, like the attribute operations, `GetChild` is something we want to be able to apply uniformly.

`GetChild` is also key to letting us define `Directory` operations recursively. For example, suppose `Node` declares a `Size` operation that returns the total number of bytes consumed by the directory (sub)tree. `Directory` could define its version of this operation as a sum of the values that its children return when their `Size` operation is called:

```
long Directory::Size () {
  long total = 0;
  Node* child;

  for (int i = 0; child = GetChild(i); ++i) {
       total += child->Size();
  }

  return total;
}
```

Directories and files illustrate the key aspects of the Composite pattern: It generates tree structures of arbitrary complexity, and it prescribes how to treat those objects uniformly. The `Applicability` section of the pattern echoes these aspects. It states that you should use `Composite` when

- You want to represent part-whole hierarchies of objects.
- You want clients to be able to ignore the difference between compositions of objects and individual objects. Clients will treat all objects in the composite structure uniformly.

The pattern's `Structure` section presents a modified OMT diagram of the canonical `Composite` class structure (see Figure 2). By "canonical" I mean simply that it represents the most common arrangement of classes that we (the Gang of Four) have observed. It can't represent the *definitive* set of classes and relationships, because the interfaces may vary when we consider certain design or implementation-driven trade-offs. (The pattern will spell those out, too.)

Figure 2 shows the classes that participate in the pattern and their static relationships. Component is the abstract base class to which our Node class corresponds. Subclass participants are `Leaf` (which corresponds to `File`) and `Composite` (corresponding to `Directory`). The arrowhead line going from `Composite` to `Component` indicates that `Composite` contains instances of type `Component`. The ball at the tip of the arrowhead indicates more than one instance; if the ball were omitted, it would mean exactly one instance. The diamond at the base of the arrowhead line means that the `Composite` aggregates its child instances, which implies that deleting the `Composite` would delete its children as well. It also implies that components aren't shared, thus assuring tree structures. The `Participant` and `Collaboration` sections of the pattern explain the static and dynamic relationships, respectively, among these participants.

`Composite`'s Consequences section sums up the benefits and liabilities of

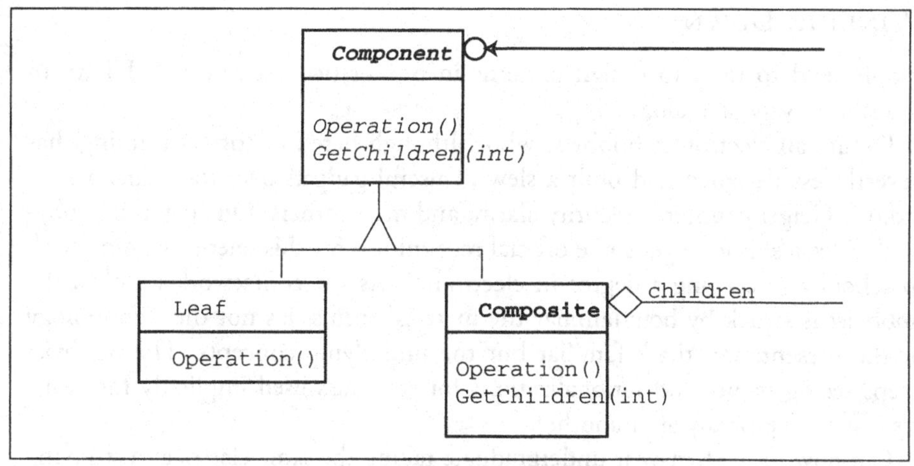

FIGURE 2. *OMT structure diagram for* `Composite`.

the pattern. On the plus side, the pattern supports tree structures of arbitrary complexity. A corollary of this property is that a node's complexity is hidden from clients: they can't tell whether they're dealing with a leaf or a composite component, because they don't have to. That makes client code more independent of the code in the components. The client is also simpler, because it can treat leaves and composites uniformly. No longer do clients have to decide which of multiple code paths to take based on the type of component. Best of all, you can add new types of components without touching existing code.

`Composite`'s down side, however, is that it can lead to a system where the class of every object looks like the class of every other. The significant differences show up only at run-time. That can make the code hard to understand, even if you are privy to class implementations. Moreover, the number of objects may become prohibitive if the pattern is applied at a low level or at too fine a granularity.

As you might have guessed, implementation issues abound for the `Composite` pattern. Some of the issues we address include:

- When and where to cache information to improve performance.
- What if any storage the `Component` class should allocate.
- What data structure(s) to use for storing children.
- Whether or not operations for adding and removing children should be declared in the `Component` class.

Winding Down

People tend to react to design patterns in one of two ways, which I'll try to describe by way of analogy.

Picture an electronics hobbyist who, although bereft of formal training, has nevertheless designed and built a slew of useful gadgets over the years: a ham radio, a Geiger counter, a security alarm, and many others. One day the hobbyist decides it's time to get some official recognition for this talent by going back to school and earning a degree in electronics. As the coursework unfolds, the hobbyist is struck by how familiar the material seems. It's not the terminology or the presentation that's familiar but the underlying concepts. The hobbyist keeps seeing names and rationalizations for stuff he's used implicitly for years. It's just one epiphany after another.

Cut now to the first-year undergraduate taking the same classes and studying the same material. The undergrad has no electronics background—lots of rollerblading, yes, but no electronics. The stuff in the course is intensely painful for him, not because he's dumb, but because it's so totally new. It takes quite a bit more time for the undergrad to understand and appreciate the material, but eventually he does, with hard work and a bit of perseverance.

If you feel like a design pattern hobbyist, more power to you. If, on the other hand, you feel more like the undergrad, take heart: the investment you make in learning good patterns will pay for itself each time you apply them in your designs. That's a promise.

Maybe electronics, with its techie connotations, isn't the best analogy for everyone. If you agree, then consider something Alfred North Whitehead said in 1943, admittedly in a different context, which might nonetheless make a more appealing connection: "Art is the imposing of a pattern on experience and our aesthetic enjoyment in recognition of the pattern."

References

1. Gamma, E., R. Helm, R. Johnson, J. Vlissides. *Design Patterns: Elements of Reusable Object-Oriented Software,* Addison-Wesley, Reading, MA, 1995.
2. Alexander, C., et al. *A Pattern Language,* Oxford University Press, New York, 1977.
3. Gamma, E. *Object-Oriented Software Development Based on ET++: Design Patterns, Class Library, Tools,* (in German), PhD thesis, University of Zurich Institut für Informatik, 1991.

Orphanage, Adoption, and Surrogates

The inaugural Pattern Hatching column introduced the `Composite` pattern, and I explained how you could use it in the design of a file system. This time I'll go a little deeper into `Composite`'s ramifications for this application. We'll look at an important trade-off in the design of the `Node` class interface, and then we'll take a shot at adding some new functionality to our fledgling design.

Composite Redux

The `Composite` pattern generates the backbone of this application. It shows us how to express the fundamental characteristics of hierarchical file systems in object-oriented terms. The pattern relates its key participants—the `Component`, `Composite`, and `Leaf` classes—through inheritance and composition in a way that supports file system structures of arbitrary size and complexity. It also lets clients treat files and directories (and whatever else might be in there) uniformly.

The key to uniformity lies in a common interface among objects in the file system. So far we have three classes of object in the design: `Node`, `File`, and `Directory`. They're related as shown in Figure 3.

Last time, I explained how operations that have clear meaning for both files and directories need to be declared in the `Node` base class. Operations for getting and setting the node's name and protection fall into this category. I also explained why we need to include an operation for accessing child nodes (`GetChild`) in the common interface, even though at first glance it doesn't seem appropriate for `File` objects. This time, we'll consider other operations that are even less obviously common.

Adopt/Orphan: Nodes and Files Need Not Apply

Before we can expect a `Directory` object to enumerate its children, it must somehow acquire them. But from where? The directory itself can't assume responsibility for creating all the children it might ever contain—the user of the file system controls such things. It's reasonable to expect clients of the file system to create files and directories and then put them where they want them. That means `Directory` objects in particular will *adopt* child nodes rather than create them. Hence `Directory` needs an interface for adopting children; something like

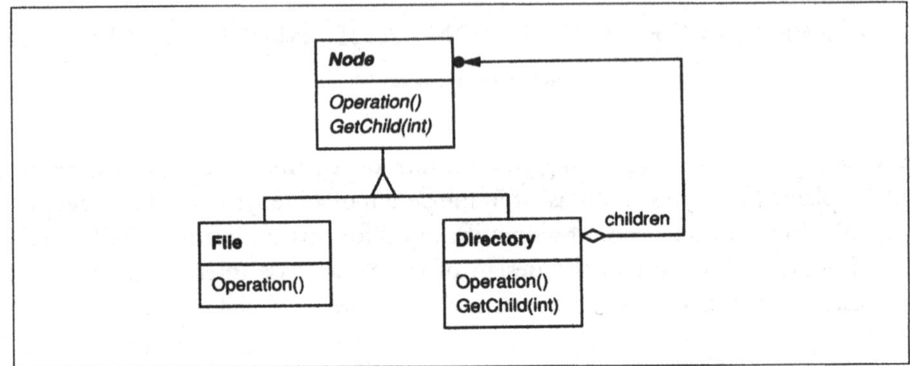

FIGURE 3. *Relationships among classes* `Node`, `File`, *and* `Directory`.

```
virtual void Adopt(Node* child)
```

will do.

When a client calls `Adopt` on a directory, the client is explicitly handing over responsibility for the given child (which may be any kind of `Node`) to the directory. Responsibility implies ownership: when the directory gets deleted, the child does also. This is the essence of the aggregation relationship (denoted by the diamond in the diagram) between the `Directory` and `Node` classes.

Now if a client can tell a directory to assume responsibility for a child, a call to *relinquish* such responsibility is probably in order. Hence:

```
virtual void Orphan(Node* child)
```

In this case `Orphan` doesn't imply that the parent directory dies . . . er, gets deleted. It just means the directory is no longer the child's parent. The child lives on, too, perhaps to be adopted shortly by another node, perhaps to be . . . deleted.

So what does this have to do with uniformity? Why can't we define these operations on `Directory` and nowhere else?

Okay, say we do that. Now consider how a client implements operations that change the file system structure. An example of such a client is a user-level command that creates a new directory. The user interface for this command is immaterial; let's assume it's just a command-line interface like the UNIX `mkdir` command. `mkdir` takes a name for the directory-to-be as an argument, like so:

```
mkdir newsubdir
```

Actually, the user can prepend any valid path to the name:

```
mkdir subdirA/subdirB/newsubdir
```

This should work as long as subdirA and subdirB exist and are directories, as opposed to files. More generally, subdirA and subdirB should be instances of Node subclasses that can have children. If this isn't true, then the user should get an error message.

How do we implement mkdir? Well, first let's assume mkdir can find out what the current directory is; that is, it can obtain a reference to the Directory object that corresponds to the user's choice of current directory.* Adding a new directory to the current one is simply a matter of creating a new Directory instance and then calling Adopt on the current directory, passing the new directory as a parameter:

```
Directory* current;
// ...
current->Adopt(new Directory("newsubdir"));
```

Simple. But what about the general case, where mkdir is supplied a nontrivial path?

This is where things get trickier. mkdir must

1. Find the subdirA object (reporting an error if it doesn't exist).

2. Find the subdirB object (reporting an error if it doesn't exist).

3. Have the subdirB object adopt the newsubdir object.

Items 1 and 2 involve iterating through the children of the current directory and those of subdirA (if it exists) in search of a node representing subdirB. At the heart of mkdir's implementation might be a recursive function that takes a path as an argument:

```
void Client::Mkdir (Directory* current, const char* path) {
  const char* subpath = Subpath(path);

  if (subpath == 0) {
    current->Adopt(new Directory(path));

  } else {
```

* The client could get the current directory object from a well-known place, like a static operation on the Node class. Accessing well-know resources is a job for the Singleton design pattern, but we'll have to leave that for a later installment.

```
        const char* name = Head(path);
        Node* child = Find(name, current);

        if (child) {
          Mkdir(child, subpath);
        } else {
          cerr << name << " nonexistent." << endl;
        }
      }
    }
```

where Head and Subpath are string manipulation routines. Head returns the first name in the path; Subpath returns everything else. The Find operation searches a directory for a child of a given name:

```
Node* Client::Find (const char* name, Directory* current)
{
  Node* child = 0;

  for (int i = 0; child = current->GetChild(); ++i) {
    if (strcmp(name, child->GetName()) == 0) {
      return child;
    }
  }
  return 0;
}
```

Note that Find must return a Node*, because that's what GetChild returns. There's nothing unreasonable about that, since a child can be either a Directory or a File. But if you've been paying attention, you'll have noticed that this little detail effectively sinks Client::Mkdir—it won't compile.

Look again at the recursive call to Mkdir. It's passed a Node*, not the Directory* it needs. The problem is that when we descend the hierarchy, we can't tell whether a child is a file or a directory. Generally this is a good thing, as long as clients don't care about the difference, but in this case it seems we do indeed care, because only Directory defines an interface for adopting and orphaning children.

But do we *really* care? Or more to the point, does the client (the mkdir command) need to care? Not really. Its charter is to either create a new directory or report failure to the user.

An Equal Opportunity Interface

What if we treat Adopt and Orphan uniformly across Node classes? "Egad!" someone reacts. "Those operations don't mean anything for leaf components like File." But how prudent is that assumption? What if down the road someone else defines a new kind of leaf component like a trash can (or, more correctly, a recycle bin) that annihilates whatever it adopts? What if adopting into a leaf means "generate an error message"? It's hard to prove that Adopt can never make sense for leaves. Same for Orphan.

On the other hand, it might make sense to argue that there's no need for separate File and Directory classes in the first place—*everything* should be a Directory—but implementation issues argue differently. Directory objects tend to have baggage that most files don't need: a data structure for storing children, cached child information for improved performance, and so forth. Experience shows that leaves tend to be more plentiful than internal nodes in many applications. That's one reason why the Composite pattern prescribes separate Leaf and Composite classes.

Let's see what happens when we define Adopt and Orphan on *all* Nodes instead of just the Directory class. We'll make these operations generate error messages by default:

```
virtual void Node::Adopt (Node*) {
  cerr << GetName() << " is not a directory." << endl;
}

virtual void Node::Orphan (Node* child) {
  cerr << child->GetName() << " not found." << endl;
}
```

These aren't necessarily the best error messages, but you get the idea. Alternatively, these operations could throw exceptions, or they could do nothing—there are lots of possibilities. Anyway, Client::Mkdir now works beautifully.[†] Notice also that this required no change to the File class.

[†] Well, almost beautifully. I confess I've ignored memory management issues in this example. Specifically, we have a potential memory leak when Adopt gets called on a leaf, bucause the client passes ownership to a node that won't accept ownerhsip. This is a general problem with Adopt, since it could fail even on Directory objects (when the client has insufficint permission, for example). The problem goes away when Nodes are reference counted, and Adopt decrements (or dosen't increment) the reference count on failure.

Here's the point: Although Adopt and Orphan might not seem to be operations that we want to treat uniformly, there's real benefit in doing so, at least in this application. The most likely alternative would have been to introduce some sort of downcast that lets the client identify the type of node:

```
void Client::Mkdir (Directory* current, const char* path) {
  const char* subpath = Subpath(path);

  if (subpath == 0) {
    current->Adopt(new Directory(path));

  } else {
    const char* name = Head(path);
    Node* node = Find(name, current);

    if (node) {
      Directory* child = dynamic_cast<Directory*>(node);

      if (child) {
        Mkdir(child, subpath);
      } else {
        cerr << name() << " is not a directory." << endl;
      }

    } else {
      cerr << name << " nonexistent." << endl;
    }
  }
}
```

See how the dynamic_cast introduced an extra control path? It's needed to handle the case where the user specified the name of a file (rather than a directory) somewhere in the path. This illustrates how nonuniformity can make clients more complicated.

BUT WHERE DO SURROGATES FIT INTO ALL THIS?

Glad you asked, because it's time we looked at adding a new feature, namely, symbolic links (a.k.a. "aliases" in Mac Finder parlance or "shadows" in OS/2 Workplace Shell). Basically, a symbolic link is a reference to another node in the file system. It's a "surrogate" for that node; it's not the node itself. If you delete the symbolic link, it goes away without affecting the node to which it refers. A symbolic link has its own access rights that may differ from the node's.

In most situations, however, the symbolic link behaves just like the node itself. If the link refers to a file, then a client can treat the link as if it were that file; that is, it can edit it and perhaps even save it through the link. If the link refers to a directory, a client can add and remove nodes from the directory by operating on the link just as though it were the directory itself.

Symbolic links are convenient. They let you access far-flung files and directories without moving or copying them, which is great for nodes that must live in one place but get used in another. We'd be remiss if our design didn't support symbolic links.

So the first question that someone who paid good money for *Design Patterns* should ask is, "Is there a pattern that helps me design and implement symbolic links?" Actually, there's a bigger question: "How do I find the right design pattern for the task at hand?" Section 1.7 in *Design Patterns* suggests several approaches:

- Consider how design patterns solve design problems. (In other words, study Section 1.6. Unfortunately, we don't have time for that this month.)
- Scan the Intent sections for something that sounds right. (A bit brute-force.)
- Study how patterns interrelate. (Still too involved for us here, but we're getting warmer.)
- Look at patterns whose purpose (creational, structural, behavioral) corresponds to what you're trying to do. (For example, adding symbolic links to a file system suggests a structural purpose.)
- Examine a relevant cause of redesign (listed on page 24 of *Design Patterns*), and apply the patterns that help you avoid it. (We're not really worried about redesign at this point.)
- Consider what should be variable in your design. For each design pattern, Table 1.2 in *Design Patterns* lists one or more design aspects that the pattern lets you vary.

If we look at the structural patterns in Table 1.2, we see that

- `Adapter` lets you vary the interface to an object,
- `Bridge` lets you vary the implementation of an object,

- `Composite` lets you vary an object's structure and composition,
- `Decorator` lets you vary responsibilities without subclassing,
- `Facade` lets you vary the interface to a subsystem,
- `Flyweight` lets you vary storage costs of objects,
- `Proxy` lets you vary how an object is accessed and/or its location, and

Maybe I'm biased, but it sure sounds like `Proxy` is our pattern. Turning to that pattern, we find the following Intent: Provide a surrogate or placeholder for another object to control access to it.

The `Motivation` section applies the pattern to the problem of delayed-loading of images (not unlike what you might want in a Web browser, for example). But it's the `Applicability` section that clinches it for us. It states that `Proxy` is applicable whenever you need a more versatile or sophisticated reference to an object than a simple pointer. It goes on to list some common situations in which it applies, including a "protection proxy" that controls access to another object—just what we need.

APPLYING PROXY

Okay, now how do we apply the `Proxy` pattern to our file system design? Looking at the pattern's `Structure` diagram (Figure 4), you'll see three key classes: an abstract `Subject` class, a concrete `RealSubject` subclass, and another concrete `Proxy` subclass. Hence we can conclude that `Subject`, `RealSubject`, and `Proxy` have compatible interfaces. The `Proxy` subclass also contains a reference to `RealSubject`.

The pattern's Participants section explains that the `Proxy` class provides an interface identical to `Subject`'s so that a `Proxy` object can substitute for the real subject. Further, the `RealSubject` is the object that the proxy represents.

Mapping these relationships back to our file system classes, it's clear that the common interface we want to adhere to is `Node`'s. (That's what the `Composite` pattern has taught us, after all.) This suggests that the `Node` class plays the part of `Subject` in the pattern. Therefore we need to define a `Node` *subclass* corresponding to the `Proxy` class in the pattern. I'll call it `Link`:

```
class Link : public Node {
public:
  Link(Node*);

  // redeclare common Node interface here
private:
  Node* _subject;
};
```

The _subject member provides the reference to the real subject. Note that we're deviating a bit from the pattern's Structure diagram, which would have the reference be of type RealSubject. In our case that would correspond to a reference of type File or Directory, but we want symbolic links to work for either kind of Node. But if you look at the pattern's description of the Proxy participant, you'll find these words:

> [Proxy] maintains a reference that lets the proxy access the real subject. Proxy may refer to a Subject if the RealSubject and Subject interfaces are the same.

And given all we've talked about so far, it is indeed the case that File and Directory share the Node interface. Therefore _subject is a pointer to a Node. Without a common interface, it's much harder to define a symbolic link that works for both files and directories. In fact, you'd probably end up defining two kinds of symbolic links that work identically, except that one is for files and the other is for directories.

The last major issue to address concerns how Link implements the Node interface. To first approximation it merely delegates each operation to the corresponding operation on _subject. For example, it might delegate GetChild as follows:

```
Node* Link::GetChild (int n) {
  return _subject->GetChild(n);
}
```

In some cases the Link may exhibit different behavior than its subject. For example, Link could implement protection operations that are independent of the subject's. In that case it could implement the operations just like File does.

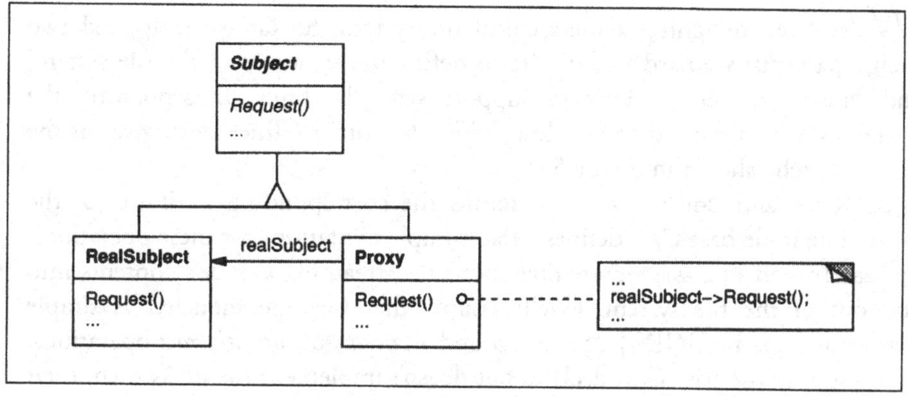

FIGURE 4.

Stay Tuned

One of the things to watch out for as a design like this evolves is the tendency to treat the base class as a dumping ground: its interface grows as operations accumulate over time. An operation or two gets added with each new file system feature. Today it's support for extended attributes; next week it's calculating a new kind of size statistic; next month it's an operation that returns an icon for a graphical user interface. Before long, `Node` is a behemoth of a class—tough to understand, maintain, and subclass.

I'll address this problem next time. We'll look at a way to add new operations to our design without modifying existing classes at all. So don't touch that dial!

Reference

1. Gamma, E., R. Helm, R. Johnson, J. Vlissides. *Design Patterns: Elements of Reusable Object-Oriented Software,* Addison-Wesley, Reading, MA, 1995.

Visiting Rights

Our ancestors are very good kind of folks, but they are the last people I should choose to have a visiting acquaintance with.

—Richard Brinsley Sheridan, *The Rivals*

We've been designing a hierarchical file system. So far we've applied two design patterns: we used Composite to define the structure of the file system, and `Proxy` showed us how to support symbolic links. Incorporating the changes we've discussed so far, along with a few other refinements, gives us the class hierarchy shown in Figure 5.

`GetName` and `GetProtection` return the corresponding attributes of the node. The node base class defines default implementations for these operations. `StreamIn` and `StreamOut` are operations for streaming a node's contents into and out of the file system. (We'll assume that files are modeled as simple bytestreams, as in UNIX.) `StreamIn` and `StreamOut` are *abstract* operations, meaning that the base class declares but doesn't implement them. As such, their

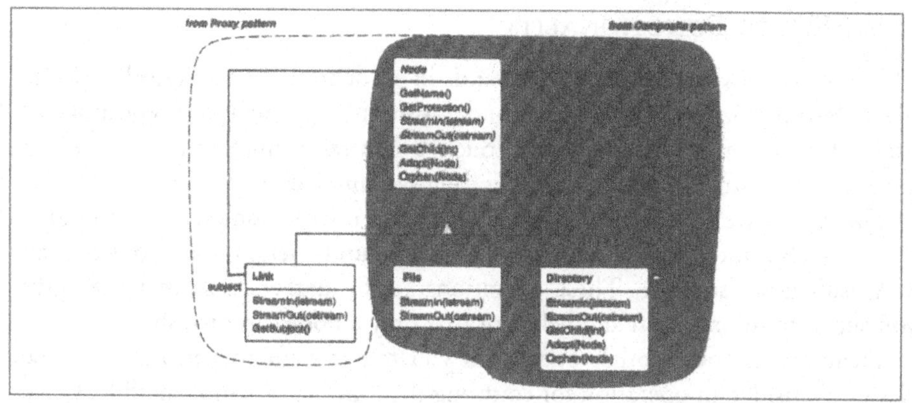

FIGURE 5.

names appear in italic. `GetChild`, `Adopt`, and `Orphan` have default implementations to make defining leaf components a bit easier.

Speaking of leaf components, recall that the `Node`, `File`, and `Directory` classes came from the `Composite` pattern. `Proxy` contributed the `Link` class, and it prescribed the `Node` class, which we already had. As a result, the `Node` class constitutes a junction of sorts between the two patterns. Whereas the other classes map to a participant of either `Proxy` or `Composite`, `Node` maps to a participant in *both* patterns: it's the `Component` in the Composite pattern, and it's the `Subject` in the `Proxy` pattern. Such dual citizenship is the mark of what Alexander calls a "dense" composition of patterns, where two or more occupy the same "space" of classes in the system.

There are plusses and minuses to this. Having multiple patterns dwell in relatively few classes lends a certain profundity to a design; much meaning is captured in a small space, not unlike good poetry. On the other hand, such density can be reminiscent of less inspired efforts. Richard Gabriel[1] puts it this way:

> [Alexandrian density] in software corresponds at least partly to highly bummed code—code where each part is doing more than one thing. Code like the code you produce when your first cut at it is two to three times too big for the RAM it needs to occupy, code like we used to have to write in the 60s and 70s in assembler.

Good point. Profound code isn't necessarily good code. Actually, Richard's concern is symptomatic of a larger problem: the pattern can get lost after it's been implemented. There's a lot to talk about here, but it'll have to wait—our file system beckons!

Open-Ended Functionality

The vast majority of user-level commands in an operating system deal with the file system in some way. And no wonder—the file system is *the* repository of user information in the computer. Such a central component is bound to engender new functionality as the operating system evolves.

The classes we've defined provide a modicum of functionality. In particular, the `Node` class interface encompasses just a few fundamental operations that all `Node` subclasses support. These operations are fundamental in that they give you access to information and behavior that only a node can furnish.

There are of course other operations you might want to perform on these classes. Consider an operation for counting the number of words in a file. Once we recognize that we need such an operation, we might be tempted to add a `GetWordCount` operation to the `Node` base class. But that'll force us to modify at least the `File` class and probably all the other classes as well. We'd prefer to add functionality without modifying (read "adding bugs to") existing code. Happily, we have streaming operations in the base class. A client of the file system can use them to examine the text in a file. Hence clients can implement word count in terms of existing operations.

In fact, I'll assert that the main challenge in designing the `Node` interface is to come up with a minimal set of operations that lets clients build open-ended functionality. The alternative—performing surgery on `Node` and its subclasses to enable each new capability—is both invasive and error-prone. It also makes the `Node` interface evolve into a hodgepodge of operations, eventually obscuring the basic properties of `Node` objects. The classes get hard to understand, extend, and use. So focusing on a suÉcient set of primitives is key to defining a simple, coherent `Node` interface.

Subclass-Specific Functionality

But what about operations that should work differently on different kinds of nodes? How can you make them external to the `Node` classes? Take the UNIX `cat` operation, for instance. It simply prints the contents of a (symbolic link to a) file to standard output, but when it's applied to a directory, it reports that the node cannot be printed, probably because a directory's textual representation doesn't look too pretty.

Since the `cat` operation's behavior depends on the type of node, it seems necessary to define a base-class operation that `Files` and `Directories` implement differently. So we change existing classes after all. Is there an alternative? Suppose we insist on taking this functionality out of the `Node` classes and putting it into a client. Then it looks like there's no choice but to introduce some kind of downcast to let the client decide which kind of node it's dealing with:

```
void Client::cat (Node* node) {
  Link* l;

  if (dynamic_cast<File*>(node)) {
    node->StreamOut(cout);    // stream out contents

  } else if (dynamic_cast<Directory*>(node)) {
    cerr << "Can't cat a directory." << endl;

  } else if (l = dynamic_cast<Link*>(node)) {
    cat(l->GetSubject());     // cat the link's subject
  }
}
```

Once again, the downcast seems unavoidable. And once again, it makes the client more complicated. True, we're deliberately putting functionality into the client instead of the `Node` classes. But in addition to the functionality itself, we're adding type tests and conditional branches—what amounts to a second level of method dispatch.

If putting the functionality into the `Nodes` themselves is distasteful, then resorting to a downcast seems downright yucky. But before we merrily hack a `cat()` operation into `Node` and its subclasses to avoid the downcast, let's look at a design pattern that offers a third alternative.

VISITOR

The intent of the `Visitor` pattern goes something like this: Represent an operation to be performed on the elements of an object structure. Visitor lets you define a new operation without changing the classes of the elements on which it operates.

The pattern's `Motivation` section talks about a compiler that represents programs in terms of abstract syntax trees. The problem in that case is to support an open-ended set of analyses like type checking, pretty-printing, and code generation without changing the classes that implement the abstract syntax trees. The compiler problem is analogous to our own, except that we're operating on file system structures instead of abstract syntax trees, and we want to do rather different things to our structures. (Then again, maybe pretty-printing a directory structure isn't so farfetched.)

At any rate, the analyses themselves don't really matter. What does matter is separating them from the Node classes without resorting to downcasts and extra control paths.

The Visitor pattern achieves this by adding just one operation to what it calls the Element participant, which in our case is the Node class:

```
virtual void Accept(Visitor&) = 0;
```

Accept lets a Visitor object visit a given node. The Visitor object encapsulates the operation to perform on the node. All concrete Element subclasses implement Accept in the same simple way. For example:

```
void File::Accept (Visitor& v) { v.Visit(this); }

void Directory::Accept (Visitor& v) { v.Visit(this); }

void Link::Accept (Visitor& v) { v.Visit(this); }
```

All the implementations look the same, but they're really different, of course. The type of the "this" parameter is different in each case. It suggests that the Visitor interface looks something like this:

```
class Visitor {
public:
  Visitor();

  void Visit(File*);
  void Visit(Directory*);
  void Visit(Link*);
};
```

The interesting property here is that when a node's Accept operation calls Visit on the Visitor object, the node effectively identifies its type to the Visitor. In turn, the Visitor operation that's called can do whatever's appropriate for that type of node:

```
void Visitor::Visit (File* f) {
  f->StreamOut(cout);
}

void Visitor::Visit (Directory* d) {
  cerr << "Can't cat a directory." << endl;
}
```

```
void Visitor::Visit (Link* l) {
  l->GetSubject()->Accept(*this);
}
```

The last operation merits some explanation. It calls `GetSubject()`, which returns the node that the link points to, that is, its subject.* We can't just tell the subject to stream itself out, because it might be a directory. Instead, we tell it to accept the visitor just like we did for the link itself. That lets the visitor act according to the type of subject. The visitor will follow any number of links in this way until it reaches a file or a directory, at which point it does the right thing.

So now we can `cat` any node simply by creating a visitor and telling the node to accept it:

```
Visitor cat;
node->Accept(cat);
```

The node's callback on the visitor will resolve to the `Visit` operation that corresponds to the node's actual type (`File`, `Directory`, or `Link`), thereby enacting the appropriate response. The bottom line is that this `Visitor` can package up functionality like the `cat` command in a single class without resorting to type tests.

Subclassing Visitor

Encapsulating the `cat` operation in `Visitor` is neat, but it still looks as though we have to change existing code if we want to do something other than `cat`-ing the file. Suppose we want to implement another command that lists the names of children in a directory, like the UNIX `ls` command. Further, the name should be suffixed by a slash if the node is a directory or by an @ symbol if it's a symbolic link.

We need to give another `Visitor`-like class visiting rights to `Node`s, but we don't want to add another `Accept` operation to the `Node` base class, and we don't have to. Any `Node` object can accept any type of `Visitor` object. The only trouble is that right now we have only one kind of `Visitor`. In the `Visitor` pattern, however, `Visitor` is actually an abstract class, and you derive a subclass for each new functionality:

---

* `GetSubject()` is specific to the `Link` class; only the `Link` class declares and implements it. So we can't access that operation when we treat links as nodes, but that isn't a problem when we use a `Visitor`, which in effect recoveres type information when it visits a node.

```
class Visitor {
public:
  virtual ~Visitor() { }

  virtual void Visit(File*) = 0;
  virtual void Visit(Directory*) = 0;
  virtual void Visit(Link*) = 0;
protected:
  Visitor();
};
```

A subclass of `Visitor` implements the `Visit` operations to do different things depending on the kind of node being visited. A `CatVisitor` subclass, for example, would implement the operations as before. We can also define a `SuffixPrinterVisitor` that prints the appropriate suffix for a node:

```
class SuffixPrinterVisitor : public Visitor {
public:
  SuffixPrinterVisitor() { }
  virtual ~SuffixPrinterVisitor() { }

  virtual void Visit(File*) { }
  virtual void Visit(Directory*)
    { cout <<    "/"; }
  virtual void Visit(Link*)
    { cout << "@";
}
};
```

Now we can use `SuffixPrinterVisitor` in a client that implements the `ls` command:

```
void Client::ls (Node* n) {
  SuffixPrinterVisitor suffixPrinter;
  Node* child;

  for (int i = 0; child = n->GetChild(i); ++i) {
    cout << child->GetName();
    child->Accept(suffixPrinter);
    cout << endl;
  }
}
```

Once we establish visiting rights by adding `Accept(Visitor&)` to the `Node` classes, we don't have to modify those classes ever again, no matter how many `Visitor` subclasses we define.

Default Implementations

We've used function overloading to give the `Visitor` operations the same name. An alternative is to encode the type of node in the `Visit` operation's name:

```
class Visitor {
public:
  virtual ~Visitor() { }

  virtual void VisitFile(File*) = 0;
  virtual void VisitDirectory(Directory*) = 0;
  virtual void VisitLink(Link*) = 0;
protected:
  Visitor();
};
```

This makes calls to these operations a little clearer, if more verbose:

```
void File::Accept (Visitor& v) { v.VisitFile(this); }

void Directory::Accept (Visitor& v) {
  v.VisitDirectory(this); }

void Link::Accept (Visitor& v) { v.VisitLink(this); }
```

A more substantial advantage comes when there's reasonable default behavior, and subclasses tend to override just a few of the operations. When we overload, subclasses must override *all* of the functions; otherwise your friendly C++ compiler will probably complain that your selective overrides hide one or more of the base class operations. We get around this problem when we give the `Visitor` operations different names. Then subclasses can redefine a subset of the `Visitor` operations with impunity.

The base class operations can implement default behavior for each type of `Node`. When the default behavior is common to two or more types, we can put the common functionality into a `VisitNode(Node*)` operation and have the other operations call it by default:

```
void Visitor::VisitNode (Node* n) {
  // common default behavior
}
void Visitor::VisitFile (File* f) {
  VisitNode(f);
}

void Visitor::VisitDirectory (Directory* d) {
  VisitNode(d);
}

void Visitor::VisitLink (Link* l) {
  VisitNode(l);
}
```

CAVEATS

There are a couple of things to consider before using the Visitor pattern.

First, ask yourself, "Is the class hierarchy I'm visiting stable?" In our case, are we constantly defining new Node subclasses or is that a rarity? Adding a new kind of Node may force us to change all the classes in the Visitor hierarchy just to add a corresponding Visit operation.

If none of your visitors care about the new subclass, and you've defined the equivalent of a VisitNode operation that provides reasonable default behavior, then this isn't a problem. But if just one kind of visitor does care, then you'll have to change it and the Visitor base class at the least. Then again, maybe multiple changes are inevitable in such circumstances. If you didn't use visitor and instead lumped the functionality into the Node hierarchy, you'd probably end up making several changes to that, too.

The second thing to realize is that the Visitor pattern introduces a circular dependency between the Visitor and Node class hierarchies. Consequently, a change to either base class interface is likely to prompt a recompile of both hierarchies. Again, this probably isn't much worse than changing a lumped base class. But in general, if you've got separate class hierarchies, you want to avoid such dependencies.

MAILBAG

Kudos to Michael Hittesdorf, who correctly points out that I neglected to change the interface to Client::Mkdir in my last column. As it stands, the example *still* won't compile. We modified the `Node` interface to include `Adopt` and `Orphan` operations, but that doesn't mean we have a `Directory*` to pass to the recursive call in `Client::Mkdir`. So that call must pass a `Node*`, not a `Directory*`. Hence:

```
void Client::Mkdir (Node* current, const char* path)
{ ... }
```

Meanwhile, Laurion Burchall[2] made some astute observations about the `Proxy` pattern in this application:

> If a file is deleted, the proxies pointing to it will have dangling pointers. The `Observer` pattern could be used to notify all proxies when a file is deleted, but this does not allow us to move a new file into the old file's location and have symbolic links still work.
>
> In UNIX and the Mac, symbolic links hold the actual name of the file they reference, not something more concrete. The proxy could hold the name of the file and a reference to the root of the file system. This could make accessing a file through the proxy expensive, though, as a name lookup would have to be performed each time.

All quite true. Keeping a pointer to the subject is efficient but probably unsatisfactory without added mechanism. The ability to replace a subject without invalidating links to it calls for a level of indirection we don't currently have. Storing the file's name instead of a pointer is a good solution, although it necessitates some kind of associative store to map the name back to the object. The overhead may not be a problem unless you have links to lots of files, or you have multiple levels of links.

Thanks, Michael and Laurion, for holding me accountable. Keep those cards and letters comin', folks!

Next Time on Pattern Hatching

We'll take a breather from our file system example to look at some principles of writing design patterns. Turns out, it's pretty easy to notice patterns in systems. The hard part is getting the patterns down on paper in a way that makes them understandable and easy to apply. We'll look at issues of content, structure, and writing style, as well as some (gentle) dos and don'ts.

References

1. Gabriel, R. Electronic mail communication, April 14,1995.
2. Burchall, L. Electronic mail communication, June 21, 1995
3. Gamma, E., R. Helm, R. Johnson, J. Vlissides. *Design Patterns: Elements of Reusable Object-Oriented Software,* Addison-Wesley, Reading, MA, 1995.

Section Two

A Focus on Programming Idioms

HOW TO WRITE BUGGY PROGRAMS

ANDREW KOENIG
ark@europa.att.com

A CASUAL GLANCE AT THE TITLE OF THIS ARTICLE MAY RAISE MORE questions than it answers. Perhaps one might ask why there is even any point in writing an article about software for horse-drawn carriages! Really, though, this article discusses techniques for writing programs that do not work. I don't want to go into why one might want to write such things; that is the subject of my companion article in *JOOP* called "When to write buggy programs." Let us just assume for the purpose of discussion that sometimes there really is a reason to write broken programs.

For our present purposes, we can distinguish three kinds of buggy programs. One is the kind that doesn't work at all; another is the kind that fails intermittently; still another is a program that appears to work reliably but may still have subtle flaws. Our first task will be to learn how to write programs that are completely broken. Later we will examine more subtle techniques for failure.

PROGRAMS THAT DON'T EVEN COMPILE

There is little challenge in writing a program that doesn't compile. Perhaps the easiest way is to hand a C++ compiler something that isn't even a C++ program at all, such as a random pile of prose.

However, although programs that don't compile at all aren't very useful, they can sometimes be fun. For example, if I take the C++ compiler on my local computer and ask it to compile a file named a.c that contains only `foo`, then the output is

```
CC a.c:
"a.c", line 1: error: bad declaration of foo—did you
                    forget a ';'?
1 error
```

Suppose we now take this helpful error message and treat it as a program? That seems like a good way to get the compiler to say interesting things to us. The result, it turns out, is this:

```
CC a.c:
"a.c", line 1: error: CC a : CC is not a type name
"a.c", line 1: error: '.' used for qualification;
                      please use '::'
"a.c", line 1: error: body of non function c
"a.c", line 2: error: syntax error
"a.c", line 2: error: syntax error
"a.c", line 2: error: bad declaration of line—did you
                      forget a ';'?
"a.c", line 2: error: syntax error
"a.c", line 2: error: syntax error
"a.c", line 2: error: body of non function error
"a.c", line 2: error: bad declaration : bad is not a type name
"a.c", line 2: error: declaration of :
                      declaration is not a type name
"a.c", line 2: error: of foo : of is not a type name
"a.c", line 2: error: syntax error
"a.c", line 2: error: did you : did is not a type name
Sorry, too many errors
14 errors
```

The penultimate line is interesting: this particular compiler throws in the towel when it has found more than some number of things wrong with a program.

Such behavior turns out to be useful in many contexts. Usually when a program has so many compilation errors, at least some of them will have been caused by the compiler making incorrect guesses about how to correct previous errors.

It is usually better to fix the first few errors the compiler has found and then try again, than to try to repair them all at once. Suppose we take this diagnostic output and compile it again? Then we get

```
CC a.c:
"a.c", line 1: error: CC a : CC is not a type name
"a.c", line 1: error: '.' used for qualification;
                      please use '::'
"a.c", line 1: error: body of non function c
"a.c", line 2: error: syntax error
"a.c", line 2: error: syntax error
```

```
"a.c", line 2: error: bad declaration of line - did you
                      forget a ';'?
"a.c", line 2: error: syntax error
"a.c", line 2: error: syntax error
"a.c", line 2: error: body of non function error
"a.c", line 2: error: CC a : CC is not a type name
"a.c", line 2: error: syntax error
"a.c", line 2: error: CC is : CC is not a type name
"a.c", line 2: error: is not : is is not a type name
"a.c", line 2: error: not a : not is not a type name
Sorry, too many errors
14 errors
```

This looks remarkably like the output from the previous try, although admittedly it isn't quite the same. However, if we repeat the process once more, the compiler output is indeed exactly the same as its input.

We have just come up with an unusual kind of self-reproducing program: a program that causes the compiler to produce a copy of the program as its diagnostic output. We have therefore transformed our program that doesn't work into one that does, merely by changing our expectations of what the program is supposed to do. In other words, we have written a self-reproducing C++ program that doesn't even need to be run.

Programs that Compile but Don't Link

Producing programs that don't compile is so easy that there's no challenge to it. A somewhat more interesting problem is to write a program that makes it through the compiler but causes the linker to complain.

The simplest such program is an empty file. Technically speaking, this is not a valid C program because every C source file must contain at least one declaration. It is, however, syntactically valid C++, and many C compilers will accept it, too.

The reason it doesn't link, of course, is that `main` is not defined anywhere. It's not much of a challenge to figure that out, of course, so let's see if it's possible to write programs that fail to link in more subtle ways.

The purpose of a linker is to match definitions and declarations. When a source file declares something and the linker finds no definition, it complains. Of course, it's not enough merely to declare something: it must usually be used as well. Thus, for example, the program

```
extern void foo();

main()
{
}
```

will happily link even though `foo` is nowhere defined; the definition is unnecessary unless `foo` is actually called. Even if a call does appear, some compilers will be clever enough to detect some cases in which the call will never be executed.

For example, my local compiler accepts

```
extern void foo()

main()
{
  if (0)
    foo();
}
```

without a squawk, and the linker likes it just fine, too.

The situation gets more interesting when the thing not defined is a virtual function. Compilers generally cannot determine whether or not a virtual function is called because such calls can be indirect.

Thus if we write something like this:

```
struct Base {
  virtual void f();
};

struct Derived: Base {
  void f();
};
```

a program that contains no direct references to `Derived::f` may nevertheless call it through an object of class `Base`.

Thus virtual functions must always be defined if any objects of their class are created, whether they (the functions or the objects) are used or not.

We can take advantage of that to write a nonlinking program:

```
struct A {
  virtual void f();
};

main()
{
  A a;
}
```

Here we hit pay dirt because compiling this program on the compiler here yields a message that seemingly has nothing to do with the problem:

```
ld: Undefined symbol
   ___vtbl__1A
```

We neglected to define `A::f`; what does this diagnostic message have to do with that?

It turns out that this particular compiler optimizes the generation of virtual function tables. From an implementation viewpoint, the idea is that every object of, say, class `A` contains a pointer to a virtual table that identifies that object as being of class `A`. The optimization is there to avoid the compiler's having to generate the contents of that virtual table for every source file that contains a declaration of class `A`. It does this by picking a particular source file and generating the virtual table in that source file only.

To do this, it has to know that there is a particular source file that will always exist. It obtains this assurance by looking for a "magic" function for each class definition, and defining the virtual table in the source file that defines that particular function. This particular compiler picks the file with the definition of the first function that is virtual and not inline.

Thus when the compiler sees

```
struct A {
   virtual void f();
};
```

it realizes that there must be a single definition of `A::f` in some source file, so when compiling that source file it will produce a definition for `A`'s virtual table as well.

When we failed to write that source file, we fooled the compiler into failing to define the virtual table. As it happens, the linker encounters that problem before it encounters the call to `f`, probably because there isn't actually a call to `f` at all.

Thus we see that even something as apparently simple as a linker error can sometimes appear to be something it isn't.

Programs that Don't Run

Because compilation and linkage checking are quite strict in C++, there isn't nearly as much fun in writing programs that fail those checks as there is in writing programs that make it all the way to execution before failing.

Even here, it is easy to induce blatant failures. As the failures become more subtle, producing them becomes more interesting. The most exciting programs are the ones that appear to work but in fact work only by coincidence.

Let's start with something simple: a program that consumes all of memory.

```
void loop()    { loop(); }
```

This little function does nothing but call itself. On many C++ implementations, that will consume unbounded memory because the implementation keeps track of each current call. On some, however, this function will run effectively forever, because the compiler is clever enough to recognize tail recursions. A tail recursion is when the very last thing a function does before returning is to call itself. Such a recursion can generally be rewritten as a `goto`, so that our `loop` function is equivalent to

```
void loop()
{
spin: gotospin;
}
```

From the viewpoint of writing buggy programs, tail recursions are useful, because they yield programs that will work on some compilers but not others, especially on machines without a lot of memory.

As it happens, some tail recursions are hard to optimize. The optimization depends on being able to throw away all the old function's memory just before calling the new one. But suppose we were to preserve a pointer to that memory, say by passing it as an argument in the recursive call? Consider, for example, the following slightly contrived function that takes two integers, `m` and `n`, and returns `m` times `n` factorial:

```
int timesfact(int m, int n)
{
    if (n == 0)
        return m;
    return timesfact (m * n, n - 1);
}
```

This function is a legitimate tail recursion that can be rewritten this way:

```
int timesfact (int m, int n)
{
    while (n != 0)
        m *= n—;
    return m;
}
```

However, if we take the original function and change it to take a *pointer* as its first argument:

```
int timesfact (int* m, int n)
{
    int mn;
    if (n == 0)
        return *m;
    mn = *m * n;
    return timesfact (&mn, n - 1);
}
```

then even though the function still has the form of a tail recursion, the tail recursion optimization is no longer possible. Functions like this have a good chance of tripping up optimizers, especially because people rarely write such things in practice.

Of course, this example isn't really fair, because it relies on the compiler to cause trouble rather than causing it directly. A much more direct way to make programs not work is by exploiting boundary errors.

Programs that Appear to Work by Coincidence

Consider, for example, the following program:

```
main()
{
    int a[10], i;
    for (i = 0; i <= 10; i++)
        a[i] = 0;
}
```

On some machines, this program appears to run and finish normally. On others, it goes into an infinite loop. The reason, of course, is that the indices of the array a run from 0 through 9, but the loop changes the value of `a[10]`.

On some machines, the "element" `a[10]` occupies a memory location that doesn't happen to be used for anything, so the program appears to work. On others, `a[10]` happens to be the same memory location as `i`, so the statement `a[i] = 0;` sets `i` to zero when `i` is 10. That starts the whole loop over again.

Of course, the whole relationship between pointers and subscripts is so deeply ingrained in C and C++ that it is hard to imagine changing it without coming up with a whole new language.

In C++, it is possible to encapsulate array operations in classes, making checking much easier and making higher level data structures as well. However, if your goal is to write programs that work some times and not others, it is hard to beat careless use of arrays and pointers as a tool.

As another example, suppose you want to implement a data structure to store a variable-length array of objects of class `Thing`. Of course, we can use a class to hide this array from its users, but how do we go about implementing it?

The clean way to do it is to define a class that contains, among other things, the length of the array and the address of its initial element:

```
class Thingarray {
    // ...
    Thing* data;
    int length;
    // ...
};
```

and then allocate such an array along these lines:

```
Thingarray::Thingarray(int n):
    data(new Thing[n]), length(n) { }
```

Remember, however, that we're trying to write unreliable programs here. One common technique for that is to insist on placing the length in memory that is adjacent to the `Thing` objects themselves. For example, imagine a structure like this:

```
struct Buggyarray {
    int length;
    Thing t[1];
};
```

Now we make the `Thingarray` class point at a `Buggyarray`:

```
class Thingarray {
    // ...
    Buggyarray* data;
    // ...
};
```

and we can allocate a `Thingarray` along these lines:

```
Thingarray::Thingarray(int n)
{
  data = (Buggyarray*) malloc
       (sizeof(Buggyarray) + n*sizeof(Thing));
  data->length = n;
  new (data->t) Thing[n];
}
```

Strictly speaking, this technique is illegal, because it accesses memory outside the bounds of the `Buggyarray` object. However, because that memory was explicitly accounted for in the call to `malloc`, it is likely to appear to work on many systems.

This technique provides some truly beautiful opportunities for failure later on. For example, if you try to run it on a C++ compiler with good debugging support, that compiler will righteously complain about trying to access memory beyond the bounds of `Buggyarray::t`. This is all to the good, as it prevents use of such compilers and thereby makes any other bugs that much harder to find. Moreover, if anyone ever introduces a virtual function into `Buggyarray`, the result is likely to be utter chaos. The reason is that C++ implementations generally store information about virtual functions in each object whose class has a virtual function. For a class like `Buggyarray`, that information is likely as not to go at the end of the object. So the compiler translates the declaration

```
struct Buggyarray {
  int length;
  Thing t [1];
};
```

into something with the approximate effect of

```
struct Buggyarray {
  int length;
  Thing t[1];
  void* __virtual_table_pointer;
};
```

Now any attempt to modify data past the end of the `Bugarray::t` member will clobber the virtual table pointer. Finding suitably creative values to put in that pointer is left as an exercise for the reader.

Conclusion

There are far more techniques for writing broken programs than there is space to describe them. This article is intended only to give a few hints. Remember, there is little challenge in writing programs that fail spectacularly.

The real fun is writing something that looks like it works, but actually conceals a serious problem that appears only later.

Of course, C++ provides a collection of tools to make such obscure problems much less likely. If instead of using subscripts and pointers directly, one uses a well-designed library class, many of these obscure problems become obvious ones. The way to deal with that is to avoid libraries.

For that matter, avoid debugging compilers and any other tools that might make these problems easier to find. Otherwise, you might unintentionally wind up with programs that actually work. What would be the challenge in that?

A Dynamic Vector Is Harder Than It Looks

Tom Cargill
cargill@spot.colorado.edu

There is a subtle bug in the `Vector` template in Glen McCluskey's recent article on template instantiation[1] that should be brought to the attention of programmers who are considering building a similar class template. The bug arises from dangling references, which may appear in a variety of circumstances. Exactly which expressions in client code will produce dangling references depends upon the order of expression evaluation, which, in general, is not well defined.

McCluskey's Vector template provides dynamically sized vectors, which grow to accommodate whatever index a client uses. The original code is:

```
template <class T> class Vector {
  int  cursize;
  T*  ptr;
  void  grow();
public:
  Vector();
  ~Vector();
  T&  operator[](int);
};

template <class T>
Vector<T>::Vector()
{
  cursize  =  10;
  ptr  =  new  T[cursize];
}
```

```
template  <class  T>
Vector<T>::~Vector()
{
  delete  ptr;
}

template <class T>
void  Vector<T>::grow()
{
  T*  p;
  int  i;

  p  =  new  T[cursize  *  2];
  for  (i  =  0;  i  <  cursize;  i++)
    p[i]  =  ptr[i];
  cursize  *=  2;
  delete  ptr;
  ptr  =  p;
}
template  <class  T>
T&  Vector<T>::operator[](int  n)
{
  if  (n  >=  cursize)
    grow();
  return  ptr[n];
}
```

Before addressing dangling references, there are two lesser problems in the code that must be corrected. First, the `delete` expressions in the destructor and in `grow()` should use the form `delete [] p` because `p` points to an array of objects[2] (p. 65 of the ARM). Second, the `if` statement in `grow()` should be a `while` statement because doubling the array size just once is not sufficient in general. With these two corrections, the code becomes:

```
template <class T> class Vector {
  int cursize;
  T* ptr;
  void grow();
public:
  Vector();
  ~Vector();
```

```
  T& operator[](int);
};

template <class T>
Vector<T>::Vector()
{
  cursize = 10;
  ptr = new T[cursize];
}

template <class T>
Vector<T>::~Vector()
{
  delete [] ptr;  // use []
}

template <class T>
void Vector<T>::grow()
{
  T* p;
  int i;

  p = new T[cursize * 2];
  for (i = 0; i < cursize; i++)
    p[i] = ptr[i];
  cursize *= 2;
  delete [] ptr;  // use []
  ptr = p;
}

template <class T>
T& Vector<T>::operator[](int n)
{
  while (n >= cursize)
    grow();
  return ptr[n];
}
```

To see the appearance of a dangling reference, consider the assignment expression

```
v[i] = v[j];
```

where `v` is a `Vector` object. The left and right sides of the assignment both yield `Vector` references, but there is no guarantee in general that the references refer to valid objects. Depending upon the order of evaluation of the expression and the execution of `grow()`, it is possible that by the time a reference is used it no longer refers to an object. A reference that no longer refers to an object is said to be a dangling reference. The situations that create dangling references are similar to those that create dangling pointers. `Vector::operator[]` generates dangling references.

A concrete code example illustrates how a dangling reference arises. First, we define class `Dummy`. Class `Dummy` has a constructor, a destructor, and a single state member. The state can be read or modified by the member functions `get()` and `set()`. (The filler member has been added to make the object large from the compiler's point of view. This prevents a `Dummy` object from being stored in a register, thereby prohibiting an optimization that may eliminate the dangling reference in an expression as simple as `v[i] = v[j]`.) The definition of `Dummy` is:

```
class Dummy {
  const char* state;
  char filler[14];
public:
  Dummy();
  ~Dummy();
  const char* get() const;
  void set(const char*);
};

Dummy::Dummy()
{
  state = "initial";
}

Dummy::~Dummy()
{
  state = "dead";
}
const char* Dummy::get() const
{
  return state;
}

void Dummy::set(const char* s)
{
  state = s;
}
```

Finally, we need a simple driver that exercises `Vector` and `Dummy`:

```
#include <iostream.h>
int main()
{
  Vector<Dummy> v;
  v[6].set("modified");
  cout << "\nv[6]: " << v[6].get();

  v[6] = v[15];

  cout << "\nv[6]: " << v[6].get();
  cout << "\nv[15]: " << v[15].get();
  cout << "\n";

  return 0;
}
```

After the assignment from `v[15]` to `v[6]`, one might expect the two objects to have the same value as the initial value from a freshly constructed `v[15]` object. However, the state of `v[6]` has not been changed by the assignment. The output from this code is:

```
v[6]: modified
v[6]: modified
v[15]: initial
```

To understand what has happened, note that the original size of the vector is 10 elements. Element 6 can be indexed from the original vector of objects, but element 15 calls for the vector to grow. With the compiler used, the target of the assignment was the *original* `v[6]` object *before* the `grow()` operation that allocated fresh memory and moved `v[6]` to a new location. In fact, the object to which the assignment is made has already executed its destructor at the end of its lifetime as a result of the delete in `grow()`. The target of the assignment is simply a piece of raw memory that has been returned to the free store.

With the compiler I used, the generated code was equivalent to:

```
Dummy& lhs = v[6];       // so far so good
Dummy& rhs = v[15];      // lhs is now dangling
lhs = rhs;               // target is not an object
```

Figure 1 shows the state of the computation after lhs has been bound; `lhs` is bound to the original `v[6]`. Figure 2 shows the state of the computation after rhs has been bound; rhs is bound to an object in the freshly allocated array,

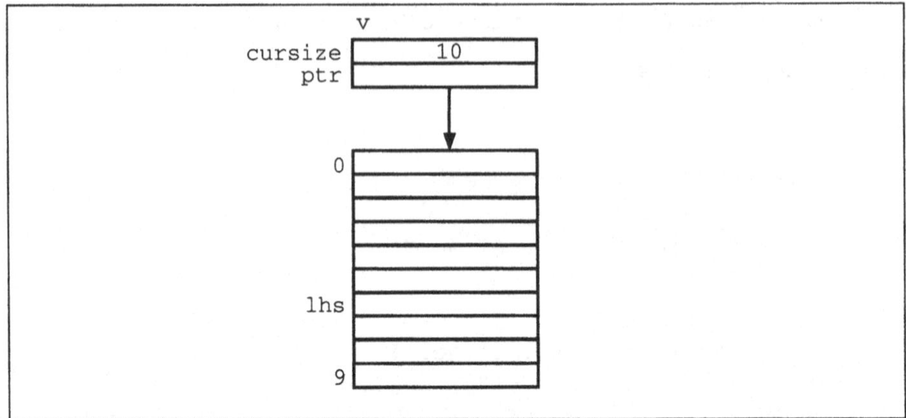

Figure 1. *The state of computation after* `lhs` *has been bound.*

while lhs remains bound to an object that is now in deallocated memory. The bindings in Figure 2 are used in the assignment.

The generated code does *not* constitute a compiler bug. The generated code follows all the rules of C++. Nor is the compiler obliged to follow this order of evaluation exactly. Another correct compiler might generate code that causes no problem for this assignment and yet generate a dangling reference in another expression.

Subtle problems due to dangling references and pointers are insidious, particularly the ones that depend upon the order of evaluation of expressions. The way to avoid the dangling reference is to leave each `T` object *in place* after its creation until the end of the lifetime of the `Vector` object. This suggests that an extra level of indirection must be introduced in `Vector`. For example, a `Vector` object could hold an array of pointers to `T`, where each element of the array points to an individually allocated `T` object. When the vector grows, a larger array of pointers is allocated, and the old pointers are copied to the bottom of the new array, while a new `T` object is allocated for each pointer in the remainder of the array. If a `T` object is relatively large, this approach may be acceptable. If a `T` object is small, the overhead of the pointers and the overhead of allocating individual `T` objects may be excessive.

A more space-efficient alternative is shown below. This `Vector` class initially allocates an array of one `T` object. When that array is found insufficient, another array of one `T` object is allocated, doubling the total number of `T` objects. Each subsequent allocation also doubles the total number of `T` objects by allocating arrays of size 2, 4, 8, and so on. At any time, the number of arrays of `T` objects is one more than the logarithm (base 2) of the total number of `T` objects. A small array of pointers records these arrays. To index to an arbitrary `T` object, `opera-`

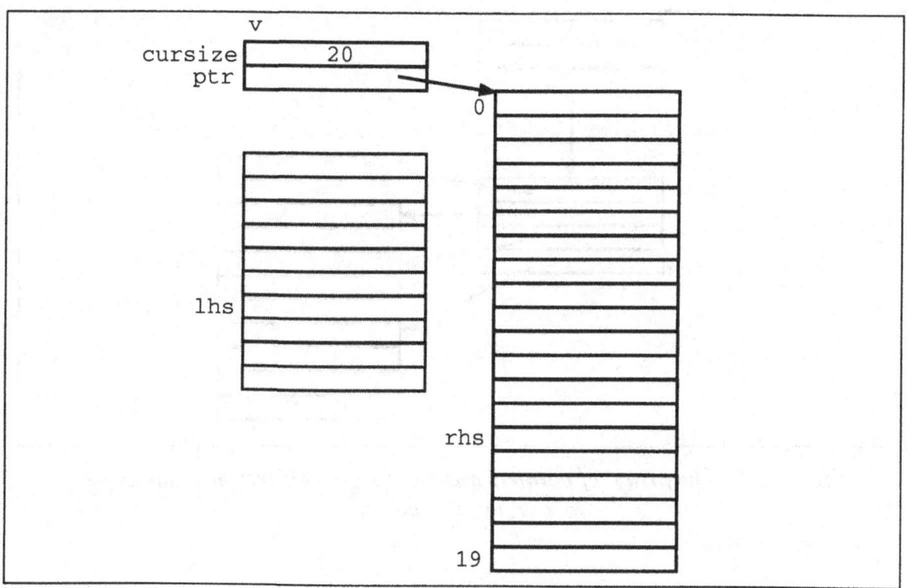

FIGURE 2. *The state of computation after* `rhs` *has been bound.*

`tor[]` must determine which array the object lies within and what its index is inside that array. The code is shown below. The array of pointers and arrays of `T` objects corresponding to a vector of 8 objects is shown in Figure 3. A private copy constructor and assignment operator are declared but left undefined to prevent copying of `Vector` objects.

```
template <class T>
class Vector {
  int cursize;
  int log2sz; // log2(cursize)
  T** ptr;
  void grow();
  Vector(const Vector<T>&);
  void operator=(const Vector<T>&);
public:
  Vector();
  ~Vector();
  T& operator[](int);
};

template <class T>
Vector<T>::Vector()
```

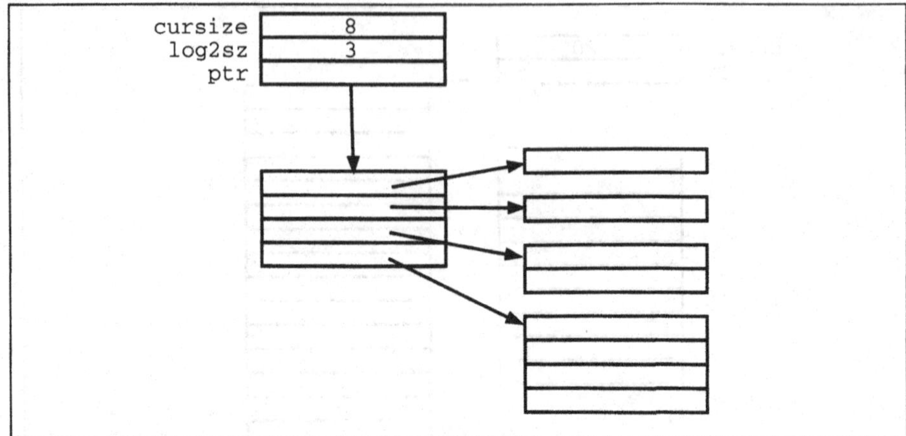

Figure 3. *The array of pointers and arrays of* `T` *objects corresponding to a vector of 8 objects.*

```
{
  ptr = new T*[1];
  ptr[0] = new T[1];
  cursize = 1;
  log2sz = 0;
}

template <class T>
Vector<T>::~Vector()
{
  while( log2sz >= 0 )
    delete [] ptr[log2sz–];
  delete [] ptr;
}

template <class T>
void Vector<T>::grow()
{
  T** p = new T*[++log2sz+1];
  for( int i = 0; i < log2sz; i++ )
    p[i] = ptr[i];
  delete [] ptr;
  ptr = p;
  ptr[log2sz] = new T[cursize];
  cursize *= 2;
}
```

```
template <class T>
T& Vector<T>::operator[](int index)
{
  while( index >= cursize )
    grow();
  int bucket = 0, mask = 0;
  while( index >= 1<<bucket )
    mask = 1<<bucket++;
  return ptr[bucket][index&(mask-1)];
}
```

This code is certainly more complicated than the original `Vector` class template. If I had a version of `Vector` that was correct, efficient, and simple, I would present it. I am interested to hear from readers who can offer improvements.

Indeed, the loop in `operator[]` can be written more efficiently at the cost of becoming more complicated. Readers who indulge in bit-twiddling may enjoy rewriting it. The basic problem is to compute the logarithm to base 2 of an arbitrary (positive) integer. ≥

References

1. McCluskey, G. An environment for template instantiation, *The C++ Report* 4(2), 1992.
2. Ellis, M., and B. Stroustrup. *The Annotated C++ Reference Manual,* Addison-Wesley, Reading, MA, 1990.

Writing Multithreaded Applications in C++

Pete Becker

About a year ago I was flying from Boston to San Jose, returning from an ANSI/ISO C++ Committee meeting. The in-flight movie was *Prelude to a Kiss,* which even Meg Ryan couldn't make interesting. I figured I had two alternatives: sleep or read. It was nine in the morning, so the chances of being able to sleep for several hours weren't very good. I pulled out Andrew Tanenbaum's, *Modern Operating Systems* and turned to the chapter on threads. Reading on a plane is always a strange experience for me. The vibration and noise put me into a mental state like that when I'm just waking up: highly imaginative and not completely rational. That's when I do some of my best design work. In this case, as I was reading Tanenbaum's discussion of the threads package in the Open Software Foundation's Distributed Computing Environment I kept thinking that the things he was talking about could be done much more easily and clearly with classes. At that time I was more interested in reading than in designing, so I didn't write down any of the details that floated through my head. A few months ago, when I had to actually create a threads package, I vaguely remembered bits and pieces of those designs and incorporated them into my classes. I don't claim to have answered all of Tanenbaum's concerns, nor those of OSF, but I'm convinced that classes can make threaded applications much easier to write and maintain.

Why Threads?

If you're a frequent CompuServe user you probably share my frustration with the off-line access programs that are most widely available. You dial in and start downloading messages, then have to wait until all of the messages have been transferred before you can start reading them and replying. That's because the access program only does one thing at a time—while it's downloading messages it can't display them. Unfortunately, there's a good reason for that restriction: doing two different things at the same time is hard. To see why, let's try to put together a skeleton for an off-line access program. Let's keep it simple: the access program needs to be able to download messages through a modem, store them in a file, sort the stored messages by date or subject according to the user's commands, and display one message at a time on the display screen. This leads immediately to three core objects for the program: a modem, a message database, and a display unit. In addition, we'll have to write the code that handles the interactions among these three objects. As a first cut, they should probably look something like this:

```
class TModem
{
public:
    const char *GetBuffer();
    int MessageWaiting() const;
    int DownloadComplete() const;
private:
    enum { MaxMsgSize=1024 };
    char buf1[MaxMsgSize];
    char buf2[MaxMsgSize];
};
```

A `TModem` object reads characters from the incoming character stream and stores them into the active text buffer. It knows enough about the message format to recognize when it has received a complete message, and when it does, it switches to the other text buffer. The user of a `TModem` object can call `MessageWaiting()` to find out if there's a complete message in one of the text buffers. `GetBuffer()` returns the address of the text buffer holding the message so that the program can copy the text into another location. `TModem` has a significant limitation: It leaves it up to the program to copy each message before the next incoming message is complete. If the program waits too long, another message will begin and `TModem` will switch to the buffer holding the previous message and overwrite it.

```
class TMessage
{
public:
    TMessage( TDate date,
              string subject, string text );
    TDate GetDate() const;
    string GetSubject() const;
    string GetText() const;
};
```

```
class TCISMessage: public TMessage
{
public:
   TClSMessage( const char *RawText );
};
```

The `TCISMessage` constructor parses the message header, pulling out the date and subject and passing them in to the `TMessage` constructor. That extra level of indirection isn't really needed here, but it's easy to do and it makes the `TMessage` class much more flexible.

```
class TMessageSet
{
public:
   void Add( TMessage NewMessage );

void SortByDate();
void SortBySubject();

TMessage operator [ ] ( unsigned index ) const;
unsigned GetMessageCount() const
      { return MessageCount; }
private:
   enum { MaxMessages = 1024 );
   TMessage Messages[MaxMessages];
  unsigned MessageCount;
```

The class `TMessageSet` holds the messages that we've downloaded. It can sort them by date and by subject, and it provides an accessor function to get at individual messages.

```
class TDisplay
{
public:
   void ShowMessage( TMessage Msg );

   void PageDown();
   void PageUp();

   void LineDown();
   void lineUp();
};
```

The class `TDisplay`, of course, displays a message on the display screen.

Hooking these three classes together to build an off-line access program is fairly straightforward:

```
TModem Modem;
TMessageSet Messages;
TDisplay Display;
unsigned CurMsg;

int ProcessKey( char ch )
{
      switch( ch )
      {
      case'n':
         CurMsg++;
         if(CurMsg>=Messages.Get MessageCount())
            CurMsg--;
         Display.ShowMessage( Messages[CurMsg] );
         return 0;
      case 'd':
         Messages.SortByDate();
         CurMsg = 0;
         Display.ShowMessage( Messages[CurMsg] );
         return 0;
      case 's':
         Messages.SortBySubject();
         CurMsg = 0;
         Display.ShowMessage( Messages[CurMsg]);
         return 0;
      case 'q':
         return 1;
      }
}
void CheckMessage()
{
   if( Modem.MessageWaiting() )
      Messages.Add(TMessage(Modem.GetBuffer()) );
}
int main()
{
   CurMsg = 0;
   Display.ShowMessage(CurMsg);
   for(;;)
```

```
        {
            if( !KeystrokeWaiting() )
                CheckMessage();
            else
            {
              char ch = tolower(GetKey());
              if( ProcessKey(ch) != 0 )
                return 0;
            }
        }
    }
```

Unfortunately, this doesn't quite work. The more messages we have in the message database, the longer it will take to sort them. If it takes too long, when we sort messages we won't call `CheckMessage()` often enough and we'll lose incoming messages.

We could fix this by sprinkling calls to `CheckMessage()` throughout the sorting code, but that's just a quick hack, not a complete solution. What happens when we add an editor for composing replies? That, too, has to call `CheckMessage()` frequently to assure we don't lose incoming messages. In fact, every function that we add has to worry about the modem. Those calls to `CheckMessage()` proliferate, and we end up with an unmaintainable mess. Clearly, something is wrong.

What's wrong is that we're not using the most appropriate technology for this job. The program has become way too complicated because we have to work around the limitations of our straight-line program model. So let's start over with a very simple version of this program and see if we can come up with a better program model.

Using Threads

Since we're trying to do two different things, we should begin with two functions:

```
void ShowMessages( void * )
{
    for(;;)
    {
        char ch = tolower(GetKey());
        if( ProcessKey(ch) != 0 )
            return;
    }
```

```
}
void ReadModem( void * )
{
    for(;;)
    {
        if( Modem.MessageWaiting() )
            Messages.Add( TMessage( Modem.GetBuffer() ) );
        if( Modem.DownloadComplete() )
            return;
    }
}
```

Each of these functions by itself is easy to understand: each one sits in a loop getting input and processing it until it's done. When we're using an operating system like OS/2 or Windows NT that supports threads we can make each of these functions a thread in our program. No additional code is needed to get them to cooperate. Every 50 milliseconds or so the operating system stops the current function, saves some information about it, and starts the other one. In `main()` we have to provide the code that creates these threads, and we have to wait until the two functions have finished their work before we exit:

```
int main()
{
HANDLE handles[2];
    handles[0] = CreateThread( &ReadModem, 0 );
    handles[1] = CreateThread( &ShowMessages, 0 );
    WaitForMultipleEvents( handles, 2 );
    cout << "Exiting.\n";
    return 0;
}
```

I've simplified the interface to the operating system here. In reality, creating a thread generally requires more than the two parameters I've shown in the call to `CreateThread()`. Check your documentation for the details of creating a thread on your particular operating system. In general, however, you create a thread by calling into the operating system and giving it the address of the function that starts your thread and a value to pass to that function. (Now you know why `ReadModem()` and `ShowMessages()` have that unused parameter: the operating system requires it, even if you don't need it.)

In this example, `main()` creates two new threads, one to read the modem and one to display messages. Then it waits for both of them to terminate.

SYNCHRONIZING THREADS

When `main()` returns, the program ends. That's why `main()` has to wait for the two new threads to terminate: if it didn't, the operating system would terminate the two threads immediately, and we wouldn't get to read any messages. This is an example of a general problem you have to watch out for when writing multithreaded code: a thread often has to wait for something to happen before it can continue execution. The operating system provides synchronization mechanisms such as `WaitForMultipleEvents()` for doing this.

We also have to be careful when we're updating data. If more than one thread has access to some piece of data, a thread may be in the middle of updating that data while another thread is trying to use it. This can lead to confusion and possibly data corruption. For instance, consider what happens when `ReadModem()` sees that a new message is available and calls the `Add()` function in our `TMessageSet` class. `Add()` might be implemented like this:

```
void TMessageSet::Add( TMessage NewMessage )
{
    if( MessageCount < MaxMessages )
      Messages[MessageCount++] = NewMessage;
}
```

There's a subtle trap here. The C++ language makes very few guarantees about when the result of incrementing `MessageCount` will be stored. In particular, it's perfectly legal for the compiler to treat this code as if it had been written like this:

```
if( MessageCount < MaxMessages )
{
    unsigned temp = MessageCount++;
    Messages[temp] = NewMessage;
}
```

Now suppose that immediately after this code increments `MessageCount` and before it copies the message into the array, the operating system interrupts this thread and switches to the `ShowMessages` thread. What happens if the message currently being displayed is the last message in the set and the user just pressed the N key to ask for the next message? `ProcessKey()` increments its message index and compares the result to the number of messages in the set. Since the other thread just incremented `MessageCount`, the current index appears to be valid, but the new message hasn't been copied yet, so there is no meaningful data at that location. At best, it displays garbage on the screen. At worst, it crashes the program. Without help from the operating system it's difficult or even impossible to code around this problem.

SEMAPHORES

Multithreaded operating systems provide semaphores to help programmers solve the problems that arise from trying to access the same data simultaneously from different threads. A semaphore acts just as a semaphore on a railroad does: It tells the thread whether it can proceed or should wait for another thread to get out of the way. In the case of our message set, we'd do something like this:

```
Semaphore sem;

void TMessageSet::Add( TMessage NewMessage )
{
    WaitForSemaphore(sem);
    if( MessageCount < MaxMessages )
        Messages[MessageCount++] = NewMessage;
    ReleaseSemaphore(sem);
}

TMessage TMessageSet::operator [ ] ( unsigned index ) const
{
        WaitForSemaphore(sem);
        TMessage result = Messages[index];
        ReleaseSemaphore(sem);
        return result;
}
```

Whenever `Add()` is called it calls `WaitForSemaphore()`. When the semaphore becomes available the operating system allows `Add()` to continue executing, but it makes a note that the semaphore is currently in use. Until `Add()` calls `ReleaseSemaphore()` any other thread that calls `WaitForSemaphore()` will not be allowed to execute. When `Add()` calls `ReleaseSemaphore()` one of the threads that is waiting for this semaphore will be allowed to resume. This guarantees that the `Add()` operation will be completed before any other thread that checks the semaphore can access the data that `Add()` is modifying.

You may have noticed that `Add()` calls `TMessageSet::operator[]()`. That function, in turn, calls `WaitForSemaphore()`, which seems like it ought to put us into a fatal deadlock: `Add()` has already locked the semaphore, so the call to `WaitForSemaphore()` in `operator[]()` should block. Once blocked, the code in `Add()` that releases the semaphore would never be executed, so the thread would be permanently blocked. That's actually not a problem because the operating system allows each thread to create multiple locks on the same semaphore. The call to `operator[]()` from `Add()` will work because both locks are being created in the same thread.

Wrapping Semaphores in Classeses

Semaphores provide the basic mechanism that allows us to protect data from multiple accesses. By themselves, however, they still leave us with one problem:

```
void Dangerous()
{
    WaitForSemaphore(sem);
    throw xmsg( "Dangerous" );
    ReleaseSemaphore(sem);
}
```

The operating system doesn't know anything about C++ exceptionss. The call to `ReleaseSemaphore()` in this function is never executed, and the semaphore remains locked. We could wrap every code block that's protected by a semaphore in a try block with a catch clause that catches every exception, unlocks the semaphore, and then rethrows the exception, but that's way too intrusive. There's a better way: Wrap the lock in a class.

```
class TMutex
{
public:
    class Lock
    {
    public:
        Lock(TMutex&);
        ~Lock();
    private:
        TMutex& mutex;
    };
    friend class Lock;
private:
    Semaphore sem;
};
TMutex::TMutex::Lock( TMutex& mtx ):
    mutex(mtx)
{
    WaitForSemaphore(mutex.sem);
}
TMutex::~TMutex()
{
    ReleaseSemaphore(mutex.sem);
}
```

Now we can write `operator[]()` like this:

```
TMutex sem;

TMessage TMessageSet::operator[ ] ( unsigned index ) const
{
    TMutex::Lock(sem);
    return Messages[index];
}
```

Similarly, `Add()` should use an object of type `TMutex::Lock` to lock and unlock the semaphore. This makes the code safe when an exception is thrown and usually simplifies it as well.

CREATING A THREAD-SAFE CLASS

We've left the semaphore object sitting in the global address space. Since its primary use is to control access to the members of `TMessageSet` it really ought to be a member of `TMessageSet`. In fact, many objects need this sort of control, so we should create a new class that can serve as a base class for classes that need to use semaphores:

```
class TMonitor
{
protected:
    class Lock
    {
    public:
        Lock(TMonitor *);
    private:
        TMutex::Lock lock;
    };
    friend class Lock;
private:
    TMutex sem;
};
TMonitor::Lock::Lock(TMonitor *mon):
TMutex::Lock(mon->sem)
{
}
```

This class holds the mutex semaphore internally, and provides a `Lock` class whose constructor locks the semaphore. The compiler-generated destructor for

`TMonitor::Lock` will call the destructor for the `TMutex::Lock` object which, in turn, will unlock the semaphore. It's used like this:

```
class TMessageSet:public TMonitor
{
public:
    TMessage operator[](unsigned index) const;
};
TMessage TMessageSet::
operator[](unsigned index) const
{
    Lock lock(this);
    return Messages[index];
}
```

The first line of every member function should create a lock. This guarantees synchronization whenever an instance of this class is used from multiple threads.

Encapsulating Thread Creation

I mentioned earlier that the mechanism for creating a thread is different on different operating systems. That makes it a prime candidate for encapsulation in a class:

```
class TThread
{
public:
    void BeginThread();
private:
    virtual void Run() = 0;
    static void Create( void *Addr );
};
void TThread::BeginThread()
{
        ::CreateThread( &TThread::Create, this );
}
void TThread::Create( void *Addr )
{
        static_cast<TThread *>(Addr)->Run();
}
```

`BeginThread()` creates a thread that executes the function `TThread::Create()`. This function cannot be an ordinary member function because the operating system doesn't know how to call ordinary member functions. We can use a static member function, however, and that's when the extra parameter that the operating system requires comes in handy. We pass the address of the `TThread` object in, and `TThread::Create()` calls the pure virtual function `Run()`. In use, the code for a thread would be in a class derived from `TThread`. For example, the global function `ReadModem()` that we looked at earlier could be encapsulated like this:

```
class TModemThread: public TThread
{
public:
   TModem Modem;
private:
   void Run();
};

void TModemThread::Run()
{
   for(;;)
   {
      if( Modem.MessageWaiting() )
         Messages.Add(
            TMessage( Modem.GetBuffer())
         );
         {( Modem.DownloadComplete() )
         return;
   }
}
```

Our function `ShowMessages()` should also be wrapped in a class:

```
class TMessageThread: public TThread
{
public:
   TMessageThread( TModem& );
private:
   void Run();
   char GetKey();
   int ProcessKey();
};
```

```
void TMessageThread::Run()
{
    for(;;)
    {
        char ch = tolower(GetKey() );
        if( ProcessKey(ch) != 0 )
            return;
    }
}
```

And now our `main()` function looks like this:

```
int main()
{
    TModemThread ModemThread;
    TMessageThreadMessage
        Thread(ModemThread.Modem);
    ModemThread.BeginThread();
    MessageThread.BeginThread();
    WaitForMultipleThreads( ModemThread,
        MessageThread );
    cout << "Exiting.\n";
    return 0;
}
```

What Have We Accomplished?

By using threads instead of explicitly calling out to the code that handles the modem, we've made our code much simpler. To use threads effectively, we had to add semaphores to our code. To make those semaphores work correctly when exceptions are thrown, we created a class to provide more robust semantics for semaphores. To make for portableour code, more portable, we pushed the operating system dependencies of creating semaphores and creating threads into classes.

Something to Think About

This column is already too long, so I won't talk about putting data members in a class derived from `TThread`, but you should think about it. What does it mean, and how would you do something similar in a multithreaded program that didn't use classes?

Bibliography

McMenamin, S. and John Palmer, *Essential Systems Analysis,* Yourdon Press, Englewood Cliffs, NJ, 1984, p. 32.

Stroustrup, B., *The C++ Programming Language,* second edition, Addison-Wesley, Reading, MA, 1991, pp. 308-14.

Tanenbaum, Andrew S., *Modern Operating Systems,* Prentice Hall, Englewood Cliffs, NJ, 1992.

Transplanting a Tree-Recursive LISP Algorithm to C++

Steve Teale
71542.2217@CompuServe.com

The other day I was trying to improve myself by doing some reading to broaden my view of the programming process. The book was *Structure and Interpretation of Computer Programs* by Harold Abelson, Gerald Jay Sussman, and Julie Sussman (MIT Press, 1985).

A small program, illustrating a typical tree-recursive process, written in the Scheme dialect of LISP caught my attention. A tree-recursive process typically uses a function that calls itself more than once, thus generating an exponentially increasing number of nested invocations. Since I don't understand LISP or Scheme in any depth, I thought I had better write a version of the program in a language I do understand, specifically C++. That way I would be sure I understood the intent behind the Scheme program.

My first attempt was successful in that it produced the correct answer, but it was highly inefficient. It led me first to think of ways in which the algorithm could be improved and then of how it could best be represented as the sort of reuseable component we should attempt to design if the potential benefits of C++ are to be realized.

Here is the original program reproduced verbatim, with my thanks to the authors and publisher for permission to use it:

```
(define (count-change amount)
        (cc amount 5))

(define (cc amount kind-of-coins)
  (cond
     ((= amount 0) 1)
     ((or (< amount 0)
```

```
    (= kinds-of-coins 0)) 0)
       (else (+
  (cc (- amount
  (first-denomination kinds-of-coins))
           kinds-of-coins)
        (cc amount (- kinds-of-coins 1))
          )
     )
   )
  )

  (define (first-denomination kinds-of-coins)
    (cond ((= kinds-of-coins 1) 1)
          ((= kinds-of-coins 2) 5)
          ((= kinds-of-coins 3) 10)
          ((= kinds-of-coins 4) 25)
          ((= kinds-of-coins 5) 50)))
```

The define statements are Scheme procedure or function definitions. For example, the first line defines a procedure called `count-change`, which takes an argument amount. The `count-change` function is evaluated using another function, `cc`, in the body of the `count-change` function. There the `cc` function is applied to two arguments, amount, and the numeric value 5.

The `cc` function takes two arguments, `amount` and `kinds-of-coins`, and has a body similar in form to a C or C++ `switch` statement. In Scheme this uses the keyword cond (for conditional). The first branch of the conditional uses the equality operator with operands `amount` and `0`. If that evaluates to `true` (`amount == 0`) `cc` evaluates to `1`. Otherwise, if `amount` is less than `0` or `kinds-of-coins` equals `0`, then `cc` evaluates to `0`. The default branch, introduced in Scheme by the `else` keyword evaluates `cc` recursively, using two calls to itself.

The program is designed to determine the number of ways to make change for some specified sum of money using pennies, nickels, dimes, quarters, and half-dollars.

The way the program works depends on the observation that the number of ways an amount `a` can be changed can be expressed as:

```
ways of changing a without using denomination d
  + ways of changing a-d using all the coins
```

It follows that the problem can be reduced recursively to a problem of changing a smaller amount with fewer kinds of coins. First, some boundary condition rules have to be set:

- If a is zero, we say there is one way to make change.
- If a is negative or the remaining number of denominations is zero, there are zero ways to make change.

A program like this would be run on a Scheme interpreter by invoking the procedure with a suitable argument:

```
==> (count-change 100)
292
```

A rather literal translation to C++ is as follows:

```
int first_denomination(kinds_of_coins)
{
  switch (kinds_of_coins) {
  case 1:
    return 1;
  case 2:
    return 5;
  case 3:
    return 10;
  case 4:
    return 25;
  case 5:
    return 50;
  }
}

long cc(int amount, int kinds_of_coins)
{
  return amount == 0 ? 1:
    ((amount < 0 || kinds_of_coins == 0)? 0:
      cc(amount
        -first_denomination(kinds_of_coins), kinds_of_coins)
      + cc(amount,kinds_of_coins-1));
}

long count_change(int amount)
{
  return cc(amount, 5);
}
```

Of course in C++—or in C, for that matter—we will need a `main()` function to exercise the function `count_change()`. The version here displays the number of ways of making change for a dollar and reports how long the calculation took:

```
// change.cpp
#include <time.h>
#include <iostream.h>

// code as above

int main()
{
  long t1 = clock();
  cout << count_change(100) << endl;
  cout << clock()-t1 << endl;

   return 0;
}
```

This program produces the same answer, 292, and runs without perceptible delay. However a tree-recursive algorithm like this takes time which is exponential in the argument to `count_change()`. For example, if the amount is changed to $10, the program goes away for some time. On my machine, it took half an hour to arrive at a result.

Although it is unlikely to speed up the program dramatically, the translation process from Scheme to C++ can be taken a stage further. The `first_denomination()` function, with its switch statement, is not the way things are done in C or C++. The function can be eliminated and replaced by a static look-up table of denominations. If the array is given an unused zeroth member, little modification to the rest of the code is required. The changed parts are as follows:

```
int first_denomination[6] = { 0, 1, 5, 10, 25, 50 };

long cc(int amount, int kinds_of_coins)
{
  return amount == 0 ? 1:
    ((amount < 0 || kinds_of_coins == 0)? 0:
      cc(amount
        -first_denomination[kinds_of_coins],
            kinds_of_coins)
      + cc(amount,kinds_of_coins-1));
}
```

As would be expected, this does not produce a dramatic improvement. All that can be expected is for it to improve the constant of proportionality in the exponential expression describing the computation time.

Tree-recursive processes are usually inefficient because they calculate the same data values repeatedly in different branches of the tree. If you put an output statement in the function `cc()` to show the values of amount and `kind_of_coins` at each call, this will be very obvious. We can make a great improvement if the algorithm is modified so that it stores any values that the `cc()` function has already calculated, in a cache.

While we are doing this, we can take the opportunity to convert the translated algorithm into a tidy C-style module. Only the `count_change()` function needs to be global. The `cc()` function and the data values can be static, and thus private to the translation unit where the change-making functions are implemented:

```
// change.h
enum coin { penny = 1, nickel = 5, dime = 10,
            quarter = 25, half_dollar = 50 };
long count_change(int amount);
```

```
// change.cpp
#include <stdlib.h>
#include <string.h>
#include <change.h>
#include <iostream.h>
```

```
const int values[6] = { 0, penny, nickel,
      dime, quarter, half_dollar };
const int denominations = 5;
static long *cc_cache;
```

The `cc()` function now has some additional code. The tests for boundary conditions are separated and made first. Then the cache is checked to see if the required value has already been calculated. If it has, the stored value is returned. Otherwise, the required value must be calculated using the recursive procedure. The result is stored in the cache:

```
static long cc(int amount, int kinds_of_coins)
{
  if (!amount) return 1;
  if (amount < 0 || !kinds_of_coins)
    return 0;
```

```
  int cell = (amount-1)*denominations
                 +kinds_of_coins-1;
  if (cc_cache[cell])
    return cc_cache[cell];
  long rv =
    cc(amount-values[kinds_of_coins],
                 kinds_of_coins)
     + cc(amount,kinds_of_coins-1);
  cc_cache[cell] = rv;
  return rv;
}
```

The count_change() function allocates the cache that is subsequently used to store values calculated by the cc() function. It also deletes the memory it allocated when it is through, so that there is no memory leakage. Otherwise, it consists only of a call to cc(). The test program remains the same:

```
long count_change(int amount)
{
  cc_cache = new long[amount*denominations];
  if (!cc_cache) {
    cerr << "Not enough memory\n";
    abort();
  }
  memset(cc_cache,0,amount*denominations*sizeof(long));
  long rv = cc(amount,denominations);
  delete cc_cache;
  return rv;
}
```

The improvement is dramatic: The $10 problem was resolved some 30,000 times faster! The ratio is not accurate because the faster program actually ran in time approximating the granularity of the system clock. This observation is not intended as a criticism of Scheme. I am sure that it must be possible to implement a cache scheme using that language also. Nevertheless, it is a stark illustration of the penalties of choosing the wrong implementation.

Up to this point we have transformed the Scheme program to the point where it now typifies good modular C programming. At this point, it is instructive to consider how the transformation to a more object-oriented style might be continued.

The change-making module could be implemented as a class. The constant data items, and the cache pointer would become static data members of the class. The `count_change()` function would be its only public function. The `cc()` function would be private. Both functions would be static class members:

```
class Change {
public:
  static int count_change(int amount);
private:
  static int cc(int amount, int kinds_of_coins);

  static const int values[6];
  static const int denominations;
  static int *cc_cache;
};
```

A transformation of this kind is no improvement on what we had. In fact, it makes the test program marginally more difficult to write, since the principal function call must now be qualified with a class name:

```
main()
{
  ...
  cout << Change::count_change(300);
  ...
}
```

Nothing has been added. C++ classes of this general form, consisting only of static members, represent modules—which was what we already had. A transformation of this kind breaks a golden rule of programming: If it's not broken, don't mend it.

If, on the other hand, we consider the present limitations of the change-making module, it is not difficult to spot an opportunity for generalization. Half-dollar coins are rare, or we may run out of dimes. So, in a program that uses the `count_change()` facility, it would be useful to be able to specify the denominations available for making change. If we add this capability, objects of the class we envisage will then have distinct states. Some instances may make change with all the coins; others, with a restricted set. A constructor will be required to initialize that state.

The choice of a constructor, or more specifically, of its argument type or types, is our principal design decision here. Three candidates are shown below:

```
class Change {
public:
```

```
    Change(int = 5);
    Change(int, int *)
    Change(int, coin, ...);
    ...
};
```

The first provides a default constructor. If the default were used, it could be assumed that all denominations of the coinage were available. A smaller value could be taken as indicating that only the corresponding smaller coins were available, so an argument value of four would mean "use pennies, nickels, dimes, and quarters." This is far from intuitive. Also, what is the constructor to do with values <= 0 or > 5?

The second attempt is intended to allow:

```
int v[4] = { penny, nickel, dime, quarter };
Change cv(4,v);
```

What happens if the first argument is incorrect or the array is uninitialized?

The third will probably make many readers wince. It is a constructor with a variable number of arguments, but it allows the quite expressive syntax:

```
Change cv(4, penny, nickel, dime, quarter);
```

However, it is subject to the same sort of criticisms as the previous one if the first argument is incorrect, or the third and subsequent arguments are of the wrong type or value.

A reasonably intuitive syntax would be:

```
Change cv(penny | nickel | dime | quarter);
```

What is more, it is relatively easy to implement this suggestion in a way that is type-safe and robust. We need an extra class, `CoinSet`, and a redefinition of `enum coin`:

```
enum coin { penny = 1, nickel = 2, dime = 4,
            quarter = 8, half_dollar = 16 };
```

The coin enumerators become bit flags. Class `CoinSet` provides a single constructor that takes an argument of type `coin`, and a bitwise `or` operator that takes the same kind of argument:

```
class CoinSet {
friend class ChangeMaker;
public:
    CoinSet(coin c) : df(c) {}
```

```
  CoinSet
  &operator|(coin c) { df |= c; return *this; }
private:
  int df;
};
const int USCoins = 5;
const CoinSet USCoinage(penny | nickel
           | dime | quarter | half_dollar);
```

Now the constructor for class `Change` can take a single argument of type `CoinSet`. It will not be possible to initialize a `Change` object other than by using the specified syntax with appropriate values:

```
class Change {
public:
  Change(const CoinSet& = USCoinage);
  int operator()(int);
private:
  int cc(int amount, int kinds_of_coins);

  static const int coins[USCoins];
  int denominations;
  int values[USCoins+1];
  int *cache;
};
```

The provision of the function call operation in the public interface of class `Change` remains to be justified. The C-style module implementation provided a single function, used as in:

```
cout << count_change(amount);
```

We criticized the postulated C++ module class because that complicated the usage, requiring instead:

```
cout << Change::count_change();
```

Without the function call operator, our user-defined type `Change` would require the introduction of three names to the test program:

```
Change changething(penny | nickel | dime);
cout << changething.count_change(300);
```

If the function call operator is overloaded this can be simplified to:

```
Change count_change(penny | nickel | dime);
cout << count_change(300);
```

This syntax is as close as we can get to the convenience of the original, given the need to initialize a class object.

Only the constructor for class `Change` is a substantial departure from what we have already presented. The functions in the C-style module are easily translated to member functions of class `Change`. The `count_change` function becomes `Change::operator()`:

```
const int Change::coins[5] = { 1, 5, 10, 25, 50 };
Change::Change(const CoinSet &c) : denominations(0)
{
  int n = c.df;
  for (int i = 0, j = 1; i < USCoins; ++i) {
    if (n & 1) {
      values[j++] = coins[i];
      ++denominations;
    }
    n >>= 1;
  }
}
```

The final test program is as follows. The problem with only pennies, nickels, and quarters making up 30 cents is sufficiently simple that we can check out the result by hand. Nine combinations of these coins make up that amount:

```
int main()
{
  ChangeMaker count_change(penny | nickel | quarter);
  cout << count_change(30) << endl;

   return 0;
}
```

This simple program demonstrates an easy way to make tree-recursive techniques more efficient. Similar improvements to such programs can often be made by devising an iterative procedure to undertake the same task. However, while the recursive algorithm is easy to specify, it is not always easy to spot the corresponding iterative technique.

The transformations involved in going from the Scheme program to the conventional C-style modular programming equivalent and then to a C++ user-defined type illustrate a number of interesting design considerations.

CLASS DERIVATION AND EMULATION OF VIRTUAL CONSTRUCTORS

DAVID JORDAN

C++ AND OTHER OBJECT-ORIENTED LANGUAGES PROVIDE SOFTWARE PACKaging mechanisms called *classes* that permit developers to build reusable components called *objects.* As object-oriented techniques become a standard software development practice, the marketplace will begin to see libraries of objects sold as tools to application developers. These libraries will be organized as collections of interrelated classes (data types) and they will permit application developers to write and integrate software much more quickly. Techniques can be used to design classes that are more reusable and extensible. In particular, they allow class consumers to extend through *class derivation* the framework of objects provided.

Classes providing "container objects" are often developed that instantiate a set of objects, placing them within some set-like construct (e.g., trees or linked-lists). The complexity of extracting and aggregating sets of objects from some external interface is hidden within the container object. The example of a container object is used in this article, but any library that instantiates objects visible to application software should consider using the technique presented.

There are many examples of libraries used by application developers that instantiate objects. Object-oriented databases and user interface management systems (UIMS) often provide such services. One may call an object-oriented database routine to extract a specific version of a CAD/CAM design, for example. The database would create a composite object that contains objects representing each of the components in the design. A specific application may need to associate additional attributes or relationships among the components in the design. Another example is a UIMS that provides applications with a front-end interface to a user who is interacting with graphical objects on the screen. Objects get instantiated by the UIMS as a result of user interactions. As in the database example, the application often needs to add properties to the objects instantiated by the UIMS.

Users of libraries usually have additional attributes that need to be associated with the objects that get instantiated by the library. Library designers sometimes realize this and provide a generic pointer (`void*`) within the data structures they create. This pointer can then be set and used by software using the library without any interference from the library itself. Unfortunately, library components often are layered and this extensibility mechanism many times gets used by one layer but not propagated to the next layer.

When this mechanism is not available, developers often resort to creating additional data structures isomorphic to those created by the library. These structures typically contain a pointer to the library object and the additional attributes that are needed. However, overhead is required to provide a mapping from the library object to the application specific object and this is awkward and inefficient.

Application developers may have the need to specify the memory location for the objects instantiated. Supported libraries usually allocate objects within the process address space, but the library user may require that the objects live in shared memory. The only way to get the library software to instantiate the objects where needed is to change its source code, which is undesirable from a maintenance standpoint.

It is not practical to require distribution of libraries in source form. Companies have a vested interest in protecting their "intellectual property," their software source code, so libraries often are only distributed in a binary form. The concept of shrink-wrap software and the resulting economics of software distribution that has occurred in the PC industry should also be used in distributing object software. There should be a corresponding notion of *shrink-wrap objects* that can be sold as libraries but be user-extensible in binary form. This will provide more motivation for the distribution and sharing of common object software across the entire software industry.

PROPOSAL

Users want to associate additional attributes with the objects that get instantiated by libraries. *Class derivation* provides the proper semantic abstraction and software mechanism for accomplishing this. The user needs to derive new types from the base types known and used by the library or container object. A mechanism is needed to cause the objects instantiated by the container object to be based on the new user defined derived type. It should not have any effect on the proper functioning of the software that causes the object to get instantiated.

The proposal is that the container object needs to provide a suite of virtual functions that can be called to return an object of the particular type used by the library. If a user needs to extend some of the objects instantiated by the container, the user derives from the base container class, redefining the virtual functions to allocate objects derived from the type allocated by the base container class. Whenever the base container class needs to instantiate an object of a particular type, it calls the virtual function to instantiate the object. Depending on the actual derived class of the container object, the proper constructor will be called for object instantiation.

Derivation of the container class provides a software layering mechanism. Each level of derivation (layer) can redefine the virtual functions causing objects of the proper derived type to be instantiated. Derivation can continue ad infinitum and the types of the objects instantiated will be based on the types required at the deepest level of derivation. No conflicts will occur among the layers of class derivation. If the container object also deallocates the objects (using the `delete` operator), the base class destructors for the objects instantiated need to be virtual.

A Hypothetical Example

A simple example illustrates the approach. Suppose the container class had two types of objects that it instantiated:

```
class Object1 {
public:
    Object1();
    virtual ~Object1();
};
class Object2 {
public:
    Object2();
    virtual ~Object2();
};
```

`Object1` and `Object2` are hypothetical names for types of objects that will be instantiated and manipulated. The object type used will be implementation specific. Note that the destructors are virtual, permitting the library to delete the object with only a pointer to the base class object.

In this example there is a class called `Container` that will provide an aggregation service, instantiating objects of type `Object1` and `Object2`:

```
class Container {
public:
  void build();
  virtual Object1      *allocObject1();
  virtual Object2      *allocObject2();
};
```

For each type of object instantiated by the `Container` class, there will be a virtual function that returns a pointer to an object of that type. The virtual functions in the base container class would return objects of the base types:

```
Object1 *
Container::allocObject1()
{ return new Object1(); }

Object2 *
Container::allocObject2()
{ return new Object2(); }
```

These virtual functions will then be called in the `build()` routine to allocate objects of the appropriate type:

```
void
Container::build()
{
    Object1 *o1;
    Object2 *o2;
       •
       •
    o1 = allocObject1();
    o2 = allocObject2();
       •
}
```

The `Container` class can then instantiate and manipulate these objects. As far as it is concerned, the objects returned are of type `Object1` and `Object2`, respectively, but the objects returned may actually be of a derived type depending on the derivation level of the `Container` class.

Why is there a separate build routine for instantiating the objects; couldn't a constructor for `Container` instantiate the objects? This would not work, due to a subtlety in the semantics of constructor invocation. Constructor invocation order proceeds from the base out to the leaves of class derivation hierarchies. When virtual functions are called within the constructors of a derivation hierarchy, the actual functions called are dependent on the current level of the particular constructor in the derivation hierarchy. Therefore, the base `Container` constructor cannot call the virtual functions and instantiate the objects required by classes derived from `Container`.

Suppose the user of the `Container` class needs additional attributes associated with `Object1` objects. The user derives a new type from `Object1` as follows:

```
class UserObj : public Object1
     {/*user class */};
```

To get the right object instantiated, the user also derives a new type from `Container`:

```
class UserContainer:
  public Container {
public:
  Object1 *allocObject1();
}

Object1 *
UserContainer: :allocObject1()
{
  return new UserObj;
}
```

The virtual function `allocObject1()` instantiates an object of type `UserObj`, which is derived from `Object1`. Then the user can allocate an object of the `Container` class:

```
main()
{
  UserContainer c;
     •
     •
  c.build();
     •
     •
}
```

The `Container` object can now instantiate and manipulate objects in the `build()` routine and manipulate objects that meet both the requirements of the `Container` and `UserContainer` classes.

Reflection

The virtual functions in the `Container` class could be considered `static member functions`, which are new features in C++ Release 2.0. Static member functions have class scope but are not invoked with nor manipulate directly any particular object of the class. An attempt was made to use `virtual static` member functions for the `allocObject` routines. The virtual functions in the `Container` class need to know the derived type of the container object to determine the appropriate virtual function to call, but the virtual function itself does not access `Container` object. `virtual static` functions are not supported in C++ Release 2.0, but ordinary virtual functions sufficed.

In the example, `UserContainer::allocObject1()` redefined the virtual function to return a `UserObj` object. If another class derives from `UserContainer` to redefine `allocObject1()`, there is no means in the language to ensure that the object instantiated is actually derived from `UserObj`. At particular levels in the class derivation hierarchy we are, in effect, wanting to change the type of the return value for some virtual functions:

```
class UserContainer:
  public Container {
public:
  UserObj *allocObject1();
};
```

But this is not possible within the C++ language. A means is needed to enforce each level of derivation from the `Container` class to derive and instantiate objects based on each level's respective base class requirements. Each level of derivation should be able to assume that the objects instantiated are derived from the type used at that level of the derivation. If this is not done, memory corruption will occur when attributes are manipulated. Each level of derivation from `Container` should therefore clearly document the type of object required at that level of the derivation hierarchy. Users deriving from a particular level of the `Container` class then need to derive the objects instantiated from the type required by the `Container` class at that level of derivation. This will ensure that the base class works properly.

The hypothetical example does not have any arguments passed to the constructor. The base `Container` class could have had arguments passed to constructors since it is at the base level that the objects are usually getting instantiated, though any level of derivation from `Container` can instantiate objects. A particular level of derivation from `Container` has no way of knowing the required arguments of any class derived from it. The attributes added by the `UserObj` class, for example, can initialize data members to a null value in the constructor. The data members can then be populated later.

Other approaches have been proposed for providing the functionality presented here. The `declare` and `implement` macros in `generic.h` can be used, but the `implement` macro requires the software in source form. The `template` addition to C++ could be used, but its proposed implementation also seems to require source code.[1] The original goal was to have the software distributed in a binary form.

Using the mechanism proposed here requires that the objects instantiated are derived from a particular type known by the creator of the container. The two mechanisms mentioned in the preceding paragraph do not have this restriction and permit containers to be generated generically. They may require that the classes implement certain functions and/or operators specified by the creator of the container, but they explicitly avoid any direct knowledge of object functionality. My mechanism assumes that the container object already has some built-in knowledge about the objects being instantiated and part of the service it is providing is the manipulation of the objects directly. Both forms are probably needed depending on the particular application.

There are two categories of virtual constructors that applications need, static and dynamic. A `static virtual constructor` would be used when an application developer wants to specify new types known at compile time and have a library be able to instantiate objects of that type, as is described here. A `dynamic virtual constructor` would provide the ability to create types on the fly. Here a running program needs to define new types dynamically at run-time and then be able to instantiate and manipulate objects of those types in the same running program. This is not completely supported by the mechanism described here. This could be done in C++ by compiling a file containing a derived class and then using incremental linkage techniques to get the classes incorporated into a running process. Software interfacing at the base class level via virtual functions could then manipulate the objects.

Conclusion

An approach has been proposed for extending the capabilities of objects that get instantiated in libraries. It is based on deriving new types of objects from those used by the library. A mechanism employing virtual functions is then used to emulate virtual constructors so that the right type of object gets instantiated. It is a simple and straightforward mechanism. This type of facility is not provided by libraries today, and users need it. It permits reliable, well tested libraries to be reused in their binary form without incurring undesired maintenance costs.

A special thanks to Jim Coplein, Tom Davison, Bill Havanas, and Tina Strouble for reviewing drafts of this article.

Reference

1. Stroustrup, B. *Parameterized Types for C++*, USENIX C++ Conference, October 1988.

Virtual Constructors Revisited

Tom Cargill
cargill@csn.org
76476.1422@compuserve.com

I would like to explore some alternatives to the code in Bruce Eckel's column on virtual constructors in the March/April [1992] issue. My goal is to rewrite the code to make it simpler, more efficient, and easier to maintain. Eckel's original code is reproduced in Listing 1. (Following Eckel's suggestion, the identifiers for the enumerators `CIRCLE`, `SQUARE`, and `TRIANGLE` have been capitalized to avoid confusion with their namesake classes.)

In reading the code in Listing 1, three things strike me immediately. First, every time a circle, square or triangle object is required, two objects must be created: a shape object and a derived object to which the shape object's `s` member points, as shown, for example, in Figure 1. This extra shape object consumes space, obviously, and time as well, because all operations to the underlying object must be delegated through the base shape object. Second, the pointer called `s` that is a member of shape is inherited by all the derived classes, even though derived objects have no use for the pointer; they use a protected base constructor that sets the pointer to null. Though less significant, this unused pointer is a further waste of space. Third, the enumeration declared in the base class and the coding of the virtual constructor in the base class depend in detail on the derived classes. If another derived class is to be added to the system, `shape::type` and `shape::shape(type)` must be recoded. Information about derived classes that must appear in the base class complicates the base class declaration. The base class should describe the common, general properties of the abstraction, not the details of the specializations. Placing information about the derived classes in the base constructor also creates a maintenance burden: What is the effect if another derived class, say, ellipse, is added, but the `ELLIPSE` case is not added to `shape::shape(type)`?

Let's examine the construction and behavior of shape objects. What is the purpose of the `shape::shape(type)` constructor? It creates a dynamic object

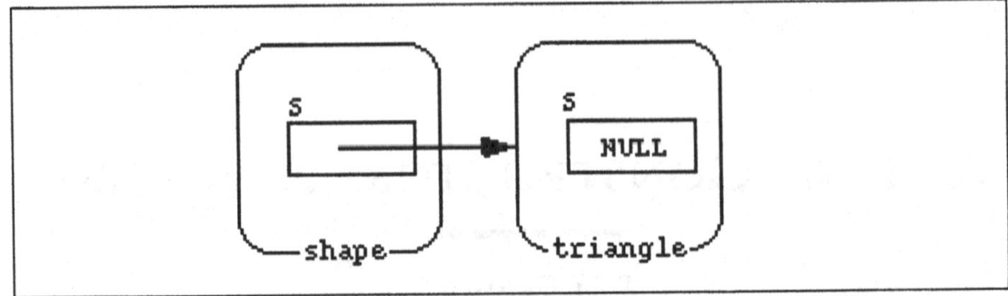

FIGURE 1. *Two objects are created.*

of the type specified by its argument, holds a pointer to that object, and calls shape's own `draw()` member function, which in turn calls `draw()` for the other object. The only operation that can be applied to the shape object during the remainder of its lifetime is `draw()`, which `shape` always delegates to the other object.

Suppose this object creation service was provided by a function rather than an object. How would the code change? The following function, `newShape()`, creates an object of the type specified by its argument and then calls the `draw()` member function of that object. The difference between `newShape()` and `shape::shape(type)` is that `newShape()` does not retain the pointer. Instead of holding the pointer, it returns the pointer to the caller.

```
shape* newShape(shape::type t)
{
  shape* S;
  switch(t) {
    case shape::CIRCLE:
      S = new circle; break;
    case shape::SQUARE:
      S = new square; break;
    case shape::TRIANGLE:
      S = new triangle; break;
  }
  S->draw();
  return S;
}
```

From a client's point of view the same service is provided: the client can call the `draw()` member function of an object of the desired type. By using a pointer directly to the derived object, there is no delegation; the client calls the virtual member function directly. The same function is executed, though more efficiently since there is no shape object acting as a go-between.

Rather than leave `newShape()` as a free-standing function, it can become part of the shape abstraction as a member function of class shape. Since `newShape()` executes to create a shape object, not on behalf of an existing one, it should be a static member function. A static member function executes on behalf of its class, not on behalf of an object. The complete program with `shape::shape(type)` replaced by `shape::newShape(type)` is shown in Listing 2. Note that `shape::S` and the protected constructor for shape are gone. The new code is smaller, creates fewer objects and executes faster, while providing all the services of the original.

Now let's turn to the information about the derived classes that appears in the base class. As mentioned above, enumerating all the derived classes in the base class clutters the base abstraction and makes its code more fragile with respect to maintenance.

As we did with the virtual constructor, we must ask, What is the purpose of the type enumeration in the base class? The enumeration is used as an argument that specifies the type of object to be created, originally to `shape::shape(type)` and now to `shape::newShape(type)`. What is needed is an argument whose value uniquely designates one of the derived classes of shape. In some languages a class is also an object. If that were true in C++ then the argument could be the class from which an object is to be instantiated. In C++ classes are not objects. The technique used in the original code is to define an enumerated type that mirrors the set of derived classes; each enumerator represents one the derived classes of shape. An alternative is to use an object of a derived class to represent the class. The only property required of the class by `newShape()` is instantiation; that is, given a class (represented by an object of the class), the function must be able to create an object of that class. Since the class is represented by an object, this is equivalent to creating a new object of the same type, or cloning the object.

To use the class-represented-by-an-object technique, a new virtual member function must be added to the base class. This function creates a dynamic object of the same class as the object that executes the function. Let the function be called `clone()`. With `clone()` added to shape, `shape::newShape()` can be greatly simplified. Instead of taking an enumerator as its argument `newShape()` takes a reference to any shape object. Instead of knowing all the derived types, `newShape()` merely clones its argument object to create the new object. The class shape and its static member function `newShape()` are rewritten as follows:

```
class shape {
public:
  static shape* newShape(const shape&);
  virtual void draw() = 0;
  virtual ~shape() {}
  virtual shape* clone() const = 0;
};

shape* shape::newShape(const shape& prototype)
{
  shape* S = prototype.clone();
  S->draw();
  return S;
}
```

This version of the program is shown in its entirety in Listing 3. Note that the base class now contains no information about its derived classes. Each derived class defines a `clone()` function that makes a new object of the corresponding type. When a new derived class must be added, the `clone()` member must be supplied. If the `clone()` member is overlooked, the derived class becomes an abstract base class, producing a compile-time error if an attempt is made to create an object. The initialization of the array in `main()` uses temporary objects as the arguments to `shape::newShape()`; the overhead of creating those temporaries can be eliminated by using static objects instead.

Two transformations have been applied to the original code. First, when a function (`shape::newShape()`) replaced an object, the total number of shape objects was reduced by a factor of two. Second, when an object replaced an enumerator as the function argument, the information about the derived classes was entirely eliminated from the base class, reducing the complexity of the base class and simplifying maintenance of the code. Let me try to generalize from these specific transformations to rules of thumb that may be applicable in other settings:

1. C++ supports object-oriented programming, but that does not mean that everything must be accomplished by an object. Some tasks are better accomplished by functions.

2. Base classes should concentrate on the common base abstraction. Don't let details of the derived classes creep into a base class.

Listing 1. The original virtual constructor code.

```
#include <iostream.h>

class shape {
  shape *S;
public:
  enum type { CIRCLE, SQUARE,
    TRIANGLE };
  shape(type); // "virtual" constructor
  virtual void draw() { S->draw(); }
  virtual ~shape() {
    cout << "~shape" << endl;
    delete S;
  }
protected:
  shape() { S = 0; }
};

class circle : public shape {
public:
  circle() {}
  void draw ()
      { cout << "circle::draw" << endl; }
  ~circle() { cout << "~circle" << endl; }
};

class square : public shape {
public:
  square() {}
  void draw ()
      { cout << "square::draw" << endl; }
  ~square() { cout << "~square" << endl; }
};

class triangle : public shape {
public:
  triangle() {}
  void draw ()
      { cout << "triangle::draw" << endl; }
  ~triangle() { cout << "~triangle" << endl; }
};
```

```
shape::shape(type t)
{
  switch(t) {
    case CIRCLE: S = new circle; break;
    case SQUARE: S = new square; break;
    case TRIANGLE: S = new triangle; break;
  }
  draw(); // virtual function call in
          // constructor
}

void main() {
  cout << "virtual constructor calls:" << endl;
  shape* s[] = {
    new shape(shape::CIRCLE),
    new shape(shape::SQUARE),
    new shape(shape::TRIANGLE)
  };
  const sz = sizeof s / sizeof *s;
  cout << "virtual function calls:" << endl;
  for(int i = 0; i < sz; i++)
    s[i]->draw();
  for(i = 0; i < sz; i++) {
    cout << "---" << endl;
    delete s[i];
  }
}
```

Listing 2. Virtual constructor replaced by static member function.

```
#include <iostream.h>

class shape {
public:
  enum type { CIRCLE, SQUARE, TRIANGLE };
  static shape* newShape(type);
  virtual void draw() = 0;
  virtual ~shape() {}
};
```

```
class circle : public shape {
public:
  circle() {}
  void draw ()
     { cout << "circle::draw" << endl; }
  ~circle() { cout << "~circle" << endl; }
};

class square : public shape {
public:
  square() {}
  void draw ()
     { cout << "square::draw" << endl; }
  ~square() { cout << "~square" << endl; }
};

class triangle : public shape {
public:
  triangle() {}
  void draw ()
     { cout << "triangle::draw" << endl; }
  ~triangle() { cout << "~triangle" << endl; }
};
shape* shape::newShape(type t)
{
  shape* S;
  switch(t) {
    case CIRCLE: S = new circle; break;
    case SQUARE: S = new square; break;
    case TRIANGLE: S = new triangle; break;
  }
  S->draw();
  return S;
}

void main() {
  shape* s[] = {
    shape::newShape(shape::CIRCLE),
    shape::newShape(shape::SQUARE),
    shape::newShape(shape::TRIANGLE)
  };
```

```
    const sz = sizeof s / sizeof *s;
    cout << "virtual function calls:" << endl;
    for(int i = 0; i < sz; i++)
      s[i]->draw();
    for(i = 0; i < sz; i++) {
      cout << "---" << endl;
      delete s[i];
    }
  }
```

LISTING 3. CLASSES REPRESENTED BY OBJECTS.

```
#include <iostream.h>

class shape {
public:
  static shape* newShape(const shape&);
  virtual void draw() = 0;
  virtual ~shape() {}
  virtual shape* clone() const = 0;
};

shape* shape::newShape(const shape& prototype)
{
  shape* S = prototype.clone();
  S->draw();
  return S;
}

class circle : public shape {
public:
  circle() {}
  void draw ()
     { cout << "circle::draw" << endl; }
  ~circle() { cout << "~circle" << endl; }

  shape* clone() const { return new circle; }
};

class square : public shape {
public:
  square() {}
```

```
  void draw ()
     { cout << "square::draw" << endl; }
  ~square() { cout << "~square" << endl; }
  shape* clone() const { return new square; }
};

class triangle : public shape {
public:
  triangle() {}
  void draw ()
     { cout << "triangle::draw" << endl; }
  ~triangle() { cout << "~triangle" << endl; }
  shape* clone() const { return new triangle; }
};

void main() {
  shape* s[] = {
    shape::newShape(circle()),
    shape::newShape(square()),
    shape::newShape(triangle())
  };
  const sz = sizeof s / sizeof *s;
  cout << "virtual function calls:" << endl;
  for(int i = 0; i < sz; i++)
    s[i]->draw();
  for(i = 0; i < sz; i++) {
    cout << "---" << endl;
    delete s[i];
  }
}
```

Initializing Static Variables in C++ Libraries

Jerry Schwarz

When a C++ class has constructors or destructors, guarantees that a "constructor" will be called when space is allocated for an object of that class, and the "destructor" when the space is freed. A pointer to the space is available within these functions. I call this guarantee the "allocation hook" and say that objects of such types are "subject to the allocation hook." For new C++ programmers the important thing to learn about constructors and destructors is not the details of the syntax used to define constructors and destructors and to cause them to be called, but the way that the allocation hook influences the language. The details of the semantics of functions that return values subject to the allocation hook and prohibitions against incorporating objects with certain types in unions are consequences of the allocation hook. Of course, in C++ it is possible to bypass the allocation hook by using casts. I ignore such bypassing of the type system in this article.

As an example of the way the allocation hook works, consider a class that serves as a buffer for I/O. The allocation hook makes it possible to arrange for pointers to be properly initialized when a buffer is created and characters to be flushed when a buffer is destroyed. This guarantee extends to objects with what the ANSI C specification calls "static storage duration": variables declared at the top level in a file or in a code block with storage class `static`. Throughout this article I will refer to such objects as *static variables.* This usage is intended to contrast with *automatic,* or *stack,* variables and should not be confused with the use of *static* by C and C++ to designate variables with file or function scope. As part of the allocation hook, the C++ compilation system arranges for constructors to be called at the beginning of (or before) main and corresponding destructors to be called from exit or when main returns.

The original C++ stream I/O package has a static variable. `cout`, that is declared in such a way that the constructor that initializes it will connect it to the UNIX standard output, and the destructor will flush waiting characters. However, there is an ordering problem. While the compilation system guarantees that the constructor for `cout` will have been called before any code in `main` is executed, there is no guarantee that `cout`'s constructor will be called before constructors for other static variables. Similarly, there is no guarantee that destructors for other static variables will be called before `cout`'s. The consequence is that extreme care is required in using `cout` in constructors or destructors.

At this point, the reader may be wondering why this is a problem for C++ streams and not for `stdio FILE`s. Indeed a little experimentation will show that stdio functions can be used with complete freedom in constructors and destructors. The answer is that the standard C library contains an exit function that flushes `stdio` buffers. The real UNIX exit function is `_exit` not `exit`. The UNIX C library developers took a lot of care to deal with the special case of `stdio`. They arranged the data structures so that they could be initialized with constants and they arranged for special code in exit. C++ tries to provide a more general mechanism.

Returning to the C++ problem: The only ordering that C++ guarantees on the constructor and destructor calls for static variables is that when two variables are defined in the same file, the constructor for the higher one (i.e., the one declared earlier in the file) will be called before the constructor for the lower and the destructor for the higher will be called after the constructor for the lower. There are no other ordering constraints. The challenge is to use this limited guarantee to solve our ordering problems. In this article I present some techniques I have developed for this purpose.

Simple Solution

As far as possible I avoid static variables subject to the allocation hook. I prefer to use such variables in a limited way to run code that will initialize the variables used by the rest of the program. The technique is sketched in this section. It is based on the observation that any file that uses a class will include the header which contains a declaration of that class. In that header I place the declaration of a static variable with file scope whose constructor will do all initializations required for use of the class. For example, suppose we have a class `Pub` that is declared in a header file, `pub.h`, and that there is a variable, `gpub`, that must be initialized before other uses of objects of the class are possible. I add a declaration of `pub_init` to `pub.h` as follows:

```
class Pub { /* ... */};
extern Pub* gpub;
class Pub_init {
private:
  static int init_count
    // static data member
    // shared by all Pub_init objects
    // initialized to 0
public:
  Pub_init();
  ~Pub_init();
};

static /* i.e. file scope */ Pub_init pub_init
```

The `Pub_init` constructor will be called to initialize the variable `pub_init`. At the same time, it will initialize `gpub`. Because `pub_init` has file static scope, there will be as many such variables as there are files that include `pub.h`. The constructors and destructors for all these variables will be called in some indeterminate order. Although there are many `pub_init` variables there will be only one object named `Pub_init::init_count`. This is a consequence of the occurrence of static in its declaration. I use this to assure that the real initialization and destruction activity is carried out only once. The code for the `Pub_init` constructor and destructor looks like

```
Pub* gpub;
Pub_init::Pub_init()
{
  if( ++init_count > 1) return;
  gpub = new Pub;
  // Manipulations of gpub.
  // and any other required initializations.
}

Pub_init::Pub_init()
{
  if ( —init_count > 0 ) return ;
  delete gpub;
  // Any other destruction
}
```

In many common cases the declaration of pub_init in pub.h is sufficient to guarantee that gpub is initialized before any use. For example, suppose we have a class Priv that contains a Pub:

```
class Priv {
private:
  Pub p;
public:
    . . .
};
```

Because classes must be declared before objects or members of that type can be declared, pub.h will be included above the declaration of Priv. The declaration of pub_init will therefore occur higher in any file than any declaration of a Priv and thus the initialization of gpub will occur before any call to a Priv constructor. Thus gpub can be used freely within Priv constructors. Similarly, the destruction of the object that gpub points at will be delayed until after all calls to a Priv destructor.

REFINEMENT

In one significant case, the technique of the previous section is inadequate. The constructor for a class K may want to use a Pub even though the class does not contain any Pubs. For example, the constructor may wish to do I/O even though the class does not contain a stream. To guarantee the required ordering in this case an initialization class for K is required. Assume that k.h contains

```
class K_init {
  static int init_count;
public:
  K_init()
  ~K_init();
};
static K_init k_init;
```

The file that defines K_init::K_init might look like

```
#include "k.h"
#include "pub.h"
static Pub_init* pinit ; // static specifies file scope
```

```
K_init::K_init()
{
  if ( ++ init_count > 1 ) return;
  pinit + new Pub_init;
  // Any other information
}

K_init::K_init()
{

  if ( --init_count > 0 ) return;
  // Any other information
  delete pinit;
}
```

Since `k_init` is declared higher in any file than any declaration of a `K`, the `K_init` constructor will be called before any `K` constructor. This, in turn, guarantees that the `Pub` initialization will be carried out by the `Pub_init` constructor before any use by a `K` constructor.

SUMMARY

The technique outlined in this note has some drawbacks.

- It is not automatic. The `init` classes must be written by hand and declarations inserted in the header file. While this is not an overwhelming task, it is easy to forget. Further. The ordering between classes, such as the construction of a `Pub_init` in `K_init::K_init`, must be enforced manually.
- Only pointers can be initialized. The careful reader will have noted that `gpub` was declared to be a pointer to a `Pub` rather than a `Pub` variable. This is because the code in `Pub_init::Pub_init` has no way to force early initialization of a variable.
- There may be a lot of calls to the `init` constructors and destructors. This may impose extra startup and termination costs, but in practice, since all but one call returns immediately, the costs are trivial.

I have been using this method for over a year and it has proved satisfactory.

OBJECTS AS RETURN VALUES

MICHAEL TIEMANN

A PREFACE TO A C COURSE TAUGHT AT STANFORD BEGINS "IN ORDER TO learn C, you have to understand it first." The same could be said of C++. C++ provides many things to many users; two prominent C++ features are support for object-oriented programming and efficiency on par with C. Trouble for many new users begins when they worry about efficiency before understanding the language as a whole.

This article was based on electronic mail exchanged over the comp.lang.c++ newsgroup. The question being raised concerns the issue of using objects at all:

I have a class `M` *for which I want to define* `operator +`*. My question(s) have to do with how I generate the temporary that contains the result, and how such a temporary gets destroyed.*

First, if my `operator +` *returns an object of class* `M`*, it has to create an object to return. If I understand things right, this will call* `operator +`*, which will return an object of class* `M` *(which was pushed onto the stack), and do a structure copy into* `c`*. All the destructors get called just fine, and no stray memory is left around, but there's the overhead of the structure copy.*

It all depends on the compiler one uses, but I know that at least the AT&T cfront and GNU C++ are smarter than this. In these compilers, the caller passes the address of the place where the new temporary should be initialized. Depending on the way it is initialized, there may be no overhead visible from the call to `operator +` at all:

```
M operator + (M x, M y)
{
  return M (x.value () + y.value ());
}
```

The result of calling M's constructor on the sum of the values is to perform initialization. There is no requirement that it construct a new object and then return that object for the caller to copy. The generated code for the caller can pass an extra parameter to operator +, saying "Here is the object I would like initialized." Operator + can initialize the object, do a simple return, and no structure copy takes place.

But you may need to do hairier things that require you to get a handle on the value you are returning:

```
M operator + (M x, M y)
{
  // calls constructor
  M tmp;
  // initialize some of tmp
  tmp.set(x.value() + y.value());

  // maybe initialize more of tmp
  if (fullmoon() )
    tmp.howl();

  // tmp is what we want, but is it
  // where we want it? No . . .
  //  . . .call to M(M&) constructor
  //  . . .or structure copy, sigh
  return tmp;
}
```

A really smart compiler could notice that tmp was the only variable feeding the return value, and substitute the hidden result parameter for tmp throughout. Another solution might be to extend the language:

```
M operator + (M x, M y)
  // calls constructor
  return tmp;
{
  // initialize some of tmp
  tmp.set(x.value() + y.value());

  // maybe initialize more of tmp
  if (fullmoon())
    tmp.howl();
```

```
    // this need do nothing, since tmp
    // *is* the return value
    return tmp;
    }
```

This extension would be very helpful when building expression-oriented classes.

Here's a commonly tried approach that doesn't work:

I've also fiddled around with trying to return a reference to an object `M`, *to avoid the structure copy. The code for* `operator + ( )` *has to allocate a pointer to an object of type* `M` *using the* `new operator`. *So, if we have some code that looks like:*

```
M a, b, c;
// some code to give a and b values
. . .
// call "m& M::operator + (M& x)"
c = a + b;
```

and we define `operator = (M&)` *to do the assignment, how can we free the space allocated by* `operator + ( )` *for the temporary result? If* `operator + ( )` *does the "delete," it may destroy some space that we meant to keep around. Also, in an expression such as* `a + b + c`, *how can the internediate temporaries be freed? The destructors get called, but how can they know to delete the space on the free store?*

These questions lead to answers on two levels. On the implementation level, the answer is "don't do this." One doesn't want to introduce a new degree of complexity (reference counting, garbage collection) to solve a problem that does not exist in the first place (needless structure copies). On a deeper level, we see the characteristic problem of not using C++ as it was intended to be used. It is one's programs one should try to outsmart, not the compiler. As a general, it can safely be assumed that no construct was added to C++ that would not have good efficiency. Return-by-value is no exception.

A follow-up to the first question was posted before I had a chance to respond. The follow-up suggested:

One thing you can do is have `operator +` *have a static local object of class* `M` *that it puts the result into. You can return a reference to this, and after you do the copy*

```
a = b + c
```

to a *from the temp the temp is not referenced anymore, so it is free to be used again whenever it is needed. You don 't have to use new or delete, and in fact the storage for the temp never has to get thrown away.*

The problem with this strategy is that it does not generalize to expressions requiring more than one temporary. For example, to evaluate `a = (b + c) * (d + e);` requires one temporary to hold the subexpression `(b + c)` and another to hold `(d + e)` to finally perform the multiplication. This problem holds even without the explicit use of subexpressions, since the technique makes the program non-reentrant: if `operator +` calls a function that can call `operator +`, the second call to `operator +` can trash the results that the first call is trying to return. This strategy is analogous to the way that an old version of the AT&T C compiler (still running on a frightening number of machines) does structure returns. Such a strategy has long been considered one of the great implementation botches of that compiler.

New users should concern themselves first with the task of mastering object-oriented programming. The language was designed so that most cases can be handled very efficiently by a reasonably smart compiler. Only after understanding how to construct object-oriented programs should one concern themselves with efficiency. At that time, one can properly identify why something is not as efficient as it could be and remedy the problem by cleanly redesigning the application, or pointing out how to fix the compiler.

I would like to thank Doug Lea for his comments on an earlier draft of this article.

Applying the Copy Constructor

Stan Lippman
stanl@fa.disney.com

Learning a new programming language begins with the mundane but necessary commitment of syntax to memory and general mastery of the mechanisms a language supports. How one names, declares, and initializes an object, for example, is something one simply just hunkers down and learns. That done, one might begin to write seemingly trivial declarations such as

```
int j = i;
```

The meaning of this declaration is clear. The programmer has defined a variable `j` set with an initial value copied from the current value of `i`. The behavior of the program (and the degree of triviality), however, cannot be determined until the context of the definition is disclosed. For example, the following program fragment is quite benign and holds no surprises for the programmer:

```
int i = 1024;
// ...
void foo()
{
   int j = i;
   // ...
```

The following program fragment, although equally well defined, introduces an additional function call into the program, which may or may not be significant, but may well surprise the unwary programmer:

```
int i = 1024;
int j = i;
```

Since the value contained within `i` cannot be evaluated by the compiler (it is only available during execution of the program), the program fragment is transformed into something like the following run-time sequence:

```
int i = 1024;
int j = 0;

// ...

// compiler generated initialization function
__sti_i_foo_c() { j = i; }
```

Does this affect the size or efficiency of the program? Yes, although its effect, in isolation, may be quite insignificant. Change the program fragment slightly, however, and suddenly the program's complexity and potential for error increases significantly:

```
extern int i;
int j = i;
```

This new program fragment is transformed during compilation in the same manner it was previously; the difference, of course, lies in the fact that `i` is now presumably defined in some other program module. This program fragment introduces an order dependency on module execution that the language does not currently guarantee! More sophisticated programming is required now to fix the order of module inclusion if the program is to execute correctly.

You may or may not have known this. If you did, no doubt you feel some sense of satisfaction in the recognition of what Andy Koenig might call a C++ pitfall. If you didn't know this, you may wish to re-inspect your code. Having the knowledge allows you to make informed implementation and design decisions. This particular program behavior is implicit in the C++ language model. What the previous few paragraphs have done is make that behavior explicit. This column (and the two previous[1,2]) are an attempt to make explicit the program behavior implicit in the C++ object model with regard to initialization of individual class objects.

SWITCH AND BAIT

Given the following program fragment

```
#include "X.h"

X foo()
{
```

```
    X xx;
    // ...
    return xx;
}
```

one might be tempted to categorically assert that

1. Every invocation of `foo()` returns xx by value.
2. Moreover, that if class `X` defines a copy constructor, that copy constructor is guaranteed to be invoked with each invocation of `foo()`.

The truth of assertion 1, however, is dependent on the definition of class `X`. The truth of assertion 2, although partially dependent on the definition of class `X`, primarily depends on the degree of aggressive optimization provided by your C++ compiler. One might, to turn things on their heads, even go so far as to assert that in a high quality C++ implementation, for non-trivial definitions of class `X`, both assertions are always false. The remainder of this column attempts to explain why.

Memberwise Initialization

Let's modify and expand the program fragment above slightly, as follows:

```
( 1 ) X foo( X x0 ) {
( 2 )    X x1 = x0;
( 3 )    // ...
( 4 )    return x1;
( 5 ) }
( 6 )
( 7 ) void bar() {
( 8 )    X x2;
( 9 )    X x3 = foo( x2 );
( 10 )   // ...
( 11 ) }
```

The declarations of `x1` (line 2) and `x3` (line 9) involve the explicit initialization of one class object with another (`x0` in one instance, the return value of a call of `foo()` in the other). In addition, there are two other less obvious examples of one class being initialized with another: the initialization of the formal argument x0 of foo() with x2 (lines 1 and 9); and the initialization of the return value of foo() with x1 (line 4).

The initialization of one class object with another is spoken of as memberwise initialization. If a copy constructor is present for the class (either declared explicitly or synthesized by the compiler), it is (nearly always) invoked to carry out the initialization. In the following sections, we look at the program transformations required by this invocation (or the optimization to remove the invocation).

THE NECESSARY BACKGROUND

A copy constructor takes as its first argument a reference of its class. Additional arguments may follow, but these must be provided with default values if the constructor is to be treated as a copy constructor. For example,

```
// ok: copy constructor declarations
X::X( const X& );
Y::Y( const Y&, int = 1024 );
```

are both valid copy constructor declarations. The following declaration, however,

```
      // no: not treated as a copy constructor
[a]     Z::Z( const Z&, int );
```

although a valid constructor declaration, is not treated as a copy constructor, since it requires two arguments rather than a single argument of the class type.

If a class does not declare a copy constructor, the compiler synthesizes a default copy constructor if the following two conditions hold:

1. No constructor requiring multiple arguments is declared that has as a first argument a reference to an object of its class. The declaration of [a], above, for example, would inhibit the synthesis of a copy constructor.

2. The class does not exhibit bitwise copy semantics (see Part 1# for a discussion of the four conditions under which bitwise copy semantics do not hold for a class).

For example, given the following class declaration:

```
class X {
public:
   char *pc;
   int val;
};
```

a synthesized copy constructor might look as follows:

```
inline
X::X( const X& xx )
  : pc( xx.pc ),
   val( xx.val ) {}
```

However, since this declaration of class `X` exhibits bitwise copy semantics, the language allows the compiler to forego the synthesis of a copy constructor. The user code initializing one object of class `X` with another, such as

```
X x1 = x0;
```

in this case can be left untransformed.

In the next three sections, we look at the instances where the copy constructor is applied, and at the program transformations that result.

Explicit Initialization

Given the definition

```
X x0;
```

the following three definitions each explicitly initialize its class object with `x0`:

```
void foo_bar() {
  X x1( x0 );
  X x2 = x0;
  X x3 = x( x0 );
  // ...
}
```

The required program transformation is two-fold:

1 Each definition is rewritten with the initialization stripped out.

2. An invocation of the class copy constructor is inserted.

`foo_bar()`, for example, after this straightforward two-fold transformation, might look as follows:

```
// possible program transformation
void foo_bar() {
  X x1;
  X x2;
  X x3;


  // compiler inserted invocations
  // of copy constructor for X
  X( &x1, x0 );
  X( &x2, x0 );
  X( &x3, x0 );
  // ...
}
```

where the call

```
X( &x1, x0 );
```

represents a call of the copy constructor

```
X::X( const X& xx );
```

with the `this` pointer made explicit and initialized with the address of `x1`.*

ARGUMENT INITIALIZATION

The Annotated C++ Reference Manual (ARM)[3] states that passing a class object as an argument to a function (or as that function's return value) is equivalent to the following form of initialization:

```
X xx = arg;
```

where `xx` represents the formal argument (or return value), and `arg` the actual argument. Therefore, given the function

```
void foo( X x0 );
```

and invocation of the form

```
X xx;
```

---

* In an implementation in which references are represented internally as pointers, this call would be further transformed to pass the address of `x0`:

```
X( &x1, &x0);
```

```
// ...
foo( xx );
```

requires that the local instance of x0 be memberwise initialized with xx. The general implementation strategy is to introduce a temporary object, initialize it with a call of the copy constructor, then pass that temporary to the function. For example, our code fragment above would be transformed as follows:

```
// compiler generated temporary
X __temp0;

// compiler invocation of copy constructor
X( &__temp0, xx );

// rewrite function call to take temporary
foo( __temp0 );
```

This transformation, however, is only half-complete as presented. Do you see the remaining problem? Think about it a moment before continuing. (In an ideally typeset article, the next paragraph would appear on the next page, or require a reader go to to some other section of the magazine).

The problem, of course, is that, given foo()'s declaration, the temporary, after being correctly initialized with the class X copy constructor, is then bitwise copied into the local instance of x0! The declaration of foo(), therefore, must also be transformed, changing the formal argument from an object to a reference of class X, as follows:

```
void foo( X& x0 );
```

Were class X to declare a destructor, it would be invoked on the temporary object following the call of foo().

Return Value Initialization

Given the following definition of bar():

```
X bar()
{
  X xx;
  // process xx ...
  return xx;
}
```

the question is how might `bar()`'s return value be copy constructed from its local object xx? Again, think about it a moment, then read on.

Stroustrup's solution in his implementation of `cfront` was a two-fold transformation:

1. Add an additional argument of type reference to the class object. This argument will hold the copy constructed 'return value.'

2. Insert an invocation of the copy constructor prior to the return statement to initialize the added argument with the value of the object being returned.

What about the actual return value, then? A final transformation rewrites the function to have it declare a void return type (that is, not to return anything). The transformation of `bar()`, following this algorithm, looks as follows:

```
// function transformation to reflect
// application of copy constructor

void
bar( X& __result )
{
  X xx;

  // compiler generated invocation
  // of default constructor
  X( &xx );

  // ... process xx

  // compiler generated invocation
  // of copy constructor
  X( &__result, xx );

    return;
}
```

Given this transformation of `bar()`, the compiler is now required to transform each invocation of `bar()` to reflect its new definition. For example,

```
X xx = bar();
```

is transformed into the following two statements:

```
X xx;
bar( xx );
```

while an invocation such as

```
bar().memfunc();
```

might be transformed into

```
// compiler generated temporary
X __temp0;
( bar( __temp0 ), __temp0 ).memfunc();
```

Similarly, if the program were to declare a pointer to function, such as

```
X ( *pf )();
pf = bar;
```

that declaration, too, needs to be transformed:

```
void ( *pf )( X& );
pf = bar;
```

Optimization at the User Level

It was Jonathan Shopiro, I believe, who first noticed a programmer optimization of a function such as `bar()` by defining a "computational" constructor. That is, rather than writing

```
X bar()
{
  X xx;
  // ... process xx using y and z
  return xx;
}
```

which requires `xx` to be memberwise copied into the compiler generated `__result`, Jonathan defined an auxiliary constructor that computed the value of `xx` directly:

```
X bar()
{
  return X( y, z );
}
```

This definition of `bar()`, when transformed, is more efficient:

```
void
bar( X &__result )
{
  X( &result, y, z );
  return;
}
```

since `__result` is directly computed, rather than copied through an invocation of the copy constructor. One drawback to this solution is the possible proliferation of specialized computational constructors. A second drawback is that some processing of an object such as xx is too complex to reasonably accomplish in a single constructor.†

Optimization at the Compiler Level

In a function such as `bar()` where all return statements return the same named value, it is possible for the compiler to itself optimize the function, substituting for the named return value the result argument itself. For example, given our original definition of `bar()`:

```
X bar()
{
  X xx;
  // ... process xx
  return xx;
}
```

`__result` is substituted for xx by the compiler:

```
void
bar( X &__result )
{
  // default constructor invocation
  X( &__result );
```

† See Scott Myers' excellent column[4] for a critique of this solution and the problem of returning objects of a class type in general.

```
    // ... process in __result directly
    return;
}
```

This compiler optimization, sometimes referred to as the function return value optimization, is described in Section 12.1.1c of the ARM (pages 300–303). It was first implemented by Walter Bright in a version of his Zortech C++ compiler (since renamed the Symantec C++ Compiler), and is now generally considered an obligatory C++ compiler optimization.

Although this optimization provides measurable performance increase, there are some programmers who strongly criticize its application. Do you see what might be their complaint? For example, imagine that you had instrumented your copy constructor such that your application depended on the symmetry of its invocation for each destructor invoked on an object initialized by copying. For example,

```
void foo()
{
    // copy constructor expected here
    X xx = bar();
    // ...
    // destructor invoked here
}
```

In this case, the symmetry is broken by the optimization, and the program, albeit faster, fails. Is the compiler at fault here for suppressing the copy constructor invocation? That is, must the copy constructor be invoked in every program situation in which the initialization of an object is achieved through copying?

A requirement such as that would levy a possibly severe performance penalty on a great many programs. For example, although the following three initializations are semantically equivalent:

```
X xx0( 1024 );
X xx1 = X( 1024 );
X xx2 = ( X ) 1024;
```

in the second and third instances, the syntax explicitly provides for a two step initialization:

1. Initialize a temporary object with 1024;

2. Copy construct the explicit object with the temporary.

That is, whereas `xx0` is initialized by a single constructor invocation

```
X( &xx0, 1024 );
```

a strict implementation of either `xx1` or `xx2` results in two constructor invocations, a temporary, and a call to the destructor of `class X` on that temporary:

```
X __temp0;
X( &__temp0, 1024 );
X( &xx1, __temp0 );
~X( &__temp0 );
```

It would have a potentially crippling effect on program efficiency were the language to prohibit the compiler from, wherever possible, optimizing away a copy constructor invocation. Even the programmer who strongly criticized the function return value optimization agreed that he would be dissatisfied with the initialization of `xx1` were it to involve three function invocations whereas `xx0`'s initialization would only take one (and both would end up with the same value).

The language permits the compiler a great deal of leeway with regard to the initialization of one class object with another. The benefit of this, of course, is more efficient code generation. What this means, however, is that as a programmer you cannot instrument a copy constructor to set conditions other member functions (or the destructor) absolutely depend on.

Summary

Application of the copy constructor requires the compiler to more or less transform portions of our program. In particular, returning an object by value for a class in which a copy constructor exists results in profound program transformations both in the definition and use of the associated function. Additionally, where possible, the compiler optimizes away copy constructor invocation. These optimizations are not only permitted by the language, but regarded by many as essential aspects of a high quality compiler. By understanding these transformations, and the likely conditions for copy constructor optimization, programmers can better control the runtime performance of their programs.

References

1. Lippman, S. C++ Primer: Default Constructor Synthesis, *C++ Report*, January, 1994.
2. Lippman, S. C++ Primer: Applying the Copy Constructor—Part 1: Synthesis, *C++ Report*, February, 1994.
3. Ellis, M. and B. Stroustrup, *The Annotated C++ Reference Manual*, Addison-Wesley, 1990.
4. Meyers, S. *Using C++ Effectively: Efficieniy and the Real World*, C++ Report, November/December, 1993.

Section Three

A Focus on Applications

O-O Benefits of Pascal to C++ Conversion

Jim Waldo

SAYING A PRODUCT IS "OBJECT ORIENTED" HAS BECOME AS MUCH A marketing necessity as a claim about the product's design. While it's considered an article of faith that "object oriented" means "good," the claim that an object-oriented product needs to be written in an object-oriented language is still open to debate. To convince people to use an object-oriented language, we need a clear comparison showing that there are things that can be done using an object-oriented language that cannot be accomplished using a non–object-oriented language. Such a comparison, however, is difficult to develop. There are arguably object-oriented systems that are not implemented using an object-oriented language, such as the X intrinsics. Object-oriented programming can also be done using algorithmic languages such as C or even Pascal. But a programmer developing an object-oriented system in a language that does not support the object-oriented paradigm rarely gains the full benefits provided by object-oriented programming.

Converting from Pascal to C++

I learned this first-hand when my group used C++ to reimplement two products written in Pascal. These projects were of particular interest because both were object-oriented in design, even in their Pascal implementations. The changeover provided the opportunity to compare both languages and learn what advantages C++ has over non–object-oriented languages. The products were a user interface management system (UIMS) and a library for building text-based applications. Both had been designed to work within the Apollo proprietary environment using the Apollo system language, a dialect of Pascal with numerous extensions.

The Projects

The UIMS was already shipping as a product (Domain Dialogue) and the text library, called the Text Management Library (TML) was in advanced beta test when management adopted the open systems approach. Development teams were told that both systems were to be "converted" so they would be portable across UNIX platforms and windowing environments. Since the flavor of Pascal in which the systems had been originally implemented was nonstandard, we were forced to pick a new language.

The engineers leading the two projects—Andrew Schulert on UIMS and myself on TML—convinced management that we should use a language that supported the object-oriented paradigm. C++ was selected as the best candidate for being available in the near future on a wide variety of platforms.

The value of the experience is the comparison of the same systems implemented in a standard language and in C++. Since both products were designed in an object-oriented fashion from the start, the designs were not greatly changed during the conversion. While some features were added, the functionality of the Pascal and C++ products was basically identical. The number of independent variables was held to a minimum; what differed in the two versions was the implementation language. Although I was more intimately involved with the reimplementation of TML than with UIMS, there is something to be learned from both. The design of the two products has been discussed before (Schulert and Erf, 1988; Waldo, 1986; Waldo, 1987).

Step One—Comparing the Object Models

The first step in the transition was to revisit the designs of both products to ensure that the object models used were the same as the object model provided by C++. With the UIMS—renamed Open Dialogue in its C++ incarnation—it was clear that the object models differed. Open Dialogue used a multiple inheritance model not supported until C++ 2.0. (When the projects began, C++ 1.1 was the only version available; it finally shipped under version 1.2). Further, Dialogue's model of multiple inheritance is more finely grained than that found even in C++ 2.0. It allows different inheritance graphs for the data contained in an object and in the behavior of the object. Open Dialogue added a mechanism for behavioral inheritance separate from the C++ inheritance mechanism and used the C++ inheritance mechanism for data inheritance (Schulert and Erf, 1988).

With TML, the object models found in the initial design and in C++ were similar. The TML class structure was a single inheritance hierarchy in which a derived object was just like its base with perhaps the addition of some data and some change in behavior.

To implement this notion inside the Pascal version required a considerable amount of code and the specification of a number of conventions users of the library would have to follow. The C++ reimplementation required none of that, since the C++ object model provided it for free within the language. We simply wrote a class definition indicating the new object inherited its attributes from a given superclass.

Step Two—Adding Persistent Objects

We then looked at what C++ didn't provide. The chief problem was that C++ didn't have, and still lacks, any notion of persistent objects—objects exist only in memory at runtime. No mechanism within the language allows saving an object to secondary storage and bringing it back. With a text library, that's an essential capability. No matter how good an editor is, if it isn't possible to save the document, people won't be interested in using it.

Our solution was not elegant, but it worked: each object was stored in a way that allowed it to be self-identifying. In effect, we added a type field to the stored data. All objects that were to be persistent were allocated at runtime to a set of heaps. That way, we could also keep track of the many pointers between the objects and, when saving those objects, convert the pointers into heap identifiers and offsets into the heaps. The heaps then became the lowest level of object that could be saved.

At the next session, when the objects were read in, the type fields allowed the creation of an object of the required type. This approach allowed us to solve some of our problems, but still didn't do everything we wanted. For example, there is still no way to save only part of a document. That will be introduced in a later release. There is an even more serious deficiency in this approach involving new classes that are added by developers as extensions of old classes: they cannot be recognized and handled appropriately by applications bound to versions of the library that were built without the extensions. This is a general problem introduced by class libraries supporting persistent objects. The problem is being worked on by a number of groups, within our organization and elsewhere.

The Paradigm Shift

Coding was an interesting process for me because I was schooled in algorithmic languages and all my work had been done in C and Pascal. Like many people, I looked at C++ and decided that it was just C with some extensions. For about four months I wrote a lot of code. Then, in what I have found is a common occurrence among programmers, I realized that all this code was just C written using C++. It wasn't object-oriented at all.

For example, I had written operations being done on objects—not within that object, but by the things relating to that object. These modules were supposedly operating on anything derived from a particular base class. In fact, within the code were requirements to know particular information about the internals of the object based on the actual derived class of the object. Management wasn't happy when it was recommended that four months' of work be scrapped. To their credit, the managers involved were soon convinced that starting over and doing the work in a correct object-oriented fashion would be better in the long run.

What surprised both the managers and the implementation teams was that doing the work in correct object-oriented fashion proved so efficient that the original production schedule was met. That, too, seems to be a common occurrence among those switching to C++.

My explanation is that, when making the original schedule, my time estimates were based on my experience in developing in non-object-oriented languages. I didn't allow for the concealed learning curve one sees with C++. The original schedule was met because the efficiency of developing in C++ made up for the time it took to learn the Zen of object-oriented programming.

The moral of this experience is not to lose heart after the Zen experience and abandon the object-oriented language. If you switch back to C, your original estimate will probably be correct, and the time it took to get to the Zen point will be the time lost in the schedule. If you keep the faith, you'll have a chance of making your schedule, because you'll be able to develop more efficiently.

Once I had made the paradigm shift and was really writing C++ code, I found some surprising differences in the writing process. I wasn't just writing in a new language—I was writing my code in a qualitatively different way. One example of this was the relative amount of time spent working on the header files and the actual code.

It's All in Your Headers

When I was writing in C or Pascal, I tended to write the header files quickly, almost without thinking about them. I would then spend the vast majority of development time working on the code. Header files tended to have the status of data structure prototypes and would get changed often as the code showed that something different was required.

Writing in C++, I found that most of my time was spent working on the header files. They were no longer simple data structure prototypes—they were prototypes of the full system behavior. They included not only the data structures but the way in which those structures could be manipulated and how they interacted. The header files defined the entire behavior of the system rather than just the data needed to code the system.

Those who are making the switch to C++ and who are accustomed to writing code the way I did (in a straight algorithmic language) may be put off by the seemingly enormous amount of time spent on the header files. However, I found that once I got to the code, it almost wrote itself. The actual functions tend to be very small, so there are many small chunks to write.

In addition, the time spent defining header files results in defining all the interactions between the objects. Concern about side effects is eliminated because there shouldn't be any—everything is self-contained. That's not always true in other languages, even though encapsulation has been championed for years. Other languages don't enforce it. C++ actually makes it harder to use side effects, while in C it's often easier to use side effects than to write another function.

Some Initial Comparisons

The 40,000 lines of the text management library were written in six months by myself and another engineer. The Pascal version, in contrast, amounted to 70,000 lines and took two years to write. The comparison isn't entirely fair, since I already knew all the challenges buried in the algorithms from the first time I wrote the package; but it isn't entirely irrelevant, either, as nearly all the code changed was to make use of the features of C++ that aided in object-oriented programming.

It should also be noted that the C++ code did more. Instead of being tied to Apollo operating and graphics systems, the library was independent of operating and graphics systems. This required adding an abstraction layer for both the operating system and graphics environment and implementing the services needed for that layer for three operating systems (UNIX System V, BSD4.2, and the Apollo Aegis OS) and two different graphics systems (the Apollo native graphics and the X Window System). Even including these extra layers, the C++ version was 40% smaller.

This reduction in code and the enforced object-oriented implementation has made the C++ version of the package much easier to change and maintain than the Pascal version. If something breaks in the C++ implementation, it's easy to determine which object and which function of that object caused the problem. When problems are fixed or changes are made, there are no unknown side effects to cause some other chunk of code to break.

From a developer's perspective, it's much easier to write an object-oriented system in a language like C++, which supports the notion of objects and contains an object model, than in a language that does not support objects. To write an object-oriented system in a non–object-oriented language, a set of conventions must be designed that define what is to be an object in that system. Some way must be designed to enforce (or encourage) and document those conventions.

In an object-oriented language, there already is an object model supported by the language and enforced by the compiler. Programmers are notoriously bad at following conventions. If they can squeeze an extra bit of performance by violating conventions, they will do so. The only way to really ensure that a programmer will follow a convention is to make the penalty for not following the convention sufficiently high. Having a compiler which refuses to generate object code when the conventions are violated is the ultimate encouragement.

The Big Payoff

We experienced significant productivity and efficiency gains simply in moving from Pascal to C++—without making use of any of the code reuse that is supposed to be the real payoff for object-oriented programming. Both systems were developed from scratch before there were any real libraries of code that could be reused. The real payoff will come when programmers begin using available building blocks and concentrating their efforts on just those objects they can do better than anyone else. Such a future requires that the building blocks share a common object model. That is encouraged if the blocks are built using an object-oriented language containing such a model.

Our experience has shown both the power and the limitations of C++ in realizing such a brave new world. An editor was built internally using Open Dialogue and TML. The editor had the usual functionality, including cut and paste, insertion and overstrike, inclusion of files, and word- and character-wrap capabilities. The code for the editor was developed by one engineer in three months and the whole thing was just over 2,000 lines of code. Most of the functionality came easily by using the objects developed in TML and Open Dialogue.

The problems arose in the editor precisely at those places where the C++ object model was lacking in features. Those features were needed by the object libraries and therefore had to be extended. Since Open Dialogue had to implement its own inheritance mechanism, it was difficult to extend the classes provided, since such extensions required learning the extended object model and following a set of conventions to stay within the model. Both object libraries had implemented their own model of persistence. While they were similar, they were not identical, so it was not possible to save the interface objects and the text objects in the same way.

Whether C++ is the wave of the future or just the latest fad remains to be seen. As an implementation language for object-oriented systems, it is already far superior to the standard system implementation languages, which do not support the object-oriented paradigm. To reach its full potential, however, will require developers to begin to reuse the code written by others. To achieve this goal will require that organizations overcome their "not invented here" orientation and begin using object libraries. It will also require a fleshing out of the object model contained in, and enforced by, the language to ensure that reuse is not only possible but easier than reinventing.

Bibliography

Jensen, Preben Fisher and Peter Juhl, 1990, "Writing a Gateway in C++," Proceedings of 1990 USENIX C++ Conference.

Russo, Vincent F., Peter W. Madany, and Roy H. Campbell, 1990, "C++ and Operating Systems Performance: A Case Study," Proceedings of 1990 USENIX C++ Conference.

Schulert, Andrew and Kate Erf, 1988, "Open Dialogue: Using an Extensible Retained Object Workspace to Support a UIMS," Proceedings of 1988 USENIX C++ Conference.

Waldo, James, 1986, "Modeling Text as a Hierarchical Object," Proceedings of 1986 Summer USENIX Conference

Waldo, James, 1987, "Using C++ to Develop a WYSIWYG Hypertext Toolkit," Proceedings of the 1987 USENIX C++ Workshop.

Zweig, Jonathan M. and Ralph E. Johnson, 1990, "The Conduit: A Communication Abstraction in C++," Proceedings of the 1990 USENIX C++ Conference.

A C++ Template-Based Application Architecture

Tasos Kontogiorgos
komtot@goldfinger.eg.gs.com

Michael Kim
mkim@goldfinger.eg.gs.com

Developing complex information systems applications in C++ has often been an experience of re-inventing the wheel. One of the reasons for this phenomenon is a lack of architectural solutions within the language that provide a foundation for IS application developers.

Tapar is an application architecture for building complex IS applications using C++. It provides an architecture for the following:

- Persistent storage of C++ objects on a relational database
- Compile-time type checked interface to the persistent storage and value management for application data types
- Memory management of C++ objects
- Mapping between object and relational models.

Persistent storage of C++ objects on a relational database allows applications developed in Tapar to leverage the mature relational database technology. There are two issues to be considered:

1. Object (logical) model to physical model mapping
2. Transaction control.

The application data type value management addresses the issues of value validation, default value generation, and compile time protection from possibly dangerous assignments. For example, Tapar will cause the compiler to issue an error if a potentially uninitialized member is assigned to a variable.

The C++ object memory management functionality ensures that only one instance of a persistent object is kept in memory and is properly shared.

A number of commercial packages that address these problems exist,[6,7] and they are very strong in some areas. However, some of them deliver their solutions by extending the C++ language or by employing code generators. Obviously, the latter approach is more acceptable albeit with problems.

Tapar does not use any facilities other than those provided by the C++ language and simple macro expansions. It maintains the C++ data model of static name resolutions thereby avoiding any sort of run time symbolic manipulations.

We will describe the three layers of Tapar. These are the object layer, the process layer and persistence.

OBJECT LAYER

The object layer supports value management. Objects have members (attributes) and members have values—the member values. We define the state of an object to be the set of all its member values. Given a class `T` we define its state space to be the set of all states that can be assigned to its objects. A certain subset of the state space of `T` is called the consistent state space and an object whose state is a member of this set is called a consistent object. A class `T` defines its consistent state space via a predicate:

```
int T::validate() const;
```

which determines if an object is consistent.

We want members to use types with properties such that we can use standard C++ capabilities to make assertions about the state of an object (e.g., consistent, based on the states of the individual member values). For this, we invoke the copy constructor of an object, which in turn invokes the copy constructors of its members.[1] If some of its members are in a erroneous state they emit errors that are interpreted to define the object state. The advantage of this method is that no explicit programming is required by an application programmer. One disadvantage is the construction of a temporary object.

Some of Tapar's elementary types are described in the following sections.

Mnd<T>

Some object members are considered mandatory. For an object to have meaning, these members must have values assigned to them. An example is dateOfBbirth in the class Human. For these members we provide the template Mnd<T>. We call T the underlying type. For a Mnd<T> the existence of its value is tested by the predicate:

```
int IsValue(const Mnd<T> &);
```

If a mandatory is empty, its copy constructor emits an error. Also, if a mandatory has a value which fails the test of being equal to itself then an error is emitted as well. This ensures that every mandatory member of an object is set and has a valid value (otherwise the object couldn't have been constructed), thus we allow a cast from a mandatory to its underlying type:

```
Mnd<T>::operator T () const;
```

This is not the case for the next type.

Opt<T>

Unlike mandatory object members, optional members do not need to have a value for the object to be meaningful. An example is the telephone number telNum in the class Human. Optional members are supported with the type Opt<T>. Opt<T> differs from Mnd<T> in that its copy constructor does not emit errors if it is empty. In addition the cast to its underlying type is undefined, to protect the application programmer from accidentally using an uninitialized value. The underlying value can be obtained with the function:

```
T IfValue(Opt<T>& v, T dflt);
```

which returns the value of v if one exists, or the default value dflt.

Example:

```
class Human {
public:
  Mnd<Date> dateOfBbirth;
  Opt<String> telNum;
};

void foo(Human h) {
  Date dt;
  String t,q;
  dt = h.dateOfBirth;  // Ok
```

```
    t = h.telNum;                   // compile  error
    q = IfValue(h.telNum,""); // Ok
}
```

`Code<E>`

Some members have values drawn from a finite domain of discrete integer values. In C++ this is expressed by an enumeration `E`. `Code<E>` supports conversions to and from `String`, code iterators, error emission on copy construction of an erroneous `Code<E>` (which can be created as a result of converting an illegal `String` value), etc.

PROCESS LAYER

Tapar distinguishes between two types of application objects: C-objects, or consistent objects, and T-objects, or temporary objects.

A C-object is a validated object known by its object identifier OID.[2] Given a class `T`, the OID of `T` is of type `ObjectID<T>`. The mapping between C-objects and their OIDs is one-to-one, which means that a C-objects has exactly one OID, which cannot be shared by any other C-object. The read-only members of a C-object are accessed via a class called `Ref<T>`,[2] which is constructed with an OID.

On the other hand, T-objects are not necessarily validated, which implies that their state can be undefined. There is no mapping between T-objects and their OIDs, such as the one that exists for C-objects. T-objects are managed by the class `Gen<T>`, which provides access to all public constant or volatile members of `T`.

The reason for this classification is the following. A C-object represents the current state of an application object, and it is made available to a number of functions some of which will make application decisions or update a database. Thus the objects made available to them should always be validated. However, these objects may need to be updated during the course of one process. Updating a C-object can only occur as an atomic operation with valid before and after states, which would be unfeasible if the volatile members of a C-object were accessible. This is the case because it is generally impossible for an object to validate its state after one single member is set, because of intra-object member dependencies. Thus we introduce the T-objects, which can be brought to the desired state, and then be promoted into a C-object. T-object promotion results to either a creation of a new C-object or the update of an existing C-object. Naturally the promotion will fail if the T-object is not consistent.

We will describe some of the process level objects.

ObjectID<T>

Every application class `T` has an OID of type `ObjectID<T>`. An OID may have one or more members. Its purpose is C-object identification within one process. To enable efficient sorting, searching, etc. an OID supports total ordering by defining the operators `==` and `<`. OIDs can be used for selecting collections of objects. This activity is supported by the function:

```
int match(const ObjectID<T> & lhs,
  const ObjectID<T> & rhs);
```

An OID serves not only the class `T` but all the classes derived from `T` as well. For this reason, in Tapar, we insist that an application class `T` be derived from its OID, thus causing all derived classes to inherit the base OID:

```
class ObjectID<Human>  {
  Mnd<String>    ssn;
};

class Human : public ObjectID<Human>
{...};
```

OIDs are also used to express relational dependencies. Consider the classes `Company` and `Employee` with the obvious one-to-many relationship. By providing the `ObjectID<Company>` with an assignment operator from an `ObjectID<Employee>` we allow the constructors of employees to find and notify the appropriate company.

ObjectTag<T>

`ObjectTag<T>` is a class derived from `ObjectID<T>` that provides a `String` description of an object. It can be very useful when we want to quickly fetch from a database a collection of object tags, and based on their descriptions decide to fetch some of the actual objects.

Ref<T>

`Ref<T>` is an object constructed with an OID that provides access to the public read only interface of the class `T` for a C-object by overloading the `-> operator`:

```
const T * Ref<T>::operator->() const;
```

`Ref<T>` implements referential transparency for the `T` objects within one process.

A `Ref<T>` maintains a pointer to the C-object it references. The referenced C-object is always aware of the `Ref<T>` objects that point to it. The actual type of the referenced object may be (and usually is) a class derived from `T`. These back-pointers allow generic implementation of arbitrary dependency graphs. For instance, an `Account` that holds `Refs` to its securities can be automatically notified once a security updates its state.

Gen<T>

`Gen<T>` creates and manages T-objects. It is similar to `Ref<T>` in that it maintains a `T` (or `T` derived) pointer but it provides read/write access to the members of `T` by overloading the `->` `operator;` `T * Gen<T>::operator->();`

Note that it returns a `T*` instead of the `const T*` returned by `Ref<T>`. `Gen<T>` supports promotion of T-objects to C-objects with the functions:

```
int Gen<T>::create();
```

which creates a new C-object and

```
int Gen<T>::update();
```

which updates the C-object with a new value.

Both of these functions perform a validation prior to any attempt to transfer state.

ERRORS

Since only a few commercial C++ compilers support exceptions, we need an alternate way to create and deliver errors. In Tapar we create errors with the class `Error` and deliver them with the class `ReturnCode`.

The class `Error` is a smart pointer to objects of the reference counted class `BaseError` that forms a root for user derived (if necessary) error classes. A `BaseError` is considered processed if one of its member functions is called, otherwise it is pending.

When an error is returned from a function, it is converted to a `ReturnCode`, a class very similar to the class `Error`:

```
ReturnCode foo()
{
  Error e;
  ...
  return e;
}
```

The conversion of an `Error e` to a `ReturnCode` annotates `e` with the history of all pending errors. Thus we can create error frames independent of the stack frames in one thread of execution. This is very useful particularly for functions that cannot return errors (e.g., constructors). `Error` frames are implemented by a class `CatchError` that provides a function `ReturnCode CatchError::get_error()` that returns the history of currently pending errors:

```
void foo() {
  CatchError c;
  // Start Error Frame
  ...
  // End Error Frame
  Error e = c.get_error();
}
```

Col<T>

Objects can be organized into a collection with the class `Col<T>`, i.e. `Col<double>`, `Col<Mnd<String>>`, `Col<ObjectID<Human>>`, `Col<Gen<Human> >` etc. One can insert or remove objects from a collection. The class `Col<T>` has a `length()` and it supports direct access to its elements using the `[] operator`:

```
T & Col<T>::operator[](int);
```

Collection elements are acted upon via functors.

Funct<T>

A functor, or procedural object,[3] is an object derived from the class:

```
template <class T> class Funct {
public:
  virtual void Func<T>::operator()
        (const T&) = 0;
  virtual int terminate();
};
```

Therefore a functor `f` is an object that can be used as a function

```
T t;
f(t);
```

Also a functor may have local state:

```
class Print : public Funct<ObjectID<T> > {
  ostream & out;

public:
  Print(ostream& o): out(o){}
  void operator()(const ObjectID<T> id){
    out << id;
  }
};
```

A collection `Col<T>` supports the function:

```
void Col<T>::apply(Funct<T> & f);
```

which applies the functor `f` to all the collection elements until either the elements are exhausted or the function `terminate()` is called for the functor `f`.

Functors become very useful in the context of database set processing by allowing the programmer to express what should happen to an individual member of a collection regardless of the iteration method. Functors can be used to implement pipes. Consider:

```
template <class T>
class Pipe:public Funct<T> {
  Col<T>  _c;

public:
  Pipe() {}
  void put(T & t) { _c.put(t);}
  operator Col<T>()& { return _c;}
};
```

and

```
template <class T>
Col<T> & operator|(Col<T> & col,
    Pipe<T> & f) {
  col.apply(f);
  return f;
}
```

Pipes can be very useful in expressing database set processing expressions such as:

```
Col<ObjectID<Security> > sec_ids;
sec_ids | DbRead | GetPrice | DbWrite;
```

where DbRead, GetPrice, and DbWrite are appropriate pipes.

Persistence

Tapar supports object persistence using SYBASE,[4] a relational database management system. The interface is based on the class DbAdaptor<T>. This is a virtual base class that defines a generic public interface. Actual adaptors, which are derived from DbAdaptor<T>, implement this interface by considering the individual class requirements as well as the actual data access mechanism that is employed.

Although it is feasible to implement a generic mechanism that interfaces C++ classes to a relational database, in many cases this mechanism will be proven suboptimal. For this reason we allow a high degree of flexibility in how adaptors are implemented. Typically, an adaptor is developed by the cooperation of a relational database architect who maintains the database schema and the class designer who maintains the class definition. The end result shields the application programmer from the esoteric details employed in the adaptor implementation.

A further degree of flexibility is introduced by parametrizing the adaptors based on the data access mechanism they use. For SYBASE such data access methods are DB-Library,[5] UniSQL[6] Persistence,[7] etc. Thus the application programmer creates adaptors of the following class:

```
template <class T, Access A>
class DbAdpt<T,A> : public DbAdaptor<T>
{...};
```

where A can be DbLib, Persistence, UniSQL, etc.

Database adaptors are further subtyped to read only and write only adaptors. These types can optimize certain database access and transaction control operations. Also database adaptors can be easily modified to provide character stream adaptors which can be used to implement GUI interfaces.[13]

In the following we will describe the methodology we have used to implement database adaptors using DB-Library that is a fairly low-level data access mechanism.

The implementation of the database adaptor is based upon the ability to create an object descriptor that allows us to transfer data from/to an object in a generic manner. Object descriptors provide an object meta model. Later on we will show how we derive the class meta model. The database publishes its own meta model as the database schema. An adaptor defines a mapping between the database meta model (schema) and the object meta model (object descriptor). This mapping is referred to as a physical-to-logical mapping. Tapar allows these mappings to be defined statically at compile time by using solely techniques within the C++ language.

In the following we will describe briefly the public interface of a database adaptor, then we will show how an object descriptor can be defined and then we will describe the physical-to-logical mappers.

Database Adaptor

Given an application root class `T` the class `DbAdaptor<T>` provides an interface to the database. Classes derived from `T` are serviced by the root adaptor.

A database adaptor can be used to fetch values from the database and deliver them into a `Gen<T>`. The delivery is always polymorphic. This means that after a read, the T-object referenced by the `Gen<T>` may be replaced by another object. The type of this object is derived from `T` and it is determined by the data read from the database.

The database adaptor can also be used to update the database via an OID. When inserting or updating, the OID should correspond to a C-object, whose values are transferred to the database. This is not necessary for deletions.

Database adaptors are constructed with objects of the class `DbConnection`. Database connections provide access to the low-level interface of the database and they are beyond the scope of this article. We mention them here because of their involvement with the transaction control. In the following we will assume the definitions:

```
ObjectID<T>       id;
Gen<T>            g;
DbAdapt<T> adpt;
Col<ObjectID<T> > col_ids;
```

Fetching

Fetching is implemented with two functions:

```
adpt.find(id);
adpt.get(g);
```

`Find` locates the object in the database, and `get` fetches its value into `g`. One may further decide to promote `g`:

```
g.create();
```

creating thus a new C-object.

SCANNING

There are two ways to scan the database. One can provide an SQL expression or have an SQL expression written automatically out of an example. The example is a partially filled `Gen<T>` that we want to match against the database:

```
char * sql;
Gen<T> g;
...
adpt.scan(sql);
```

or

```
adpt.scan(g);
```

After the database is scanned, we can obtain the results by executing the function `next()` in a loop:

```
while(adpt.next(g)) {
// do something with g
}
```

UPDATING, DELETING, AND INSERTING

Updating, deleting, and inserting are supported with the functions `update()`, `remove()`, and `insert()` correspondingly by passing an OID. Obviously, only leaf classes can and should affect the database. Otherwise, object validation would have been meaningless.

SET PROCESSING

In the context of processing database query results the term set processing refers to dealing with collections rather than using set theory. Some examples in this category follow. The `next()` loop after a `scan()` can be replaced by

```
adpt.CachCollection(col_ids);
```

which receives the values scanned, creates, or updates the corresponding C-objects and updates the collection of OIDs, with the ones that were successfully processed.

Given a collection of OIDs one can fetch the values of their corresponding objects by

```
adpt.FindAndCach(col_ids);
```

Some adaptors may decide to support this function with a simple loop over the individual OIDs of the collection and invoke the `find()` and `get()` for each one of them. Other adaptors may decide to employ other strategies that optimize the database accesses. In either case, the application programmer is shielded from these considerations.

Other set processing functions use OID collections for inserting, removing, updating, etc.

Transaction Control

Transaction control is provided by the class `UoW`, or Unit of Work. A `UoW` is created for a database connection. Its construction initiates a database transaction. After a `UoW` is created its state is considered to be open. An open transaction can be closed by either committing with the function `UoW::commit()` or aborting with the function `UoW::rollback()`. It is an error to call either of these functions on a closed unit of work. It is also an error to close a unit of work when other newer (nested) units of work are still open. This error will result in aborting all nested units of work. The destructor of an open unit of work closes it by calling `UoW::rollback()`.

Object Meta-Model

Most systems that interface C++ with databases rely either on extensions of the language or on code generators.[6–9] Our approach is to create simple macros that guide the C++ compiler to synthesize[10] the code required to provide the object descriptions necessary for interfacing the database.

Member Descriptor

Assume we have an application class `T` with a member of type `X`:

```
class T {
   X x;
};
```

We want to define the signature of a function that moves data from or to an object:

```
typedef void (*MvVal)(void * obj, void * val, Dir);
```

where

```
enum Dir { from, to}
```

For our example we can define:

```
void f(void *o, void *v, Dir d) {
  T * tp = (T *)o;
  X * xp = (X *)v;
  if (d == to)
    tp->x = (*xp);
  else
    *xp = tp->x;
}
```

We define a class that binds together the name of a member with the corresponding `MvVal`:

```
class MemberDscr { public:
  String name();
  MvVal mvVal();
}
```

We define the following template:

```
MemberDscr (*MDF)();
int FC;
void F(MemberDscr);
template <class X, MDF f>
class Mbr : public X {
public:
  Mbr() {if (FC) F(f());}
};
```

This template has two interesting properties. It has the same memory layout as that of the class `X` and under some condition `FC!=0` the empty constructor will supply the function `F()` with a member descriptor. The function `F` then may collect the member descriptors to implement a meta model.

If an application class `T` has members of types based on the class `Mbr<X,f>`, then we can construct a description for that class, simply by setting `FC=1` and creating an empty `T` instance that will enable us to collect all its member descriptors. This is possible because we rely on the C++ compiler to synthesize[10] the code required for traversing the default constructors of the all members in a class. Otherwise, we would have to rely on the application programmer to provide this code or use a code generator.

One simplification we made is the signature of `MvVal`. In reality this function does not use `void*` arguments to move values but another class called `MemoryRegion`, which is typed and is supported with polymorphic assignments from and to application types. This class implements the conversions from the database native types to the application ones. Also, the actual `MemberDscr` class is richer in properties and enables compile time checks to ensure that the database types are compatible with the application ones. This topic however lies beyond the scope of this article.

The application class developer is free to intermix `Mbr` template based members with members of other types. The `Mbr`-based ones would be interfaced to the database automatically. We have found this methodology more user friendly than the code generation one.

OBJECT DESCRIPTOR

The collection of all member descriptors of an object defines its meta-model, which we call object descriptor. A member of an object descriptor can be identified either by name (which gives us a limited symbolic run time access to the object structure and of course requires some kind of name conflict resolution) or by the value of the `MvVal`, which uniquely identifies a member of a given class and is a compile-time constant that can be used to derive statically defined physical-to-logical mappers.

Object descriptors annotate the `Type_info` associated with the typeid of every application class. A `DbAdaptor<T>` forms the union of all object descriptors for the `T` derived types. This union is used by the physical-to-logical mapper.

PHYSICAL-TO-LOGICAL MAPPER

The database schema can be transformed into a C++ class called `Schema` whose members are classes corresponding to tables. These classes have members that correspond to the table columns. Thus we create a static C++ representation of the database schema. `Schema` allows us to statically map a selected number of columns form a table to a set of member descriptors for a class. This mapping is implemented by a class called `Row`. A set of rows defines the physical-to-logical mapper. A mapper associates individual member descriptors with table columns. A mapper also identifies the typeid implied from a set of database results.

PROCESSING DATABASE RESULTS

After the execution of a query, the database sends back the results in a form that makes it possible to associate datums with column names and their corresponding types. The mapper can bind these datums to individual member descriptors and provide the typeid implied by the values of these datums. Then the database adaptor simply enacts these bindings to transfer data from the datums via the object descriptor associated with the typeid to the receiving object memory. At this point the `DbAdaptor<T>` and the `Gen<T>` cooperate by manipulating the object pointer to point to an object of the class defined by the typeid.

Databases usually have ways to indicate the absence of a value in a column. This information is passed back to the `Mnd<T>` or `Opt<T>` members.

CONCLUSION

Tapar has been used to deliver one IS application successfully, and we are in the process of developing another Tapar-based, large-scale IS application. We expect that new applications will clearly indicate to us the areas that need improvement.

We have encountered a number of problems with the existing C++ compilers and their template implementation. Apart from compiler bugs, the template instantiation time has been a problem. Eventually we had to rely on manual instantiations and our experience in time savings has been similar to the one reported by Stroustrup.[12] We are looking forward to a template instantiation operator.

ACKNOWLEDGMENTS

Jacob Friedman initiated many of the ideas we have presented in this article. His advice was crucial, especially in the area of the database application development.

Shaun Codner and Brian Kolaci have given us valuable suggestions.

REFERENCES

1. Lippman S. Applying the copy constructor, *C++ Report,* March 1994.
2. Cattell R. *Object Data Management,* Addison-Wesley, 1994.
3. Shopiro J. Seminar view-graphs.
4. Sybase, Inc. *SYBASE Reference Manual,* Emeryville, CA, 1993.
5. Sybase, Inc. *DB_Library/C Reference Manual,* Emeryville, CA, 1993.
6. UniSQL, Inc. *UniSQL/X Database Management System Product Description,* Austin, TX, 1993.

7. Persistence, Inc. *Persistence Technical Overview,* San Mateo, CA, 1993.
8. Grossman M. Object I/0 and runtime type information via automatic code generation in C++, *Journal of Object-Oriented Programming,* July 1993.
9. ACM OOPSLA '88, *ET++-An Object-Oriented Application Framework in C++,* San Diego, Sept. 1988.
10. Lippman S. Default constructor synthesis, *C++ Report,* Jan.1994.
11. Stroustrup B., and Lenkov D. *Runtime type identification for C++,* C++ Report, March 1992.
12. Stroustrup, B. *The Evolution of C++,* Addison-Wesley, 1994.
13. Kontogiorgos T, *GUIs and Atom Iterators—C++ Objects and GUI,* C++ World 93, Dallas, 1993.

An Object-Oriented Framework for I/O

Bill Berg
bilber@vnet.ibm.com

Ed Rowlance
rowlance@pipeline.com

Input/output is a natural area for the application of object-oriented design and programming. The domain contains a wealth of physical items (buses, cards, devices, media) and logical entities (connections, protocols, buffers, messages) that are easy to pick up and grab as objects.

As the IBM Rochester laboratory approached the task of moving the AS/400 operating system from the proprietary-based processor architecture used since its introduction to a new RISC-based architecture, we realized there would be a significant number of changes required in the lower layers. We had also become very aware of some of the limitations of the old software design related to I/O support:

- Dependence on physical addressing for identication of hardware
- Usage of type and model information for checking characteristics
- Poor localization of software impact when adding new I/O features or hardware

Along with these limitations, there was a general sense that we needed to start down a path that would allow us to open our I/O to vendor attachment. We were no longer able to keep up with the rapid additions of new hardware and software technologies using only in-house development, and needed to get on a path where the addition of I/O support to the system by other companies, or at least IBM sites, was possible.

In 1990, the IBM lab in Rochester had decided on C++ as the strategic language for internal development and had began building on our experience with object-based programming (abstract data types). As we looked at the requirements and amount of code change required to meet them, we decided that we needed to rewrite significant portions of the code that would support I/O on the new machine. Object-oriented design and C++ were the logical choice for development. This article describes the framework that resulted from this effort.

We take our definition of framework from Booch[2]: "A framework is a collection of classes that provide a set of services for a particular domain; a framework thus exports a number of individual classes which clients can use or adopt."

Currently, support for tape, optical and DASD devices is included in the first release, and we will be able to use the framework to add future I/O classes and subclasses to the system. To date there are 225 KLOC of C++ and 2300 classes in the framework.

This article covers the main elements of our framework:

- Hardware drivers
- I/O drivers
- Hardware resource information

We will also discuss our experiences in introducing an object-oriented framework into the existing procedural operating system and will touch on some of the key idioms that we made use of in the project.

Background

The existing operating system for the AS/400 can be divided into two large pieces, OS/400 and the system licensed internal code (SLIC; see Figure 1). SLIC supports an architected interface for OS/400 called the *machine interface* (MI), which is effectively a very-high-level instruction set. It is this MI instruction set that is targeted by the compilers, rather than the actual hardware instructions. It is up to a translator that is part of SLIC to translate these MI programs into a combination of hardware instructions and SLIC calls.

The hardware structure for I/O on AS/400 consists of a proprietary bus with high function adapters attached to it called *I/O processors* (or IOPs). All IOPs have at least one processor on them, running their own internal operating systems and specialized adapter hardware onboard for attachment of devices. Components of the operating system in SLIC communicate with components of the IOP's operating system via logical connections that are provided by a

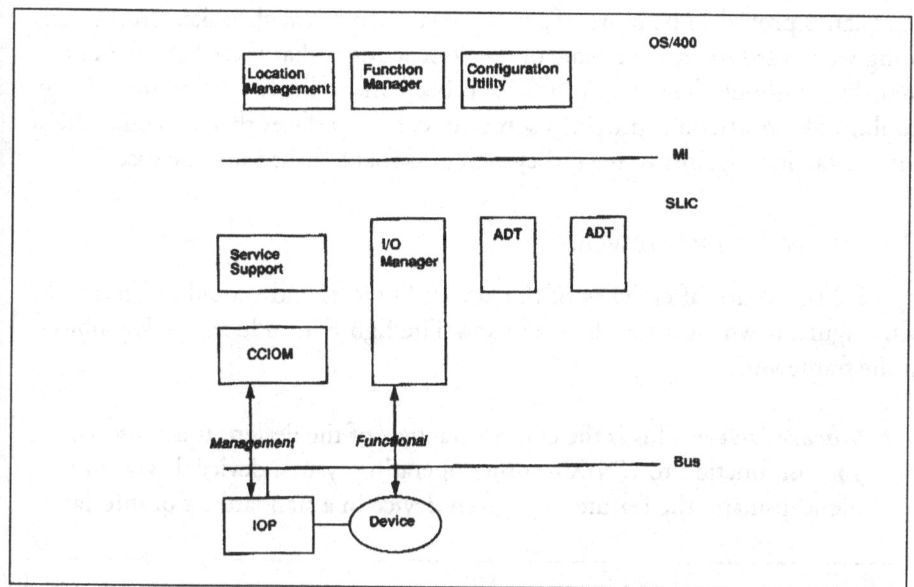

FIGURE 1. *AS/400 internal architecture before introduction of I/O framework.*

transport mechanism component. There can be several functional connections between SLIC and an IOP existing at one time but only one management connection per IOP.

AS/400 is an object-*based* system. The objects in the AS/400 are more precisely *abstract data types* or ADTs from the MI perspective. Each hardware device that can be used by OS/400 is represented by an ADT that is intended to abstract the hardware. ADTs are provided for devices, controllers, networks, and sessions. From an MI view, these are real ADTs that consist of data and code. Below the MI however, they are implemented as global data structures that SLIC components are free to read and modify at will.

Our design was bounded at the top by the MI, and to some degree by the usage of the ADTs within SLIC. Since most of the SLIC legacy code remains procedural, the I/O framework was required to work well with that code. We gained significant experience with interfacing procedural code with new OO/C++ code. In most cases, this involved providing legacy interfaces into the OO framework. While we could not make any extensive changes in the MI interface in order to avoid massive customer and IBM code impacts, we were able to add several new machine instructions and modify others to remove hardware dependencies from the interface.

At the bottom of the design we were bounded to some degree by the architectures that define how we interface to IOPs and devices. In general, these boundaries proved to be more of a warm coat than a straightjacket. In the early going we tended to chafe at some of the "restrictions" that these boundaries created, but without them we would have been more likely to run into design trouble. The restrictions provided some concrete interfaces that we could check our abstractions against to see if they were reasonable in at least one case.

Overview of Framework

Figure 2 shows an "after" view of the key I/O objects and should be contrasted with Figure 1, which is the "before" view. The figure introduces the key objects in the framework:

Hardware Driver. This is the core abstraction of the design. It is quite analogous in function to UNIX or other operating system device drivers in that it encapsulates the features of a given device in a standard set of interfaces.

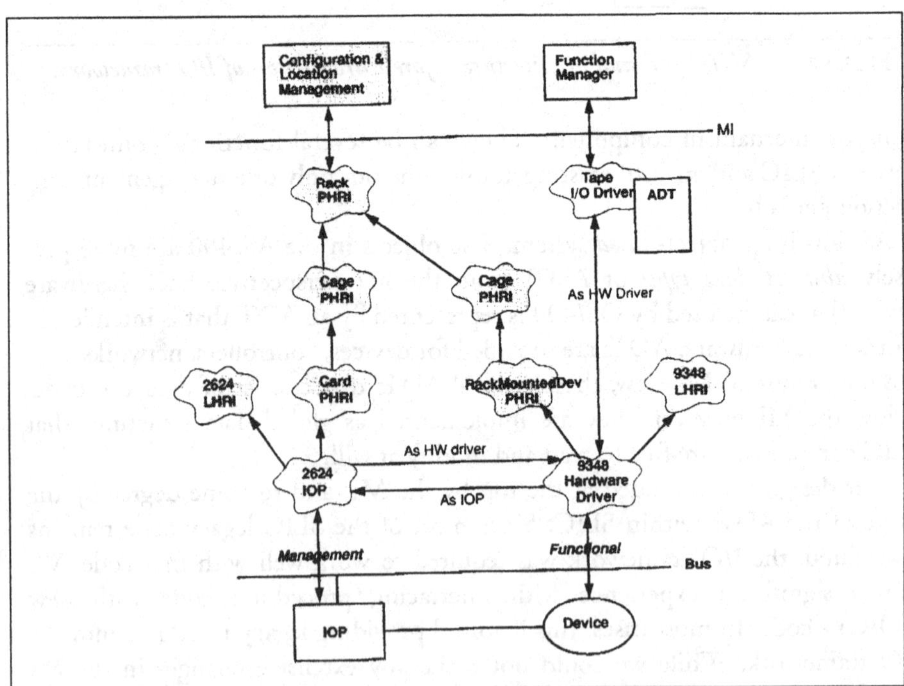

Figure 2. *High-level view of I/O framework. The arrows in the figure indicate "uses" relationships. In some cases, they are labeled with "As xxxx" to indicate the class that they view the object as. Objects that provide a support role are shaded to differentiate those that are in the functional path.*

I/O Driver. This allows the hardware driver to be operating system independent. While the hardware driver looks down at the hardware, the I/O Driver looks up at the operating system. In an operating system with multiple personalities, there would likely be a subclass of I/O driver per personality, but only a single hardware driver per device.

Hardware resource information (HRI) objects provide information that is needed for configuration and service. They are the primary mechanism that allowed us to remove the hardware dependencies from the MI. There are two kinds of HRI:

1. Logical HRI (LHRI) objects provide information about the functionality of the hardware attached to the system.
2. Packaging HRI (PHRI) objects provide information about the packaging for a given piece of hardware.

We will go into some detail on each of these key objects in the rest of this article.

There are other objects in the framework that perform a supporting role. In general, clients that are just doing I/O on the system are unaware of these objects. They are included for completeness, but will be described in less detail (see "Support Staff: IOPs, Statistics, Service" later in the article).

Figure 3 shows the abstract relationship of our framework to the rest of the system. The framework has two clients:

1. The clients that will use the framework. In the "AS/400 centric" view of our framework, these clients are the I/O drivers, a smattering of SLIC components, and the MI instructions that will deal with the HRI domain. If we extend the view and postulate a "portable framework," we see that

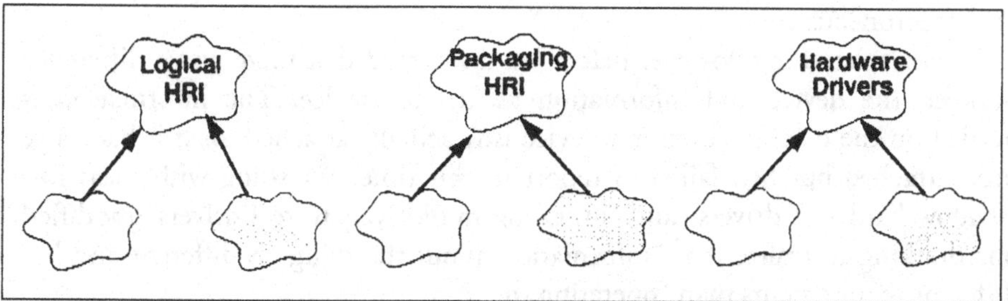

FIGURE 3. *Framework clients. The shaded boxes indicate classes added by a framework extender.*

we have a difficulty with the HRI objects, since the new system may not have anything that interfaces to them. If we stick with the localized view, the clients at this level are protected from changes in the I/O framework by the abstract base classes that interface at this level. We can tell how good a job we did by how much new function can be added to the bottom of the framework while still keeping them protected.

2. The framework extenders or inheritors. The clients at this level are programmers that aim to extend the framework by adding new sub-classes to support new I/O facilities. How easily they can accomplish this is one of the measures of the success of the framework.

Doing the Work: Hardware Drivers

Hardware driver objects are the core of the new design. They are the abstract view of a piece of hardware that we want to provide attachment for, and the base class for a given type of I/O gear must provide the "essence" of that kind of I/O gear as it's interface. It is the hardware driver that provides "open, close, read, write" for a given type of I/O gear in a general enough way so as to be a stable abstraction, but in a specific enough manner so that all the essential characteristics of that type of device are provided.

Our work with the I/O framework is in agreement with the observation of Booch[2]: "In our experience, the design of classes and objects is an incremental, iterative process. Frankly, except for the most trivial abstractions, we have never been able to define a class exactly right the first time."

From the current perspective it is hard to believe that we were once so foolish to believe that the hardware driver would be the only abstraction needed to model a piece of hardware. At one level, the fact that the existing procedural I/O manager components did more than support a single device probably led us to that erroneous view.

It wasn't very long however before we discovered that there was a difference between the device and information about the device. The information is needed on the machine even if a device isn't actually attached, or if it had once been attached but had failed to report in this time. Wrestling with ideas like "shadow hardware drivers" and "mutating minidrivers to real drivers" modified our thinking to realize that "information about the thing" is different and has different requirements than "operating the thing."

As a general rule, we discovered that when we ran into a fairly difficult problem with a class, the solution often involved the creation of a new class structure that was related to the class with the problem. HRI came first after hardware

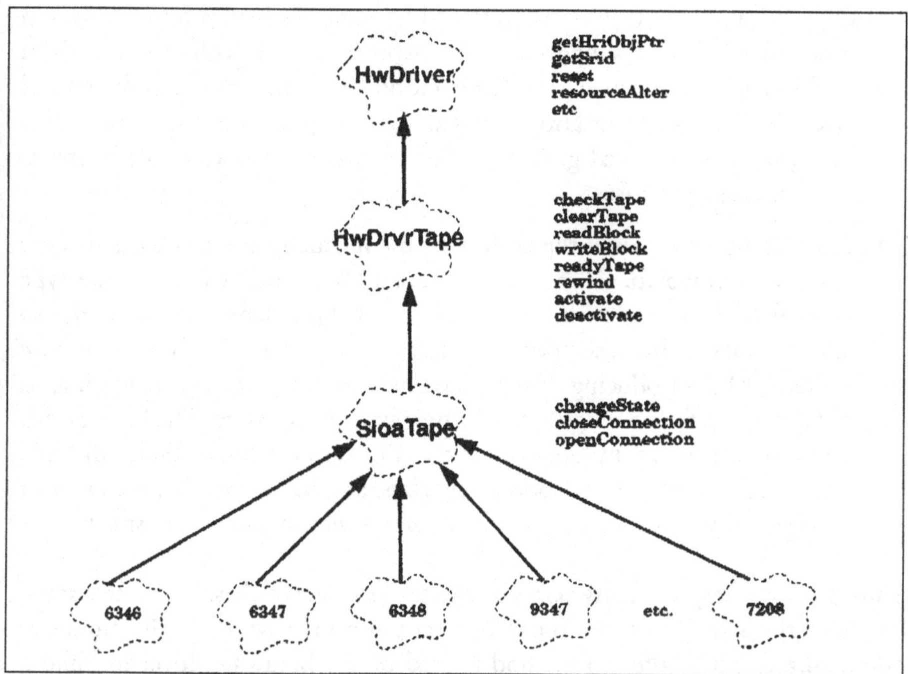

FIGURE 4. *Class hierarchy for hardware driver. A sampling of methods is shown next to the class where they are first defined. The numbered classes at the bottom of the hierarchy are the concrete classes.*

drivers, and we then later split that into packaging and logical subclasses as we discovered that the requirements of the packaging information were related, yet different enough from the logical information to warrant a new class.

A class hierarchy diagram for a typical hardware driver class (in this case `Tape`) is shown in Figure 4. A discussion of each base class follows:

- All hardware driver classes inherit from the `HwDriver` abstract base class. The abstraction presented at this level is "a piece of I/O hardware." The methods defined here are mostly administrative in nature and the only clients of this class are other hardware drivers.
- `HwDrvrTape` is the class that is useful to a tape client. It is this class that is used by the `Tape` I/O Driver, which is the chief client. The methods defined here are intended to provide "all the functions you need and no more" for doing I/O to tape.
- Storage I/O Architecture `Tape` (`SioaTape`) is not visible to clients. Since all of the tape drives that are currently attached to the AS/400 follow a

single architecture (SIOA) from the SLIC view, we have a lot of common code for all drivers supported. `SioaTape` is a "code collector class." In addition to the "normal" implementation of all public methods, several protected methods are also provided that support the public methods. This provides increased granularity for concrete classes to override operations in exception cases.

- The numbered classes at the bottom of the hierarchy are the classes that are actually instantiated. These concrete classes are typed based on the type number of the device itself. One of the original problems that we set out to solve was one of hardware dependence. It is somewhat of a paradox that we "solved" it by introducing a guaranteed hardware dependency of needing to add a subclass for every instance of a new type of hardware. The blow of this decision is softened by our use of the Constructor Jump Table Idiom,[1,2] which makes it very easy to add a new class, and by the fact that the amount of code that we have needed to add for any device to date is very small.

Figure 5 shows a representative class declaration for one of these concrete classes. We pulled the actual code into the class description to show the small amount of code required. The protected method is used by the hardware driver to build a command that is type specific to get the density from the device on the functional path. Normally the information is returned on the management path via the report status table (RST) command that appears in the code fragment.

If one was going to extend the framework by adding a new tape drive that brought direct SCSI into the processor, rather than using the SIOA interface, the following steps would be followed (see Figure 6):

- Inherit a new `ScsiTape` from `HwDrvrTape` and handle the SCSI protocol operations at that level. Be sure to include appropriate protected methods to allow leaf classes to override operations that may vary on a device basis.
- Create a leaf subclass that provides unique support for the SCSI device being added.

Note that even though the implementation of this new class of tape drives might be substantially different (except for function implemented in the `HwDriver` class), the contract to the users of `HwDriver` is preserved and would not change.

Hardware driver objects are instantiated one for one with the actual devices that are attached to the system (and powered on) based on information provided by the IOPs. Provision is also made for devices being added or deleted

```
//IoHwDev6346 – Leaf class for 6346 Cartridge Tape
class IoHwDev6346 : public IoTapeSioa {
public:
   // CONSTRUCTOR
   IoHwDev6346(Io=HwIop *myIop                  //pointer to IOP
      IoRstEntry myRst,                          //Rst is information reported to
                                                   the hardware
      IpcfServiceController &iobuId              //connection to the device
      Srid parentSrid,                           //System Resource ID of parent
                                                   driver
      IpcfGuaranteedExchangeCapacity snum,       //ipcf details
      IpcfGuaranteedExchangeCapacity tnum,       //ipcf details
      Srid aSrid)                                //system resource ID for this
                                                   device
      :IoTapeSioa(myIop, myRst, iobuId, snum, tnum, 0, 0, 0, aSrid){}
void createHri(IoTape *tapeProxy)                                          /
    {myHri = new(SystemHeap) IoHriDev6346(mySrid, rst, tapeProxy, iop);}
protected:
   enum { Density=0x2000 }
   IoTapeDensity getCartDensity() {return Density;}
   //build a special command for this type of drive
   IoTaWhenDone* xSetTapeParms(IoTaParms *parms, IoTapeResponse *r);
};//END Class
```

FIGURE 5. *Source code for a concrete class of tape hardware driver.*

(powered off) during normal operation of the system such that at any point in time there is one and only one Hardware driver object representing a particular real device on the system. This capability eliminates the need for manual configuration at the "device reporting level." When coupled with higher-level facilities the function is similar to, but more extensive than, the "plug and play BIOS" that has been suggested for personal computers.

Impedance Matching: I/O Drivers

Having a perfectly good piece of hardware, or even a really great abstraction of piece of hardware isn't enough for today's operating systems. There can be many different operating environments on the system that all need to use the same hardware, each with their own unique "personality." In our environment, there was an emerging requirement to make hardware look like it was designed for other operating systems in addition to OS/400. Although we thought we did a pretty good job of abstracting the hardware into hardware drivers, we found there was more to be done to produce an abstraction palatable to the operating system designers.

We first thought of doing subclasses of hardware drivers for the different operating system personalities, but that quickly got messy. Added to that is the problem that the requirements at the hardware driver level for speed, storage economy, and the ability to operate in restricted environments tend to be at odds with what the higher level clients want. Hardware drivers sometimes need to run in non-pageable or restricted paging environments, while OS/400 needed to access the old MI ADTs that require paging to beavailable before they could be touched.

Our solution was another class of objects called I/O Drivers. These "impedance-matching" objects allowed us to provide a custom interface to the old AS/400 clients, without being constrained in our desire to provide the best hardware driver abstraction that we could. They also provide for a multipersonality future where we can have I/O Drivers for each kind of operating system supported by the hardware.

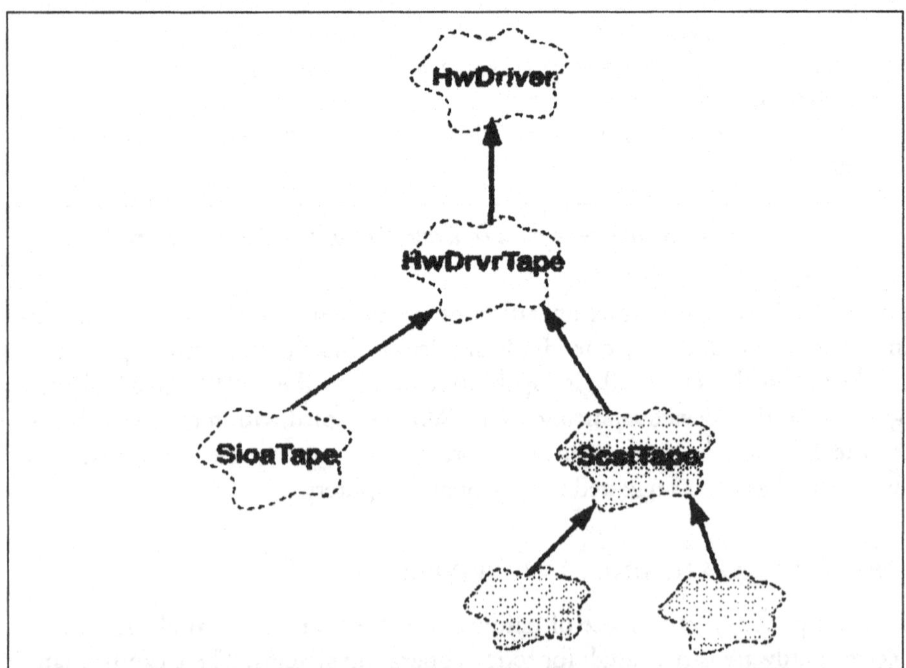

Figure 6. *Possible changes to tape class hierarchy for SCSI. The shaded classes are those that would be added to support a non-SIOA type of tape drive.*

Figure 7 shows a class hierarchy for the I/O driver class. The I/O driver represents a view of a class of I/O devices, so it is quite abstract. All I/O drivers will interface with hardware drivers, but the rules of engagement for the client interface are radically different. For the AS/400 the I/O drivers deal with encapsulation of the ADTs and the MI instructions that OS/400 and our clients expect to see. For an OS/2 personality their interface would be quite different, and different again for a POSIX personality.

There is no I/O driver for the DASD. The AS/400 manages all the DASDs as part of a single-level storage address space. DASD devices are not exposed at the MI as "I/O capable." Storage is allocated as part of object creation and is managed entirely by SLIC. The DASD hardware drivers interface only to the storage management component that implements the address model for the AS/400.[5]

Systems Management: Hardware Resource Information

AS/400 has a strong heritage of providing extensive capability to find, configure, and service the hardware attached to the system. In the past, those facilities came at a rather high cost to the operating system. More than 100 KLOC of

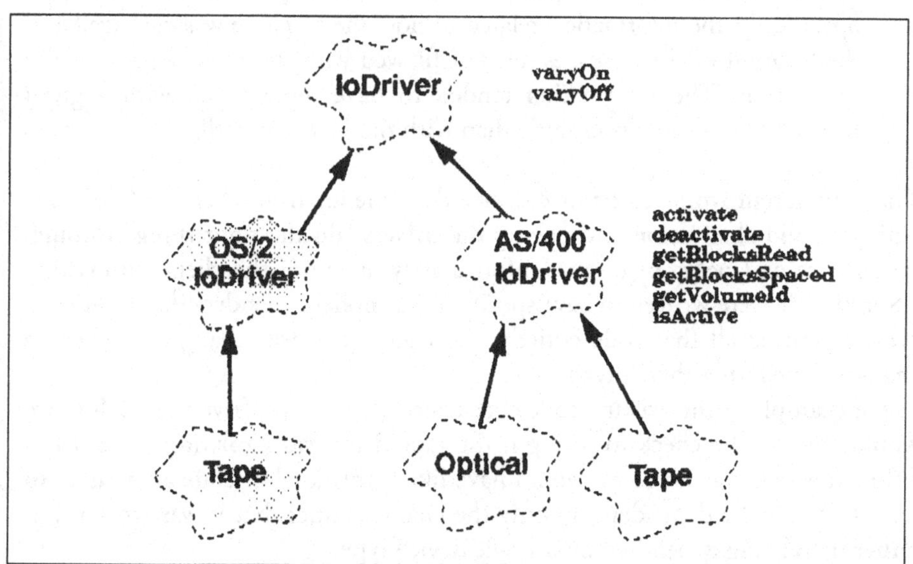

FIGURE 7. *Class hierarchy for I/O drivers. The shaded objects indicate how the hierarchy could be extended to support other operating systems that needed to use the same hardware.*

code, much of it above the MI and highly hardware dependent, was devoted to finding, identifying, and tracking hardware attached to the system.

HRI provides the same or better facilities below the MI so that we reduce the hardware dependencies above the MI, and provide better information about the hardware in cases where we are unable to IPL OS/400 due to the missing devices. We provided this information by adding inspector methods to the hardware driver class originally. We ran into the following difficulties with that approach:

- There was a requirement to provide information about hardware components for which there would be no hardware driver present on the system. There are two cases where this could happen:

  a. Static information about a hardware component that was not yet installed on the system but where the user wanted to preconfigure the device.

  b. Information about a piece of hardware that had not reported in on this IPL. Since this could represent a piece of failed hardware (as opposed to removed), saved information from a previous IPL would be retrieved and used.

- Some of the information required by the operating system did not fit well with the logical view of the hardware represented by `Hardware Drivers`. Specifically, the information related to how the machine was packaged and the location of the packages did not fit well with the `Hardware Driver` abstraction. The information tended to have more to do with a given release of the system packaging than with the I/O gear itself.

The new design works to remove device dependency from client code by providing a solid abstraction and having the drivers "do the right thing" through inheritance and polymorphism. Unfortunately, many of the clients in existing AS/400 code were written to have specific type/model dependencies. In order to avoid rewriting all that code entirely, the client code was changed to check a characteristic rather than a type.

For example, if the existing code checked to see if a tape drive was a 2440, we would convert the check to seeing if the tape drive was a cartridge tape drive. While not going as far as we would have liked, this level of code allowed us to have I/O code be dependent on only the characteristics that it was written for, rather than being dependent on a single device type.

The large amount of characteristic information that had to be exposed with this technique made it important that we split this stopgap interface away from the primary driver abstractions. This technique also factors heavily into our

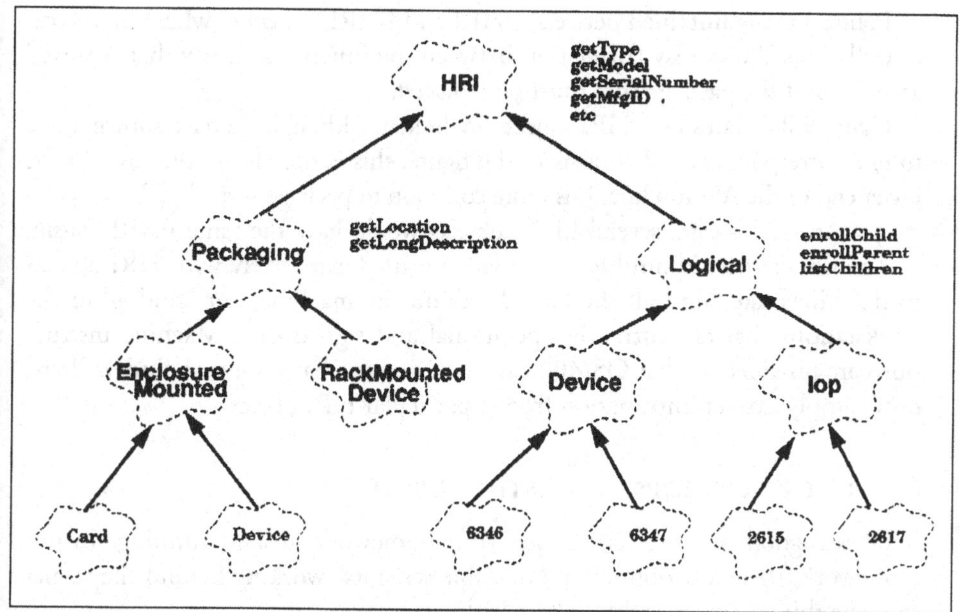

FIGURE 8. *Class hierarchy for hardware resource information (HRI).*

decision to require code be installed for every type of I/O gear that we support, since we need to insure support for the ability to check characteristics.

Figure 8 shows the hardware resource information (HRI) class hierarchy. Most clients access either the packaging hardware resource information (PHRI) class or the logical hardware resource information (LHRI) class.

PHRI objects contain information about how the hardware is packaged and where these packages are located in physical space. The main requirement for this information is related to servicing or upgrading the system rather than operating it. LHRI objects contain the functional or operational information about the hardware that is used by the clients for characteristic checking.

The HRI objects are linked together when they are instantiated with "parent and children pointers." Together the objects themselves and these linkages provide a topological representation of the system.* Siblings can be easily found by asking a parent for pointers to all of its children. Note that the two domains are not identical since a package may have no function (at least as far as the operating system is concerned) but a functional entity *must* reside in some sort of package.

* Note that the hardware drivers are also linked together to represent the topology of the system, but with less completeness since there are no hardware drivers for special constructs such as the system processor, service processor, etc.

Pointers are maintained between PHRI and LHRI "cousins" where they exist, as well. This allows easy correlation between the functional entity that reported an error and the package that must be replaced.

Figure 9 illustrates how HRI objects are linked. Although we have shown a one to one correspondence of cousins in the figure, this is not always the case. In the lower end of the AS/400 line, it is quite common to package several IOPs on a single planar. In this case, several LHRI objects would have the same PHRI cousin.

The finder/filter idiom (described later) is used extensively with HRI objects to do things like "find all the tape drives on the machine," or "find all of the workstations that are currently operational and signed on." Machine instructions are provided so that OS/400 can issue queries that resolve to finder/filters, or to simply extract information from a particular HRI object.

Support Staff: IOPs, Statistics, Service

It takes a good support staff to get your framework up and running. In our framework, there are a bunch of "invisible servants" working behind the scenes to make things run smoothly. These include:

IOP Objects. AS/400 uses fairly complex outboard processors to perform our I/O. The IOP objects manage (encapsulate) the management functions of these processors.

Service Objects. These objects "shadow" the Hardware Driver objects. They are designed to perform service functions on the hardware and are instantiated the first time service is required on a hardware component.

Device Statistics Objects. These objects initiate, perform, and terminate statistics gathering operations for devices. Device statistics objects exist for all hardware components that provide statistics.

Volume Statistics Objects. These objects are instantiated by hardware drivers that encapsulate removable media devices (tape, optical, etc.). They are used to collect statistics on a particular volume of media.

Persistence

In our framework, only I/O drivers and HRI objects have to deal with retaining portions of data across IPLs (persistence). I/O Drivers deal with persistence by piggy-backing off the old ADTs that the I/O Drivers logically encapsulate. Since these ADTs have always been persistent, and continue to be in our model,

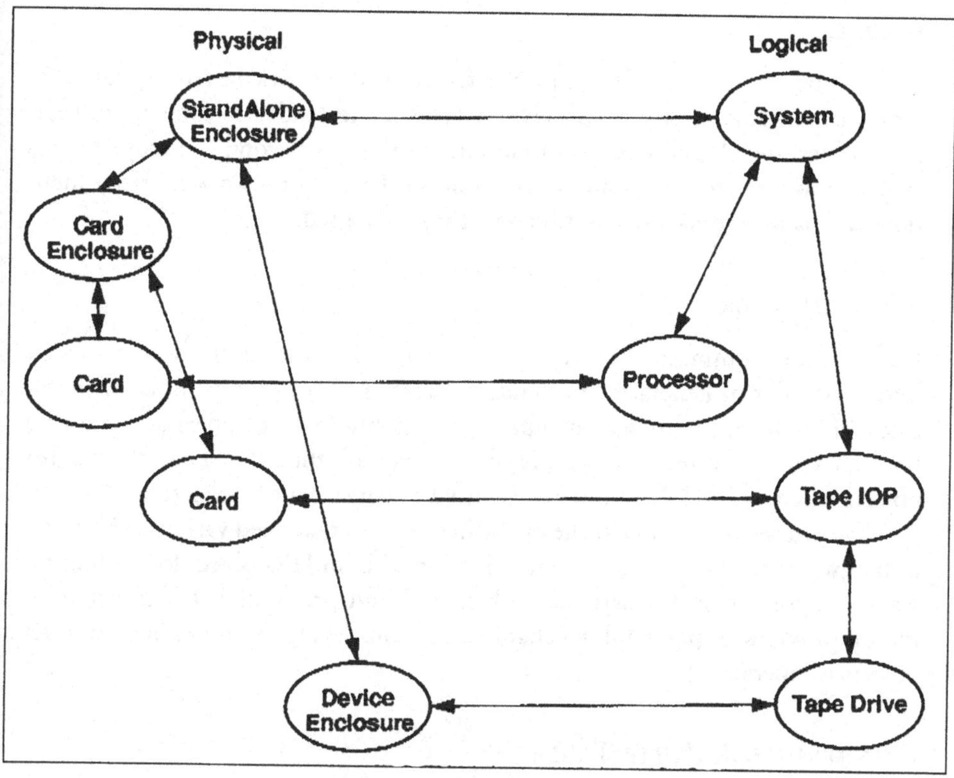

FIGURE 9. *Linking of HRI objects to represent system topology.*

the I/O Drivers are able to store persistent information there.

HRI objects are originally instantiated using vital product data reported to the IOP object by the hardware. Once something has reported in, it becomes the responsibility of the operating system to remember that device as part of the system so that we can diagnose a possible hardware problem if a device fails to report in the future. The mechanism for this detection is to save critical data portions of each HRI object so that it can be partially reconstructed on IPL, even if the hardware it represents fails to report.

When an HRI object is constructed, it calls a global function to save the critical data portions to disk. On subsequent IPLs, this table of saved data is compared with the HRI objects instantiated at IPL to see if any HRI objects are missing that were present previously. If any are found, they are called with a special constructor that enrolls them on a list of "missing" hardware that can be examined by a system operator.

Idioms

As we progressed in the design of our framework, we discovered several techniques or "idioms" that proved to be very useful and tended to show up in multiple places. detailed discussion of any one of these is beyond the scope of this article. however, since they are so useful in our framework, we will brieôy mention the major idioms and describe how they were used.

Finder/Filter

Perhaps more commonly known as Generator and Predicate, this idiom uses an iterator (finder or generator) to iterate through a list of objects. filter or predicate objects accept an object as input (presumably from a finder) and return a boolean that indicates whether the object "passed" the filter. Logical operator objects (such as `And` or `Or`) can also be used to construct complex filters.

There are several clients in the operating systems that need various subset lists of hardware attached to the system.† Since there is an HRI object for each hardware component on the system (both logical and packaging), the finder/filter idiom provides a powerful mechanism for producing a subset list of HRI objects to operate on.

Constructor Jump Table

Coplein[1] refers to this idiom as Virtual Constructors. We found it to be extremely useful in our domain since it provides for the ability to add new classes to the framework at runtime (via table entries). Also, since the typing of our objects is based on information provided at run time (by the hardware), the ability to pass a parameter on construction that determines the type of the object constructed, was very useful.

Proxy Objects

Also known as Envelope and Letter, we found two uses for this idiom. Some of the hardware components on the AS/400 can be removed or replaced without powering down the system or forcing an IPL. When this event happens (called a Resource Alter), the IOP object is notified and initiates the construction of a hardware driver object for the new or changed resource.

---

† Such as "all the tape drives on the sytem" or "all devices attached to this ocntroller" or even "the system console."

For the case where the new hardware reporting in is a replacement for some other hardware component, the clients that have cached pointers to obsolete hardware drivers must be notified to update their pointers.

To avoid the necessity for the client update, we used the proxy object idiom. Each hardware driver object has a proxy object with the same public contract as the hardware driver itself. Clients call methods on the proxy that in turn call the same method on the real hardware driver.

When it becomes necessary to replace a hardware driver (because of a change in the hardware), it is only necessary to update the pointer held by the proxy object. No client update is needed.

`WhenDone` Objects

The nature of I/O tends to cause many of the interactions between components to be asynchronous. The operating system does not want to wait while the disk spins or the arm positions itself over the correct track. Instead, the client prefers to invoke a method to initiate the operation with a quick return, and then be notified later when the operation is completed.

The `WhenDone` idiom (called "callbacks" in Coplein[1]) proved to be well suited for this environment. Parameter lists for methods that are asynchronous include a parameter of type `WhenDone`. Initiation of the operation is performed when the method is called and executes under the client's thread of execution. When the requested operation is completed, the Server invokes the `Done` method on this object, which executes under the server's thread. Since the client provides the `WhenDone` object, it has complete flexibility in what is executed at operation complete.

Potential Future Improvements

Although there are many areas in our framework where incremental design improvements could be made (and in fact some will be made), there is one area where it appears the framework itself may be deficient.

The division of the device drivers into "abstract the hardware" (hardware drivers) and "match the operating system" (I/O drivers) seems to be something that is going to get a lot of use. We wish that we had thought to create a comparable division in the HRI domain. While the HRI objects will allow us to advance our capability for the AS/400, we need to work to try to abstract that kind of information so that it can be applied to other OS personalities.

Conclusion

We have been very pleased with our first large-scale experience with both object orientation and C++. After some initial performance and object code size scares, the I/O framework seems to be stabilizing nicely. We continue to work to create more commonality within the framework with things like command and response objects. We believe that the success we have experienced is largely due to natural fit of I/O to the object-oriented paradigm.

Acknowledgment

We would like to acknowledge the advice and counsel of Marshall Cline of Paradigm Shift, Inc. in the development of our framework. His training and consultation were indispensable to the success of our project.

References

1. Coplien, J. *Advanced C++ Programming Styles and Idioms,* Addison-Wesley, Reading, MA.
2. Booch, G. *OO Analysis with Design,* second ed., Benjamin/Cummings, Redwood City, CA.
3. Koskimies, K., and J. Vihavainen. The problem of unexpected subclasses, *Journal of Object-Oriented Programming,* Oct. 1992.
4. Sorward, Sthei, Shopiro. *Adding New Code to a Running C++ Program,* 1990 USENIX Conference.
5. French, R. E., *et al. System/38 Machine Storage Management,* IBM System/38 Technical Developments.
6. Gamma, E., R. Helm, R. Johnson, and J. Vlissides. *Design Patterns,* Addison Wesley, Reading, MA, 1995.

DISTRIBUTED OBJECT COMPUTING IN C++

STEVE VINOSKI
vinoski@ch.hp.com

DOUG SCHMIDT
schmidt@cs.wustl.edu

WELCOME TO THE FIRST EDITION OF OUR NEW OBJECT INTERCONNECtions column concerning distributed object computing (DOC) and C++. In this column, we will explore a wide range of topics related to DOC. Our goal is to demystify the terminology and dispel the hype surrounding DOC. In place of hype, we will focus on object-oriented principles, methods, and tools that are emerging to support DOC using C++. We plan to investigate and describe various tools and environments that are available commercially. In addition, we will discuss detailed design and implementation problems that arise when using C++ to create DOC solutions. The field of DOC is already broad and is still growing rapidly. Therefore, we will have plenty of material to cover in the coming months. If there's any topic in particular that you'd like us to cover, please send us email at object_connect@ch.hp.com.

It has been claimed that distributed computing can improve

- Collaboration through connectivity and interworking
- Performance through parallel processing
- reliability and availability through replication
- Scalability and portability through modularity
- Extensibility through dynamic configuration and reconfiguration
- Cost effectiveness through resource sharing and open systems.

Our experiences and the experiences of others have shown that distributed computing can indeed offer these benefits when applied properly. However, developing distributed applications whose components collaborate efficiently, reliably, transparently, and scalably is a complex task. Much of this complexity arises from limitations with conventional tools and techniques used to develop distributed application software. Many standard network programming mechanisms (e.g., BSD sockets and Windows NT named pipes) and reusable component libraries (e.g., Sun RPC) lack type-safe, portable, reentrant, and extensible interfaces. For example, both sockets and named pipes identify endpoints of communication using weakly-typed I/O handles. These handles increase the potential for subtle runtime errors since compilers can't detect type mismatches at compile-time.

Another source of development complexity arises from the widespread use of functional decomposition. Many distributed applications are developed using functional decomposition techniques that result in nonextensible system architectures. This problem is exacerbated by the source code examples in popular network programming textbooks being based on functional-oriented design and implementation techniques.

So, in this world full of hollow buzzwords and slick marketing hype, it is natural to ask what object-oriented technology contributes to the domain of distributed computing. The short answer is that object-oriented technology provides distributed computing with many of the same benefits (such as encapsulation, reuse, portabability, and extensibilty) as it does for nondistribuited computing.

In fact, it is often more natural to use object-oriented techniques in the domain of distributed computing than it is for nondistributed computing. This is due to the inherently decentralized nature of distributed computing. In conventional nondistributed applications, there is often a temptation to sacrifice abstraction and modularity for a perceived increase in performance. For example, many programmers use global variables or access fields in structures directly to avoid the overhead of passing parameters and calling functions, respectively.

In distributed computing, however, performance optimizations based on direct access to global resources are extremely difficult to develop and scale. Research and development on operating system support for distributed shared memory, for example, not yet ready for large-scale system development. Therefore, most distributed applications interoperate by passing messages. There are many variations on this message passing theme (e.g., RPC, remote event queues, bytestream communication, etc.). However, it doesn't require much of a stretch of the imagination to recognize that message passing in distributed computing is very similar to method invocation on an object in object-oriented programming.

With this observation in mind, let's discuss several of the key features of DOC:

Providing many of the same enhancements to procedural RPC *toolkits that object-oriented languages provide to conventional procedural programming languages:* Distributed object computing enhances procedural RPC toolkits (such as Sun RPC and the OSF DCE) by supporting object-oriented language features. These features include encapsulation, interface inheritance, parameterized types, and object-based exception handling. Encapsulation promotes the separation of interface from implementation. This separation is crucial for developing highly extensible architectures that decouple reusable application-independent mechanisms from application-specific policies. Interface inheritance and parameterized types promote reuse and emphasize commonality in a design. Object-based exception handling often simplifies program logic by decoupling error-handling code from normal application processing.

Enabling interworking between applications at higher levels of abstraction: Distributed applications have traditionally been developed using relatively low-level mechanisms. Common mechanisms include the TCP/IP protocol, the socket transport layer programming interface, and the `select` event demultiplexing system call. These low-level mechanisms provide applications with reliable, untyped, point-to-point bytestream services. In general, these services are optimized for performance, rather than ease of programming, reliability, flexibility, and extensibility.

A primary objective of DOC is to enable developers to program distributed applications using familiar techniques such as method calls on objects. Ideally, accessing the services of a remote object should be as simple as calling a method on that object. For example, if object `foo` provides a service `bar`, we'd like to use `bar` by simply writing `foo->bar()`.

A surprisingly large number of fairly complicated components must be developed to support remote method invocation on objects transparently. These components include directory name servers, object request brokers (ORBs), interface definition language compilers, object location and startup facilities, multithreading facilities, and security mechanisms. In subsequent columns, we will define these terms and illustrate how these components work together to solve real-world problems.

Providing a foundation for building higher-level mechanisms that facilitate the collaboration among services in distributed applications: Supporting transparent remote object method invocation is only the first step in the long journey into the realm of distributed object computing. An increasing number of distributed applications require more sophisticated collaboration mechanisms. These mechanisms include common object services such as global naming, event filtering, object migration, transactional messaging, reliable group communication, and quality of service facilities. More advanced tools will support electronic mail, visualization, collaborative work, and concurrent engineering.

When all these provisions of DOC are realized and standardized, we may very well finally see the long-awaited arrival of "plug and play" software components and "Software ICs." Object vendors will be able to market various implementations of industry-standard interfaces, and users will be able to mix and match those components, investing in the ones that they believe best fulfill their needs. Until that time, however, there is still quite a bit of work to do. Only recently have the very lowest levels of support for DOC, such as object request brokers, become commonplace in the market.

But What About C++?

So far, we've barely even mentioned C++. In future columns, we'll discuss ways in which C++ may be used to simplify distributed object computing. We believe that when used properly, C++ is well-suited for the construction of both distributed object support systems and the object components themselves. C++ combines high-level abstractions with the efficiency of a low-level language like C. Many of the emerging frameworks and environments for distributed object computing are based on C++, due to its widespread availability and appeal. For example, commercial tools such as several CORBA ORBs, HP OODCE, and OLE/COM, as well as freely-available software toolkits such as ILU from Xerox PARC and the ADAPTIVE Communication Environment (ACE), support object-based distributed programming using C++.

Certain C++ features are well-suited for programming distributed objects. For example, abstract base classes, pure virtual inheritance, virtual functions, and exception handling help to separate object interfaces from object implementations. However, the lack of other features in C++ increases the complexity of developing robust and concise distributed applications. For instance, support for garbage collection would greatly reduce memory management complexity. Likewise, `before` and `after` methods would enable greater control over the marshaling and demarshaling of parameters passed to remote method calls. In the coming months, we will discuss C++ language idioms that have been successfully used in practice to address certain C++ limitations.

Next Time

In our next column we will compare and contrast different ways to use C++ to solve a representative distributed programming application. We'll compare several solutions, ranging from using the sockets C language network programming interface, to using C++ wrappers for sockets, all the way up to the use of a CORBA object request broker (ORB). The example will illustrate the various trade-offs between efficiency, extensibility, and portability involved with each approach.

DOC by Example: Modeling Distributed Object Applications

In our first column, we discussed several promising benefits of using object-oriented (OO) technology and C++ to develop extensible, robust, portable, and efficient distributed application software. However, the OO marketplace is often long on promises and short on viable solutions. Therefore, we'd like to start moving the discussion from the abstract to the concrete. In our next several columns, we'll present an extended example that compares and contrasts different ways of using C++ and DOC to solve a representative distributed programming application.

Our example centers around a financial services system, whose distributed architecture is shown in Figure 1. We'll focus on a stock trading application that enables investment brokers to query stock prices, as well as buy shares of stock. As shown in Figure 1, the quote server that maintains the current stock prices is physically remote from brokers, who work in various geographically distributed sites. Therefore, our application must be developed to work efficiently, robustly, and securely across a variety of wide area networks (WAN) and local area (LAN) networks. We selected the stock trading application since the issues involved in analyzing, designing, and implementing it are remarkably similar to many other types of distributed applications.

Distributing application services among networks of computers offers many potential benefits. However, implementing robust, efficient, and extensible distributed applications is more complex than building standalone applications. A significant portion of this complexity is due to the fact that developers must consider new design alternatives and must acquire many new skills.

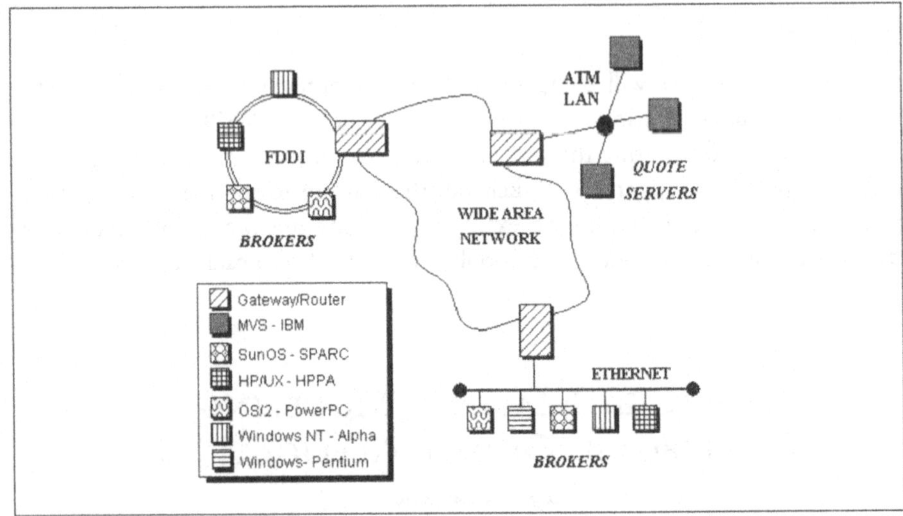

FIGURE 1. *Distributed architecture of financial services system.*

Realizing the potential benefits of DOC requires both strategic and tactical skills/ Strategic skills involve mastering design patterns¤ and architectural techniques that exist in the domain of distributed computing. This month's column focuses on the strategic issues underlying the distributed computing requirements and environment of our stock trading application. Tactical skills involve mastering tools such as OO programming languages like C++ and OO DOC frameworks (such as CORBA, OODCE, and OLE/ COM). CORBA is an emerging standard for distributed object computing sponsored by the OMG,‹ OODCE is a C++ framework for the OSF Distributed Computing Environment (DCE),› and OLE/COM is Microsoft's technology for integrating distributed objects.fi Subsequent columns will focus on tactical issues by evaluating detailed design and programming techniques used for the client-side and server-side of our example distributed application.

APPLICATION DISTRIBUTED COMPUTING ENVIRONMENT AND REQUIREMENTS

A good systems analysis begins by capturing the requirements of an application, and modeling the essential elements in its environment. This section discusses the distributed computing requirements of our stock trading application, as well as key characteristics of the distributed computing environment in which it operates. Along the way, we indicate how these requirements and environmental characteristics motivate and shape many reusable components and features found in DOC frameworks.

Distributed Computing Environment Characteristics

The distributed computing environment (shown in Figure 1) in which the stock trading application runs may be characterized as follows.

Broker Cients and Quote Servers Run on Separate Computers

These computers are joined by a heterogeneous internetwork of LANs and WANs (such as Ethernet, FDDI, and ATM). The network protocol stack connecting the distributed application components may be based on one of any WAN and LAN protocol families such as TCP/IP, X.25, ISO OSI, and Novell IPX/SPX. All these protocol families support end-to-end communication. However, they have subtly different characteristics and constraints that complicate software portability and interoperability. For example, TCP/IP is a bytestream transport protocol that ignores application message boundaries, whereas IPX/SPX maintains message boundaries

Writing applications that operate transparently across different protocol stacks is often tedious and error-prone. Ideally, a DOC framework should shield applications from knowledge of these types of protocol-level details. OODCE is particularly strong in this area since it was designed to run over many protocol stacks. First-generation CORBA and OLE/COM implementations, in contrast, have not addressed protocol stack transparency as vigorously. This complicates the development and deployment of highly portable applications that run on multiple transport protocols.

Clients and Servers May Be Heterogeneous End Systems

These end systems may run on various hardware platforms (such as PA-RISC, Intel 80≈86, DEC Alpha, SPARC, or the Power PC). Different hardware platforms possess instruction sets with either little-endian and big-endian byte orders. To improve application portability, DOC frameworks typically provide tools such as interface definition languages (IDLs) and IDL compilers. These tools generate code that automatically marshals and demarshals method parameters. This process converts binary data to and from, respectively, a format that is recognizable throughout a heterogeneous system of computers with instruction sets containing different byte orders.

The broker clients and quote servers may also run on different operating systems (such as variants of UNIX, Windows NT, OS/2, or MVS). These operating systems provide different sets of features (such as multi-threading, shared memory, and GUIs) and different system call interfaces (such as POSIX or Win32).

DOC frameworks provide different levels of support for shielding applications from differences in heterogeneous OS features and interfaces. Several DOC frameworks provide portable interfaces for certain OS-level features (such as the thread interface available with OODCE). However, other OS features (such as text file I/O, shared memory, and graphics) are often not standardized by DOC frameworks. OLE/COM addresses OS heterogeneity by the focusing primarily on a relatively homogeneous OS platform (i.e., the Win32 family of APIs).

CORBA does not attempt to define a standard set of interfaces to OS features, ostensibly to give users the freedom to select their favorite OS tools. They may, however, define a standard set of interfaces for accessing DOC framework features, such as CORBA's Dynamic Invocation Interface (DII). The DII allows a client to access the request mechanisms provided by an Object Request Broker (ORB). Applications use the DII to dynamically issue requests to objects without requiring interface-specific stubs to be linked into the application. This allows clients to make use of services that are "discovered" at runtime.

It remains to be seen which of these different approaches to heterogeneity will be embraced by the marketplace.

Application Requirements for Distributed Computing

All DOC frameworks provide reusable components that simplify the development of distributed applications. These components elevate the level at which applications are designed and implemented. This enables application domain experts to focus on application-specific aspects of the problem (such as determining user-friendly interfaces for trading stocks), rather than wrestling with low-level communication details.

Our stock trading application has a number of distributed computing requirements. Many other types of distributed applications have similar requirements. Figure 2 shows some of the DOC components that we use in this section to motivate and explain our application's distributed computing requirements. Some of these components are specific to our application (such as the stock quoter, stock trader, and trading rules objects), and would typically be developed in-house. Other components are more generic (such as the printer, network time, location broker, authenticator, and heartbeat monitor objects), and are often provided by a DOC framework.

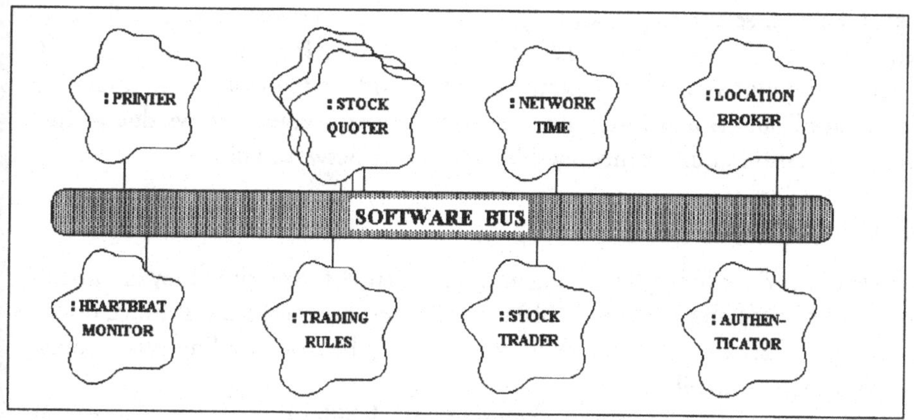

FIGURE 2. *DOC components.*

High Reliability

Distributed applications often require substantial effort to achieve levels of reliability equivalent to those expected from stand-alone applications. Detecting service failures in a stand-alone application is relatively straightforward. For example, if a service fails gracefully, the caller is usually notified by a designated return value.

In contrast, detecting failures in distributed applications is often extremely complicated. For example, separate components in our stock trading application possess incomplete knowledge of global system state (such as the current price of a stock). By the time this information becomes available it may no longer be valid. This is a serious problem for distributed applications (such as an algorithmic trading system) that may exhibit transient inconsistencies due to caching on clients and/or servers.

Distributed transaction monitors, such as DCE-based Encina from Transarc, help to improve the reliability of a distributed application by ensuring that changes to system state occur atomically, consistently, and repeatably. In practice, our stock quote application would undoubtedly use some type of transaction service to ensure reliability. The OMG recently standardized on a Transaction Object Service.° Few, if any, ORB vendors have yet to offer an implementation of it with their ORB products, however. OLE/COM doesn't provide support for distributed transaction monitoring.

Developing services that are resilient to independent host and network failures is also difficult. For instance, distributed applications are designed to tolerate some amount of variation in network transmission delay. Thus, a client may not detect an abnormal server termination until after valuable information is lost. Likewise, server responses may get lost in the network, causing clients to retransmit duplicate requests. Isis RDO· is a DOC framework that supports reliable distributed object computing. It provides "fail-stop" semantics that ensure applications can distinguish reliably between request delays due to network congestion and lost messages due to host or network failures.

High Availability

Brokers earn their living by buying and selling stocks. Any time they are unable to access current stock prices or place trades their business suffers. Since downtime is generally unacceptable, it is essential that the stock trading system operate with high availability.

One technique for improving application availability is to replicate services in multiple locations throughout a network. For example, the stock quote object in Figure 2 is replicated to ensure a market data feed was always accessible (we've duplicated the `Stock Quoter` object in the figure to illustrate the replication).

Another technique for improving availability is to invoke applications under the control of a heartbeat monitor. This service detects and automatically reinvokes an application if it terminates unexpectedly. The Orbix+Isis ORB supports transparent replication and reinvocation of CORBA objects.

Object Location and Selection

Traditional stand-alone applications generally identify their constituent services via memory addresses that point to objects and subroutines. In contrast, distributed applications require more elaborate mechanisms for naming and locating their remote services.

A traditional scheme for addressing remote services involves Internet (IP) host addresses and communication port numbers However, this mechanism is generally inadequate for large-scale distributed systems since it is difficult to administer in a portable and unambiguous manner. For example, "port 5000" does not necessarily refer to the same service on separate host machines configured by different vendors or by network administrators.

DOC frameworks generally provide location brokers that allow clients to access remote object services via higher-level names (rather than by low-level memory addresses or IP/port numbers), and traders that allow remote objects to be selected based on the desired characteristics of the services they provide.

Location brokers and traders simplify distributed system administration and promote more flexible and dynamic placement of services throughout a network by automating distributed object selection.

If a service has been replicated for improved reliability or availability, applications may use a location broker or trader to determine the most appropriate service provider. For example, the OODCE Cell Directory Service (CDS) can be considered to be a type of trader service. CDS supports the selection of remote services based upon a set of interfaces and objects associated with each service. In the stock quote application, the client may rely on a trader to help it locate a stock quote service that also happens to support the stock trading service attribute. Likewise, a broker might use the service attributes to print a postscript document by determining which printer(s) possess the postscript attribute and/or by determining which printer has the shortest queue. Using service attributes to select the shortest queue is an example of *load balancing,* described in the following paragraph.

Load Balancing

A bottleneck may result if many services are configured into the server-side of the application and too many active clients simultaneously access these services. Conversely, configuring many services into the client-side may also result in a bottleneck since clients often execute on cheaper, less powerful host machines.

In general, it is difficult to determine the relative processing characteristics of application services a priori since workloads may vary over time. Therefore, load balancing techniques that enable developers to experiment with different application service partitioning and placement policies may be necessary. These techniques are supported by flexible distributed OS mechanisms that migrate services to other host machines either statically at installation-time or dynamically during runtime. Fully automated dynamic load balancing is still primarily a research topic,* and few commercial DOC frameworks support it.

Security

Distributed applications are generally more vulnerable to security breaches than are stand-alone applications since there are more access points for an intruder to attack. For example, most shared-media networks (such as Ethernet, token ring, and FDDI) provide limited built-in protection against cable tapping and promiscuous-mode "packet snooping" tools. Likewise, distributed applications must guard against a client or server masquerading as another entity in order to access unauthorized information.

---

* Unfortunately, there are several overloaded terms here! Location brokers and traders in DOC framework are quite different from stock brokers and traders, though they share some striking similarities.

DOC frameworks provide various forms of authentication (e.g., Kerberos), authorization (e.g., OODCE access control lists), and data security (e.g., DES encryption). As of this writing, CORBA offers no standard security service, but technology submissions proposing a Security Object Service are due to the OMG Object Services Task Force by February 1995, with the selection of the standard to follow (hopefully) sometime within 1995.

Synchronous Communication and Threading

The communication between a broker client and a quote server may be performed synchronously. In other words, while a client application is querying the database for a stock quote, or waiting to place a trade, it need not perform additional processing. This requirement helps to simplify the client-side program structure since multithreading and asynchronous I/O may be avoided. Both of these techniques tend to decrease portability and increase development and debugging effort.

It may be necessary to use multi-threading for the server-side of the stock trading application, however. Multi-threading helps to improve throughput and performance in circumstances where multiple clients make service requests simultaneously. We'll cover server-side threading issues in a future column.

OODCE and OLE/COM both have provisions for multi-threading (OODCE via DCE pthreads and OLE/COM via Win32 threads). The OMG CORBA standard, on the other hand, considers threading to be outside of its scope. Certain CORBA ORBs (such as Orbix) provide hooks that integrate threading into an application in a relatively transparent and portable manner.

Deferred Activation

Deferred activation is a technique that activates only those objects that are actually requested to perform services on the behalf of clients. Such activation, which is completely transparent to the client, is needed in large-scale networks to allow finite computing resources (such as memory and CPU cycles) to be used efficiently. Objects that are not currently in use may remain dormant, knowing that they will be activated if necessary.

Support for deferred activation is useful for certain types of objects in our stock trading application such as trading rules illustrated in Figure 2. Certain trading rules may only be required under circumstances that occur infrequent (such as a major market correction). By activating these objects "on demand," the the load on host process systems may be reduced significantly.

A conforming CORBA ORB is required to activate certain types of objects when requests arrive for them, if the objects are not already up and running.

Likewise, DCE provides a similar service via its "DCE daemon" (dced), which is modeled after the Internet superserver inetd Windows NT and OLE/COM provide a service control management facility that initiates and controls network services on a Windows NT endsystem.

Binary Data Exchange

The stock trading application passes binary data between little- and big-endian machines. Therefore, marshaling and unmarshaling must be performed for requests and responses have fields that contain binary values. As described previously, all DOC frameworks perform these tasks reasonably well.

As you can see, the requirements for a distributed application like our stock trading example are numerous and complex, perhaps to the point of being overwhelming. The DOC frameworks and systems discussed in this article provide varying degrees of support for these requirements. In general, the current generation of commercially available DOC frameworks handle certain requirements fairly well (such as network heterogeneity, object location and selection, synchronous communication and threading, deferred activation, security, and binary data exchange). Other requirements are not handled as thoroughly at this point (such as OS heterogeneity, reliability and availability, load balancing, and interoperability). Naturally, there are exceptions to these generalizations (e.g., Isis supports fault tolerant DOC and OODCE handles interoperability quite well). We expect the next-generation DOC frameworks to provide more comprehensive and better integrated support for common distributed application requirements.

Conclusion

In this column, we analyzed the distributed computing environment and requirements of a representative distributed stock trading application. Using this application, we identified a number of common object services that help satisfy the distributed computing requirements of many emerging applications. In our next several articles, we will evaluate various programming techniques for the client-side and the server-side of our example application. We'll compare several solutions, ranging from using the conventional sockets network programming interface (which is written in C), to using C++ wrappers for sockets, all the way up to using the CORBA Interface Definition Language (IDL) and a CORBA ORB. Each solution illustrates various tradeoffs between extensibility, robustness, portability, and efficiency.

In future columns we'll cover the DOC frameworks and features mentioned previously in much greater detail. Our goal is to be as comprehensive and unbiased as possible. Please let us know if we've failed to mention your favorite

DOC framework, or if you feel that we've misrepresented the features and functionality of certain tools and technologies. As always, if there are any distributed object topics that you'd like us to cover in future articles, please send us email at object_connect@ch.hp.com.

References

1. Booch, G. *Object Oriented Analysis and Design with Applications* (second ed.), Benjamin/Cummings, Redwood City, CA , 1993.
2. Gamma, E., R. Helm, R. Johnson, and J. Vlissides, *Design Patterns: Elements of Reusable Object-Oriented Software,* Addison-Wesley, Reading, MA, 1994.
3. Object Management Group, *The Common Object Request Broker: Architecture and Specification,* version 1.2, 1993.
4. Dilley, J. OODCE: A C++ framework for the OSF distributed computing environment, *Proceedings of the Winter Usenix Conference,* USENIX Association, Jan. 1994.
5. Microsoft Press, Redmond, WA, *Object Linking and Embedding Version 2 (OLE2) Programmer's Reference,* Vols. 1 and 2, 1993.
6. Stevens, W. R. UNIX *Network Programming,* Prentice Hall, Englewood Cliffs, NJ, 1990.
7. Custer, H. *Inside Windows NT,* Microsoft Press, Redmond, WA, 1993.
8. Object Management Group, *Common Object Services Specification,* Vol. 1, version 94-1-1, 1994.
9. Isis Distributed Systems, Inc., *Isis Users's Guide: Reliable Distributed Objects for C++,* Marlboro, MA, Apr. 1994.
10. Birman, K. and R. van Renesse. *Reliable Distributed Computing with the Isis Toolkit,* IEEE Computer Society Press, Los Alamitos, CA, 1994.
11. C. Horn, The Orbix Architecture, tech. rep., IONA Technologies, Aug. 1993.
12. Schmidt, D. C., and T. Suda. An object-oriented framework for dynamically configuring extensible distributed communication systems, *IEE/BCS Distributed Systems Engineering Journal* (Special Issue on Configurable Distributed Systems), vol.2, pp. 280–293, Dec. 1994.
13. Microsoft Press, *Microsoft Win32 Programmer's Reference,* Microsoft Press, Redmond, WA, 1993.

Comparing Alternative Distributed Programming Techniques

Steve Vinoski
vinoski@ch.hp.com

Doug Schmidt
schmidt@cs.wustl.edu

There are are various programming techniques for developing distributed applications, which we examine and evaluate in this article. The requirements for a representative distributed application in the financial services domain have been outlined in previous articles (see preceding article). This application enables investment brokers to query the price of a stock, as well as to buy shares of stock. As shown in Figure 1, the quote service that maintains the current stock prices is physically remote from brokers, who work in geographically distributed sites. Therefore, our application must work efficiently, robustly, and securely across various wide area (WAN) and local area (LAN) networks.

We selected the stock trading application because the issues raised by analyzing, designing, and implementing it are representative of the issues that arise when developing many other types of distributed applications. Some issues we identified in our previous column were platform heterogeneity, high system reliability and availability, flexibility of object location and selection, support for transactions, security, and deferred process activation, and the exchange of binary data between different computer architectures.

After identifying many requirements and problems we must tackle to create a distributed stock trading application, it's time to look at some actual code. This month's column examines various distributed programming techniques used for the client-side of the stock trading application (our next column will explore server-side techniques). Below, we compare several solutions that range from

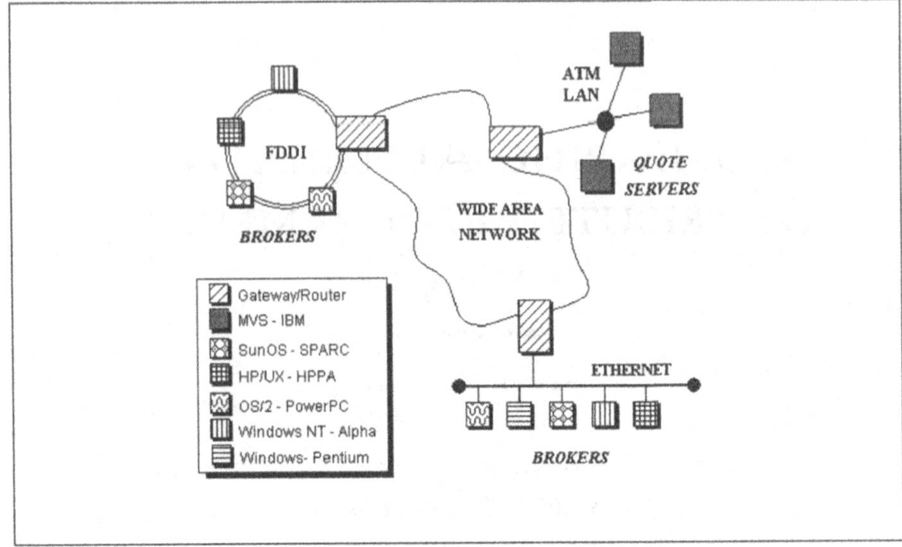

FIGURE 1. *Distributed architecture of financial services systems.*

using the socket network programming interface (which is defined using the C programming language), to using C++ wrappers for sockets, all the way up to using a distributed object computing (DOC) solution. The DOC solution is based upon the CORBA interface definition language (IDL) and a CORBA Object Request Broker (ORB). Each solution illustrates various trade-offs between extensibility, robustness, portability, and efficiency.

THE SOCKET SOLUTION

Distributed applications have traditionally been written using network programming interfaces such as sockets or TLI. Sockets were developed in BSD UNIX to interface with the TCP/IP protocol suite.[1] Transport Layer Interface (TLI) is another network programming interface available on System V UNIX platforms. Our primary focus in this article is on sockets since it is widely available on many platforms, including most variants of UNIX, Windows, Windows NT, OS/2, Mac OS, etc.

From an application's perspective, a socket is an endpoint of communication that is bound to the address of a service. The service may reside on another process or on another computer in a network. A socket is accessed via an I/O descriptor, which is an unsigned integer handle that indexes into a table of open sockets maintained by the OS.

The standard socket interface is defined using C functions. It contains several dozen routines that perform tasks such as locating address information for network services, establishing and terminating connections, and sending and receiving data. In-depth coverage of sockets and TLI can be found in Stevens.[2]

Socket/C Code

The following code illustrates the relevant steps required to program the stock quote program using sockets and C. We first create two C structures that define the schema for the quote request and quote response, respectively:

```
#define MAXSTOCKNAMELEN 100

struct Quote_Request
{
  long len;                           /* Length of the
                                         request. */
  char name[MAXSTOCKNAMELEN];         /* Stock name. */
};

struct Quote_Response
{
  long value;                         /* Current value of the
                                         stock. */
};
```

Next, we've written a number of C utility routines. These routines shield the rest of the application from dealing with the low-level socket API. The first routine establishes a connection with a stock quote server at a port number passed as a parameter to the routine:

```
// WIN32 already defines this.
#if defined (unix)
typedef int HANDLE;
#endif /* unix */

int connect_quote_server (const char server[],
                          u_short port)
{
  struct sockaddr_in addr;
  struct hostent *hp;
  HANDLE sd;

  /* Create a local endpoint of communication. */
  sd = socket (PF_INET, SOCK_STREAM, 0);
```

```
  /* Determine IP address of the server */
  hp = gethostbyname (server);

  /* Setup the address of server. */
  memset ((void *) &addr, 0, sizeof addr);
  addr.sin_family = AF_INET;
  addr.sin_port = htons (port);
  memcpy (&addr.sin_addr, hp->h_addr, hp->h_length);

  /* Establish connection with remote server. */
  connect (sd,
       (struct sockaddr *) &addr, sizeof addr);
  return sd;
}
```

Even though we've omitted most of the error handling code, the routine shown above illustrates the many subtle details required to program at the socket level.

The next routine sends a stock quote request to the server:

```
void send_request (HANDLE sd,
  const char stock_name[])
{
  struct Quote_Request req;
  size_t w_bytes;
  size_t namelen;
  int n;

  /* Determine the packet length. */
  namelen = strlen (stock_name);
  if (namelen > MAXSTOCKNAMELEN)
   namelen = MAXSTOCKNAMELEN;
  strncpy (req.name, stock_name, namelen);
  /* Convert to network byte order. */
  req.len = htonl (sizeof req.len + namelen);

  /* Send data to server, handling "short-writes". */
  for (w_bytes = 0; w_bytes < req.len; w_bytes += n)
    n = send (sd, ((char *) &req) + w_bytes,
      req.len - w_bytes, 0);
}
```

Since the length field is represented as a binary number the `send_request` routine must convert the message length into network byte order. The example uses stream sockets, which are created via the `SOCK_STREAM` socket type directive. This choice requires the application code to handle "short-writes" that may occur due to buffer constraints in the OS and transport protocols.* To handle short-writes, the code loops until all the bytes in the request are sent to the server.

The following `recv_response` routine receives a stock quote response from the server. It converts the numeric value of the stock quote into host byte order before returning the value to the caller:

```
void recv_response (HANDLE sd, long *value)
{
  struct Quote_Response res;

  recv (sd, (char*)&res.value, sizeof res.value, 0);
  /* Convert to host byte order */
  *value = ntohl (res.value);
}
```

The `print_quote` routine shown below uses the C utility routines defined above to establish a connection with the server. The host and port addresses are passed by the caller. After establishing a connection, the routine requests the server to return the current value of the designated `stock_name`.

```
void print_quote (const char server[],
          u_short port,
          const char stock_name[])
{
  HANDLE sd;
  long value;

  sd = connect_quote_server (server, port);
  send_request (sd, stock_name);
  recv_response (sd, &value);
  display ("value of %s stock = $%ld\n",
       stock_name, value);
}
```

This routine would typically be compiled, linked into an executable program, and called as follows:

```
print_quote ("quotes.nyse.com", 5150, "ACME ORBs");

/* Might print: "value of ACME ORBs stock = $12" */
```

* Sequence packet sockets (SOCK_SEQPACKET) could be used to preserve message boundaries, but this type of socket is not available on many operating systems.

Evaluating the Socket Solution

Sockets are a relatively low-level interface. As illustrated in the code above, programmers must explicitly perform the following tedious and potentially error-prone activities:

- ***Determining the addressing information for a service.*** The service addressing information in the example above would be inflexible if the user must enter the IP address and port number explicitly. Our socket code provides a glimmer of flexibility by using the `gethostbyname` utility routine, which converts a server name into its IP number. A more flexible scheme would automate service location by using some type of name service or location broker.

- ***Initializing the socket endpoint and connecting to the server.*** As shown in the `connect_quote_server` routine, socket programming requires a nontrivial amount of detail to establish a connection with a service. Moreover, minor mistakes (such as forgetting to initialize a socket address structure to zero) will prevent the application from working correctly.

- ***Marshaling and unmarshaling messages.*** The current example exchanges relatively simple data structures. Even so, the solution we show above will not work correctly if compilers on the client and server hosts align structures differently. In general, developing more complicated applications using sockets requires significant programmer effort to marshal and unmarshal complex messages that contain arrays, nested structures, or floating point numbers. In addition, developers must ensure that clients and servers don't get out of sync as changes are made.

- ***Sending and receiving messages.*** The code required to send and receive messages using sockets is subtle and surprisingly complex. The programmer must explicitly detect and handle many error conditions (such as short-writes), as well as frame and transfer record-oriented messages correctly over bytestream protocols such as TCP/IP.

- ***Error detection and error recovery.*** Another problem with sockets is that they make it hard to detect accidental type errors at compile-time. Socket descriptors are "weakly-typed," i.e., a descriptor associated with a connection-oriented socket is not syntactically different from a descriptor associated with a connectionless socket. Weakly-typed interfaces increase the potential for subtle runtime errors since a compiler cannot detect using the wrong descriptor in the wrong circumstances. To save space, we omitted much of the error handling code that would normally exist. In a production system, a large percentage of the code would be dedicated to providing robust error detection and error recovery at runtime.

- ***Portability.*** Another limitation with the solution shown above is that it hard-codes a dependency on sockets into the source code. Porting this code to a platform without sockets (such as early versions of System V UNIX) will require major changes to the source.
- ***Secure communications.*** A real-life stock trading service that did not provide secure communications would not be very useful, for obvious reasons. Adding security to the sockets code would exceed the capabilities of most programmers due to the expertise and effort required to get it right.

THE C++ WRAPPERS SOLUTION

Using C++ wrappers (which encapsulate lower-level network programming interfaces such as sockets or TLI within a type-safe, object-oriented interface) is one way to simplify the complexity of programming distributed applications. The C++ wrappers shown below are part of the `IPC_SAP` interprocess communication class library.[3] `IPC_SAP` encapsulates both sockets and TLI with C++ class categories.

C++ Wrapper Code

Rewriting the `print_quote` routine using C++ templates simplifies and generalizes the low-level C code in the `connect_quote_server` routine, as shown below:

```
template <class CONNECTOR, class STREAM, class ADDR>
void print_quote (const char server[],
    u_short port,
    const char stock_name[])
{
  // Data transfer object.
  STREAM peer_stream;

  // Create the address of the server.
  ADDR addr (port, server);

  // Establish a connection with the server.
  CONNECTOR con (peer_stream, addr);
```

```
    long value;

    send_request (peer_stream, stock_name);
    recv_response (peer_stream, &value);
    display ("value of %s stock = $%ld\n",
        stock_name, value);
}
```

The template parameters in this routine may be instantiated with the IPC_SAP C++ wrappers for sockets as follows:

```
print_quote<SOCK_Connector, SOCK_Stream, INET_Addr>
    ("quotes.nyse.com", 5150, "ACME ORBs");
```

SOCK_Connector shields application developers from the low-level details of establishing a connection. It is a factory[4] that connects to the server located at the INET_Addr address and produces a SOCK_Stream object when the connection completes. The SOCK_Stream object performs the message exchange for the stock query transaction and handles short-writes automatically. The INET_Addr class shields developers from the tedious and error-prone details of socket addressing shown in the "Socket/C Code" section.

The template routine may be parameterized by different types of IPC classes. Thus, we solve the portability problem with the socket solution discussed in the "Socket/C Code" section. For instance, only the following minimal changes are necessary to port our application from an OS platform that lacks sockets, but that has TLI:

```
print_quote<TLI_Connector, TLI_Stream, INET_Addr>
    ("quotes.nyse.com", 5150, "ACME ORBs");
```

Note that we simply replaced the SOCK* C++ class wrappers with TLI* C++ wrappers that encapsulate the TLI network programming interface. The IPC_SAP wrappers for sockets and TLI offers a conformant interface. Template parameterization is a useful technique that increases the flexibility and portability of the code. Moreover, parameterization does not degrade application performance since template instantiation is performed at compile-time. In contrast, the alternative technique for extensibility using inheritance and dynamic binding exacts a runtime performance penalty in C++ due to virtual function table lookup overhead.

The send_request and recv_request routines also may be simplified by using C++ wrappers that handle short-writes automatically, as illustrated in the send_request template routine below:

```
template <class STREAM>
void send_request (STREAM &peer_stream,
                   const char stock_name[])
{
  // Quote_Request's constructor does
  // the dirty work...
  Quote_Request req (stock_name);

  // send_n() handles the "short-writes"
  peer_stream.send_n (&req, req.length ());
}
```

Evaluating the C++ Wrappers Solution

The IPC_SAP C++ wrappers improve the use of sockets and C for several reasons. First, they help to automate and simplify certain aspects of using sockets (such as initialization, addressing, and handling short-writes). Second, they improve portability by shielding applications from platform-specific network programming interfaces. Wrapping sockets with C++ classes (rather than standalone C functions) makes it convenient to switch wholesale between different IPC mechanisms by using parameterized types. In addition, by combining inline functions and templates, the C++ wrappers do not introduce any measurable overhead compared with programming with socket directly.

However, the C++ wrappers solution, as well as the sockets solution, both suffer from the same costly drawback: too much of the code required for the application has nothing at all to do with the stock market. Moreover, unless you already have a C++ wrapper library like `IPC_SAP`, developing an OO communication infrastructure to support the stock quote application is prohibitively expensive. For one thing, stock market domain experts may not know anything at all about sockets programming. Developing an OO infrastructure either requires them to divert their attention to learning about sockets and C++ wrappers, or requires the hiring of people familiar with low-level network programming. Each solution would typically delay the deployment of the application and increase its overall development and maintenance cost.

Even if the stock market domain experts learned to program at the socket or C++ wrapper level, it is inevitable that the requirements for the system would eventually change. For example, it might become necessary to combine the stock quote system with a similar, yet separately developed, system for mutual funds. These changes may require modifications to the request/response message schema. In this case, the original solution and the C++ wrappers solution would require extensive modifications. Moreover, if the communication infrastructure of the stock quote system and the mutual funds system were each custom-developed, interoperability between the two would very likely prove impossible. Therefore, one or both of the systems would have to be rewritten extensively before they could be integrated.

In general, a more practical approach may be to use a distributed object computing (DOC) infrastructure built specifically to support distributed applications. In the following section, we motivate, describe, and evaluate such a DOC solution based upon CORBA. In subsequent columns, we'll examine solutions based on other DOC tools and environments (such as OODCE[5] and OLE/COM[6]).

The CORBA Solution

Overview of CORBA

An Object Request Broker (ORB)[7] is a system that supports distributed object computing in accordance with the OMG CORBA specification (currently CORBA 1.2,[8] although major pieces of CORBA 2.0 have already been completed). CORBA delegates much of the tedious and error-prone complexity associated with developing distributed applications to its reusable infrastructure. Application developers are then freed to focus their knowledge of the domain upon the problem at hand.

To invoke a service using CORBA, an application only needs to hold a reference to a target object. The ORB is responsible for automating other common communication infrastructure activities. These activities include locating a suitable target object, activating it if necessary, delivering the request to it, and returning any response back to the caller. Parameters passed as part of the request or response are automatically and transparently marshaled by the ORB. This marshaling process ensures correct interworking between applications and objects residing on different computer architectures.

CORBA object interfaces are described using an Interface Definition Language (IDL). CORBA IDL resembles C++ in many ways, though it is much simpler. In particular, it is not a full-ðedged programming language. Instead, it is a declarative language that programmers use to define object interfaces, operations, and parameter types.

An IDL compiler automatically translates CORBA IDL into client-side "stubs" and server-side "skeletons" that are written in a full-ðedged application development programming language (such as C++, C, Smalltalk, or Modula 3).

These stubs and skeletons serve as the "glue" between the client and server applications, respectively, and the ORB. Since the IDL programming language transformation is automated, the potential for inconsistencies between client stubs and server skeletons is reduced significantly.

CORBA Code

The following is a CORBA IDL specification for the stock quote system:

```
module Stock {
  exception Invalid_Stock {};

  interface Quoter {
    long get_quote (in string stock_name)
      raises (Invalid_Stock);
  };
};
```

The `Quoter` interface supports a single operation, `get_quote`. Its parameter is specified as an `in` parameter, which means that it is passed from the client to the server. IDL also permits `inout` parameters, which are passed from the client to the server and back to the client, and `out` parameters, which originate at the server and are passed back to the client. When given the name of a stock as an input parameter, `get_quote` either returns its value as a `long` or throws an `Invalid_Stock` exception. Both `Quoter` and `Invalid_Stock` are scoped within the `Stock` module to avoid polluting the application namespace.

A CORBA client using the standard OMG Naming service to locate and invoke an operation on a `Quoter` object might look as follows[†]:

```
// Introduce components into application namespace.
using namespace CORBA;
using namespace CosNaming;
using namespace Stock;

// Forward declaration.
Object_var bind_service (int argc, char *argv[],
    const Name &service_name);
```

[†] Note the use of the using namespace construct in this code to introduce scoped names into the application namespace; those unfamiliar with this construct should consult Bjarne Stroustrup's *Design and Evolution of C++* [12] for more details.

```
int main(int argc, char *argv[])
 {
   // Create desired service name
   const char *name = "Quoter";
   Name service_name;
   service_name.length(1);
   service_name[0].id = name;

   // Initialize and locate Quote service.
   Object_var obj =
     bind_service (argc, argv, service_name);

   // Narrow to Quoter interface and away we go!
   Quoter_var q = Quoter::_narrow (obj);

   const char *stock_name = "ACME ORB Inc.";

   try {
       long value = q->get_quote (stock_name);
       cout << "value of " << stock_name
          << " = $ "
          << value << endl;
     return 0;
   } catch (Invalid_Stock &) {
     cerr << stock_name
        << " is not a valid stock name!\n";
     return 1;
   }
 }
```

This application binds to the stock quote service, asks it for the value of ACME ORBs, Inc. stock, and prints out the value if everything works correctly. Several steps are required to accomplish this task. First, a `CosNaming::Name` structure representing the name of the desired service must be created. A `CosNaming::Name` is a `sequence` (which are essentially dynamically-sized arrays) of `CosNaming::NameComponents`, each of which is a `struct` containing two strings members, `id` and `kind`. In our application, we're only using the `id` member, which we set to the string "Quoter," the name of our service. Before the object reference returned from our utility routine `bind_service` can be used as a `Quoter`, it must be narrowed[††] to the `Quoter` interface. Once this is

[††] Narrowing to a derived interface is similar to using the C++ `dynamic_cast<T>` operator to downcast from a pointer to a base class to a pointer to a derived

done, the get_quote operation is called inside a try block. If an exception occurs, the catch block for the Invalid_Stock exception prints a suitable error message and exits. If no exception is thrown, the value returned is displayed on the standard output as the current value of the stock of ACME ORBs, Inc.

To simplify our application, the details of initializing the ORB and looking up object references in the Naming service have been hidden inside the bind_service utility function. Here's how it might be implemented:

```
Object_var bind_service (int argc, char *argv[],
    const Name &service_name)
  {
   // Get reference to name service.
   ORB_var orb = ORB_init (argc, argv, 0);
   Object_var obj =
     orb->resolve_initial_references ("NameService");
   NamingContext_var name_context =
     NamingContext::_narrow (obj);

   // Find object reference in the name service.
   return name_context->resolve (service_name);
}
```

To obtain an object reference to the Naming service, bind_service must first obtain a reference to the ORB. It accomplishes this by calling ORB_init. This is a standard routine defined in the CORBA namespace—it returns an ORB object reference. Using this object reference, the application then invokes resolve_initial_references. This routine acts as a miniature name service provided by the ORB for certain well-known object references. From this it obtains an object reference to the name service. The resolve_initial_references call returns an object reference of type CORBA::Object (the base interface of all IDL interfaces). Therefore, the return value must be narrowed to the more derived interface type, CosNaming::NamingContext, before any of the naming operations can be invoked on it.

Once the NamingContext object reference has been obtained, the service_name argument is passed to the resolve operation on the NamingContext. Assuming the name is resolved successfully, the resolve operation returns to the caller an object reference of type CORBA::Object for the Quoter service.

---

class. In the OMG C++ language mapping, the result of a successful narrow operation is a new object reference statically typed to the requested derived interface.

Evaluating the CORBA Solution

The preceding example illustrates how the client-side code deals directly with the application-related issues of obtaining stock quotes, rather than with the low-level communication-related issues. Therefore, the amount of effort required to extend and port this application will be reduced. This should not come as a surprise, since the CORBA solution significantly raises the level of abstraction at which the solution is developed.

Of course, the CORBA solution is not perfect. The use of CORBA has several potential drawbacks that are important to understand and evaluate carefully before committing to use it on a commercial project:

- ***Learning Curve.*** The level of abstraction at which our CORBA solution is developed is much higher than that of the socket-based solution. However, CORBA does not totally relieve the stock market domain expert of being able to program DOC software in C++. CORBA introduces a range of new concepts (such as object references, proxies, and object adapters), components and tools (such as interface definition languages, IDL compilers, and object request brokers), and features (such as exception handling and interface inheritance). Depending on developer experience, it may take a fair amount of time to ramp-up to using CORBA productively. As with any other software tool, the cost of learning the new technology must be amortized over time and/or successive projects.
- ***Interoperability and portability.*** Interoperability between different ORBs has traditionally been a major problem with CORBA. This problem was solved recently when the OMG approved an Interoperability protocol.[9] However, few if any ORBs actually implement the Interoperability protocol at this time. Therefore, interoperability will remain a real problem for CORBA-based applications in the near future.

  Likewise, portability of applications from ORB to ORB will be limited until conformance becomes more commonplace. The OMG just recently approved the IDL-to-C++ language mapping, the Naming service, and the ORB Initialization service (e.g., `ORB_init` and `resolve_initial_references`). However, like the standard Interoperability protocol mentioned above, at this time few if any commercially-available ORBs actually provide services conforming to these standards.
- ***Security.*** Any ORB hoping to serve as the distributed computing infrastructure for a real stock trading system must address the need for security within the system. Unfortunately, few if any of the CORBA ORBs

available today address this issue, since the OMG has not yet standardized on a Security Service. However, given that the OMG Object Services Task Force is currently evaluating several proposals for such a service, a standard OMG security specification should be available by late 1995 or early 1996.

- ***Performance.*** The performance of the stock quote application may not be as good as that of the socket-based or C++ wrapper-based applications. In particular, the ORB is not tuned specifically to this application. In addition, we are accessing the Naming service, which probably requires one or more remote invocations of its own.

  For large-scale distributed software systems, the small loss in microlevel efficiency is often more than made up for by the increased extensibility, robustness, maintainability, and macro-level efficiency. In particular, a well designed CORBA implementation may actually improve performance by recognizing the context in which a service is accessed and automatically applying certain optimizations.

  For example, if an ORB determines that a requestor and a target object are co-located in the same address space, it may eliminate marshaling and IPC and simply invoke the target object's method directly. Likewise, if the ORB determines that the requestor and target object are located on the same host machine, it may suppress marshaling and pass parameters via shared memory rather than using a message-passing IPC mechanism. Finally, even if the requestor and target object are on different machines, an ORB may optimize marshaling if it recognizes that the requestor and target host support the same byte ordering.

All the optimizations listed above may be performed automatically without requiring a developer to modify the application. In general, manually programming this degree of flexibility using sockets, C, or C++ would be too time-consuming to justify the development effort.

Coping with Changing Requirements

Designing software that is resilient to change is a constant challenge for developers of large-scale systems. A primary motivation for DOC is to simplify the development of flexible and extensible software. Software with these two qualities adapts more easily to inevitable changes in requirements and environments during the lifetime of applications in large distributed systems.

A major benefit of using CORBA rather than sockets or C++ wrappers is revealed when application requirements change. For example, imagine that after deploying the first version of the stock quote application, the customer requests certain requirement changes described below.

Adding New Features

New features are inevitably added to successful software applications. For instance, end-users of the stock quote application might request additional query operations, as well as the ability to place a trade (i.e., to automatically buy shares of stock) along with determining the current value.

Many new features will modify the request and response formats. For example, additional information may be returned in a query, such as the percentage that the stock has risen or fallen in value since the start of the day and the volume of trading that has taken place (i.e., number of shares traded).

```
interface Quoter {
  long get_quote (in string stock_name,
                  out double percent_change,
                  out long trading_volume)
  raises (Invalid_Stock);
};
```

In contrast, adding new parameters to the original socket or C++ wrapper solution requires many tedious changes to be performed manually. For example, the `struct` defining the request format must change, necessitating a rewrite of the marshaling code. This modification may introduce inconsistencies into the source code that cause runtime failures. In addition, handling the marshaling and unmarshaling of the floating point `percent_change` parameter can be tricky.

Format changes (such as the adding parameters to methods) typically require recompiling both client and server software in many ORB development environments. Often, this is undesirable since tracking down all the deployed binaries may be hard. In addition, it may not be possible to take the system down for upgrade. Therefore, a less obtrusive method for managing changes involves creating new interfaces. For example, rather than adding parameters as shown above, a `get_stats` operation could simply be added to a new derived interface:

```
interface Stat_Quoter
    : Quoter // a Stat_Quoter IS-A Quoter
{
  void get_stats (in string stock_name,
    out double percent_change,
```

```
    out long trading_volume)
  raises (Invalid_Stock);
};
```

CORBA's support for interface inheritance enables it to satisfy the "open/closed" principle of OO library design.[10] By using inheritance, existing clients may continue using the old interface (i.e., existing library components are "closed," which ensures backwards compatibility). Conversely, clients requiring the new features and services use the new one (i.e., the library components are "open" to future extensions).

As an example of adding a trading interface, we could define a new CORBA IDL interface called `Trader` in the `Stock` module:

```
interface Trader {
  void buy (in string name,
            inout long num_shares,
            in long max_value)
  raises (Invalid_Stock);

  void sell (in string name,
             inout long num_shares,
             in long min_value)
  raises (Invalid_Stock);
};
```

The `Trader` interface provides two methods, `buy` and `sell`, that are used to trade shares of stock with other brokers.

By using CORBA IDL's support for multiple inheritance, an interface describing a full service broker might then be defined in the `Stock` module as follows:

```
interface Broker : Stat_Quoter, Trader {};
```

The `Broker` interface now supports all the operations of all the `Stat_Quoter`, `Quoter`, and `Trader` interfaces.

Note that adding this functionality to either the C or C++ socket solution would probably require extensive changes to all existing code to incorporate the new features. For example, it would be necessary to define several new request and response message formats. In turn, these changes would require modifying and recompiling the client and server applications.

Improving Existing Features

In addition to adding new features, let's consider changes occurring after extensive day-to-day usage and performance benchmarking of the trading application. Based on experience and end-user feedback, the following changes to existing features might be proposed:

- ***Server location independence.*** The socket and C++ wrapper code shown earlier "hard-codes" the server name and port number of the service into the application. However, the application can be much more flexible if it delays binding the name to the service until runtime. Run-time binding to the service can be accomplished in CORBA by a client locating the object reference of the service using a *Naming service* or a *Trader service.*

  A Naming service manages a hierarchy consisting of pairs of names and object references. The desired object reference can be found if its name is known. An example of this type of name service is the `CosNaming` name service used in the CORBA example shown above.

  A Trader service can locate a suitable object given a set of attributes for the object, such as supported interface(s), average load and response times, or permissions and privileges.

  Run-time binding allows the application to locate and use the server with the lightest load, or the closest server in order to minimize network transmission delays. In addition, once the Naming or Trading services are developed, debugged, and deployed they can be reused by subsequent distributed applications.

- ***Bulk requests.*** rather than sending each quote request individually, it may be much more efficient to send an entire sequence of requests and receive a sequence of responses in order to minimize network traffic.

In CORBA, this type of optimization may be expressed succinctly using CORBA IDL `sequences`. While retaining backwards compatibility, we can extend our `Quoter` interface to incorporate this change using CORBA IDL inheritance and IDL sequences as follows:

```
interface Bulk_Quoter
  : Stat_Quoter // A Bulk_Quoter IS-A Stat_Quoter
{
  typedef sequence<string> Names;
  struct Stock_Info {
    string       name;
    long         value;
```

```
      double       change;
      long         volume;
    };
    typedef sequence<Stock_Info> Info;

    exception No_Such_Stock {
      Names stock; // List of invalid stock names
    };

    void bulk_quote (in Names stock_names,
                     out Info stock_info)
    raises (No_Such_Stock);
  };
```

Notice how CORBA exceptions may contain user-defined fields that provide additional information about the causes of a failure. For example, in the `Bulk_Quoter` class the `No_Such_Stock` exception contains a sequence of strings indicating which stock names were invalid.

Conclusion

In this article, we examined several different techniques for developing the client-side of a distributed stock trading application. In general, the example illustrates how the CORBA-based DOC solution improves extensibility and robustness by relying on an ORB infrastructure built to support communication between distributed objects without unduly compromising efficiency. Relying on an ORB in this manner is not unlike relying on a good general-purpose library (such as the C++ Standard Templates Library[11]) for nondistributed C++ applications. The ORB allows the application developer to focus mainly on the application and not worry nearly as much about the infrastructure required to support it.

Note that CORBA is only one of several key technologies that are emerging to support DOC. In future articles, we will discuss other OO toolkits and environments (such as OODCE and OLE/COM) and compare them with CORBA in the same manner that we compared sockets to CORBA. Before we do that, though, we need to discuss various aspects of the server-side of our financial services application, which we will tackle in our next column. The server-side implements the various methods defined in the CORBA IDL interfaces.

As always, if there are any topics that you'd like us to cover, please send us email at object_connect@ch.hp.com.

References

1. Leffler, S.J., M. McKusick, M. Karels, and J. Quarterman. *The Design and Implementation of the 4.3BSD UNIX Operating System,* Addison-Wesley, 1989.
2. Stevens, W. R. *UNIX Network Programming,* Prentice Hall, Englewood Cliffs, NJ, 1990.
3. Schmidt, D. C. IPC_SAP; An Object-Oriented Interface to Interprocess Communications Services, *C++ Report,* Vol. 4, Nov.-Dec. 1992.
4. Gamma, E., R. Helm, R. Johnson, and J. Vlissides. *Design Patterns: Elements of Reusable Object-Oriented Software,* Addison-Wesley, Reading, MA, 1994.
5. Dilley, J. OODCE: A C++ framework for the OSF distributed computing environment, in *Proceedings of the Winter Usenix Conference,* USENIX Association, Jan. 1994.
6. Microsoft Press, *Object Linking and Embedding Version 2 (OLE2) Programmer's Reference,* Volumes 1 and 2, Microsoft Press, Redmond, WA, 1993.
7. Vinoski, S. Distributed object computing with CORBA, *C++ Report,* 5(6), Jul.–Aug. 1993.
8. Object Management Group, *The Common Object Request Broker: Architecture and Specification,* 1.2, 1993.
9. Object Management Group, *Universal Networked Objects,* TC Document 94-9-32, Sept. 1994.
10. Meyer, B. *Object Oriented Software Construction,* Prentice Hall, Englewood Cliffs, NJ, 1989.
11. Stepanov, A. and M. Lee. "The Standard Template Library," Tech. Rep. HPL-94-34, Hewlett-Packard Laboratories, Apr. 1994.
12. Stroustrup, B. *Design and Evolution of C++,* Addison-Wesley, Reading, MA, 1994.

COMPARING ALTERNATIVE SERVER PROGRAMMING TECHNIQUES

STEVE VINOSKI
vinoski@ch.hp.com

DOUG SCHMIDT
schmidt@cs.wustl.edu

SEVERAL TECHNIQUES FOR DEVELOPING CLIENT/SERVER APPLICATIONS ARE examined and evaluated in this column to illustrate key aspects of distributed programming. The application we're examining enables investment brokers to query the price of a stock from a distributed quote database. Our two previous columns outlined the distributed computing requirements of this application and examined several ways to implement the client-side functionality. In this article, we compare several ways to program the server-side of this application.

The solutions we examine range from using C, `select`, and the sockets network programming interface; to using C++ wrappers for `select` and sockets; to using a distributed object computing (DOC) solution based on the OMG's Common Object Request Broker Architecture (CORBA). Along the way, we'll examine various tradeoffs between extensibility, robustness, portability, and efficiency for each of the three solutions.

SERVER PROGRAMMING

Developers who write the server-side of an application must address certain topics that client-side developers may be able to ignore. One such topic is demultiplexing of requests from multiple clients. For example, our stock quote server can be accessed simultaneously by multiple clients connected via communication protocols such as TCP/IP or IPX/SPX. Therefore, the server must be capable of receiving client requests over multiple connections without blocking indefinitely on any single connection.

A related topic that server programmers must address is concurrency. The two primary types of server concurrency strategies[1,2] are distinguished as follows:

- *Iterative servers,* which handle each client request in its entirety before servicing subsequent requests. While processing the current request, an iterative server typically queues new client requests. An iterative design is most suitable for short-duration services that exhibit relatively little variation in their execution time. Internet services like `echo` and `daytime` are commonly implemented as iterative servers.
- *Concurrent servers,* which handle multiple client requests simultaneously. Concurrent servers help improve responsiveness and reduce latency when the rate at which requests are processed is less than the rate at which requests arrive at the server. A concurrent server design may also increase throughput for I/O-bound and/or long-duration services that require a variable amount of time to execute. Internet services like `telnet` and `ftp` are commonly implemented as concurrent servers.

Concurrent servers generally require more sophisticated synchronization and scheduling strategies than iterative servers. For the example application in this column, we'll assume that each stock quote request in the server executes quickly. Therefore, an iterative server design will suffice to meet our response and throughput requirements. Moreover, as shown below, our synchronization and scheduling strategies are simplified by using an iterative server.

We'll use the UNIX `select` event demultiplexing system call to provide a simple round-robin scheduler. The `select` call detects and reports the occurrence of one or more connection events or data events that occur simultaneously on multiple communication endpoints (e.g., socket handles). The `select` call provides coarse-grained concurrency control that serializes event handling within a process or thread. This eliminates the need for more complicated threading, synchronization, or locking within our server.

In-depth coverage of sockets and `select` appears in Stevens.[2] In future columns we'll discuss how to extend our solutions to incorporate more sophisticated concurrency and demultiplexing strategies.

The Socket Server Solution

Socket/C Code

The following code illustrates how to program the server-side of the stock quote program using sockets, select, and C. The following two C structures define the schema for quote requests and quote responses:

```
#define MAXSTOCKNAMELEN 100

struct Quote_Request
{
  long len; /* Length of the request. */
  char name[MAXSTOCKNAMELEN]; /* Stock name. */
};

struct Quote_Response
{
  long value; /* Current value of the stock. */
  long errno; /* 0 if success, else errno value. */
};
```

These structures are exchanged between the client-side and server-side of the stock quote programs.

Next, we've written four C utility routines. These routines shield the rest of the application from dealing with the low-level socket interface. To save space, we've omitted most of the error handling code. Naturally, a robust production application would carefully check the return values of system calls, handle unexpected connection resets, and insure that messages don't overflow array bounds.

The first routine receives a stock quote request from a client:

```
// WIN32 already defines this.
#if defined (unix)
typedef int HANDLE;
#endif /* unix */

int recv_request (HANDLE h,
    struct Quote_Request *req)
{
  int r_bytes, n;
  int len = sizeof *req;

  /* Recv data from client, handle "short-reads". */
  for (r_bytes = 0; r_bytes < len; r_bytes += n) {
    n = recv (h, ((char *) req) + r_bytes, len - r_bytes, 0);
    if (n <= 0) return n;
  }
  /* Decode len to host byte order. */
  req->len = ntohl (req->len);
  return r_bytes;
}
```

The length field of a `Quote_Request` is represented as a binary number that the client's `send_request` encoded into network byte order. Therefore, the server's `recv_request` routine must decode the message length back into host byte order using `ntohl`. In addition, since we use the bytestream-oriented TCP protocol, the server code must explicitly loop to handle "short-reads" that occur due to buffer constraints in the OS and transport protocols.

The following `send_response` routine sends a stock quote from the server back to the client. It encodes the numeric value of the stock quote into network byte order before returning the value to the client, as follows:

```
int send_response (HANDLE h, long value)
{
  struct Quote_Response res;
  size_t w_bytes;
  size_t len = sizeof res;

  // Set error value if failure occurred.
  res.errno = value == -1 ? htonl (errno) : 0;
  res.value = htonl (value);

  /* Respond to client, handle "short-writes". */
  for (w_bytes = 0; w_bytes < len; w_bytes += n) {
    n = send (h, ((const char *) &res) + w_bytes,
              len - w_bytes, 0);
    if (n <= 0) return n;
  }
  return w_bytes;
}
```

As with `recv_request`, the server must explicitly handle short-writes by looping until all the bytes in the response are sent to the client.

The `handle_quote` routine uses the C functions shown above to receive the stock quote request from the client, look up the value of the stock in an online database, and return the value to the client, as follows:

```
extern Quote_Database *quote_db;
long lookup_stock_price (Quote_Database *,
          Quote_Request *);

void handle_quote (HANDLE h)
{
  struct Quote_Request req;
  long value;
```

```
    if (recv_request (h, &req) == 0)
      return 0;

    /* ... lookup stock in database. */
    value = lookup_stock_price (quote_db, &req);

    return send_response (h, value);
  }
```

The handle_quote function illustrates the synchronous, request/response style of communication between clients and the quote server. In a future column we'll illustrate how to develop asynchronous "publish/subscribe" communication mechanisms that notify consumers automatically when stock values change.

The next routine creates a socket server endpoint that listens for connections from stock quote clients. The caller passes the port number to listen on as a parameter:

```
HANDLE create_server_endpoint (u_short port)
{
  struct sockaddr_in addr;
  HANDLE h;

  /* Create a local endpoint of communication. */
  h = socket (PF_INET, SOCK_STREAM, 0);

  /* Setup the address of the server. */
  memset ((void *) &addr, 0, sizeof addr);
  addr.sin_family = AF_INET;
  addr.sin_port = htons (port);
  addr.sin_addr.s_addr = INADDR_ANY;

  /* Bind server port. */
  bind (h, (struct sockaddr *) &addr, sizeof addr);

  /* Make server endpoint listen for connections. */
  listen (h, 5);
  return h;
}
```

The main function shown below uses the C utility routines defined above to create an iterative quote server. The select system call demultiplexes new connection events and data events from clients. Connection events are handled directly in the event loop, which adds the new HANDLE to the fd_set used by select. Data events are presumed to be quote requests, which trigger the handle_quote function to return the latest stock quote from the online database. Note that data events are demultiplexed using a round-robin scheduling policy that dispatches the handle_quote function in order of ascending HANDLE values.

```
int main(int argc, char *argv[])
{
  u_short port /* Port to listen for connections. */
    = argc > 1 ? atoi(argv[1]) : 10000;

  /* Create a passive-mode listener endpoint. */
  HANDLE listener = create_server_endpoint(port);
  HANDLE maxhp = listener + 1;

  /* fd_sets maintain a set of HANDLEs that
     select() uses to wait for events. */
  fd_set read_hs, temp_hs;
  FD_ZERO(&read_hs);
  FD_ZERO(&temp_hs);
  FD_SET(listener, &read_hs);

  for (;;) {
    HANDLE h;
    /* Demultiplex connection and data events */
    select(maxhp, &temp_hs, 0, 0, 0);

    /* Check for stock quote requests and
      dispatch the quote handler in
      round-robin order. */
    for (h = listener + 1; h < maxhp; h++)
    if (FD_ISSET(h, &temp_hs))
      if (handle_quote(h) == 0)
      /* Client's shutdown. */
      FD_CLR(h, &read_hs);

    /* Check for new connections. */
    if (FD_ISSET(listener, &temp_hs)) {
      h = accept(listener, 0, 0);
      FD_SET(h, &read_hs);
      if (maxhp <= h)
        maxhp = h + 1;
    }
```

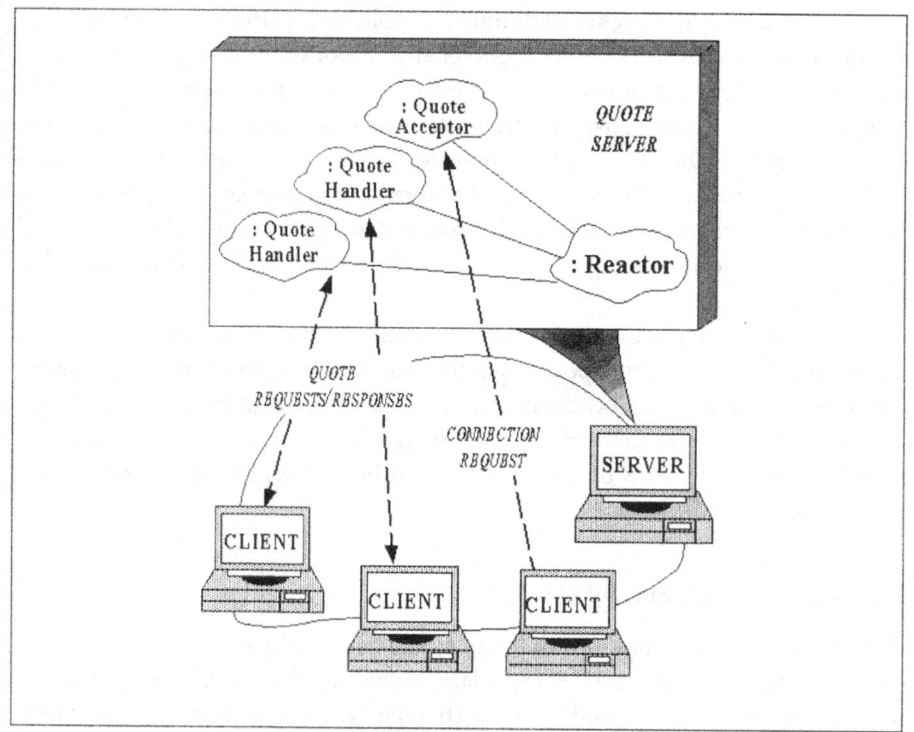

FIGURE 1. *The C++ wrapper architecture for the stock quote server.*

```
    temp_hs = read_hs;
    }
    /* NOTREACHED */
}
```

The main program iterates continuously accepting connections and returning quotes. Once a client establishes a connection with the server it remains connected until the client explicitly closes down the connection. This design amortizes the cost of establishing connections since clients can request multiple quote values without reconnecting.

Evaluating the Socket Solution

Programming with C, sockets, and `select` as shown above yields relatively efficient sequential programs. However, sockets and `select` are low-level interfaces. Our previous column described the many communication-related activities that must be performed by programs written at this level. Briefly, these activities include initializing the socket endpoints, establishing connections, marshaling and unmarshaling of stock quote requests and responses, sending and receiving messages, detecting and recovering from errors, and providing security.

In addition to these activities, the server must also perform demultiplexing and concurrency. Directly programming `select` to demultiplex events is particularly problematic.[3] The `select` call requires programmers to explicitly handle many low-level details involving bitmasks, descriptor counts, time-outs, and signals. In addition to being tedious and error-prone, `select` is not portable across OS platforms.

Another drawback with the current structure of the quote server is that it hard-codes the application-specific service behavior directly into the program. This makes it hard to extend the current solution (e.g., changing from an iterative to a concurrent server) without modifying existing source code. Likewise, it is hard to reuse any pieces of this solution in other servers that implement similar, but not identical, services.

The C++ Wrappers Solution

Using C++ wrappers is one way to simplify the complexity of programming network servers. C++ wrappers encapsulate lower-level network programming interfaces such as sockets and select with type-safe, object-oriented interfaces. The `IPC_SAP`,[4] `Reactor`,[3,5] and `Acceptor`[6] C++ wrappers shown below are part of the ACE object-oriented network programming toolkit. IPC_SAP encapsulates sockets and TLI network programming interfaces; the Reactor encapsulates the select and poll event demultiplexing system calls; and the Acceptor combines IPC_SAP and the Reactor to implement a reusable strategy for establishing connections passively.*

C++ Wrapper Code

This section illustrates how the use of C++ wrappers improves the reuse, portability, and extensibility of the quote server. Figure 1 depicts the following three components in the quote server architecture:

1. `Reactor`—defines a mechanism for registering, removing, and dispatching `Event_Handlers` (such as the `Quote_Acceptor` and `Quote_Handler`

---

* Communication software is typified by asymmetric connection behavior between clients and servers. In general, servers listen passively for clients to initiate connections actively.

described below). The `Reactor` encapsulates the `select` and `poll` event demultiplexing system calls with an extensible and portable callback-driven object-oriented interface.

2. `Quote_Acceptor`—a factory that implements the strategy for accepting connections from clients, followed by creating and activating `Quote_Handlers`.

3. `Quote_Handler`—interacts with clients by receiving quote requests, looking up quotes in the database, and returning responses. `Quote_Handlers` can be implemented as either passive or active objects, depending on how they are configured.

Both the `Quote_Acceptor` and `Quote_Handler` inherit from the `Reactor`'s `Event_Handler` base class. This enables the `Reactor` to callback to their `handle_input` methods when connection events and data events arrive, respectively.

We'll start by showing the `Quote_Handler`. This template class inherits from the reusable `Svc_Handler` base class in the ACE toolkit. A `Svc_Handler` defines a generic interface for a communication services that exchange data with peers over network connections. For the stock quote application, `Svc_Handler` is instantiated with a communication interface that receives quote requests and returns quote values to clients. As shown below, it uses the `IPC_SAP` `SOCK_Stream` C++ wrapper for TCP stream sockets. `IPC_SAP` shields applications from low-level details of network programming interfaces like sockets or TLI.

```
template <class STREAM,      // IPC interface
          class ADDR,        // Addressing interface
          class SYNCH>       // Synchronization interface

class Quote_Handler
  : public Svc_Handler<STREAM, ADDR, SYNCH>
    // ACE base class defines "STREAM peer_;"
{
public:
  Quote_Handler (Quote_Database *db): db_ (db) {}

  // This method is invoked as a callback by
  // the Reactor when data arrives from a client.
  virtual int handle_input (HANDLE) {
    return this->handle_quote ();
  }
```

```
  virtual int handle_quote (void) {
    Quote_Request req;

    if (this->recv_request (req) <= 0)
        return -1;

    long value = this->db_->lookup_stock_price (req);

    return this->send_response (value);
  }

  virtual int recv_request (Quote_Request &req) {
    // recv_n handles "short-reads"
    int n = this->peer_.recv_n (&req, sizeof req);
    if (n > 0)
      /* Decode len to host byte order. */
      req.len (ntohl (req.len ()));
    return n;
  }

  virtual int send_response (long value) {
    // The constructor performs the error checking
    // and network byte-ordering conversions.
    Quote_Response res (value);

    // send_n handles "short-writes".
    return this->peer_.send_n (&res, sizeof res);
  }
private:
  Quote_Database *db_;
};
```

The next class is the `Quote_Acceptor`. This class is a `typedef` that supplies concrete template arguments for the reusable `Acceptor` connection factory from the ACE toolkit shown below:

```
template <class SVC_HANDLER, // Service handler
  class ACCEPTOR,            // Passive connection factory
  class ADDR>                // Addressing interface
class Acceptor
{
public:
  // Initialize a passive-mode connection factory.
  Acceptor (const ADDR &addr): peer_acceptor_ (addr) {}
```

```
    // Implements the strategy to accept connections from
    // clients, and creating and activating SVC_HANDLERs
    // to process data exchanged over the connections.

    int handle_input (void) {
      // Create a new service handler.
      SVC_HANDLER *svc_handler = this-make_svc_handler ();
      // Accept connection into the service handler.
      this->peer_acceptor_.accept (*svc_handler);

      // Delegate control to the service handler.
      svc_handler->open ();
      }

      // Factory method to create a service handler.
      // The default behavior allocates a SVC_HANDLER.
      // Subclasses can override this to implement

      // other policies (such as a Singleton).
      virtual SVC_HANDLER *make_svc_handler (void) {
      return new SVC_HANDLER;
    }

    // Returns the underlying passive-mode HANDLE.

    virtual HANDLE get_handle (void) {
      return this->peer_acceptor_.get_handle ();
    }

  private:
    ACCEPTOR peer_acceptor_;
    // Factory that establishes connections passively.
  };
```

The `Quote_Acceptor` class is formed by parameterizing the `Acceptor` template with concrete types that (1) accept connections (e.g., `SOCK_Acceptor` or `TLI_Acceptor`) and (2) perform the quote service (`Quote_Handler`). Note that using C++ classes and templates makes it efficient and convenient to conditionally choose between sockets and TLI, as shown below:

```
  // Conditionally choose network programming interface.
  #if defined (USE_SOCKETS)
  typedef SOCK_Acceptor ACCEPTOR;
  typedef SOCK_Stream STREAM;
  #elif defined (USE_TLI)
```

```
typedef TLI_Acceptor ACCEPTOR;
typedef TLI_Stream STREAM;
#endif /* USE_SOCKET */

// Make a specialized version of the Acceptor
// factory to handle quote requests from clients.
// Since we are an iterative server we can use the
// ACE "Null_Synch" synchronization mechanisms.
typedef Acceptor <Quote_Handler <STREAM,
                   INET_Addr,
                   Null_Synch>,
                   ACCEPTOR, INET_Addr>
      Quote_Acceptor;
```

A more dynamically extensible method of selecting between sockets or TLI can be achieved via inheritance and dynamic binding by using the Abstract Factory or Factory Method patterns described in Gamma *et al.*[7] An advantage of using parameterized types, however, is that they improve runtime efficiency. For example, parameterized types avoid the overhead of virtual method dispatching and allow compilers to inline frequently accessed methods. The downside, of course, is that template parameters are locked in at compile time, templates can be slower to link, and they usually require more space.

The `main` function uses the components defined above to implement the quote server:

```
int main (int argc, char *argv[])
{
  u_short port = argc > 1 ? atoi (argv[1]) : 10000;

  // Event demultiplexer.
  Reactor reactor;

  // Factory that produces Quote_Handlers.
  Quote_Acceptor acceptor (port);

  // Register acceptor with the reactor, which
  // calls the acceptor's get_handle() method)
  // to obtain the passive-mode HANDLE.
  reactor.register_handler (&acceptor, READ_MASK);

  // Single-threaded event loop that dispatches
  // all events as callbacks to the appropriate
  // Event_Handler subclass object (such as
  // the Quote_Acceptor or Quote_Handlers).
```

```
  for (;;)
    reactor.handle_events ();

  /* NOTREACHED */
  return 0;
}
```

After the `Quote_Acceptor` factory has been registered with the `Reactor` the application goes into an event loop. This loop runs continuously handling client connections, quote requests, and quote responses, all of which are driven by callbacks from the `Reactor`. Since this application runs as an iterative server in a single thread there is no need for additional locking mechanisms. The `Reactor` implicitly serializes `Event_Handlers` at the event dispatching level.

Evaluating the C++ Wrappers Solution

Using C++ wrappers to implement the quote server is an improvement over the use of sockets, `select`, and C for the following reasons:

- ***Simplify programming.*** Low-level details of programming sockets (such as initialization, addressing, and handling short-writes and short-reads) can be performed automatically by the `IPC_SAP` wrappers. Moreover, we eliminate several common programming errors by not using `select` directly.[3]

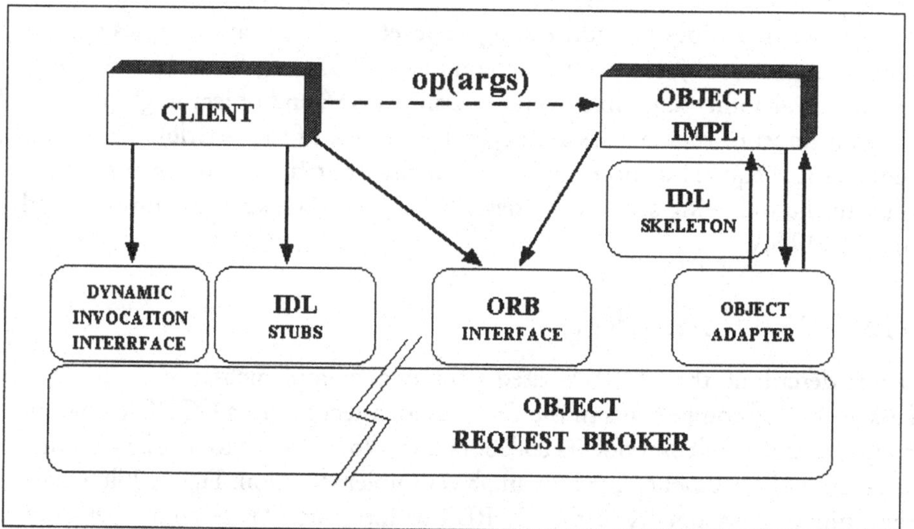

FIGURE 2. *Key components in the CORBA architecture.*

- *Improve portability.* By shielding applications from platform-specific network programming interfaces. Wrapping sockets with C++ classes (rather than stand-alone C functions) makes it easy to switch wholesale between different network programming interfaces simply by changing the parameterized types to the `Acceptor` template. Moreover, the code is more portable since the server no longer accesses `select` directly. For example, the `Reactor` can be implemented with other event demultiplexing system calls (such as SVR4 UNIX `poll`, WIN32 `WaitForMultipleObjects`, or even separate threads).[8]
- *Increase reusability and extensibility.* The `Reactor`, `Quote_Acceptor`, and `Quote_Handler` components are not as tightly coupled as the version given earlier. Therefore, it is easier to extend the C++ solution to include new services, as well as to enhance existing services. For example, to modify or extend the functionality of the quote server (e.g., to adding stock trading functionality), only the implementation of the `Quote_Handler` class must change.

In addition, C++ features like templates and inlining ensure that these improvements do not penalize performance.

However, even though the C++ wrapper solution is a distinct improvement over the C solution it still has the same drawbacks as the C++ wrapper client solution we presented in our last column: too much of the code required for the application is not directly related to the stock market. Moreover, the use of C++ wrappers does not address higher-level communication topics such as object location, object activation, complex marshaling and demarshaling, security, availability and fault tolerance transactions; and object migration and copying (most of these topics are beyond the scope of this article). To address these issues requires a more sophisticated distributed computing infrastructure. In the following section, we describe and evaluate such a solution based upon CORBA.

THE CORBA SOLUTION

Before describing the CORBA-based stock quoter implementation we'll take a look at the key components in the CORBA architecture. In a CORBA environment, a number of components collaborate to allow a client to invoke an operation `op` with arguments `args` on an object implementation. Figure 2 illustrates the primary components in the CORBA architecture. These components are described below:

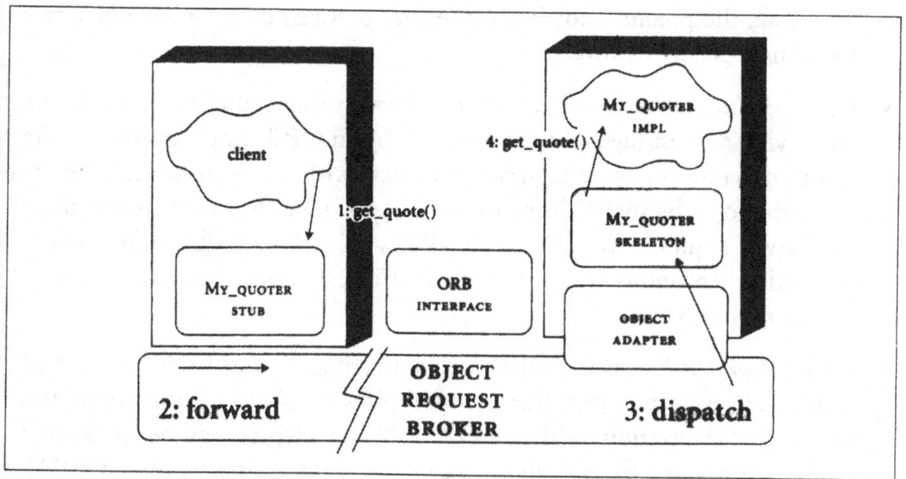

FIGURE 3. *CORBA request flow throughout the ORB.*

- ***Object Implementation.*** Defines operations that implement an OMG-IDL interface. We implement our examples using C++. However, object implementations can be written in other languages such as C, Smalltalk, Ada95, Eiffel, etc.
- ***Client.*** This is the program entity that invokes an operation on an object implementation. Ideally, accessing the services of a remote object should be as simple as calling a method on that object, i.e., `obj->op(args)`. The remaining components in Figure 2 support this behavior.
- ***Object Request Broker (ORB).*** When a client invokes an operation the ORB is responsible for finding the object implementation, transparently activating it if necessary, delivering the request to the object, and returning any response to the caller.
- ***ORB Interface.*** An ORB is a logical entity that may be implemented in various ways (such as one or more processes or a set of libraries). To decouple applications from implementation details, the CORBA specification defines an abstract interface for an ORB. This interface provides various helper functions such as converting object references to strings and back, and creating argument lists for requests made through the dynamic invocation interface described below.
- ***OMG-IDL stubs and skeletons.*** OMG-IDL stubs and skeletons serve as the "glue" between the client and server applications, respectively, and the ORB. The OMG-IDL programming language transformation is automated.

Therefore, the potential for inconsistencies between client stubs and server skeletons is greatly reduced.

- *Dynamic Invocation Interface (DII).* Allows a client to directly access the underlying request mechanisms provided by an ORB. Applications use the DII to dynamically issue requests to objects without requiring IDL interface-specific stubs to be linked in. Unlike IDL stubs (which only allow RPC-style requests) the DII also allows clients to make nonblocking deferred synchronous (separate send and receive operations) and oneway (send-only) calls.
- *Object Adapter.* Assists the ORB with delivering requests to the object and with activating the object. More importantly, an object adapter associates object implementations with the ORB. Object adapters can be specialized to provide support for certain object implementation styles, (e.g., OODB object adapters, library object adapters for nonremote (same-process) objects, etc).

Below, we outline how an ORB supports diverse and flexible object implementations via object adapters and object activation. We'll cover the remainder of the components mentioned previously in future columns.

Object Adapters

A fundamental goal of CORBA is to support implementation diversity. In particular, the CORBA model allows for diversity of programming languages, OS platforms, transport protocols, and networks. This enables CORBA to encompass a wide-spectrum of environments and requirements.

To support implementation diversity, an ORB should be able to interact with various types and styles of object implementations. It is hard to achieve this goal by allowing object implementations to interact directly with the ORB, however. This approach would require the ORB to provide a very "fat" interface and implementation. For example, an ORB that directly supported objects written in C, C++, and Smalltalk could become very complicated. It would need to provide separate foundations for each language or would need to use a least-common-denominator binary object model that made programming in some of the languages unnatural.

By having object implementations plug into object adapters (OAs) instead of plugging directly into the ORB, bloated ORBs can be avoided. Object adapters can be specialized to support certain object implementation styles. For example, one object adapter could be developed specifically to support C++ objects.

Another object adapter might be designed for object-oriented database objects. Still another object adapter could be created to optimize access to objects located in the same process address space as the client.

Conceptually, object adapters fit between the ORB and the object implementation (as shown in Figure 2). They assist the ORB with delivering requests to the object and with activating the object. By specializing object adapters, ORBs can remain lightweight, while still supporting different types and styles of objects. Likewise, object implementors can choose the object adapter that best suits their development environment and application requirements. Therefore, they incur overhead only for what they use. As mentioned above, the alternative is to cram the ORB full of code to support different object implementation styles. This is undesirable since it leads to bloated and potentially inefficient implementations.

Currently, CORBA specifies only one object adapter: the Basic Object Adapter (BOA). According to the specification, the BOA is intended to provide reasonable support for a wide spectrum of object implementations. These range from one or more objects per program to *server-per-method* objects, where each method provided by the object is implemented by a different program. Our stock quoter object implementation below is written in a generic fashion—the actual object implementations and object adapter interfaces in your particular ORB may vary.

Object Activation

When a client sends a request to an object, the ORB first delivers the request to the object adapter that the object's implementation was registered with. How an ORB locates both the object and the correct object adapter and delivers the request to it depends on the ORB implementation. Moreover, the interface between the ORB and the object adapter is implementation-dependent and is not specified by CORBA.

If the object implementation is not currently "active" the ORB and object adapter activate it before the request is delivered to the object. As mentioned previously, CORBA requires that object activation be transparent to the client making the request. A CORBA-conformant BOA must support four different activation styles:

- ***Shared server.*** Multiple objects are activated into a single server process.
- ***Unshared server.*** Each object is activated into its own server process.
- ***Persistent server.*** The server process is activated by something other than

the BOA (e.g., a system boot-up script) but still registers with the BOA once it's ready to receive requests.

- *Server-per-method.* Each operation of the object's interface is implemented in a separate server process.

In practice, BOAs provided by commercially available ORBs do not always support all four activation modes. We'll discuss issues related to the BOA specification below.

Our example server described below is an unshared server since it only supports a single object implementation. Once the object implementation is activated, the object adapter delivers the request to the object's skeleton. Skeletons are the server-side analog of client-side stubs† generated by an OMG-IDL compiler. The skeleton selected by the BOA performs the callback to the implementation of the object's method and returns any results to the client. Figure 3 illustrates the request flow from client through ORB to the object implementation for the stock quoter application presented below.

CORBA Code

The server-side CORBA implementation of our stock quote example is based on the following OMG-IDL specification:

```
// OMG-IDL modules are used to avoid polluting
// the application namespace.

module Stock {
  // Requested stock does not exist.
  exception Invalid_Stock {};

  interface Quoter {
    // Returns the current stock value or
    // throw an Invalid_Stock exception.
    long get_quote (in string stock_name)
      raises (Invalid_Stock);
  };
};
```

In this section we'll illustrate how a server programmer might implement this

† Stubs are also commonly referred to as "proxies" or "surrogates."

OMG-IDL interface and make the object available to client applications.

Our last column illustrated how client programmers obtain and use object references supporting the `Quoter` interface to determine the current value of a particular `stock_name`. Object references are opaque, immutable "handles" that uniquely identify objects. A client application must somehow obtain an object reference to an object implementation before it can invoke that object's operations. An object implementation is typically assigned an object reference when it registers with its object adapter.

ORBs supporting C++ object implementation typically provide a compiler that automatically generates server-side skeleton C++ classes from IDL specifications (e.g., the `Quoter` interface). Programmers then integrate their implementation code with this skeleton using inheritance or object composition. The `My_Quoter` implementation class shown below is an example of inheritance-based skeleton integration:

```
// Implementation class for IDL interface.

class My_Quoter
     // Inheritance from an automatically-generated
     // CORBA skeleton class
   : virtual public Stock::QuoterBOAImpl
{
public:
   My_Quoter (Quote_Database *db) : db_ (db) {}

   // Callback invoked by the CORBA skeleton.
   virtual long get_quote (const char *stock_name)
     throw (Stock::Invalid_Stock) {
     long value =
       this->db_->lookup_stock_price (stock_name);
     if (value == -1)
       throw Stock::Invalid_Stock();
     return value;
   }
private:
   // Keep a pointer to a quote database.
   Quote_Database *db_;
};
```

`My_Quoter` is our object implementation class. It inherits from the `Stock::QuoterBOAImpl` skeleton class. This class is generated automatically from the original IDL `Quoter` specification. The `Quoter` interface supports a single operation: get_quote. Our implementation of get_quote relies on an external database object that maintains the current stock price. Since we are single-threaded we don't need to acquire any locks to access object state like this->db_.

If the lookup of the desired stock price is successful the value of the stock is returned to the caller. If the stock is not found, the database lookup_stock_price function returns a value of –1. This value triggers our implementation to throw a Stock::Invalid_Stock exception.

The implementation of get_quote shown above uses C++ exception handling (EH). However, EH is still not implemented by all C++ compilers. Thus, many commercial ORBs currently use special status parameters of type CORBA::Environment to convey exception information. An alternative implementation of My_Quoter::get_quote could be written as follows using a CORBA::Environment parameter:

```
long
My_Quoter::get_quote (const char *stock_name,
      CORBA::Environment &ev)
{
  long value =
    this->db_->lookup_stock_price (stock_name);
  if (value == -1)
    ev.exception (new Stock::Invalid_Stock);
  return value;
}
```

This code first attempts to look up the stock price. If that fails it sets the exception field in the CORBA::Environment to a Stock::Invalid_Stock exception. A client can also use CORBA::Environment parameters instead of C++ EH. In this case the client is obligated to check the Environment parameter after the call returns before attempting to use any values of out and inout parameters or the return value. These values may be meaningless if an exception is raised.

If the client and object are in different address spaces, they don't need to use the same exception handling mechanism. For example, a client on one machine using C++ EH can access an object on another machine that was built to use CORBA::Environment parameters. The ORB will make sure they interoperate correctly and transparently.

The main program for our quote server initializes the ORB and the BOA, defines an instance of a My_Quoter, and tells the BOA it is ready to receive requests by calling CORBA::BOA::impl_is_ready, as follows:

```
// Include standard BOA definitions.
# include <corba/orb.hh>

// Pointer to online stock quote database.
extern Quote_Database *quote_db;

int main (int argc, char *argv[])
{
  // Initialize the ORB and the BOA.
  CORBA::ORB_var orb = CORBA::ORB_init (argv, argv, 0);
  CORBA::BOA_var boa = orb->boa_init (argc, argv, 0);

  // Create an object implementation.
  My_Quoter quoter (quote_db);

  // Single-threaded event loop that handles CORBA
  // requests by making callbacks to the user-supplied
  // object implementation of My_Quoter.
  boa->impl_is_ready ();
  /* NOTREACHED */
  return 0;
}
```

After the executable is produced by compiling and linking this code it must be registered with the ORB. This is typically done by using a separate ORB-specific administrative program. Normally such programs let the ORB know how to start up the server program (i.e., which activation mode to use and the pathname to the executable image) when a request arrives for the object. They might also create and register an object reference for the object. As illustrated in our last column, and as mentioned above, clients use object references to access object implementations.

Evaluating the CORBA Solution

The CORBA solution illustrated above is similar to the C++ wrappers solution presented earlier. For instance, both approaches use a callback-driven event-loop structure. However, the amount of effort required to maintain, extend, and port the CORBA version of the stock quoter application should be less than the C sockets and C++ wrappers versions. This reduction in effort occurs since CORBA raises the level of abstraction at which our solution is developed. For example, the ORB handles more of the lower-level communication-related tasks.

These tasks include automated stub and skeleton generation, marshaling and demarshaling, object location, object activation, and remote method invocation and retransmission. This allows the server-side of the CORBA solution to focus primarily on application-related issues of looking up stock quotes in a database.

The benefits of CORBA become more evident when we extend the quote server to support concurrency. In particular, the effort required to transform the CORBA solution from the existing iterative server to a concurrent server is minimal. The exact details will vary depending on the ORB implementation and the desired concurrency strategy (e.g., thread-per-object, thread-per-request, etc.). However, most multi-threaded versions of CORBA (such as MT Orbix[9]) require only a few extra lines of code. In contrast, transforming the C or C++ versions to concurrent servers will require more work. A forthcoming column will illustrate the different strategies required to multithread each version.

Our previous column also described the primary drawbacks to using CORBA. Briefly, these drawbacks include the high learning curve for developing and managing distributed objects effectively, performance limitations,[10] as well as the lack of portability and security. One particularly problematic drawback for servers is that the BOA is not specified very thoroughly by the CORBA 2.0 specification.[11]

The BOA specification is probably the weakest area of CORBA 2.0. For example, the body of the `My_Quoter::get_quote` method in the CORBA section is mostly portable. However, the name of the automatically-generated skeleton base class and the implementation of `main` remain very ORB-specific. Our implementation assumed that the constructor of the `Stock::QuoterBOAImpl` base skeleton class registered the object with the BOA. Other ORBs might require an explicit object registration call. These differences between ORBs exist because registration of objects with the BOA is not specified at all by CORBA 2.0.

The OMG ORB Task Force is well aware of this problem and has issued a request for proposals (RFP) asking for ways to solve it. Until it's solved (probably mid-to-late 1996), the portability of CORBA object implementations between ORBs will remain problematic.

CONCLUSION

In this column, we examined several different programming techniques for developing the server-side of a distributed stock quote application. Our examples illustrated how the CORBA-based distributed object computing (DOC) solution simplifies programming and improves extensibility. It achieves these benefits by relying on an ORB infrastructure that supports communication between distributed objects.

A major objective of CORBA is to let application developers focus primarily on application requirements, without devoting as much effort to the underlying communication infrastructure. As applications become more sophisticated and complex, DOC frameworks like CORBA become essential to produce correct, portable, and maintainable distributed systems.

CORBA is one of several technologies that are emerging to support DOC. In future articles, we will discuss other OO toolkits and environments (such as OODCE and OLE/COM) and compare them with CORBA in the same manner that we compared sockets and C++ wrappers to CORBA. In addition, we will compare the various distributed object solutions with more conventional distributed programming toolkits (such as Sun RPC and OSF DCE).

As always, if there are any topics that you'd like us to cover, please send us email at object_connect@ch.hp.com.

References

1. Schmidt, D. C. A domain analysis of network daemon design dimensions, *C++ Report*, 6(3), 1994.
2. Stevens, W. R. *UNIX Network Programming*, Englewood Cliffs, NJ:Prentice Hall, 1990.
3. Schmidt, D. C. The reactor: An object-oriented interface for event-driven UNIX I/O multiplexing (Part 1 of 2), *C++ Report, 5(2),* 1993.
4. Schmidt, D. C. IPC_SAP: An object-oriented interface to interprocess communication services, *C++ Report*, 4(9), 1992.
5. Schmidt, D. C. The object-oriented design and implementation of the reactor: A C++ wrapper for UNIX I/O multiplexing (Part 2 of 2), *C++ Report*, 5(7), 1993.
6. Schmidt, D. C. Acceptor and connector: Design patterns for active and passive establishment of network connections, in *Workshop on Pattern Languages of Object-Oriented Programs at ECOOP '95*, (Aarhus, Denmark), Aug. 1995.
7. Gamma, E., R. Helm, R. Johnson, and J. Vlissides. *Design Patterns: Elements of Reusable Object-Oriented Software*, Reading, MA, Addison-Wesley, 1994.

8. Schmidt, D. C. and P. Stephenson. Using design patterns to evolve system software from UNIX to Windows NT, *C++ Report*, 7(3), 1995.

9. Horn, C. The Orbix Architecture. tech. rep., IONA Technologies, Aug. 1993.

10. Schmidt, D. C., T. Harrison, and E. Al-Shaer. Object-oriented components for high-speed network programming, in *Proceedings of the Conference on Object-Oriented Technologies*, (Monterey, CA), USENIX, June 1995.

11. Object Management Group. The Common Object Request Broker: Architecture and Specification, 2.0 (draft) ed., May 1995.

Section Four

A Focus on Language

MEMORY MANAGEMENT IN C++

NATHAN C. MYERS
myersn@roguewave.com

MEMORY USAGE IN C++ IS AS THE SEA COME TO LAND: A TIDE ROLLS IN and sweeps out again, leaving only puddles and stranded fish. At intervals, a wave crashes ashore; but the ripples never cease.

Many programs have little need for memory management: They use a fixed amount of memory or simply consume it until they exit. The best that can be done for such programs is to stay out of their way. Others, including most C++ programs, are much less deterministic, and their performance can be profoundly affected by the memory management policy they run under. Unfortunately, the memory management facilities provided by many system vendors have failed to keep pace with growth in program size and dynamic memory usage.

Because C++ code is naturally organized by class, a common response to this failure is to overload member operator new for individual classes. In addition to being tedious to implement and maintain, however, this piecemeal approach can actually hurt performance in large systems. For example, applied to a tree-node class, it forces nodes of each tree to share pages with nodes of other (probably unrelated) trees, rather than with related data. Furthermore, it tends to fragment memory by keeping large, mostly empty blocks dedicated to each class. The result can be a quick new/delete cycle that accidentally causes virtual memory thrashing. At best, the approach interferes with system-wide tuning efforts.

Thus, while detailed knowledge of the memory usage patterns of individual classes can be helpful, it is best applied by tuning memory usage for a whole program or major subsystem. The first part of this article describes an interface that can ease such tuning in C++ programs. Before tuning a particular program, however, it pays to improve performance for all programs by improving the global memory manager. The second part of this article covers the design of a global memory manager that is as fast and space-efficient as per-class allocators.

But raw speed and efficiency are only the beginning. A memory management library written in C++ can be an organizational tool in its own right. Even as we confront the traditional problems involving large data structures, progress in operating systems is yielding different kinds of memory—shared memory, memory-mapped files, persistent storage—which must be managed as well. With a common interface to all types of memory, most classes need not know the difference. This makes quite a contrast with systems of classes hard-wired to use only regular memory.

Global Operator New

In C++, the only way to organize memory management on a larger scale than the class is by overloading the global operator new. To select a memory management policy requires adding a placement argument, in this case a reference to a class which implements the policy:

```
extern void* operator new(size_t, class Heap&);
```

When we overload the operator new in this way, we recognize that the regular operator `new` is implementing a policy of its own, and we would like to tune it as well. That is, it makes sense to offer the same choices for the regular operator `new` as for the placement version.

In fact, one cannot provide an interesting placement operator `new` without also replacing the regular operator `new`. The global operator `delete` can take no user parameters, so it must be able to tell what to do just by looking at the memory being freed. This means that the operator `delete` and all operators `new` must agree on a memory management architecture.

For example, if our global operators `new` were to be built on top of `malloc()`, we would need to store extra data in each block so that the global operator `delete` would know what to do with it. Adding a word of overhead for each object to `malloc()`'s own overhead (a total of 16 bytes, on most RISCs), would seem a crazy way to improve memory management. Fortunately, all this space overhead can be eliminated by bypassing `malloc()`, as will be seen later.

The need to replace the global operators `new` and `delete` when adding a placement operator `new` has profound effects on memory management system design. It means that it is impossible to integrate different memory management architectures. Therefore, the top-level memory management architecture must be totally general, so that it can support any policy we might want to apply. Total generality, in turn, requires absolute simplicity.

An Interface

How simple can we get? Let us consider some declarations. `Heap` is an abstract class:

```
class Heap {
  protected:
    virtual ~Heap();
  public:
    virtual void* allocate(size_t) = 0;
    static Heap& whatHeap(void*);
};
```

The static member function `whatHeap(void*)` is discussed later. `Heap`'s abstract interface is simple enough. Given a global `Heap` pointer, the regular global operator `new` can use it:

```
extern Heap* __global_heap;

inline void*
operator new(size_t sz)
  { return ::__global_heap->allocate(sz); }
```

Inline dispatching makes it fast. It's general, too; we can use the `Heap` interface to implement the placement operator `new`, providing access to any private heap:

```
inline void*
operator new(size_t size, Heap& heap)
  { return heap.allocate(size); }
```

What kind of implementations might we define for the `Heap` interface? Of course, the first must be a general-purpose memory allocator, class `HeapAny`. (`HeapAny` is the memory manager described in detail in the second part of this article.) The global heap pointer, used by the regular operator `new` defined above, is initialized to refer to an instance of class `HeapAny`:

```
extern class HeapAny __THE_global_heap;
Heap* __global_heap = &__THE_global_heap;
```

Users, too, can instantiate class HeapAny to make a private heap:

```
HeapAny& myheap = *new HeapAny;
```

and allocate storage from it, using the placement operator `new`:

```
MyType* mine = new(myheap) MyType;
```

As promised, deletion is the same as always:

```
delete mine;
```

Now we have the basis for a memory management architecture. It seems that all we need to do is provide an appropriate implementation of class `Heap` for any policy we might want. As usual, life is not so simple.

COMPLICATIONS

What happens if `MyType`'s constructor itself needs to allocate memory? That memory should come from the same heap, too. We could pass a heap reference to the constructor:

```
mine = new(myheap) MyType(myheap);
```

and store it in the object for use later, if needed. However, in practice this approach leads to a massive proliferation of `Heap&` arguments—in constructors, in functions that call constructors, everywhere!—which penetrates from the top of the system (where the heaps are managed) to the bottom (where they are used). Ultimately, almost every function needs a `Heap&` argument. Applied earnestly, the result can be horrendous. Even at best, such an approach makes it difficult to integrate other libraries into a system.

One way to reduce the proliferation of `Heap&` arguments is to provide a function to call to discover what heap an object is on. That is the purpose of the the `Heap::whatHeap()` static member function. For example, here's a `MyType` member function that allocates some buffer storage:

```
char* MyType::make_buffer()
{
  Heap& aHeap = Heap::whatHeap(this);
  return new(aHeap) char[BUFSIZ];
}
```

(If this points into the stack or static space, `whatHeap()` returns a reference to the default global heap.)

Another way to reduce `Heap` argument proliferation is to substitute a private heap to be used by the global operator `new`. Such a global resource calls for careful handling. Class `HeapStackTop`'s constructor replaces the default heap with its argument, but retains the old default so it can be restored by the destructor:

```
class HeapStackTop {
  Heap* old_;
```

```
public:
  HeapStackTop(Heap& h);
  ~HeapStackTop();
};
```

We might use this as follows:

```
{ HeapStackTop top = myheap;
  mine = new MyType;
}
```

Now space for the `MyType` object, and any secondary store allocated by its constructor, comes from `myheap`. At the closing brace, the destructor `~HeapStackTop()` restores the previous default global heap. If one of `MyType`'s member functions might later want to allocate more space from the same heap, it can use `whatHeap()`; or the constructor can save a pointer to the current global heap before returning.

Creating a `HeapStackTop` object is very clean way to install any global memory management mechanism: a `HeapStackTop` object created in `main()` quietly slips a new memory allocator under the whole program.

Some classes must allocate storage from the top-level global heap regardless of the current default. Any object can force itself to be allocated there by defining a member operator `new`, and can control where its secondary storage comes from by the same techniques described above.

With `HeapStackTop`, many classes need not know about `Heap` at all; this can make a big difference when integrating libraries from various sources. On the other hand, the meaning of `Heap::whatHeap()` (or a `Heap&` member or argument) is easier to grasp; it is clearer and, therefore, safer. While neither approach is wholly satisfactory, a careful mix of the two can reduce the proliferation of `Heap&` arguments to a reasonable level.

Uses for Private Heaps

But what can private heaps do for us? We have hinted that improved locality of reference leads to better performance in a virtual memory environment and that a uniform interface helps when using special types of memory.

One obvious use for private heaps is as a sort of poor man's garbage collection:

```
Heap* myheap = new HeapTrash;
... // lots of calls to new(*myheap)
delete myheap;
```

Instead of deleting objects, we discard the whole data structure at one throw. The approach is sometimes called lifetime management. Since the destructors are never called, you must carefully control what kind of objects are put in the heap; it would be hazardous to install such a heap as the default (with `HeapStackTop`) because many classes, including iostream, allocate space at unpredictable times. Dangling pointers to objects in the deleted heap must be prevented, which can be tricky if any objects secretly share storage among themselves. Objects whose destructors do more than just delete other objects require special handling; the heap may need to maintain a registry of objects that require "finalization."

But private heaps have many other uses that don't violate C++ language semantics. Perhaps the quietest one is simply to get better performance than your vendor's `malloc()` offers. In many large systems, member operator new is defined for many classes just so they may call the global operator new less often. When the global operator new is fast enough, such code can be deleted, yielding easier maintenance, often with a net gain in performance from better locality and reduced fragmentation.

An idea that strikes many people is that a private heap could be written that is optimized to work well with a particular algorithm. Because it need not field requests from the rest of the program, it can concentrate on the needs of that algorithm. The simplest example is a heap that allocates objects of only one size. As we will see later, however, the default heap can be made fast enough that this is no great advantage. A mark/release mechanism is optimal in some contexts (such as parsing), if it can be used for only part of the associated data structure.

When shared memory is used for interprocess communication, it is usually allocated by the operating system in blocks larger than the objects that you want to share. For this case, a heap that manages a shared memory region can offer the same benefits that regular operator new does for private memory. If the interface is the same as for non-shared memory, objects may not need to know they are in shared memory. Similarly, if you are constrained to implement your system on an architecture with a tiny address space, you may need to swap memory segments in and out. If a private heap knows how to handle these segments, objects that don't even know about swapping can be allocated in them.

In general, whenever a chunk of memory is to be carved up and made into various objects, a heap-like interface is called for. If that interface is the same for the whole system, other objects need not know where the chunk came from. As a result, objects written without the particular use in mind may safely be instantiated in very peculiar places.

In a multithreaded program, the global operator new must carefully exclude other threads while it operates on its data structures. The time spent just getting and releasing the lock can itself become a bottleneck in some systems. If each thread is given a private heap that maintains a cache of memory available without locking, the threads need not synchronize except when the cache becomes empty (or too full). Of course, the operator `delete` must be able to accept blocks allocated by any thread.

A heap that remembers details about how or when objects in it were created can be very useful when implementing an object-oriented database or remote procedure-call mechanism. A heap that segregates small objects by type can allow them to simulate virtual function behavior without the overhead of a virtual function table pointer in each object. A heap that zero-fills blocks on allocation can simplify constructors.

Programs can be instrumented to collect statistics about memory usage (or leakage) by substituting a specialized heap at various places in a program. Use of private heaps allows much finer granularity than the traditional approach of shadowing `malloc()` at link time.

In the second part of this article, we will explore how to implement `HeapAny` efficiently, so that `malloc()`, the global operator `new(size_t)`, the global operator `new(size_t, Heap&)`, and `Heap::whatHeap(void*)` can be built on it.

MEMORY MANAGEMENT IN C++ PART 2

Many factors work against achieving optimal memory management. In many vendor libraries, memory used by the memory manager itself for bookkeeping can double the total space used. Fragmentation, where blocks are free but unavailable, can also multiply the space used. Space matters, even today, because virtual memory page faults slow down your program (indeed, your entire computer), and swap space limits can be exceeded just as real memory can.

A memory manager can also waste time in many ways. On allocation, a block of the right size must be found or made. If made, the remainder of the split block must be placed where it can be found. On deallocation, the freed block may need to be coalesced with any neighboring blocks, and the result must be placed where it can be found again. System calls to obtain raw memory can take longer than any other single operation; a page fault that results when idle memory is touched is just a hidden system call. All these operations take time, time spent not computing results.

The effects of wasteful memory management can be hard to see. Time spent thrashing the swap file doesn't show up on profiler output and is hard to attribute to the responsible code. Often, the problem is easily visible only when memory usage exceeds available swap space. Make no mistake: Poor memory management can multiply your program's running time or so bog down a machine that little else can run.

Before buying (or making your customer buy) more memory, it makes sense to see what can be done with a little code.

Principles

A memory manager project is an opportunity to apply principles of good design. Separate the common case from special cases, and make the common case fast and cheap and other cases tolerable. Make the user of a feature bear the cost of its use. Use hints. Reuse good ideas.

Before delving into detailed design, we must be clear about our goals. We want a memory manager that satisfies the following criteria:

- ***Speed.*** It must be much faster than existing memory managers, especially for small objects. Performance should not suffer under common usage patterns, such as repeatedly allocating and freeing the same block.
- ***Low overhead.*** The total size of headers and other wasted space must be a small percentage of total space used, even when all objects are tiny. Repeated allocation and deallocation of different sizes must not cause memory usage to grow without bound.
- ***Small working set.*** The number of pages touched by the memory manager in satisfying a request must be minimal to avoid paging delays in virtual memory systems. Unused memory must be returned to the operating system periodically.
- ***Robustness.*** Erroneous programs must have difficulty corrupting the memory manager's data structures. Errors must be flagged as soon as possible and not allowed to accumulate. Out-of-memory events must be handled gracefully.
- ***Portability.*** The memory manager must adapt easily to different machines.
- ***Convenience.*** Users mustn't need to change code to use it.

- ***Flexibility.*** It must be easily customized for unusual needs without imposing any additional overhead.

Techniques

Optimal memory managers would be common if they were easily built. They are scarce, so you can expect that a variety of subtle techniques are needed even to approach the optimum.

One such technique is to treat different request sizes differently. In most programs, small blocks are requested overwhelmingly more often than large blocks, so both time and space overhead for them is felt disproportionately.

Another technique results from noting that only a few different sizes are possible for very small blocks, so that each such size may be handled separately. We can even afford to keep a vector of free block lists for those few sizes.

A third is to avoid system call overhead by requesting memory from the operating system in big chunks, and by not touching unused (and possibly paged-out) blocks unnecessarily. This means data structures consulted to find a block to allocate should be stored compactly, apart from the unused blocks they describe.

The final—and most important—technique is to exploit address arithmetic that, while not strictly portable according to language standards, works well on all modern flat-memory architectures. A pointer value can be treated as an integer, and bitwise logical operations may be used on it to yield a new pointer value. In particular, the low bits may be masked off to yield a pointer to a header structure that describes the block pointed to. In this way, a block need not contain a pointer to that information. Furthermore, many blocks can share the same header, amortizing its overhead across all. (This technique is familiar in the LISP community, where it is known as *page-tagging.*)

A Design

The first major feature of the design is suggested by the last two techniques above. We request memory from the operating system in units of a large power of two (e.g., 64K bytes) in size, and place them so they are aligned on such a boundary. We call these units *segments.* Any address within the segment may have its low bits masked off, yielding a pointer to the segment header. We can treat this header as an instance of the abstract class `HeapSegment`:

```
class Heapsegment {
```

```
public:
  virtual void free(void*) = 0;
  virtual void* realloc(void*) = 0;
  victual Heap& owned_by(void*) = 0;
};
```

The second major feature of the design takes advantage of the small number of small-block sizes possible. A segment (with a header of class `HeapPageseg`) is split up into pages, where each page contains blocks of only one size. A vector of free lists, with one element for each size, allows instant access to a free block of the right size. Deallocation is just as quick; no coalescing is needed. Each page has just one header to record the size of the blocks it contains, and the owning heap. The page header is found by address arithmetic, just like the segment header. In this way, space overhead is limited to a few percent, even for the smallest blocks, and the time to allocate and deallocate the page is amortized over all usage of the blocks in the page.

For larger blocks, there are too many sizes to give each a segment, but such blocks may be packed adjacent to one another within a segment, to be coalesced with neighboring free blocks when freed. (We will call such blocks *spans*, with a segment header of type `HeapSpanseg`.) Fragmentation, the proliferation of free blocks too small to use, is the chief danger in span segments, and there are several ways to limit it. Because the common case, small blocks, is handled separately, we have some breathing room: Spans may have a large granularity, and we can afford to spend more time managing them. A balanced tree of available sizes is fast enough that we can use several searches to avoid creating tiny unusable spans. The tree can be stored compactly, apart from the free spans, to avoid touching them until they are actually used. Finally, aggressive coalescing helps reclaim small blocks and keep large blocks available.

Blocks too big to fit in a segment are allocated as a contiguous sequence of segments; the header of the first segment in the sequence is of class `HeapHugeseg`. Memory wasted in the last segment is much less than might be feared; any pages not touched are not even assigned by the operating system, so the average waste for huge blocks is only half a virtual-memory page.

Dispatching for deallocation is simple and quick:

```
void operator delete(void* ptr)
{
  long header = (long)ptr & MASK;
  ((HeapSegment* ) header) ->free (ptr)
}
```

`HeapSegment::free()` is a virtual function, so each segment type handles deallocation its own way. This allows different Heaps to coexist. If the freed pointer does not point to allocated memory, the program will most likely crash immediately. (This is a feature. Bugs that are allowed to accumulate are extremely difficult to track down.)

The classical C memory management functions, `malloc()`, `calloc()`, `realloc()`, and `free()` can be implemented on top of `HeapAny` just as was the global operator new. Only `realloc()` requires particular support.

The only remaining feature to implement is the function `Heap::whatHeap(void* ptr)`. We cannot assume that `ptr` refers to heap storage; it may point into the stack, or static storage, or elsewhere. The solution is to keep a bitmap of allocated segments, one bit per segment. On most architectures this takes 2K words to cover the entire address space. If the pointer refers to a managed segment, `HeapSegment::owned_by()` reports the owning heap; if not, a reference to the default global heap may be returned instead. (In the LISP community, this technique is referred to as BBOP, or "big bag o' pages.")

Pitfalls

Where we depart from the aforementioned principles of good design, we must be careful to avoid the consequences. One example is when we allocate a page to hold a small block: We are investing the time to get that page on behalf of all the blocks that may be allocated in it. If the user frees the block immediately, and we free the page, then the user has paid to allocate and free a page just to use one block in it. In a loop, this could be much slower than expected. To avoid this kind of thrashing, we can add some hysteresis by keeping one empty page for a size if there are no other free blocks of that size. Similar heuristics may be used for other boundary cases.

Another pitfall results from a sad fact of life: Programs have bugs. We can expect programs to try to free memory that was not allocated or that has already been freed, and to clobber memory beyond the bounds of allocated blocks. The best a regular memory manager can do is to throw an exception as early as possible when it finds things amiss. Beyond that, it can try to keep its data structures out of harm's way, so that bugs will tend to clobber users' data and not the memory manager's. This makes debugging much easier.

Initialization, always a problem for libraries, is especially onerous for a portable memory manager. C++ offers no way to control the order in which libraries are initialized, but the memory manager must be available before anything else. The standard iostream library, with a similar problem, gets away by using some magic in its header file (at a sometimes intolerable cost in startup time), but we don't have even this option, because modules that use the global operator new are not obliged to include any header file. The fastest approach is to take advantage of any non-portable static initialization ordering available on the target architecture. (This is usually easy.) Failing that, we can check for initialization on each call to operator new or `malloc()`. A better portable solution depends on a standard for control of initialization order, which seems (alas!) unlikely to appear.

Dividends

The benefits of careful design often go beyond the immediate goals. Indeed, unexpected results of this design include a global memory management interface that allows different memory managers to coexist. For most programs, though, the greatest benefit beyond better performance is that all the ad hoc apparatus intended to compensate for a poor memory manager may be ripped out. This leaves algorithms and data structures unobscured, and allows classes to be used in unanticipated ways.

Acknowledgments

The author thanks Paul McKenney and Jim Shur for their help in improving this article.

MEMORY MANAGEMENT, DLLS, AND C++

PETE BECKER

ANYONE WHO HAS MADE THE TRANSITION FROM DOS PROGRAMMING to Windows programming can tell you that one of the most diffcult aspects of Windows programming is memory management. Fortunately for all of us, with the release of Windows 3.1, real-mode Windows doesn't exist anymore, so the most complicated aspects of Windows memory management have gone away. There are still some tricky areas that you have to be aware of, though, and in this article I'm going to describe one of them.

FOR THOSE OF YOU WHO DON'T DO WINDOWS

I don't either—not much, anyway. But I won't write about things I don't use, so trust me: If this weren't applicable elsewhere, I wouldn't be writing about it. This article really isn't about Windows, it's about memory management and multiple heaps. If that's a subject that interests you, read on.

A SIMPLE LIST

Suppose you have a template for a family of `List` classes. You've been given the job of extending that template so that you can create special `List` instantiations in Windows Dynamic Link Libraries (DLLs). What changes do you need to make? Of course, the place to start is with the existing code:

```
// LIST.H
#include <_defs.h>

template <class T>
struct _CLASSTYPE Node
```

```
{
  Node<T> _FAR *next;
  T data;
  Node( Node _FAR *nxt, T dta ) :
    next(nxt), data(dta) {}
};

template <class T>
class _CLASSTYPE List
{
  Node<T> _FAR *head;
public:
  List() : head(0) {}
  ~List();
  void add( T data )
    { head = new Node<T>( head, data ); }
  void removeHead();
  T peek() const
    { return head->data; }
  int isEmpty() const
    { return head == 0; }
};

template <class T>
List<T>::~List()
{
  while( head != 0 )
    removeHead();
}

template <class T>
void List<T>::removeHead()
{
  Node<T> _FAR *temp = head->next;
  delete head;
  head = temp;
}
```

The macros _CLASSTYPE and _FAR are defined in the header _DEFS.H. When compiling a DOS application, their expansions are empty. To see this template in action, let's write a simple application that uses it:

```
// DEMO.CPP
#include <fstream.h>
#include "list.h"

int main()
{
  ofstream out( "demo.out" );
  List<int> intList;
  intList.add(1);
  intList.add(2);
  while( !intList.isEmpty() )
    {
    out << intList.peek() << endl;
    intList.removeHead();
    }
  return 0;
}
```

To compile and link this program under DOS, use the following command line:

```
bcc demo
```

This builds DEMO.EXE, which runs the way you'd expect.

Building a DLL

Putting the code that implements a list of integers into a DLL is easy:

```
// INTLIST.CPP
#include "list.h"
typedef List<int> IntList;
```

Building the DLL is a little more complicated:

```
bcc -WD -D_CLASSDLL -ml -Jgd intlist.cpp libmain.cpp
implib intlist.lib intlist.dll
```

These two lines build the DLL and the import library. The -WD switch tells the compiler to build a DLL. The -D_CLASSDLL is used in _DEFS.H to determine how to expand _CLASSTYPE and _FAR. When building a DLL, if _CLASSDLL is defined, _CLASSTYPE becomes _export, which tells the compiler to export all the members of all classes that are defined in the file. _FAR becomes _far, which is necessary to be able to pass data pointers between the main module and the DLL. -Jgd tells the compiler to generate code for all template instantiations encountered in the source file. In combination with the typedef in INTLIST.CPP, this forces the code for List<int> to be generated in the file INTLIST.OBJ. LIBMAIN.CPP contains the LIBMAIN() entry point that Windows requires in a DLL. After the DLL has been built, the IMPLIB command builds an import library that describes all the entry points defined in the DLL. This will be used when we build the main module. To build the main module, we do the following:

```
bcc -WS -D_CLASSDLL -ml -lC -Jgx demo intlist.lib
```

This creates DEMO.EXE. The -WS switch says to create a Windows executable using smart callbacks. Defining _CLASSDLL in a Windows executable makes _CLASSTYPE expand to _huge, which is needed when accessing imported classes. -lC makes imports case sensitive, which is always needed for C++ code. -Jgx creates external references for all templates, rather than expanding the code in the current file. This means that when DEMO is linked, the linker will use the entry points defined in INTLIST.LIB, which in turn will tell Windows to load INTLIST.DLL when the program is run. Unfortunately, DEMO.EXE has a serious problem.

The Problem

The problem is that List<T>::add() is an inline function. Since it is called from the main module, its code is expanded in the main module. When it creates a new Node<T>, it allocates space for the node from the main module's heap. List<T>::removeHead(), on the other hand, is not inline. It's code is in INTLIST.DLL. When it tries to delete the node, it deletes it from the DLL's heap. Since the node wasn't allocated from the DLL's heap, this doesn't make sense. If you're lucky, the program will crash immediately. If you're not, it will continue to run and crash later.

Simple Solutions

The simplest solution is to not make List<T>::add() inline and to put it into the DLL instead. Applied broadly, that means never inlining anything unless you're convinced that you won't run into problems. That will eliminate the conflict, but at the price of severely limiting the usefulness of inline functions. A better solution is to attack the problem at its source. The conflict arises because an object can be allocated on one module'sheap and deleted from another's. If we make this impossible, the problem won't arise. So the first cut at this solution is to make sure every Node<int> is allocated and deleted from the DLL's heap. That sounds very much like a class-specific `operator new()` and `operator delete()`:

```
// LIST.H
template <class T>
struct _CLASSTYPE Node
{
  Node<T> _FAR *next;
  T data;
  Node( Node _FAR *nxt, T dta ) :
    next(nxt), data(dta) {}
  void _FAR *operator new( size_t sz );
  void operator delete( void _FAR *ptr );
};

template <class T>
void _FAR *Node<T>::operator new( size_t sz )
{
  return ::operator new( sz );
}

template <class T>
void Node<T>::operator delete( void _FAR *ptr )
{
  ::operator delete( ptr );
}
```

If we make these changes to `LIST.H` we'll have a `Node<T>` that will be allocated and deleted consistently, regardless of whether it is created in an inline function or directly from code in the DLL. The underlying problem we are trying to solve relates to memory management, and this solution isolates memory management from the rest of the class. Because it isolates the specific problem and provides a mechanism that deals directly with that problem, it is a much better solution than avoiding inline functions.

Generalizing the Solution

This solution is still a long way from what it should be, though. If we were to recompile this code as a DOS application, we'd still have overhead of `Node<T>::operator new()` calling the global `operator new()`, even though this step is no longer necessary. How can we get rid of this overhead when we don't need it? One possibility is to use the preprocessor to insert or remove `operator new()` and `operator delete()` from the definition of `Node`. I won't give you sample code for doing this because I think it's a terrible solution. Any time you use the preprocessor to change the definition of a class, you're in danger of creating modules with inconsistent definitions. This usually happens when you change one `#define` and don't recompile the entire program. The conditionalized class has one definition in some modules and a diïerent definition in the others. In some cases that's harmless, and in others it results in code that won't compile, but most of the time it will quietly create code that doesn't work correctly. If there's no way to avoid using the preprocessor to change the definition of a class, be sure to encapsulate those changes in simple macros, like `_CLASSTYPE` above. In this case, we can handle memory management in a much better manner. Macros aren't needed.

```
// LIST.H
template <class T, class Alloc>
struct _CLASSTYPE MNode : public Alloc
{
  MNode<T,Alloc> _FAR *next;
  T data;
  MNode( MNode<T,Alloc> _FAR *nxt, T dta ) :
    next(nxt), data(dta) {}
};

template <class T, class Alloc>
class _CLASSTYPE MList
{
  MNode<T,Alloc> _FAR *head;
public:
  MList() : head(0) {}
  ~MList();
  void add( T data )
    { head = new MNode<T,Alloc>( head, data ); }
  void removeHead();
  T peek() const
    { return head->data; }
  int isEmpty() const
    { return head == 0; }
};

template <class T,class Alloc>
```

```
MList<T,Alloc>::~MList()
{
  while( head != 0 )
    removeHead();
}

template <class T,class Alloc>
void MList<T,Alloc>::removeHead()
{
  MNode<T,Alloc> _FAR *temp = head->next;
  delete head;
  head = temp;
}

class _CLASSTYPE IntListAllocator
{
public:
  void _FAR *operator new( size_t sz );
  void operator delete( void _FAR *ptr );
};

class _CLASSTYPE DOSAllocator
{
public:
  void _FAR *operator new( size_t sz )
    { return ::operator new( sz ); }
  void operator delete( void _FAR *ptr )
    { ::operator delete( ptr ); }
};
```

By adding a memory manager class as a base class for `Node` and passing the actual memory manager class as a parameter to the `MNode` template, . we get the greatest possible flexibility. Note that the member functions of `DOSAllocator` are inline. When this version of the memory manager is used, there is no added overhead. The Windows version of our DLL code now looks like this:

```
// INTLIST.CPP
#include "list.h"
typedef MList<int,IntListAllocator> IntList;

void *IntListAllocator::operator new( size_t sz )
{
  return ::operator new( sz );
}
```

```
void IntListAllocator::operator delete( void *ptr )
{
  ::operator delete( ptr );
}
```

and the main module looks like this:

```
// DEMO.CPP
#include <fstream.h>
#include "list.h"

int main()
{
  ofstream out( "demo.out" );
  MList<int,IntListAllocator> intList;
  intList.add(1);
  intList.add(2);
  while( !intList.isEmpty() )
    {
    out << intList.peek() << endl;
    intList.removeHead();
    }
  return 0;
}
```

The only line that had to be changed in the main module was the definition of `intList`, which now specifies the memory manager that is to be used for the list. The DOS version, of course, would use `DOSAllocator` instead of `IntListAllocator`. This means that the DOS version and the Windows version of the list have different names: `MList<int,IntListAllocator>`, and `MList<int,DOSAllocator>`. This prevents the problem with inconsistent class def initions I mentioned eariler. If the program attempts to use two different memory managers, the result will be two different classes, not one class with two different definitions.

SUPPORTING EXISTING CODE

The final step is to make sure that code written with the original `List` template still works. We could just leave it as is, but that would mean that we'd have two sets of code to maintain. Since the new template `MList` supports all the behavior that the old template `List` does, we can reimplement the old template with the new one. That's a straightforward change to make, so I won't rewrite all the code for you, but here's what it looks like:

```
// LIST.H
#include <_defs.h>

template <class T, class Alloc>
class _CLASSTYPE MNode
{
// same as above
};

template <class T, class Alloc>
class _CLASSTYPE MList
{
// same as above
};

template <class T>
class Node : public MNode<T,DOSAllocator>
{
};

template <class T>
class List : public MList<T,DOSAllocator>
{
};
```

Something to Think About

When I was planning this article, I was going to use an `Array` class as the example. I decided against it because it has an extra complication the `List` class doesn't have. Let's assume that we will never try to instantiate an `Array<T>` for a type `T` that does not have a default constructor. Here's what the code might look like:

```
#include <assert.h>

template <class T, class Alloc>
class Node : public Alloc
{
  T data;
```

```
  public:
    Node() {}
    Node( T t ) : data(t) {}
    void operator = ( T t ) { data = t; }
    operator const T() const { return data; }
  };

  template <class T, class Alloc>
  class Array
  {
    Node *data;
    unsigned size;
  public:
    Array( unsigned sz );
    ~Array() { delete [] data; }
    T& operator [] ( unsigned index );
  };

  template <class T, class Alloc>
  Array<T,Alloc>::Array( unsigned sz )
  {
    size = sz;
    data = new Node[sz];
    assert( data != 0 );
  }

  template <class T, class Alloc>
  Array<T,Alloc>::~Array()
  {
    delete [] data;
  }

  template <class T, class Alloc>
  T& Array<T,Alloc>::operator [] ( unsigned index )
  {
    assert( index < size );
    return data[index];
  }
```

Aside from possible inadequacies in class Node, why doesn't this work? How could you make it work?

IMPLEMENTING NEW AND DELETE

STEPHEN D. CLAMAGE
steve@taumet.com

IN THIS COLUMN WE'LL TALK ABOUT THE CONSIDERATIONS THAT GO INTO implementing the built-in C++ memory-management routines. In particular, we'll find out what has to happen when the programmer uses new and delete. There is more to it than might seem obvious at first.

Let me stress at the outset that we are talking, as always, about what the C++ implementor must provide as part of an integrated C++ system. We will not be directly discussing how to do your own memory management as part of a C++ application. In particular we'll discuss tricks and conspiracies between the compiler and the runtime support library. The library needn't be written in portable C++ code, and usually parts of it are very dependent on the particular compiler and operating system.

THANKS FOR THE MEMORY . . .

The first consideration is basic management of raw memory. There must be a mechanism for getting the memory and making it available for reuse. There are many different strategies for managing this "heap" memory), and we are not going to go into that here. Entire chapters of textbooks are devoted to this subject.

Let's assume that our C++ implementation is built on, or concurrently with, a C implementation. The C library will have, in particular, functions `malloc` and `free`. We certainly hope that these routines were implemented carefully and that they are reliable and reasonably efficient.

We want new and delete to coexist peacefully with these C routines. That is, if a program uses both `malloc/free` and `new/delete`, we don't want them to interfere with each other by corrupting one another's data structures. Either they will be completely independent, or one set of routines will be implemented in terms of the other set. Please note that we do not want or expect to mix new and free or malloc and delete on the same object, only that both styles of memory management may be used in the same program.

An earlier article in this series talked about how we wanted our C++ implementation to coexist with the native C and our own C implementation. This meant that any of several different versions of malloc (and free) might be linked into any given program. If this was going to work at all, the C++ library version of operator new must call malloc, and operator delete must call free, accepting whichever versions were ultimately linked.

Operator New

The ARM[2] describes in some detail the global version of operator new. Since we have decided to implement new in terms of malloc, it will wind up looking like Listing 1. There are two versions of the global operator new, one that allocates storage and one that is called for a new-expression with "placement" syntax.

Recall that the simplest placement syntax looks like this:

```
T* p = new (address) T
```

It results in a call to operator new(size_t, void*). The effect is to construct a T object at the given address without actually doing any memory allocation. The purpose of this is to allow an object to be constructed at a given address. C++ does not allow you to call a constructor directly, but a placement new-expression lets you get that effect.

This is a good place to review what is sometimes a source of confusion. A new-expression is a C++ language construct using the keyword new, which (usually) allocates storage for and possibly initializes an object or array of objects. Among other things, the compiler invokes some version of operator new in evaluating a new-expression. Operator new is an ordinary C++ function that is responsible only for allocating raw storage. The programmer may define different versions of this function to be invoked under differing circumstances. Listing 1 shows the default library versions of operator new.

The basic version of operator new tries to allocate storage with (in this implementation) the C library function malloc. If that succeeds, we are done. Otherwise, if a "new-handler" function has been installed by the programmer, that function is called and the allocation is tried again. If there is no new-handler, operator new returns a null pointer to indicate failure. Usually a new-handler does not return. If it does, it must somehow arrange for more storage to be made available or "de-install" itself to avoid an infinite loop. In this implementation there is no default new-handler.

LISTING 1. GLOBAL OPERATOR `new` AND OPERATOR `delete`

```
//  set by set_new_handler()
extern void (*__new_handler) ();

//  default basic version of operator new
void* operator new(size_t size)
{
    if( size == 0)
      size = 1; // return a unique value for new(0)

    void *retval;
    while( 1 ) {
      retval = malloc(size);
      if( __new_handler == 0  ||  retval  != 0 )
          break;

      __new_handler();
      // if handler returns, try again
    }
    return retval;
}

//  default "placement" version of operator new
void* operator new(size_t, void* addr)
{
    return addr;
}

//  default version of operator delete
void operator delete(void* p)
{
    // redundant check for null pointer
    if( p ) free(p);
}
```

One other point: operator `new` must return a different pointer each time it is called, even when asked for zero bytes. The simplest way to implement this (if not the most space-efficient) is to change the requested size from 0 to 1. Early printings of the ARM incorrectly said that zero was returned for a request of zero bytes; the error was corrected in later printings. The question is sometimes raised whether different unique values for each such request or always the same unique value should be returned. The forthcoming C++ standard will make clear that a different unique value is required. (Of course, once allocated storage has been deleted, it may be supplied again by subsequent allocation requests.)

Part of the fun of C++ is that the language definition is a moving target. As I write this article, the C++ Committee is contemplating a change in the specification of operator `new`. It will probably be defined to raise an exception when it cannot allocate storage, rather than return zero. Implementations will undoubtedly make the old behavior available so as not to break existing programs. For example, the library could use the version of operator `new` given here, and install a default `new`-handler that throws an exception. By removing the `new`-handler, that is, by calling `set_new_handler(0)`, the user could get the old behavior. It would be left up to implementors to specify) whether and how programmers could get the old behavior which would no longer comply with the standard.

Operator Delete

In this implementation, there is nothing for operator `delete` to do but call the C library `free`. Since a null pointer may be the object of a delete, this function must accept the null pointer and do nothing. In Standard C, `free` must also accept a null pointer argument and do nothing, but not all C libraries are standard in this regard. If this default library version of operator delete must work in such an environment, it must make a possibly redundant check as shown in Listing 1.

Array Locatoin and Deletion

When an array of objects is allocated with a new expression, the compiler must generate code to accomplish several things:

1. Raw storage must be allocated for the array.
2. If the object has a constructor, it must be used to create each object in the array.
3. The number of objects allocated may need to be renumbered for a later `delete` expression.

Our old friend operator new is the basic storage allocator, so that takes care of step 1. For step 2, the compiler has all the information it needs in the new expression to construct the array of objects. Partly because of the information that needs to be saved in step 3, it is convenient to add a private helper function to the C++ library that does all the work. The compiler just generates a call to this helper function, which we will get to in a moment.

If the element type of the array has a destructor, that destructor must be used to destroy each object in the array when it is deleted. Since the `delete` expression does not contain any information about the size of the array, it must somehow be recorded for later use; thus, step 3. If the array element type does not have a destructor, step 3 can be skipped.

You may recall that in earlier versions of C++, the delete expression provided the number of elements in the array. That is, for a new expression like

```
T *p new T [20];
```

there would be a delete expression like

```
delete [20]  p;
```

Beginning with AT&T C++ release 2.1 the `delete` expression no longer specified a size. This is now officially part of the language. It was felt that specifying the size in two places was error-prone and that it placed a burden on the programmer to save the size somehow, which could be very inconvenient. Instead, we now require the C++ runtime system to remember the size.

Digression

Here are some ugly details about getting objects constructed and destroyed correctly. It's not for the faint of heart, and you call safely skip down to the next section if you wish.

A given class constructor or destructor might be invoked to construct or destroy an entire object or just a base class sub-object. Consider the following:

```
class vbase { . . .};
class base1 : virtual public vbase { . . .}
class deriv : public base1 { . . .}
base1 B;
deriv D;
```

When object B is constructed, the constructor for base1 must first construct the virtual base class vbase. When object D is constructed, the constructor for deriv must first construct the virtual base class vbase, then construct base class base1. This time, the (same) constructor for base1 must not invoke the constructor for vbase. This implies that some extra information must be passed along to the base1 constructor so that it knows what to do. Similar considerations apply to the destructors. The usual implementation is for constructors and destructors to have an extra hidden parameter, known only to the compiler.

It would be possible always to have this extra parameter, which has the advantage of uniformity. It has the disadvantage of making a more complicated calling sequence than necessary when there are no virtual base classes in the hierarchy. The compiler always knows whether a given class has any virtual base classes. The usual implementation then is to provide the extra parameter in constructors and destructors of any class which has a virtual base class, and not otherwise.

This is another reason why constructors and destructors are special, by the way. You know that they have a this parameter, but they might also have an extra parameter that doesn't show up anywhere but the generated code.

The helper functions we were discussing for operator new and operator delete (I really did have a reason for this digression) must call constructors and destructors, but there isn't a uniform calling sequence. This means that there might be two versions of these helper functions: one for classes with virtual bases, and one for classes without. Because such details are implementation-specific and really very minor, we will discuss only the simpler case without virtual base classes.

While we are digressing, let's consider what happens when the constructor that must be used has default parameters. Recall that an array of class objects must be initialized with the default constructor. Our helper functions assume that the default constructor has no user-defined parameters. In early versions of C++, the default constructor was not allowed to have any user-defined parameters. In more recent versions of C++, the default constructor is allowed to have user-defined parameters provided they all have default values.

Suppose we have a class like this:

```
class Tau {
   . . .
   Tau(const char* = "Easy as", double = 3.1416);
};
```

and we create an array like this:

```
Tau* Metric = new Tau[10]; // subliminal advertisement,
```

Looking at Listing 2, there does not seem to be any way to communicate the number, type, and values of the defaulted argument and pass them through to the constructor that must be called. We use yet another compiler trick. The compiler creates a phony constructor like this (in pseudocode):

```
// phony constructor calls default constructor
Tau::Tau()  {
  this->Tau("Easy as", 3.1416);
}
```

Of course, you can't write this function in C++, but it is never written at all; the compiler just emits code for it.

The compiler must take care not to enter this phony constructor into the overloaded list of constructors for `Tau`, because it would cause ambiguities (there would be two constructors which could be called with no arguments). The function is just quietly used for array initialization, and only the compiler knows about it. The address of this phony constructor is passed to the helper routines for new expressions.

By the way, I mentioned earlier that different versions of helper routines might be needed to handle classes with and without virtual base classes. The compiler could instead generate phony constructors along the lines just discussed to call the real constructor with an extra parameter. The helper function gets the address of the phony constructor and never knows the difference.

MEMORIES OF THE WAY WE WERE . . .

How shall we remember the array size so that destructors get called for each object in the array? There are quite a few design choices here, and different implementations use different methods.

I am told that the method used in the AT&T 2.1 compiler was to keep an associative array of pointer values and array sizes. When an array of objects with destructors was allocated with a new expression, the address and number of objects was entered into the associative array. When the array was deleted, the pointer was looked up in the table and the number of objects to be deleted was found.

An alternative method, which is more efficient in both space arid time, is to allocate a little extra space and store the number of objects there. That is, the `vector-new` helper function would look in part like this, omitting needed casts and ignoring errors:

LISTING 2. Vector new AND delete helper func-

```
//  type corresponding to a destructor
typedef . . . dptr;

// type corresponding to a constructor
typedef . . . cptr;

//  associative array element; details omitted
struct data { . . .
    dptr dtor;
};

//  Add item to the associative array of allocated
//  objects, return 0 on failure, 1 on success.
static int
add_vector(void *addr, size_t size, int count,
           dptr dtor)
{
    if( addr  ==  0 )
      return 0; // original allocation failed
    if( no room in table and cannot expand it )
      return 0; // out of memory
    . . . add data to table; code not shown
    return 1;   // success
}

//  Allocate and construct a vector of
//  objects having destructors.
//  Return the address, 0 on failure.
void * _vector_new_(size_t size, // size of object
    int count, // how many objects
    cptr ctor, // constructor for class
    dptr dtor // destructor for class
)
{
    void *ptr = operator new(size * count);
    if( ! add_vector(ptr, size, count, dtor) )
      return 0;   // fails if ptr == 0
```

```
    if( ctor != 0 )
      for( char *p = (char *) ptr; --count >= 0;
           p += size )
        ctor(p); // call constructors
    return ptr;
}

//  match delete with corresponding allocated object
//  if found, remove entry from table and return
//  pointer to it; otherwise return 0
Static
data* cvheck_addr(void *addr, size_t Size)
{
    ... code not shown
}

//  Destroy a vector of objects on the heap, and
//  release storage. called only if there is a
//  destructor.
void _vector_delete_(void *ptr, // address of array
         size_t size // size of each object
)
}
    if( ptr == 0 )
      return;
    data* loc = check_addr(ptr, size);
    if( ! lot ) {
       ... report error
       abort();
    }
    else  {
      int count = loc->count;
      for( char *p = ( char *)ptr + ((size_t)count-1)*size;
          --count >= 0; p -= size)
        loc->dtor(p); // call destructors
      operator delete(ptr); // delete allocated space
    }
}
```

```
p = operator new(size + sizeof(int));
*p = count;
p += sizeof(int);
. . . call  'count' constructors starring at  'p'
return p;
```

The `vector-delete` helper function would look, in part, like this:

```
count = *(p - sizeof(int));
. . . call 'count' destructors starting at 'p'
operator delete(p - sizeof(int));
```

This method avoids the storage overhead of the extra data in the associative array, and the time overhead of looking up the pointer in the array. Nevertheless, we did not choose this efficient method.

Look what happens in the presence of various kinds of errors. If the static type of the pointer is wrong, the wrong destructor may be called, and the step size through the array is wrong. If the pointer was not allocated by `vector-new`, whatever happens to be at the pointed-to location is used as the count of destructor calls, and the wrong pointer value is passed to operator `delete`. These all have disastrous results. Of course, what ought to happen in these circumstances is undefined, so this implementation violates no requirements.

Pointer errors are notoriously hard to find, so we elected to provide some checks in this case to help the programmer. For example, the problems might arise from implicit casts to a base-class pointer:

```
class Derived : public Base { . . . };
Derived *p = new Derived[10];
  . . .
finishup(p); // deletes the array of classes
```

If function `finishup` takes a pointer to `Base`, there would be no warning from the compiler and no obvious indicator of a possible error like an explicit cast in the source code. Yet the destructor for `Base` rather than for `Derived` is called, and it is called for objects spaced `sizeof(Base)` rather than `sizeof(Derived)` apart in the array. The method we chose gives us a chance to catch the error at the delete rather than getting bizarre behavior later. The vector-new helper function, which we called `_vector_new_`, is invoked by the compiler in response to a vector allocation like this:

```
T *p = new T [count]
```

but only if type `T` has a destructor. The function takes as parameters the size of `T`, the count, and the address of the constructor and destructor for `T`. As shown in Listing 2, it stores the size, count, and address of the destructor in an associative array. If there is a constructor, the function calls it count times, stepping through the array by the provided size.

If type `T` does not have a destructor, we don't need to keep track of the array size. The compiler calls a helper function similar to `_vector_new`, but which only calls the constructors. If type `T` doesn't have a constructor either, then the compiler can generate a simple call to operator new to get uninitialized storage. This is the case for the basic types and for C-like structs. Of course, the implementation could elect to keep track of these array allocations to provide error checking, but we did not do this.

Notice that this helper function can't be called from ordinary C++ code, since it needs the address of a constructor and destructor as arguments. The compiler secretly passes the address of functions for `_vector_new_` to call in a way consistent with the way constructors are called. The helper function doesn't "know" that this is a constructor address. The compiler can break language rules internally, since it knows all about the implementation. Of course, we have to be careful that the compiler and the helper functions are kept in agreement.

The vector-delete helper function, `vector_delete`, is called by the compiler in response to a vector de-allocation like this:

```
delete [] p;
```

but only if the static type of p has a destructor. The function takes as parameters the value of `p` and `sizeof(*p)`. If the pointer is not in the associative array, or if the pointer is in the array but the size does not match, we know there is some kind of error. The array may have been deleted already, the object might not have been allocated as a vector, the address might be just plain wrong, or the static type of p might not match the static type used to when allocating the array. We report the fact of an error and abort the program. (A future version might raise an exception.) If all is well, the function calls the destructor for each element of the array. Notice that we are careful to destroy the objects in the reverse order of their construction.

What are the runtime costs of this error checking? We have to search an associative array to find the address, and we store three extra words of data. If there are a lot of dynamically allocated array objects in a program, this might be expensive.

But let's look at this more carefully. The overhead is incurred only for arrays of objects having destructors, allocated with a new expression. How often does that occur in programs? It seemed to us that dynamic arrays would normally be simple types, or would be allocated and deallocated once each. That is, we would expect there to be very few entries in the associative array, and deallocation of arrays of complex objects would occur very seldom in any program. Besides, the cost of searching the associative array is negligible compared to the cost of destroying the objects, not to mention the call to operator `delete`.

In fact, that is why we only keep track of objects having destructors. We considered providing all this checking for every allocation, but the runtime cost would be too high to provide as the normal implementation.

Finally, let's consider one more language change. The C++ Committee has voted to add a new syntax for dynamic array allocation. Under current language rules, arrays of objects are allocated only with the global operator `new`, even if the class has its own operator `new`. The new syntax will allow a class-specific operator new to be specified for an array of objects. This has only a small impact on our implementation. All we need to do is to modify the helper functions to take an extra parameter specifying the allocation or de-allocation function to use.

Conclusion

Although implementing the semantics of `new` and `delete` in C++ may appear to be straightforward, it requires some tricks in the compiler and runtime system. The implementor must take care to get the right things done in the right order, and may need to take into account peculiarities of the C++ runtime library as well. When all this is carefully done, the C++ programmer can make full use of the flexible dynamic memory allocation available in the language.

References

1. Clambake, S. Making a combined C and C++ implementation, *C++Report* 4(9): 22–26, 1992.
2. Ellis, M.A., and B. Stroustrup. *The Annotated C++ Reference Manual*, Addison-Wesley, Reading, MA, 1990.

Exception Handling: Behind the Scenes

Josée Lajoie
josee@vnet.ibm.com

This is the first part of a two-part article that will review some of the language features provided in C++ to support exception handling as well as review the underlying mechanisms an implementation must provide to support these features. I believe that one understands better the behavior of the C++ exception handling features if one understands the work happening behind the scenes—the work performed by the compiler and during runtime to support C++ exception handling.

Basic Concepts

The C++ exception handling mechanism is a runtime mechanism that can be used to communicate between two unrelated (often separately developed) portions of a C++ application. One portion of the application, usually one performing specialized work (for example, a class library), can detect an exceptional situation that needs to be communicated to the portion of the application which controls or synchronizes the work underway. The exception is the means by which the two portions of the application communicate. If a function notices that an exceptional situation has occurred, it can raise an exception and hope that one of its callers will be capable of handling the exception.

C++ provides three basic constructs to support exception handling:

- A construct to raise exceptions (the *throw expression*);
- A construct to define the exception handler (the *catch block*);
- A construct to indicate sections of code that are sensitive to exceptions (the *try block*).

Let's look at an example to see how these constructs can be used. Let's assume that a math library provides an `OutOfRange` exception.

```
// Math Library
class OutOfRange { }; // Exception class
```

A function in the math library will throw this exception if the operands it receives have values that are not in the acceptable range of values for the operation the function performs. For example, the `math_f` function in the math library will throw an exception if its operand is less than 0.

```
int math_f(int i) {
  if (i < 0)
    throw OutOfRange();
  // otherwise, normal processing continues
}
```

The construct: `throw OutOfRange();` is the throw expression. It is the statement that actually raises the exception.

When an exception is thrown, an exception handler is searched for from the throw point up through the chain of functions calling the function throwing the exception, until a handler for the exception is found.

A user of the `math_f` function can indicate that exceptions need to be detected by enclosing the code using the `math_f` function in a try block as follows:

```
extern int first;
void f() {
  try {
    int result = math_f(first);
  }
  catch (OutOfRange) {
    // If we get here, the operand passed to the
    // math_f library function is less than 0
  }
  //1
}
```

The construct:

```
catch (OutOfRange) {
  // ...
}
```

is the exception handler, or the catch block as it is described in C++. The type in parentheses (here, '`(OutOfRange)`') specifies the type of exception the handler handles. The handler is entered only if an `OutOfRange` exception is thrown by the code in the try block (or thrown by functions called by the code in the try block).

The C++ exception handling mechanism is said to be non-resumptive; that is, once the exception is handled, execution continues at the end of the list of handlers (on line //1 in the preceding example). The execution of the program does not resume where the exception was thrown.

Because the list of callers is searched for a handler, the immediate caller of the function throwing the exception doesn't have to be capable of handling the exception. This capability may be supported by a function further up the call chain. For example:

```
extern int first;
void f() {
  int result = math_f(first);
}
void g() {
  f();
}
void h() {
  try {
    g();
  }
  catch (OutOfRange) {
    // ...
  }
}
```

Here `h()` is the function that will handle the `OutOfRange` exception thrown by the `math_f` function, even though `h()` does not call the `math_f` function directly.

An exception handler can throw an exception to request that another function higher up in the call chain handle the exception. Because exception handlers can themselves throw exceptions, an exception is considered handled immediately after its handler is entered. For example:

```
extern int first;
void f() {
```

```
    try {
      ... math_f(first) ...
    }
    catch (OutOfRange) { //1
      throw OutOfRange();
    }
  }
```

The `OutOfRange` exception thrown by `'math_f'` is considered handled when the `'OutOfRange'` catch block in `'f'` is entered. This implies that if another `'OutOfRange'` exception is thrown by the code in the catch block, a new exception is thrown and a handler is searched in the call chain of function `f()`. The handler on line //1 is not examined again and cannot handle the new `OutOfRange` exception. This prevents infinite loops from happening in the exception handling system.

When an exception is handled, any other handler that may exist for the exception is not relevant. For example:

```
extern int first;
void f() {
  int result = math_f(first);
}
void g() {
  try {
    f();
  }
  catch (OutOfRange) {
    // ...
  }
}
void h() {
  try {
    g();
  }
  catch (OutOfRange) {
    // ...
  }
}
```

Here, both functions `g()` and `h()` are capable of handling an `OutOfRange` exception. If the `math_f` function throws an exception, the handler in function `g()` will handle the exception, because `g()` is the first function encountered (while going up `math_f's` call chain) that contains a handler for `OutOfRange` exceptions.

The class library we have used until now is very simple. One must assume that real-life class libraries will provide more than just one exception class. More than one catch block may therefore be associated with a particular try block.

```
// Exception classes
class OutOfRange { };
class DivideByZero { };

// math_f may throw OutOfRange exception
int math_f(int);
// divide may throw DivideByZero exception
double divide(double, double);

void f() {
  try {
    ... math_f(i) ...
    ... divide(d1,d2) ...
  }
  catch (OutOfRange) {
  }
  catch (DivideByZero) {
  }
}
```

In this example, the first catch block is entered if the `math_f` function throws an `OutOfRange` exception while the second catch block is entered if the divide function throws a `DivideByZero` exception.

There may seem to be a resemblance between exception handling and function calls. A throw expression behaves somewhat like a function call, the catch block somewhat like a function definition. The main difference between these two mechanisms is that all the information necessary to set up a function call is available at compile time, while this is not true for the exception handling mechanism. C++ exception handling requires runtime support. For example, for an ordinary function call, the compiler knows at the point of call which function will actually be called. For exception handling, the compiler doesn't know for a particular throw expression which function the catch block resides in and where execution will resume after the exception has been handled. These decisions happen at runtime. The compiler must therefore leave some information around for the proper decisions to take place. The compiler generates data structures to hold the information needed during runtime to handle C++ exception handling.

BASIC IMPLEMENTATION SUPPORT

We will now look at the work an implementation does behind the scenes, both at compile time and at runtime. To help with the description, let's use a code example that combines some of the language features presented earlier:

```
// Exception classes
class OutOfRange { };
class DivideByZero { };

// math_f may throw OutOfRange exception
int math_f(int);
// divide may throw DivideByZero exception
double divide(double, double);

void f() {
  try {
    ... math_f(i) ...
    ... divide(d1,d2) ...
  }
  catch (OutOfRange) { /* ... */ }
}
void g() {
  try {
    f();
  }
  catch (DivideByZero) { /* ... */ }
}
```

TYPE DESCRIPTORS

As shown earlier, the decision to match an exception thrown with the proper handler is based on type. Because this type matching is performed at runtime, the compiler must encode at compile time some exception handling;type information about the type of the exception thrown. This information is used at runtime to search for a handler.

Type encoding must therefore take place when the C++ compiler encounters a throw expression: the compiler creates a type descriptor describing the type of the exception thrown. If an exception is actually thrown at runtime, the type descriptor is used by a runtime routine to find the proper handler for the exception.

Similar work is done at the catch point: the compiler creates a type descriptor describing the type of the handler. At runtime, during the search for a handler, the type descriptor representing the thrown exception is compared with the type descriptor of the different handlers available until a match is found.

There are many possible ways an implementation can encode the types of the exceptions thrown or the types handled by the catch blocks. One possibility is to encode the types in type descriptors using character strings. This would give, for the preceding example, the type descriptors shown in Table 1.

Stack Unwinding

To find the proper handler for an exception, the stack unwinding routine must know the state of every active function it encounters while unwinding the stack. The state of a function can be determined by answering a set of questions which can be summarized as follows:

1. Does the current function have an active try block? That is, is the function call that threw the exception contained in a try block?
2. If the function contains an active try block, can any of the corresponding exception handlers handle the thrown exception? That is, does the type descriptor of the thrown exception match the type descriptor of any of the handlers (catch block) associated with this try block?

TABLE 1. *Character Strings Can Be Used to Encode the Types in Type Descriptors.*

C++ Statement	Descriptor
`throw OutOfRange();`	`"OutOfRange"`
`throw DivideByZero();`	`"DivideByZero"`
`catch (OutOfRange) {}`	`"OutOfRange"`
`catch (DivideByZero) {}`	`"DivideByZero"`

For these questions to be answered, a function must register—as execution proceeds through its statements—the important events taking place. What is an important event? An important event is an event that influences the answer to the questions listed above. For example, since the runtime routine needs to know when execution is proceeding from within a try block, entering and leaving a try block is considered an important event. One can decompose a function into regions, each region being delimited by an important event. So far, we only have listed entering and leaving a try block as the important events. We will see other important events later on; but for now, we will keep using the try block entry and exit as the only important events to be remembered.

Let's decompose the program shown above into function regions:

```
void f() {
  // Region f::0

  try {
    // Region f::1

    ... math_f(i) ...
    ... divide(d1,d2) ...
  }
  // Region f::0

  catch (OutOfRange) { /* ... */ }}

void g() {
  // Region g::0

  try {
    // Region g::1

    f();
  }
  // Region g::0

  catch (DivideByZero) { /* ... */ }
}
```

Each function contains two regions: a region 0 where there is no active try block, and a region 1 delimited by the start and the end of a try block. Every region is associated with a set of actions that must be executed by the runtime

TABLE 2. *Table of Regions Queried at Runtime*

For function `f`:
Region `f::0`
— Nothing needs to be done

Region `f::1`
— There is an active try block
— The handlers associated with the try block must be examined to find a proper handler for the exception thrown: the type descriptor of the exception thrown must match the type descriptor of one of the handlers for this search to succeed.

For function `g`:
Region `g::0`
— Nothing needs to be done

Region `g::1`
— There is an active try block
— The handlers associated with the try block must be examined to find a proper handler for the exception thrown: the type descriptor of the exception thrown must match the type descriptor of one of the handlers for this search to succeed.

routines if an exception ever originates from within the region. For the example above, the set of actions associated with the different function regions are shown in Table 2.

There are different means for an implementation to know the limits of a function region. A range of program counter values can be used to determine the start and the end of a function region. A state variable can also be used where the state variable is given a particular value depending on the region in which program execution is taking place.

How does the runtime routine for stack unwinding become aware of these regions, and how can it know which action to take if an exception is thrown from within one of these regions? Each function is associated with a table that describes its regions and the actions to be taken if an exception thrown ever originates from within one of its regions. That is, to go back to the example above, the first table in Table 2 is associated with function `f` and the second with function `g`; these tables are queried at runtime to identify which actions must be taken when the stack is unwound.

To get a better idea of how these tables are used at runtime, let's go through our example assuming that the math library function `'divide'` throws a `DivideByZero` exception. The following steps are undertaken at runtime:

At the throw point in function `math_f`:

R1. A type descriptor "`DivideByZero`" is created to represent the exception thrown by the divide function.

During stack unwinding:

R2. Stack unwinding proceeds in order to find a handler for the exception. The first function queried is the divide function itself. Since the divide function doesn't contain any try block, the function contains no region that requires special actions to be taken.

R3. Stack unwinding must proceed to the next enclosing function.

While examining `f`'s table of regions (in Table 2, above):

R4. Using a state variable or the program counter, the runtime routine recognizes that execution was proceeding in region `f::1` when the exception was thrown. The table entry for region `f::1` is examined: it indicates that there is an active try block and that the handler for this try block must be examined.

R5. The handler is examined and no match is found between the type descriptor of the exception thrown ("`DivideByZero`") and the type descriptor of the handler ("`OutOfRange`").

R6. Stack unwinding must proceed to the next enclosing function.

While examining `g`'s table of regions (Table 2, above):

R7. Using a state variable or the program counter, the runtime routine recognizes that execution was proceeding in region `g::1` when the exception was thrown. The table entry for region `g::1` is examined: it indicates that there is an active try block and that the handler for this try block must be examined.

R8. The handler is examined and a match is found between the type descriptor of the exception thrown and the type descriptor of the handler. The handler is entered.

RESOURCE MANAGEMENT

Let's examine other language features that cause the table of regions for a function to be augmented. Resource management requires that these tables provide more information. What is resource management? When allocating a resource in a function, users want the resource to be deallocated properly even if the function is abnormally terminated by a thrown exception. For example:

```
void f() {
  // Acquire resource A
  try {
    ... math_f(i) ...
    ... divide(d1,d2) ...
  }
  catch (OutOfRange) { /* ... */ }
  // release resource A
}

void g() {
  // Acquire resource B
  try {
    f();
  }
  catch (DivideByZero) { /* ... */ }
  // release resource B
}
```

is resource A properly released when the divide function throws an exception? C++ guarantees that any destructor for local variables is properly called when the stack is unwound. This ensures that resources acquired by functions are properly released when a function is abnormally terminated by a thrown exception. This facility implies that the user of a class does not need to write explicit exception handling code, because the clean up work is done automatically:

```
void f() {
  A a;// Acquires resource A
  try {
    ... math_f(i) ...
    ... divide(d1,d2) ...
  }
  catch (OutOfRange) { /* ... */ }

      // Releases resource A
      // Calls ~A() for a
}
```

```
void g() {
  B b; // Acquires resource B
  try {
    f();
  }
  catch (DivideByZero) { /* ... */ }

      // Releases resource B
      // Calls ~B() for b
}
```

If the divide function throws a `DivideByZero` exception, since the function `'f'` doesn't provide a handler for the exception thrown, `'f'` is exited while the stack is unwound. This doesn't prevent local object `'a'` from being properly destroyed.

How does an implementation guarantee that the destructors for local class objects are called?

The list of questions to be answered during stack unwinding (provided earlier) needs to be augmented. An additional question needs to be added to the end of this list. This question must be answered for every function that is examined while going up through the chain of callers during stack unwinding:

3. If the exception cannot be handled by this function and the function must be abnormally exited because the unwinding needs to proceed further up the call chain, do destructors for any local object need to be called?

Constructor calls and destructor calls therefore become important events that need to be remembered for stack unwinding to proceed properly. Because of these new important events, functions need to be decomposed into more granular regions:

```
void f() {
  // Region f::0

  A a; // Acquires resource A
  // Region f::1

  try {
    // Region f::2
```

```
        ... math_f(i) ...
        ... divide(d1,d2) ...
    }
    // Region f::1

    catch (OutOfRange) { /* ... */ }

        // Releases resource A
        // Calls ~A() for a
        // Region f::0
}

void g() {
    // Region g::0

    B b;// Acquires resource B
    // Region g::1

    try {
        // Region g::2

        f();
    }
    // Region g::1

    catch (DivideByZero) { /* ... */ }

        // Releases resource B
        // Calls ~B() for b
        // Region g::0
    }
```

Each function contains three regions: a region 0, where there is no active try block and where no class object has been constructed; a region 1, where a local class object has been constructed; and a region 2, delimited by the start and the end of a try block. Because of these new regions, the set of actions associated with each function region differs slightly from the ones presented earlier. The function tables need to be modified as shown in Table 3.

The table for function `g` is identical to function `f`'s table. These function tables will be used at runtime to identify the actions that need to take place

TABLE 3. *Table for functions* `f`
Region `f::0` — Nothing needs to be done Region `f::1` — A's destructor needs to be called for the automatic class object 'a' Region `f::2` — There is an active try block — The handlers associated with the try block must be examined to find a proper handler for the exception thrown: the type descriptor of the exception thrown must match the type descriptor of one of the handlers for this search to succeed. — If no handler is found, A's destructor must be called for the automatic class object 'a'.

when the stack is unwound. To go back to our earlier example where the math library function divide throws a `DivideByZero` exception, the runtime would use the new function tables as follows:

. . .

During stack unwinding:

R2 and **R3** as before: the first function examined is function `f`.

While examining `f`'s table of regions:

R4, R5 and **R6** as before: the table indicates that there is an active try block. After examining the type of the handler, no match is found.

RNEW. The destructor for the automatic variable `'a'` is executed before function `'f'` is exited, and before the stack is unwound any further.

While examining `g`'s table of regions:

R7 and **R8** as before: the table indicates that there is an active try block. After examining the type of the handler, a match is found and the handler is entered.

Notice that `RNEW` describes the only additional action performed at runtime when function `'f'` is abnormally exited when a `DivideByZero` exception is thrown by the divide function. This new action ensures that the local object `'a'` is destroyed properly when the stack is unwound.

Summary

This is the first part of a two-part article that reviews some of the language features provided in C++ to support exception handling and that reviews some of the underlying mechanisms necessary to support these features. In the first part of this article, we reviewed the data structures generated by a C++ compiler that enable the C++ runtime to make the proper decisions when processing exceptions. In the second part of this article, we will review the consequences of having C++ exceptions be objects. Stay tuned.

Acknowledgments

Many thanks to Kim Knuttila, who reviewed and provided many of the ideas presented in this article.

Many people contributed to IBM's implementation of C++ exception handling. Many years of ideas, discussions, comments, suggestions have gone by. A paper on exception handling cannot be published by one of their teammates without recognizing the whole team as well. In particular, Mark Mendell deserves the major credit for all the work he has done to implement C++ exception handling in the RS/6000 C++ compiler.

Exceptions and Windowing Systems

Pete Becker

I've never enjoyed moving. It's a tedious chore that should only rarely be undertaken and never cheerfully. It was 9 o'clock at night in the middle of February, with a foot of snow on the ground and another snowstorm on the way. I was tired and cold.

I had just pulled my rented truck up to a toll booth on the Massachusetts Turnpike. The toll taker told me that the driver who had come through the booth ahead of me had been a state trooper who had told him that I had to have flashing lights on the car that I was towing. If I didn't fix it the trooper would give me a ticket.

Fixing it wouldn't be easy: the battery in my car was dead and I hadn't gotten a lighting harness when I rented the truck. The toll taker suggested that I pull over into a clear space ahead and figure out what I could do. I pulled over, and after I calmed down a little I figured out how to do it. I grabbed the jumper cables out of my trunk, disconnected the power cables from the battery in my car, clamped the two clamps on one end of the jumper cables to the power cables, and wrapped all the exposed metal in packaging tape so it wouldn't short out.

I snaked the cable out to the back of the truck, taping it to the tow bar. Then I stripped the insulation off the two wires to which the lighting harness was supposed to hook up to, clamped the jumper cables to the wires, and added more tape. I started the truck's engine and turned on the headlights. I went back to my car and turned on the emergency flashers. They worked, drawing their power from the truck through the jumper cables. I climbed into the truck and drove off into the snowstorm.

Of course, if I had had the right lighting harness I could have hooked the two electrical systems together without having to tear anything apart. Since I didn't have it, I had to make my own hooks into the electrical systems in my car and in the truck. That's not the way either one of them was designed to work, but I didn't have the right tool, so I had to improvise.

Programmers learn, sooner or later, that making the pieces of a program work as independently as possible makes maintenance much easier. That's why everyone says, for example, that global data is bad. Global data is a path for interaction between different parts of a program, and it's a path that's hard to control. It encourages improvising, which in turn creates interdependencies that are hard to trace.

Object-oriented programming teaches us that the right tool for handling these problems is encapsulation. Interactions between different parts of a program should be handled through well designed objects with purely functional interfaces. In many cases, however, interactions between different parts of a program arise in more subtle ways.

Sometimes the hard part of fixing such problems is recognizing that there's an interaction in the first place. This is especially true in event-driven windowing systems, where the sequence of execution is largely determined by the windowing system and not by the program itself.

EVENT-DRIVEN PROGRAMMING

When the user of an event-driven program presses a key or clicks a mouse button or does anything else that the program should know about, the windowing system creates a message that contains information about that event. All input from the user and from the windowing system comes to the program from these messages. At its most basic level, an event-driven program consists of a message loop and a message handler. The message loop is usually quite simple: It asks the windowing system whether there is a message waiting to be handled, and when there is one, it tells the windowing system to dispatch it. When programming for Microsoft Windows, a simple version of the message loop typically looks like this:

```
MSG msg;
while( GetMessage( &msg, 0, 0, 0 ))
   {
   DispatchMessage( &msg);
   }
```

The call to `GetMessage()` doesn't return until there is a message ready for the application. This allows the windowing system to run other applications when there are no messages waiting to be handled by the current application. `GetMessage()` returns 0 when the user terminates the application. When that happens, the while loop terminates, and the program can do whatever cleanup is needed before shutting down.

Of course, messages are not of much use unless there's a place to send them. In most cases messages are sent to windows that the windowing system creates at the request of the application. When the application requests creation of a window, one of the things that it has to tell the windowing system is what function to call when there are messages to be processed by that window. The windowing system determines which window should receive a message based on the type of the event that generated the message. For example, when the user clicks a mouse button, the window directly under the mouse cursor at the time of the click should get the message. The windowing system figures out which window it is, and puts an identifier for that window into the message. `DispatchMessage()` uses that identifier to determine which message handler to call. In Windows, a typical message handler looks something like this:

```
long WndProc( HWND hwnd,
    UNIT message,
    WPARAM wParam,
    LPARAM lparam)
{
switch( message )
  {
  case WM_PAINT:
    // code to paint window goes here
    return 0;
    break;
  default:
    return DefWindowProc( hwnd,
      message,
      wParam,
      lParam );
  }
}
```

The original message, which was packed in the `struct MSG`, will be split into four pieces, which are passed as parameters to this function. The second parameter contains a number that tells what event occurred to trigger this message. Under Windows, for example, a `WM_PAINT` message is sent whenever a portion of the window needs to be redrawn. This happens, for example, when someone moves another window that was covering part of this window. The program responds to this message by drawing the part of the window that was exposed by the move.

Throwing Exceptions

If we're writing the message handler in C++ we have to be alert to the possibility that the code that handles some of the windowing system's messages might throw exceptions, so the result would be that the program would terminate. That's not a very friendly thing to do, at least, not without giving some sort of explanation to the user, so we ought to add some exception handling to the program. The obvious place to do that is in the message loop. We might try something like this:

```
MSG msg;
while( GetMessage( &msg, 0, 0, 0 ))
  {
  try {
    DispatchMessage( &msg);
    }
  catch( . . .)
    {
    MessageBox( 0,
      "Unhandled Exception",
      0,
      MB_OK);
    abort();
    }
  }
```

This code catches any exceptions that are thrown by the message handler and puts up a pop-up message telling the user that there was an unhandled exception. Once the user clicks the OK button the application terminates. This is a rather abrupt way to end an application. Let's try something that gives the user a little more flexibility:

```
MSG msg;
while( GetMEssage( &msg, 0, 0, 0))
  {
  try {
    DispatchMessage( & msg);
```

```
        }
    catch( . . .)
        {
        int res = MessageBox( 0,
            "Unhandled Exception, Continue Anyway?",
            0,
            MB_YESNO);
        if( res != IDYES)
            abort();
        }
    }
```

This call to `MessageBox()` puts up a box with two buttons, one marked "Yes" and one marked "No." Now when the code throws an exception, the user gets the option to abort the program or continue executing. Of course, in a real application you'd have to figure out whether the error that caused the exception required terminating, and only let the user choose in the case of nonfatal errors.

But there's a much more fundamental problem in this code: We don't know whether there's a wiring harness running from the message handler back to the message loop. The message loop called `DisptachMessage()`, which called `WndProc()`, `WndProc()` threw an exception. Any destructors that needed to be called in `WndProc()` were called, and then execution jumped to the catch clause in the message loop. Unless `DispatchMessage()` has been written with exceptions in mind, anything that it expected to be able to do after `Wndproc()` returned won't get done. That leads to unpredictable behavior.

Programs that run on windowing systems that support exceptions can use the native exception handling to eliminate this problem. In fact, if your compiler uses the native exception handling as its underlying mechanism for handling C++ exceptions, you don't need to worry about this problem at all. The wiring harness has been provided for you, and everything integrates smoothly. But if you're using a windowing system that doesn't support exceptions, such as 16-bit Windows, you've got a problem.

Constraining Exceptions

One way to solve this problem is to constrain exceptions so that they do not cross the boundary into the windowing system. Instead of putting the try block in the message loop, put it in the message handler:

```
long WndProc(HWND hwnd,
    UINT message,
```

```
        WPARAM wParam,
        LPARAM lparam)
    {
    try {
      switch( message)
        {
        case WM_PAINT:
          // code to paint window goes here
          return 0;
        default:
          return DefWindowProc( hwnd,
                     message,
                     wParam,
                     lParam);
        }
      }
    catch( . . .)
      {
      int res = MessageBox( 0,
        "Unhandled Exception, Continue Anyway?",
        0,
        MB_YESNO);
      if(res != IDYES)
        abort();
      else
        return 0;
      }
    }
```

By catching exceptions inside `WndProc` we prevent unhandled exceptions from being thrown across the windowing system.

Breaking the Exception Model

This solution works fine when you're writing all the code yourself. It poses some problems when it's contained inside an application framework that you're using as the core of your program, where it isn't as visible to you. You may find that the catch clauses that you use in your own code to handle problems that you know how to fix sometimes don't catch things. Application frameworks take care of the grunt work of writing the window procedure and maintaining that awful switch statement. When you use a framework you typically write something like this:

```
class TNewWindow : public Twindow
{
public:
  void EvPaint();
private:
  DECLARE_RESPONSE_TABLE( TNewWindow);
};
DEFINE_RESPONSE_TABLE( TNewWindow, TWindow)
EV_WM_PAINT,
END_RESPONSE_TABLE;
void TNewWindow::EvPaint()
{
try {
  TWindow::DoSomeProcessing();
  }
catch( . . .)
  {
  // handle the exception
  }
}
```

The `DEFINE_RESPONSE_TABLE1` macro builds a message response table for the class `TNewWindow`. The application framework provides a message handler that uses these message response tables to figure out which member function to call when it receives a message. In this case, the handler will call `EvPaint()` whenever it receives a `WM_PAINT` message. This version of `EvPaint()` tries to be smart about exceptions. It provides its own try block and a catch clause that will catch any exceptions that are thrown during execution of its try block.

Even so, you may find that some exceptions end up getting caught in the message handler rather than in `EvPaint()`. That's because some of the functions provided by the application framework are implemented by sending messages to the windowing system. That, in turn, results in a nested call to the message handler. If `TWindow::DoSomeProcessing()` sends a message and the program throws an exception during that nested call, the exception will be caught by the nested invocation of the message handler and won't make its way out to the catch clause in `EvPaint()`.

One solution to this problem is for the framework vendor simply to document this behavior. That's not really a good answer, though, because it fundamentally breaks the model of how exceptions are supposed to work in C++. Programmers shouldn't have to distort their code to work around features provided by a library. A better solution is for the framework to provide its own wiring harness.

Fixing the Exception Model

The problem is that code that is invoked from inside a nested message handler can throw exceptions that should be propagated back to the calling code. It's only when the exception reaches the outermost message handler that the framework should intervene visibly. The wiring harness that we need to build should be able to carry exceptions that are thrown by a nested message handler back to the point where the message that caused the exception was sent. We need to catch exceptions in the nested handler, translate them into a form that won't confuse the windowing system, and throw them again when we get back into our own code. Like this:

```
long WndProc( HWND hwnd,
  UINT message,
  WPARAM wParam,
  LPARAM lparam)
{
try {
  // message dispatching code goes here
  }
catch( . . .)
  {
  if(OutermostHandler())
    // put up message box
  else
    {
    SaveException();
    return 1;
    }
  }
}
void TWindow::DoSomeProcessing()
{
  SendMessage();
}
void TWindow::SendMessage()
{
  ::SendMessage();     // invokes mested message handler
  if(ExceptionSaved())
    RethrownException();
}
```

The function `OutermostHandler()` is a good place holder for the logic to determine whether we're in the outermost message handler. This would typically be done by querying a variable that holds the current nesting level. `SaveException()`, `ExceptionSaved()`, and `RethrowException()` are left as an exercise for the reader.

Where We've Been

Throwing exceptions through code that wasn't designed to handle them can cause problems. One way of eliminating these problems is to catch all exceptions before returning to code in the foreign system. This works, but often results in exceptions being caught earlier than users of a library expect them to be. A better solution to this problem is to provide a wiring harness that transfers the exceptions across the foreign code while still allowing the foreign code to execute its normal return sequence. This preserves the C++ model of exceptions without skipping any cleanup that the foreign system needs to do.

Exception Handling: A False Sense of Security

Tom Cargill
cargill@csn.org
71574,1374@compuserve.com

I suspect that most members of the C++ community vastly underestimate the skills needed to program with exceptions and therefore underestimate the true costs of their use. The popular belief is that exceptions provide a straightforward mechanism for adding reliable error handling to our programs. On the contrary, I see exceptions as a mechanism that may cause more ills than it cures. Without extraordinary care, the addition of exceptions to most software is likely to diminish overall reliability and impede the software development process.

The "extraordinary care" demanded by exceptions originates in the subtle interactions among language features that can arise in exception handling. Counterintuitively, the hard part of coding exceptions is not the explicit throws and catches. The really hard part of using exceptions is to write all the intervening code in such a way that an arbitrary exception can propagate from its throw site to its handler, arriving safely and without damaging other parts of the program along the way.

In the October 1993 issue of the *C++ Report,* David Reed argues in favor of exceptions saying, "Robust reusable types require a robust error handling mechanism that can be used in a consistent way across different reusable class libraries." While entirely in favor of robust error handling, I have serious doubts that exceptions will engender software that is any more robust than that achieved by other means. I am concerned that exceptions will lull programmers into a false sense of security, believing that their code is handling errors when in reality the exceptions are actually compounding errors and hindering the software.

To illustrate my concerns concretely I will examine the code that appeared in Reed's article. The code (*C++ Report* 5(8): 42, October 1993) is a `Stack` class template. To reduce the size of Reed's code for presentation purposes, I have made two changes. First, instead of throwing `Exception` objects, my version simply throws literal character strings. The detailed encoding of the `sException` object is irrelevant for my purposes because we will see no extraction of information from an exception object. Second, to avoid having to break long lines of source text, I have abbreviated the identifier `current_index` to top. Reed's code follows. Spend a few minutes studying it before reading on. Pay particular attention to its exception handling. (Hint: Look for any of the classic problems associated with delete, such as too few delete operations, too many delete operations or access to memory after its delete.)

```
template <class T>
class Stack
{
  unsigned nelems;
  int top;
  T* v;
public:
  unsigned count();
  void push(T);
  T pop();

  Stack();
  ~Stack();
  Stack(const Stack&);
  Stack& operator=(const Stack&);
};

template <class T>
Stack<T>::Stack()
{
  top = -1;
  v = new T[nelems=10];
  if( v == 0 )
    throw "out of memory";
}

template <class T>
Stack<T>::Stack(const Stack<T>& s)
```

```
{
  v = new T[nelems = s.nelems];
  if( v == 0 )
    throw "out of memory";
  if( s.top > -1 ){
    for(top = 0; top <= s.top; top++)
      v[top] = s.v[top];
    top--;
  }
}
template <class T>
Stack<T>::~Stack()
{
  delete [] v;
}

template <class T>
void Stack<T>::push(T element)
{
  top++;
  if( top == nelems-1 ){
    T* new_buffer = new T[nelems+=10];
    if( new_buffer == 0 )
      throw "out of memory";
    for(int i = 0; i < top; i++)
      new_buffer[i] = v[i];
    delete [] v;
    v = new_buffer;
  }
  v[top] = element;
}
template <class T>
T Stack<T>::pop()
{
  if( top < 0 )
    throw "pop on empty stack";
  return v[top--];
}

template <class T>
unsigned Stack<T>::count()
```

```
{
  return top+1;
}

template <class T>
Stack<T>&
Stack<T>::operator=(const Stack<T>& s)
{
  delete [] v;
  v = new T[nelems=s.nelems];
  if( v == 0 )
    throw "out of memory";
  if( s.top > -1 ){
    for(top = 0; top <= s.top; top++)
      v[top] = s.v[top];
    top--;
  }
  return *this;
}
```

My examination of the code is in three phases. First, I study the code's behavior along its "normal," exception-free execution paths, those in which no exceptions are thrown. Second, I study the consequences of exceptions thrown explicitly by the member functions of `Stack`. Third, I study the consequences of exceptions thrown by the `T` objects that are manipulated by `Stack`. Of these three phases, it is unquestionably the third that involves the most demanding analysis.

NORMAL EXECUTION PATHS

Consider the following code, which uses assignment to make a copy of an empty stack:

```
Stack<int> y;
Stack<int> x = y;
assert( y.count() == 0 );
printf( "%u\n", x.count() );

<outputs>

17736
```

The object `x` should be made empty, since it is copied from an empty master. However, `x` is not empty according to `x.count()`; the value `17736` appears because `x.top` is not set by the copy constructor when copying an empty object. The test that suppresses the copy loop for an empty object also suppresses the setting of top. The value that top assumes is determined by the contents of its memory as left by the last occupant.

Now consider a similar situation with respect to assignment:

```
Stack<int> a, b;
a.push(0);
a = b;
printf( "%u\n", a.count() );

<outputs>

1
```

Again, the object a should be empty. Again, it isn't. The boundary condition fault seen in the copy constructor also appears in `operator=`, so the value of a.top is not set to the value of `b.top`. There is a second bug in `operator=`. It does nothing to protect itself against self-assignment, that is, where the left-hand and right-hand sides of the assignment are the same object. Such an assignment would cause `operator=` to attempt to access deleted memory, with undefined results.

Exceptions Thrown by Stack

There are five explicit throw sites in `Stack`: four report memory exhaustion from operator `new`, and one reports stack underflow on a `pop` operation. (`Stack` assumes that on memory exhaustion operator `new` returns a null pointer. However, some implementations of operator new throw an exception instead. I will probably address exceptions thrown by operator `new` in a later column.)

The throw expressions in the default constructor and copy constructor of `Stack` are benign, by and large. When either of these constructors throws an exception, no `Stack` object remains and there is little left to say. (The little that does remain is suffciently subtle that I will defer it to a later column as well.)

The throw from `push` is more interesting. Clearly, a `Stack` object that throws from a `push` operation has rejected the pushed value. However, when rejecting the operation, in what state should `push` leave its object? On push failure, this stack class takes its object into an inconsistent state, because the increment of top precedes a check to see that any necessary growth can be accomplished. The stack object is in an inconsistent state because the value of top indicates the presence of an element for which there is no corresponding entry in the allocated array.

Of course, the Stack class might be documented to indicate that a throw from its push leaves the object in a state in which further member functions (count, push and pop) can no longer be used. However, it is simpler to correct the code. The push member function could be modified so that if an exception is thrown, the object is left in the state that it occupied before the push was attempted. Exceptions do not provide a rationale for an object to enter an inconsistent state, thus requiring clients to know which member functions may be called.

A similar problem arises in operator=, which disposes of the original array before successfully allocating a new one. If x and y are Stack objects and x=y throws the out-of-memory exception from x.operator=, the state of x is inconsistent. The value returned by a.count() does not reflect the number of elements that can be popped off the stack because the array of stacked elements no longer exists.

Exceptions Thrown by T

The member functions of Stack<T> create and copy arbitrary T objects. If T is a built-in type, such as int or double, then operations that copy T objects do not throw exceptions. However, if T is another class type there is no such guarantee. The default constructor, copy constructor, and assignment operator of T may throw exceptions just as the corresponding members of Stack do. Even if our program contains no other classes, client code might instantiate Stack<Stack<int>>. We must therefore analyze the effect of an operation on a T object that throws an exception when called from a member function of Stack.

The behavior of Stack should be "exception neutral" with respect to T. The Stack class must let exceptions from T propagate correctly through its member functions without causing a failure of Stack. This is much easier said than done.

Consider an exception thrown by the assignment operation in the for loop of the copy constructor:

```
template <class T>
Stack<T>::Stack(const Stack<T>& s)
{
  v = new T[nelems = s.nelems]; // leak
  if( v == 0 )
    throw "out of memory";
  if( s.top > -1 ){
```

```
    for(top = 0; top <= s.top; top++)
      v[top] = s.v[top]; // throw
    top--;
  }
}
```

Since the copy constructor does not catch it, the exception propagates to the context in which the `Stack` object is being created. Because the exception came from a constructor, the creating context assumes that no object has been constructed. The destructor for `Stack` does not execute. Therefore, no attempt is made to delete the array of `T` objects allocated by the copy constructor. This array has leaked. The memory can never be recovered. Perhaps some programs can tolerate limited memory leaks. Many others cannot. A long-lived system, one that catches and successfully recovers from this exception, may eventually be throttled by the memory leaked in the copy constructor.

A second memory leak can be found in `push`. An exception thrown from the assignment of `T` in the `for` loop in `push` propagates out of the function, thereby leaking the newly allocated array, to which only `new_buffer` points:

```
template <class T>
void Stack<T>::push(T element)
{
  top++;
  if( top == nelems-1 ){
    T* new_buffer = new T[nelems+=10]; // leak
    if( new_buffer == 0 )
      throw "out of memory";
    for(int i = 0; i < top; i++)
      new_buffer[i] = v[i]; // throw
    delete [] v;
    v = new_buffer;
  }
  v[top] = element;
}
```

The next operation on `T` we examine is the copy construction of the `T` object returned from `pop`:

```
template <class T>
T Stack<T>::pop()
{
  if( top < 0 )
```

```
        throw "pop on empty stack";
    return v[top--]; // throw
}
```

What happens if the copy construction of this object throws an exception? The pop operation fails because the object at the top of the stack cannot be copied (not because the stack is empty). Clearly, the caller does not receive a T object. But what should happen to the state of the stack object on which a pop operation fails in this way? A simple policy would be that if an operation on a stack throws an exception, the state of the stack is unchanged. A caller that removes the exception's cause can then repeat the pop operation, perhaps successfully.

However, pop does change the state of the stack when the copy construction of its result fails. The post-decrement of top appears in an argument expression to the copy constructor for T. Argument expressions are fully evaluated before their function is called. So top is decremented before the copy construction. It is therefore impossible for a caller to recover from this exception and repeat the pop operation to retrieve that element off the stack.

Finally, consider an exception thrown by the default constructor for T during the creation of the dynamic array of T in operator=:

```
template <class T>
Stack<T>&
Stack<T>::operator=(const Stack<T>& s)
{
    delete [] v; // v undefined
    v = new T[nelems=s.nelems]; // throw
    if( v == 0 )
        throw "out of memory";
    if( s.top > -1 ){
        for(top = 0; top <= s.top; top++)
        v[top] = s.v[top];
        top--;
    }
    return *this;
}
```

The delete expression in operator= deletes the old array for the object on the left-hand side of the assignment. The delete operator leaves the value of v undefined. Most implementations leave v dangling unchanged, still pointing to the old array that has been returned to the heap. Suppose the exception from T::T() is thrown from within this assignment:

```
{
  Stack<Thing> x, y;
  y = x; // throw
} // double delete
```

As the exception propagates out of `y.operator=`, `y.v` is left pointing to the deallocated array. When the destructor for y executes at the end of the block, `y.v` still points to the deallocated array. The delete in the `Stack` destructor therefore has undefined results—it is illegal to delete the array twice.

AN INVITATION

Regular readers of this column might now expect to see a presentation of my version of `Stack`. In this case, I have no code to offer, at least at present. Although I can see how to correct many of the faults in Reed's `Stack`, I am not confident that I can produce an exception-correct version. Quite simply, I don't think that I understand all the exception-related interactions against which `Stack` must defend itself. Rather, I invite Reed (or anyone else) to publish an exception-correct version of `Stack`. This task involves more than just addressing the faults I have enumerated here because I have chosen not to identify all the problems that I found in `Stack`. This omission is intended to encourage others to think exhaustively about the issues and perhaps uncover situations that I have missed. If I did offer all of my analysis, while there is no guarantee of it completeness, it might discourage others from looking further. I don't know for sure how many bugs must be corrected in `Stack` to make it exception-correct.

STANDARD C++ TEMPLATES: NEW AND IMPROVED, LIKE YOUR FAVORITE DETERGENT :-)

JOSÉE LAJOIE
josee@vnet.ibm.com

AT THE NOVEMBER 1993 MEETING IN SAN JOSE, THE ANSI/ISO C++ Standards Committee did a major review of the template chapter. Because templates were first adopted by the committee more than 3 years ago, many implementations supporting templates have become available, and templates have been heavily used by the user community. As a result of this, many questions regarding templates and their use were brought forward to the committee. The template chapter in the committee's working paper was basically the same as the template chapter (chapter 14) published in the *Annotated C++ Reference Manual* (ARM).[1] Very few changes had been applied to the chapter. The committee decided that a major review of the template chapter was needed.

The clarifications and changes adopted by the committee mostly affect the area of name look up in template definitions and the area of template instantiation and specialization. In this article, I will review these changes as well as other minor clarifications regarding template parameters that the committee adopted.

These changes affect some of the basic concepts regarding templates, and, as a result of these changes, you should expect that implementations will modify the support they provide for templates and that the template chapter(s) of many tutorial books on C++ will be updated.

You should also be aware that the committee has not completed the review of the template chapter. The committee is still working on clarifications, especially in the area of function overload resolutions, where the committee is considering clarifying how template functions and ordinary functions interact during function overloading. These clarifications will be considered by the committee at the next meeting. Meanwhile, I will present in this column the changes that have already been adopted.

TEMPLATE PARAMETERS

Many C++ users felt that the previous template chapter left many questions regarding template parameters unanswered. The committee clarified many of these questions at the San Jose meeting.

As before, a template parameter may be either a type or a non-type parameter. In the following example:

```
template<class T, int i> class X {
};
```

`T` is a template type parameter and `i` is a template nontype parameter. The committee clarified that the name of a template parameter belongs to the scope of the template definition, and the parameter name is reserved in the scope of the template definition as well as in any scope nested within the template definition:

```
template<class T1, class T2> class X {
  int T1;              //1: error
  void f( ) {
    typedef int T2; //2: error
  }
};
```

The declaration on line //1 is in error because it declares a template member to have the same name as one of the template parameters. The effect of line //2 may surprise you more: line //2 is also in error even though the name `T2` is not redeclared directly in the scope of the template definition but rather in one of its nested scopes, here, in the scope of the class template member function `f`. This is a consequence of the clarification adopted by the committee that prohibits the redeclaration of a template parameter name in any scope nested within the template definition.

The scope of a template parameter extends from its point of declaration until the end of its template and can therefore be used in the declaration of subsequent template parameters:

```
template<class T, T* p> class X { };
```

In this template definition, the type `T` is used to declare the second template parameter p to be of type pointer to `T`, where the type represented by `T` will be determined when the template is instantiated.

As I said above, the scope of a template parameter name extends from its point of declaration, therefore the name of a template parameter cannot be used to declare preceding template parameters. For example:

```
template<T* p, class T> class X { }: // error
```

This template definition is in error because when the compiler sees the declaration of the first template parameter `p`, the name `T` is not in scope, and the declaration causes a syntax error.

The committee also clarified that template nontype parameters of reference type are allowed:

```
template<int& ri> class X { }; // OK
```

Only objects or functions with external linkage can be used as template arguments for template parameters of reference type. This is not new: this requirement on template arguments was already specified in the old template chapter, and the committee did not modify this rule at the San Jose meeting. Especially, the committee confirmed that a temporary cannot be created to initialize a template parameter of reference type. For example:

```
template<int& ri> class X { };
template<const int& cri> class Y { };

int i;
static int si;

X<i> x1         //1: OK
X<1> x2;        //2: error
X<si> x3:       //3: error
Y<1> y1;        //4: error
```

Line //1 is OK because the object i used as the template argument is a global object with external linkage, and line //3 is in error because the object si used as the template argument has internal linkage. The result of line 4 // may be the most surprising: even though the parameter `cri` of class template `Y` is of type reference to const int, a temporary cannot be created to initialize the template parameter and the instantiation of Y<1> is m error.

Because template nontype parameters are to be used as "constant values" during template instantiation, some restrictions were imposed by the committee on the use of these parameters. A template nontype parameter cannot be assigned to or in any other way have its value changed. For example:

```
template<class T, int i> class X {
    void f( ) {
        i++ error
    }
} ;
```

line //1 is in error because it attempts to modify the template nontype parameter i.

Also, to enforce this "constant value" behavior for template nontype parameters, the committee imposed another restriction: a template nontype parameter that is not of reference type cannot explicitly have its address taken.

```
template<int i> class X {
    int f( ) {
        int* p = &i:      // error
    }
};
```

That is, a template nontype parameter is a value, not an object; it cannot be modified nor can it have its address taken.

Finally, the committee approved a minor extension for template parameters that most implementations seem to already support: default arguments for template parameters (either type or nontype parameters) can be specified in a class template declaration or definition. For example:

```
template<class T = int> class X;
```

Most of the rules already enforced for function default arguments apply to template default arguments as well.

Rule 1: If a default argument is specified for a template parameter, all subsequent parameters must have default arguments supplied in this or previous declarations of the template.

For example, the following declaration of the class template X:

```
template<class T1 = int, class T2> class X: // error
```

is in error because no declaration of the template provides a default argument for the template parameter T2.

Rule 2: A template parameter may not be given a default argument by two different declarations in the same scope. For example:

```
template<class T = int> class X;
template<class T = int> class X; // error
```

Here, the second declaration of the class template X is in error even though the two declarations provide the same default argument for the template parameter T.

When referring to a class template for which default arguments are available for every template parameter, the template argument list can be left empty. Empty brackets (<>) must, however, be used to refer to such a template:

```
X<> *ps1 //1: ok, X<int> *ps1;
X *ps2;         //2: syntax error
```

On line //2, the name X does not refer to the template class X, and the statement on line //2 has a syntax error.

As I said above, default arguments for template parameters are only allowed for class templates. A function template cannot have default arguments specified for its template parameters. This is because default arguments are not necessary for function template parameters; the template arguments are deduced from the type of the arguments with which the function is called. For example:

```
template<class T> T f(T) { }
...f(3)...
```

the type of the template type parameter T is 'int'. This type is deduced by looking at the type of the argument '3' specified on the function call. If T had a default argument, it would be of no help. The implementation would still use the type of argument '3' to determine which instantiation of the template function f should be called or generated. Allowing default arguments for function template parameters would therefore burden the language without providing users with any useful feature, and the committee therefore decided against allowing them.

NAME LOOK UP IN TEMPLATE DEFINITIONS

Old versions of the template chapter didn't dearly specify when to bind a name used either explicitly or implicitly inside a template definition. For example:

```
template<class T> class X {//1
public:
  void f(T t) {
    g(1);
    g(t);
    i++;
  }
};
class complex { ... };
X<complex> xc;          //2
```

what do the names `i`, `g`, `operator++`, refer to in the definition of template `X`? Are these names bound when the template is instantiated at point //2? This solution, that is, to bind names in a template definition when the template is instantiated, is the current status quo that most implementations have adopted. However, this solution gives a somewhat unpredictable behavior to template definitions. A template may have many users, and it may have many instantiation points. It is impossible to tell when the template is defined which name will be present at the instantiation point. It is impossible to tell to which declarations the names in the template definition will bind when the template is used. This makes reading and writing templates harder because the reader or the author of the template definition cannot predict the meaning the template definition will have when the template is instantiated.

The other obvious solution, that is, to bind all names at the template definition point (point //1) is also not possible. The names that depend on the template parameters cannot be bound until the template arguments are provided. For example, one cannot know which function is referred to by the name `g` in the statement:

```
g(t);
```

until the argument for the template parameter `T` is known.

Because the two solutions listed above have important limitations, the committee decided to adopt a hybrid solution: to bind as many names as possible at the template definition point (//1) and then bind the rest at the instantiation point (//2) but only accept names (at //2) that depend on a template parameter.

The committee chose this solution because it is simple, it supports better static-type checking because it gives template definitions a more predictable behavior, and it is safer for the class library provider.

Let's examine the consequences of this new-name binding rule on the meaning of template definitions. First, the names used in a template definition will now be looked up in the scope enclosing the template definition. If a name is found in this enclosing scope, the name used in the template definition will be the one declared in this enclosing scope. For example:

```
void g(int);                    //1
int i = 33;                     //2
template<class T> class X {
public:
  void f(T t) {
    g(1);                       //3: calls g(int)
      // declared in            //1
    i++;                        //4: refers to global i
  }
};
```

In this example, the statement `g(1)` on line //3 will call the global function `g(int)` declared on line //1, and the statement `i++` on line // 4 will refer to global `i` declared on line //2.

What happens if a given name used in a template definition can be bound to two different declarations, one visible in the template definition, the other visible at the point of instantiation? Worse, what happens if the name visible at the point of instantiation would be a "better match" than the name bound to in the template definition? Does program validity influence name look up on names used in template definitions? I will briefly answer these questions by saying that for names that do not depend on a template argument, name look up is always done when the template is defined, and source code validity does not affect the outcome of the name look up done in the template definition.

To clarify all this, lets look at an example:

```
void g(double);                 //1
template<class T> class X {
public:
  void f(T t) {
    g(1);                       //2: calls g(double)
      // declared in            //1
```

```
        i++;                 //3: i is not declared
                             // error
    }
};
int i;                       //4
void g(int);                 //5
main( ) {
X<char> x;
  x.f('a');
}
```

In this example, the statement `g(1)` on line //2 will call the global function `g(double)` declared on line //1 this, even though this function is not an exact match for the call on line //2, and this, even though the function `g(int)` declared on line //5 and visible at the point of instantiation would be a better match for the call. Thus, the name binding process in a template definition is never postponed to see if name binding at the point of instantiation will provide a better match. Name binding in the template definition always takes place unless the name in question depends on a template argument.

This state of affairs is made even more obvious if we look at the statement on line //3 the name `i` used in this statement is not declared. This name binding causes the statement on line //3 to be an error. Implementations are mandated to see `i` on line //3 as an undeclared name. Implementations cannot decide to bind the name `i` later at the point of instantiation even if this later binding makes the program a valid C++ program, because the name `i` would then bind to the integer `i` declared on line //4.

As mentioned earlier, the only names that are bound at the point of instantiation are the names dependent on a template parameter. A name is "dependent" on a template parameter `T` if discarding `T`'s declaration makes the name in the template definition bind differently. For example:

```
void g(double);                  //1
template<classT> class X {
public:
  void f(T t) {
    g(t);                        //2: calls g(char)
      // declared in             //3
  }
};
void g(char);                    //3
main( ) {
```

```
X<char> x;
  x.f('a');
}
```

Here, the function called by the statement `g(t)` on line //2 is the function `g(char)` declared on line //3. Because the resolution of the call depends on the type of `t`, and because the type of `t` is dependent on the type of the template parameter `T`, the name resolution for the function `g` (in the statement `g(t)`) will only be done when `X<char>::f(char)` is instantiated.

There are situations when one would like to postpone the binding of a name until the template is instantiated. To do this, one must ensure that the name referenced is explicitly made dependent on the template parameter. For example:

```
template<class T> class x: public T {
...
f(5);
...
};]
```

Some would like to be able to bind `f` at the point of instantiation so that `f(5)` would call `T`'s `f` in preference to a global function `f`. If one wants to refer to `T`'s `f`, one must write the call as `T::f(5)`. This syntax forces name binding for `f` to be delayed until the template is instantiated.

Finally, the committee also adopted some clarifications for the use of the template name itself. Within the scope of a template, the name of the template is equivalent to the name of the template qualified by the template parameter. For example:

```
template<class T> class X {
  X* p1; //1: means X<T>* p1;
  X<T>* p2;
};
```

In this template definition, a use of the name `X` means `X<T>`. This implies that line //1 declares `p1` to be a pointer to `X<T>` and that the pointers `p1` and `p2` point to the same type.

This clarification also implies that if the class template `X` has a cer-defined constructor, it can be defined as

```
template<class T> class X {
  x<T>( ) { }
  // equivalent to: X( ) { }
};
```

that is, the constructor for X can be referred to as X( ) or X<T>( ) interchangeably in the definition of the class template.

This clarification also applies to template specializations:

```
struct X<int>
  X*p1                  //1: means X<int>* p1;
  X<int>( ) { }         //2: equivalent to X( ) { }
};
```

in the definition of this template specialization, a use of the name X refers to the name of the template qualified by the template argument X<int> and the constructor for X can be referred to as X( ) or X<int>( ) interchangeably.

TEMPLATE INSTANTIATIONS AND SPECIALIZATIONS

Another area of the template chapter that was greatly affected by the decisions adopted by the committee in San Jose is the area related to template instantiations and specializations.

As a preamble to the discussion, I would like to present two extensions that the committee adopted in San Jose. The first extension allows users to provide for the automatic instantiation of static data members of class templates. Users can now provide template definitions for static data members as they always could for member functions of class templates. For example:

```
template<class T> class X {
  static T s;
};
template<class T> T X<T>::s = 0; //1
```

Line //1 provides a template definition for the static data member X<T>::s. Users can then refer to the member s of a specialization of the class template X and cause the proper definition of s to be generated automatically. For example, referring to s in an expression as follows:

```
...X<int>::s...
```

will cause the definition of X<int>::s to be generated automatically and will not require the user to provide an explicit definition for the static data member as it was required by the old template chapter.

The second extension allows users to explicitly specify the template arguments, when referring to a template function name, exactly as template arguments are specified in uses of class templates. For example, template arguments can be specified in a call by qualifying the template function name by the list of template arguments as follows:

```
template<class T> void g(T);
void f(int i, double d) {
  g<int>(i);            //1: calls g(int)
  g<double>(d);         //2: calls g(double)
}
```

The name of the template function `g<int>` used on line //1 requests that the function `g(int)` be called, while the name of the template function `g<double>` used on line //2 requests that the function `g(double)` be called.

The use of this new syntax is optional. Users are not required to specify explicitly the template arguments. They can still choose to have the template arguments deduced from the function arguments. For example, the definition for function `f` above could be rewritten as follows, and its meaning would be unchanged:

```
void f(int i, double d) {
  g(i);         //1: calls g(int)
  g(d);         //2: calls g(double)
```

This new extension allows a template parameter to be used exclusively as the return type of a function template. For example, in the following:

```
template<class T1, class T2> T1 h(T2);
  void f(int i) {
    h<double,int>(i); // double h(int)
  }
```

the template parameter `T1` is not used in the function template parameter list. This is ok, because an explicit template argument specification can be used to indicate the type of the template argument for the parameter `T1`. This technique is used in the example above, and the argument specification `h<double,int>` on the call explicitly indicates that `T1` (that is, the return type of function `h`) is type double.

If an explicit argument specification is used to name a function template, the arguments are associated with the template parameters in declaration order. For example, in the call to h in the example above, the first type specified in the explicit specification is type double; it is the type associated with the first template parameter T1. The second type specified, type int, is associated with the second template parameter T2.

Trailing arguments can be left out of the explicit argument specification if they can be deduced from the type of the arguments provided on the function call. For example:

```
template<class T1, class T2> T1 h(T2);
void f( )
{
  h<int, char *> ("aa");     //1
  h<int> ("aa");             //2: T2 is char *
  h("aa");                   //3: error
}
```

The call on line //1 provides an explicit template specification for the template parameters T1 and T2: the type int is associated with type T1 and the type char* is associated with type T2. The call on line //2 only provides an explicit template specification for the template parameter T1: the type int is associated with type T1. This is ok, because the type associated with type T2 can be deduced to be char* using the function argument "aa". The call on line //3 is in error, because the template parameter T1 cannot be deduced by looking at the type of the arguments specified on the call.

With explicit template argument specification, conversions are now possible for arguments passed to template functions. If the type of a template argument has been fixed by an explicit specification, a conversion will be performed by the compiler to convert the function argument to the type specified by the explicit argument specification. For example:

```
template<class T> void f(T);
class complex {
  complex(double);            1//
};
void g( )
  f<complex>(1);              //2: ok
// f<complex>(complex(1));
}
```

In this example, the call on line //2 will cause the template function f(complex) to be instantiated, this, even though the argument passed to the function is of type int. Because the type of the template argument is fixed by the explicit argument specification f<complex>, the compiler searches for a possible conversion from int to complex. Because this conversion is defined by the constructor declared on line //1, the compiler will perform the conversion implicitly, making the call on line //1 a perfectly valid call to the template function f(complex).

We are now ready to describe the clarifications and changes the committee adopted on template instantiations and specializations. Let's first examine the clarifications that relate to implicit instantiations. An implicit instantiation (sometimes just simply called instantiation) is a class, function, or static data member that is implicitly generated by an implementation using the template definition. For example:

```
template<class T> class X { };
template<class T> void f(T);
X<int> x;              //1: implicit instantiation
int i;
f(i);                  //2: implicit instantiation
f<double>(i);          //3: implicit instantiation
```

Line //1 causes the template class X<int> to be implicitly instantiated using the template definition for X. Both lines //2 and //3 use the definition for the function template f(T). The function call on line //2 causes the template function f(int) to be implicitly instantiated while the call on line //3 causes the template function f(double) to be implicitly instantiated.

The committee clarified that not every use of a template causes the implementation to provide an implicit instantiation for the class, function, or static data member. Only if the template is referenced in a context that requires the class, function, or static data member to be defined will the template be implicitly instantiated. If the template is referenced in a context that allows incomplete types, the template will not be instantiated. For example:

```
template <class T> class X { }
x<int>* px;           //1
*px;                  //2
X<char> g(int);       //3
int h(X<double>);     //4
g(33);                //5
```

Line //1 doesn't cause the template class X<int> to be instantiated. Because a pointer can be declared to point to an incomplete type, an implementation will not perceive the pointer declaration on line //1 as being an instantiation request. Line //2, however, uses the pointer in a way that requires the pointer type to be defined, and an implementation will perceive this statement as an instantiation request for the template class `X<int>`.

Lines //3 and //4 are handled like line //1 line //3 refers to the template class `X<char>` and line //4 refers to the template class `X<double>`, but because both statements do not refer to the template classes in a way that requires these types to be defined, the statements will not cause the instantiations of types `X<char>` and `X<double>`. If these functions are called, as is done in the statement on line //5, the implementation instantiates the template classes.

When a class is implicitly instantiated, the class member functions (including the inline member functions), and the static data members that are themselves defined as templates are not implicitly instantiated. These members of class templates are only implicitly instantiated themselves when they are first used. For example:

```
template<class T> class X{
public:
  void f(T t) { }
  void g(T t) { }
};
X<int> x;       //1
x.f(3);         //2
```

Line //1 defines an object of type `X<int>`. Because this definition requires that the type `X<int>` be defined, the class `X<int>` will be instantiated. However, its inline member function `X<int>::f(int)` is not implicitly instantiated until it is called by the statement on line //2. The inline member function `X<int>::g(int)` will not be instantiated because it is never used.

A user may choose to provide in the source code of a program an explicit definition for a template class, function, or static data member. This explicit definition is called an explicit specialization. For example:

```
class X<int> { };             //1
int f<double>(double) { }  //2
int f<int>(int);              //3
f(4);                         //4
```

Line //1 defines the explicit specialization X<int> for the class template X<T>, and line //2 defines the explicit specialization f(double) for the function template f(T). Line //3 declares the explicit specialization f(int) for the function template f(T). This declaration indicates that the user will provide the definition for the explicit specialization somewhere else. Implementations cannot instantiate a template if the declaration of a specialization has been provided by the user. In this example, the implementation cannot instantiate the template when the function f(int) is called on line //4. The call on line //4 will call the explicit specialization declared on line //3.

Some have wondered how instantiations and specializations intermix across compilation units. If a user provides a specialization somewhere in a program, is it always guaranteed to be used? Must implementations be aware of specializations provided in other compilation units and prevent unnecessary instantiations in this compilation unit? For example:

```
  // --- file 1 ---
template<class T> class X{ };
X<int> x;                    //1
  // --- file 2 ---
template<class T> class X{ };
class X <int> { };           //2
extern X<int> x;             //3
```

Must the implementation be aware that the specialization on line //2 is present in the program while processing the declaration on line //1? That is, must the declaration of x on line //1 refer to the instantiation of X<int> or the specialization of X<int> defined in file 2?

The committee decided that a piece of code will use a specialization only if the specialization is declared before the template is used. If a declaration of a specialization is not in scope, the use of a template will cause the template to be instantiated. That is, to go back to the example provided previously, the declaration on line //1 will refer to the instantiation of the type X<int>.

What is the result of this rule on the multiple declarations of x provided in file 1 and 2 of the previous example? Lines //1 and //3 will refer to two different definitions of X<int>. Line //1 therefore declares x to be of a different type than the declaration on line //3. This causes the program above to be erroneous, because it violates the C++ requirement that multiple declarations for a single global object be identical.

The committee members realized that, in addition to implicit instantiation and explicit specialization, almost every implementation offers a mechanism that allows explicit instantiations of templates, that is, that allows users to force the instantiation of a template for a particular set of template arguments. Something like:

```
#pragma generate_here X<int>
```

which requests that the template `X` be generated according to the template definition with an argument of type int.

Why do implementations provide such mechanism for explicit instantiations? Well, relying exclusively on implicit instantiations has problems. It slows down the compile and link times of many applications, sometimes to the point that development is hindered by the use of templates; when implicit instantiations are used, users have trouble predicting what the compile and link times will be. Also, some development environments still have some difficulty in providing support for implicit instantiations.

Because the use of explicit instantiations is so widespread, the committee decided to provide users with a standard mechanism to support explicit instantiations. C++ will now provide the following syntax to support explicit instantiations:

```
template 'specialization'
```

For example, the statement:

```
template class X<int>;
```

is a request for an explicit instantiation of the `type X<int>`, and the statement:

```
template int f<int>(int);
```

is a request for an explicit instantiation of the template function `f(int)`.

Even though the language now provides a mechanism for explicit instantiation, the language will not require that this mechanism be used. Users can decide to exclusively use implicit instantiation and their program will continue to work. Users may choose to use explicit instantiation to obtain better code generation or faster and more predictable compile and link times, but the choice remains optional. Users should be aware, though, that a program can explicitly instantiate a template only once and cannot both explicitly instantiate and explicitly specialize a template. Doing so will cause the program to have undefined behavior.

One should be aware that the explicit instantiation of a class implies that all its member functions and all its static data members that are themselves templates will also be explicitly instantiated. It is, therefore, not possible to both explicitly instantiate a class and to specialize some of its members for a given set of template arguments. For example:

```
template<class T> class X {
public:
  void f(T t) { }
};
template class X<int>;      //1
void X::f<int>(int) { }     //2: error
```

Line //1 causes the explicit instantiation of the class `X<int>` as well as the explicit instantiation of its member function `X<int>::f(int)`. Line //2 is in error because it provides an explicit specialization for a function that has already been instantiated as a consequence of the instantiation request on line //1. The statement on line //2 violates the C++ rule that requires that a C++ entity get only one definition per program.

A New and Useful Template Technique: "Traits"

Nathan Myers
myersn@roguewave.com

Support for internationalization was one of the mandates to the ANSI/ISO C++ Standard Library working group at its inception. What this would mean wasn't clear at the time and has only gradually become clear over the course of five years. One thing we have discovered it to mean is that any library facility which operates on characters must be parameterized on the character type, using templates.

Parameterizing existing iostream and string classes on the character type turned out to be unexpectedly difficult. It required inventing a new technique, which has since been found to be unexpectedly useful in a variety of applications.

The Problem

Let us begin with the problem: In the iostream library, the interface to `streambuf` (as in `stdio` before it) depends on a value "EOF," which is distinct from all character values. In traditional libraries, therefore, the type of EOF was `int`, and the function that retrieves characters returned an `int`:

```
class streambuf {
  ...
  int sgetc();   // return the next character, or EOF
  int sgetn(char*, int N);   // get N characters
};
```

What happens when we parameterize `streambuf` on the character type? We need not only a type for the character, but for the type of the EOF value. Here's a start:

```
template <class charT, class intT>
class basic_streambuf {
  ...
  intT sgetc();
  int sgetn(charT*, int N);
};
```

The extra template parameter clutters things up. Users of iostream don't care what the end-of-file mark is, or its type, and shouldn't need to care. Worse, what value should `sgetc()` return at end-of-file? Must that be another template parameter? The effort is getting out of hand.

The "Trait" Technique

This is where the new technique comes in. Instead of accreting parameters to our original template, we can define another template. Because the user never mentions it, its name can be long and descriptive:

```
template <class charT>
struct ios_char_trait { };
```

The default `trait` class template is empty; what can anyone say about a generalized character type? However, for real character types, we can specialize the template and provide useful semantics:

```
struct ios_char_trait<char> {
  typedef char char_type;
  typedef int int_type;
  static inline int_type eof() { return EOF; }
};
```

Notice that `ios_char_trait<char>` has no data members; it only provides public definitions. Now we can define our `streambuf` template, using the trait template:

```
template <class charT>
class basic_streambuf {
  public:
    typedef ios_char_trait<charT> traits_type;
    typedef traits_type::int_type int_type;
    int_type eof() { return traits_type::eof(); }
    ...
    int_type sgetc();
    int sgetn(charT*, int N);
};
```

Except for the `typedefs`, this looks much like the previous declaration. But notice that it only has one template parameter, the one that interests users. The compiler looks up information about the character type in the character's `trait` class. Code that uses the new template looks the same as before, except that some variables are declared differently.

To put a new character type on a stream, we need only specialize `ios_char_trait` for the new type. For example, let's add support for wide characters:

```
struct ios_char_trait<wchar_t> {
  typedef wchar_t char_type;
  typedef wint_t int_type;
  static inline int_type eof() { return WEOF; }
};
```

Strings may be generalized exactly the same way.

This technique turns out to be useful anywhere that a template must be applied to native types, or to any type for which you cannot add members as required for the template's operations.

Another Example

Before elaborating on the technique, let us see how it might be applied elsewhere. This example is also drawn from the ANSI/ISO C++ Standard.*

* Todd Veldhuizen credits John Barton and Lee Nackman for this usage.

First, imagine writing a numerical analysis library, that should work on float, double, and long double numeric types. Each type has a maximum exponent value, an "epsilon," a mantissa size, and so on. These parameters are all defined in the standard header file `<float.h>`, but a template parameterized on the doesn't know whether to refer to `FLT_MAX_EXP` or `DBL_MAX_EXP`. A trait template with specializations solves the problem cleanly:

```
template <class numT>
struct float_trait { };

struct float_trait<float> {
  typedef float float_type;
  enum { max_exponent = FLT_MAX_EXP };
  static inline float_type epsilon() {
                  return FLT_EPSILON; }
  ...
};
struct float_trait<double> {
  typedef double float_type;
  enum { max_exponent = DBL_MAX_EXP };
  static inline float_type epsilon() {
                  return DBL_EPSILON; }
  ...
};
```

Now we can refer to "`max_exponent`" without knowing whether it is for a float, a double, or your own class type. Here's a matrix template, for instance:

```
template <class numT>
class matrix {
 public:
  typedef numT num_type;
  typedef float_trait<num_type> traits_type;
  inline num_type epsilon() {
        return traits_type::epsilon(); }
  ...
};
```

Notice that in all the examples thus far, each template provided public `typedef`s of its parameters, and also anything that depended on them. This is no accident: in a wide variety of situations, the parameters used to instantiate a template are not available, and can only be retrieved if provided in the template declaration. The moral: always provide these `typedefs`.

Default Template Arguments

The preceding examples are about as far as we can go with 1993-vintage compilers. However, a minor extension approved at the meeting in November 1993 and already implemented in recent compiler releases from some vendors allows us to go much further.

The extension simply allows default parameters to templates. Some compilers have long supported numeric default template parameters. The syntax is obvious; the power it provides may not be. Here is an example drawn from Stroustrup's *Design and Evolution of C++* (page 359).[†] First, we assume a trait-like template `CMP`:

```
template <class T> class CMP {
  static bool eq(T a, T b) { return a == b; }
  static bool lt(T a, T b) { return a < b; }
};
```

and an ordinary string template:

```
template <class charT> class basic_string;
```

Now we can define a `compare()` function on such strings:

```
template <class charT, class C = CMP<charT> >
int compare(const basic_string<charT>&,
    const basic_string<charT>&);
```

I have omitted implementation details here, because I want to draw your attention to the parameters to `compare<>()`. First, notice that the second parameter, C, defaults not just to a class, but to an instantiated template class. Second, notice that the parameter to that template is the previous parameter! This

---

[†] Note: the first edition has typographical errors in this example; if you have that edition, the correction may be found in Doug Schmidt's "Virtual Interview" with Bjarne Stroustrup in *C++ Report* Vol. 6, No. 6.

would not be allowed in a function declaration, but it is explicitly legal for template parameters.

This allows us to call `compare()` on two strings using the default definitions of `eq()` and `lt()`, or substitute our own definitions (such as a case-insensitive comparison). We can do the same thing with our `streambuf` template:

```
template <class charT, class traits =
ios_char_trait<charT> >
class basic_streambuf {
 public:
  typedef traits traits_type;
  typedef traits_type::int_type int_type;
  int_type eof() { return traits_type::eof(); }
  ...
  int_type sgetc();
  int sgetn(charT*, int N);
};
```

This allows us to substitute different trait for a particular character type—which may be important, if (for instance) the end-of-file mark value must be different for a different character set mapping.

Runtime Variable Trait

We can generalize even further. We haven't seen the constructor for `basic_streambuf` yet:

```
template <class charT, class traits =
ios_char_trait<charT> >
class basic_streambuf {
  traits traits; // member data
  ...
  public:
  basic_streambuf(const traits& b = traits())
    : traits(b) { ... }

  int_type eof() { return trait.eof(); }
};
```

By adding a default construct or parameter, we can use a trait template parameter that may vary not only at compile time, but at runtime. In this case, the call to "`trait.eof()`" may call a static member function of `traits`, or a regular member function. A nonstatic member function can use values passed in from the constructor and saved.[††]

Notice that nothing has become harder to use, because the defaults result in traditional behavior; but when you need greater flexibility, you can have it. And in every case you get optimal code—the extra flexibility costs nothing at runtime unless it's used.

SUMMARY

The "trait" technique is useful immediately, on any compiler that supports templates. It provides a convenient way to associate related types, values, and functions with a template parameter type without requiring that they be defined as members of the type. A simple language extension dramatically (and upward-compatibly) extends the technique to allow greater flexibility, even at runtime, at no cost in convenience or efficiency.

REFERENCES

1. Stroustrup, B. *Design and Evolution of C++*, Addison-Wesley, Reading, MA, 1993.
2. Barton, J.J., and L.R. Nackman, *Scientific and Engineering C++*, Addison-Wesley, Reading, MA, 1994.

[††] This final example is not actually found in the Draft Standard.

USING C++ TEMPLATE METAPROGRAMS

TODD VELDHUIZEN
todd@cybervision.kwnet.on.ca

THE INTRODUCTION OF TEMPLATES TO C++ ADDED A FACILITY WHEREBY the compiler can act as an interpreter. This makes it possible to write "programs" in a subset of C++ that are interpreted at compile time. Language features such as for loops and if statements can be replaced by template specialization and recursion. The first examples of these techniques were written by Erwin Unruh and circulated among members of the ANSI/ISO C++ standardization committee.[1] These programs didn't have to be executed—they generated their output at compile time as warning messages. For example, one program generated warning messages containing prime numbers when compiled.

Here's a simple example that generates factorials at compile time:

```
template<int N>
class Factorial {
public:

  enum { value = N * Factorial<N-1>::value };
};

class Factorial<1> {
public:
  enum { value = 1 };
};
```

Using this class, the value `N!` is accessible at compile time as `Factorial<N>::value`. How does this work? When `Factorial<N>` is instantiated, the compiler needs Factorial<N-1> in order to assign the enum "value." So it instantiates Factorial<N-1>, which in turn requires Factorial<N-2>, requiring Factorial<N-3>, and so on until Factorial<1> is reached, where template specialization is used to end the recursion. The compiler effectively performs a for loop to evaluate N! at compile time.

Although this technique might seem like just a cute C++ trick, it becomes powerful when combined with normal C++ code. In this hybrid approach, source code contains two programs: the normal C++ runtime program, and a *template metaprogram* that runs at compile time. Template metaprograms can generate useful code when interpreted by the compiler, such as a massively inlined algorithm—that is, an implementation of an algorithm that works for a specific input size, and has its loops unrolled. This results in large speed increases for many applications.

The next section presents a simple template metaprogram that generates a bubble-sort algorithm.

AN EXAMPLE: BUBBLE SORT

Although bubble sort is a very inefficient algorithm for large arrays, it's quite reasonable for small N. It's also one of the simplest sorting algorithms. This makes it a good example to illustrate how template metaprograms can be used to generate specialized algorithms. Here's a typical bubble sort implementation, to sort an array of ints:

```
inline void swap(int& a, int& b)
{
  int temp = a;
  a = b;
  b = temp;
}

void bubbleSort(int* data, int N)
{
  for (int i = N - 1; i > 0; --i)
  {
    for (int j = 0; j < i; ++j)
    {
      if (data[j] > data[j+1])
```

```
            swap(data[j], data[j+1]);
        }
    }
}
```

A specialized version of bubble sort for `N=3` might look like this:

```
inline void bubbleSort3(int* data)
{
    int temp;

    if (data[0] > data[1])
    { temp = data[0]; data[0] = data[1]; data[1] = temp; }
    if (data[1] > data[2])
    { temp = data[1]; data[1] = data[2]; data[2] = temp; }
    if (data[0] > data[1])
    { temp = data[0]; data[0] = data[1]; data[1] = temp; }
}
```

To generate an inlined bubble sort such as the above, it seems that we'll have to unwind two loops. We can reduce the number of loops to one, by using a recursive version of bubble sort:

```
void bubbleSort(int* data, int N)
{
    for (int j = 0; j < N - 1; ++j)
    {
        if (data[j] > data[j+1])
            swap(data[j], data[j+1]);
    }
    if (N > 2)
        bubbleSort(data, N-1);
}
```

Now the sort consists of a loop, and a recursive call to itself. This structure is simple to implement using some template classes:

```
template<int N>
class IntBubbleSort {
public:
```

```
    static inline void sort(int* data)
    {
      IntBubbleSortLoop<N-1,0>::loop(data);
      IntBubbleSort<N-1>::sort(data);
    }
};
class IntBubbleSort<1> {
public:
    static inline void sort(int* data)
    { }
};
```

We invoke `IntBubbleSort<N>::sort(int* data)` to sort an array of `N` integers. This routine calls a function `IntBubbleSortLoop<N-1,0>::loop(data)`, which will replace the for loop in `j`, then makes a recursive call to itself. A template specialization for `N=1` is provided to end the recursive calls. We can manually expand this for `N=4` to see the effect:

```
static inline void IntBubbleSort<4>::sort(int* data)
{
  IntBubbleSortLoop<3,0>::loop(data);
  IntBubbleSortLoop<2,0>::loop(data);
  IntBubbleSortLoop<1,0>::loop(data);
}
```

The first template argument in the `IntBubbleSortLoop` classes (3,2,1) is the value of `i` in the original version of `bubbleSort()`, so it makes sense to call this argument `I`. The second template parameter will take the role of `j` in the loop, so we'll call it `J`. Now we need to write the `IntBubbleSortLoop` class. It needs to loop from `J=0` to `J=I-2`, comparing elements `data[J]` and `data[J+1]` and swapping them if necessary:

```
template<int I, int J>
class IntBubbleSortLoop {

private:
  enum { go = (J <= I-2) };

public:
  static inline void loop(int* data)
```

```
    {
    IntSwap<J,J+1>::compareAndSwap(data);
    IntBubbleSortLoop<go ? I : 0, go ? (J+1) :
  0>::loop(data);
    }
  };
  class IntBubbleSortLoop<0,0> {
  public:
    static inline void loop(int*)
    { }
  };
```

Writing a base case for this recursion is a little more difficult, since we have two variables. The solution is to make both template parameters revert to 0 when the base case is reached. This is accomplished by storing the loop flag in an enumerative type (`go`), and using a conditional expression operator (`?:`) to force the template parameters to 0 when `go` is false. The class `IntSwap<I,J>` will perform the task of swapping `data[I]` and `data[J]` if necessary. Once again, we can manually expand `IntBubbleSort<4>::sort(data)` to see what is being generated:

```
static inline void IntBubbleSort<4>::sort(int* data)
{
  IntSwap<0,1>::compareAndSwap(data);
  IntSwap<1,2>::compareAndSwap(data);
  IntSwap<2,3>::compareAndSwap(data);
  IntSwap<0,1>::compareAndSwap(data);
  IntSwap<1,2>::compareAndSwap(data);
  IntSwap<0,1>::compareAndSwap(data);
}
```

The last remaining definition is the `IntSwap<I,J>::compareAndSwap()` `routine`:

```
template<int I, int J>
class IntSwap {

public:
  static inline void compareAndSwap(int* data)
```

```
    {
      if (data[I] > data[J])
        swap(data[I], data[J]);
    }
  };
```

The `swap()` routine is the same as before:

```
inline void swap(int& a, int& b)
{
  int temp = a;
  a = b;
  b = temp;
}
```

It's easy to see that this results in code equivalent to:

```
static inline void IntBubbleSort<4>::sort(int* data)
{
  if (data[0] > data[1]) swap(data[0], data[1]);
  if (data[1] > data[2]) swap(data[1], data[2]);
  if (data[2] > data[3]) swap(data[2], data[3]);
  if (data[0] > data[1]) swap(data[0], data[1]);
  if (data[1] > data[2]) swap(data[1], data[2]);
  if (data[0] > data[1]) swap(data[0], data[1]);
}
```

In the next section, the speed of this version is compared to the original version of `bubbleSort()`.

PRACTICAL ISSUES

Performance

The goal of algorithm specialization is to improve performance. Figure 1 shows benchmarks comparing the time required to sort arrays of different sizes, using the specialized bubble sort versus a call to the `bubbleSort()` routine. These benchmarks were obtained on an 80486/66-MHz machine running Borland C++ V4.0. For small arrays (3 to 5 elements), the inlined version is 7 to 2.5 times faster than the `bubbleSort()` routine. As the array size gets larger, the advantage levels off to roughly 1.6.

The curve in Figure 1 is the general shape of the performance increase for algorithm specialization. For very small input sizes, the advantage is very good since the overhead of function calls and setting up stack variables is avoided. As the input size gets larger, the performance increase settles out to some constant value that depends on the nature of the algorithm and the processor for which code is generated. In most situations, this value will be greater than 1, since the compiler can generate faster code if array indices are known at compile time. Also, in superscalar architectures, the long code bursts generated by inlining can run faster than code containing loops, since the cost of failed branch predictions is avoided.

In theory, unwinding loops can result in a performance loss for processors with instruction caches. If an algorithm contains loops, the cache hit rate may be much higher for the nonspecialized version the first time it is invoked. However, in practice, most algorithms for which specialization is useful are invoked many times, and hence are loaded into the cache.

The price of specialized code is that it takes longer to compile, and generates larger programs. There are less tangible costs for the developer: the explosion of a simple algorithm into scores of cryptic template classes can cause serious debugging and maintenance problems. This leads to the question: is there a better way of working with template metaprograms? The next section presents a better representation.

A Condensed Representation

In essence, template metaprograms encode an algorithm as a set of production rules. For example, the specialized bubble sort can be summarized by this "grammar," where the template classes are nonterminal symbols, and C++ code blocks are terminal symbols:

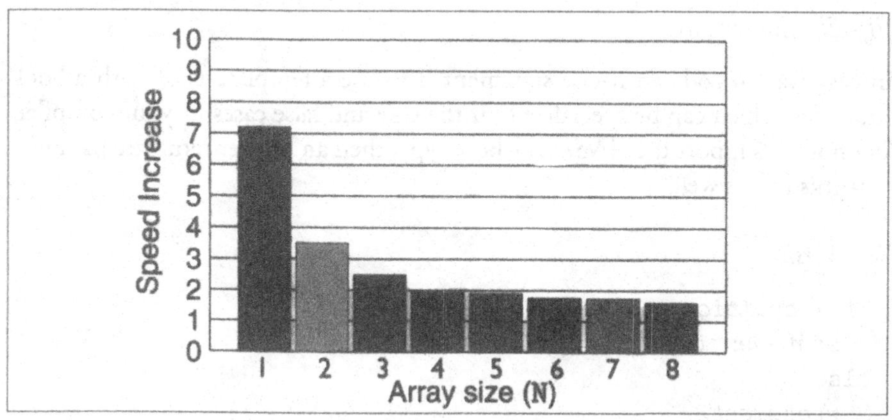

FIGURE 1. *Performance increase achieved by specializing the bubble sort algorithm.*

```
IntBubbleSort<N>:
  IntBubbleSortLoop<N-1,0> IntBubbleSort<N-1>

IntBubbleSort<1>:
  (nil)

IntBubbleSortLoop<I,J>:
  IntSwap<J,J+1> IntBubbleSortLoop<(J+2<=I) ? I : 0,
    (J+2<=I) ? (J+1) : 0>

IntBubbleSortLoop<0,0>:
  (nil)

IntSwap<I,J>:
  if (data[I] > data[J]) swap(data[I],data[J]);
```

Although this representation is far from elegant, it is more compact and easier to work with than the corresponding class implementations. When designing template metaprograms, it's useful to avoid thinking about details such as class declarations, and just concentrate on the underlying production rules.

Implementing Control Flow Structures

Writing algorithms as production rules imposes annoying constraints, such as requiring the use of recursion to implement loops. Though primitive, production rules are powerful enough to implement all C++ control flow structures, with the exception of goto. This section provides some sample implementations.

If/If–Else Statements

An easy way to code an if-else statement is to use a template class with a bool parameter, which can be specialized for the true and false cases. If your compiler does not yet support the *ANSI* C++ bool type, then an integer template parameter works just as well.

C++ Version

```
if (condition)
  statement1;
else
  statement2;
```

Template Metaprogram Version

```
// Class declarations
template<bool C>
class _name { };

class _name<true> {
public:
  static inline void f()
  { statement1; }    // true case
};

class _name<false> {
public:
  static inline void f()
  { statement2; }    // false case
};

// Replacement for 'if/else' statement:
_name<condition>::f();
```

The template metaprogram version generates either `statement1` or `statement2`, depending on whether condition is true. Note that since condition is used as a template parameter, it must be known at compile time. Arguments can be passed to the `f()` function as either template parameters of `_name`, or function arguments of `f()`.

Switch Statements

Switch statements can be implemented using specialization, if the cases are selected by the value of an integral type:

C++ Version

```
int i;

switch(i)
{
  case value1:
    statement1;
    break;
```

```
    case value2:
      statement2;
      break;

    default:
      default-statement;
      break;
}
```

Template Metaprogram Version

```
// Class declarations
template<int I>
class _name {
public:
  static inline void f()
  { default-statement; }
};

class _name<value1> {
public:
  static inline void f()
  { statement1; }
};

class _name<value2> {
public:
  static inline void f()
  { statement2; }
};

// Replacement for switch(i) statement
_name<I>::f();
```

The template metaprogram version *generates* one of `statement1`, `statement2`, or *`default-statement`* depending on the value of `I`. Again, since `I` is used as a template argument, its value must be known at compile time.

Loops

Loops can be implemented with template recursion. The use of the `go` enumerative value avoids repeating the condition if there are several template parameters:

C++ Version

```
int i = N;

do {
  statement;
} while (—i > 0);
```

Template Metaprogram Version

```
// Class declarations
template<int I>
class _name {
private:
  enum { go = (I-1) != 0 };

public:
  static inline void f()
  {
     statement;
     _name<go ? (I-1) : 0>::f();
  }
};

// Specialization provides base case for recursion
class _name<0> {
public:
  static inline void f()
  { }
};

// Equivalent loop code
_name<N>::f();
```

The template metaprogram generates statement N times. Of course, the code generated by statement can vary depending on the loop index `I`. Similar implementations are possible for while and for loops. The conditional expression operator `(?:)` can be replaced by multiplication, which is trickier but more clear visually (i.e. `_name<(I- 1)*go>` rather than `name_<go ? (I-1) : 0>`).

Temporary Variables

In C++, temporary variables are used to store the result of a computation that one wishes to reuse, or to simplify a complex expression by naming subexpressions. Enumerative types can be used as named expressions for template metaprograms, although they are limited to integral values. For example, to count the number of bits set in the lowest nibble of an integer, a C++ implementation might be:

```
int countBits(int N)
{
  int bit3 = (N & 0x08) ? 1 : 0,
    bit2 = (N & 0x04) ? 1 : 0,
    bit1 = (N & 0x02) ? 1 : 0,
    bit0 = (N & 0x01) ? 1 : 0;

  return bit0+bit1+bit2+bit3;
}

int i = countBits(13);
```

Writing a template metaprogram version of this function, the argument `N` is passed as a template parameter, and the four temporary variables (`bit0`, `bit1`, `bit2`, `bit3`) are replaced by enumerative types:

```
template<int N>
class countBits {
  enum {
      bit3 = (N & 0x08) ? 1 : 0,
      bit2 = (N & 0x04) ? 1 : 0,
      bit1 = (N & 0x02) ? 1 : 0,
      bit0 = (N & 0x01) ? 1 : 0 };

public:
  enum { nbits = bit0+bit1+bit2+bit3 };
};

int i = countBits<13>::nbits;
```

Compile-Time Functions

Many C++ optimizers will use partial evaluation to simplify expressions containing known values to a single result. This makes it possible to write compile-time versions of library functions such as `sin()`, `cos()`, `log()`, etc. For example, to write a sine function that will be evaluated at compile time, we can use a series expansion:

$$\sin x = x - \begin{bmatrix} 3 \\ x \\ \overline{3!} \end{bmatrix} = \begin{bmatrix} 5 \\ x \\ \overline{5!} \end{bmatrix} = \begin{bmatrix} 7 \\ x \\ \overline{7!} \end{bmatrix} + K$$

A C implementation of this series might be:

```
// Calculate sin(x) using j terms:
float sine(float x, int j)
{
  float val = 1;

  for (int k = j - 1; k >= 0; —k)
    val = 1 - x*x/(2*k+2)/(2*k+3)*val;

  return x * val;
}
```

Using our production rule grammar analogy, we can design the corresponding template classes needed to evaluate `sin  x` using `J=10` terms of the series. Letting `x = 2*Pi*I/N`, which permits us to pass x using two integer template parameters (`I` and `N`), we can write

```
Sine<N,I>:
  x * SineSeries<N,I,10,0>
SineSeries<N,I,J,K>:
  1-x*x/(2*K+2)/(2*K+3) * SineSeries<N*go, I*go,J*go,
(K+1)*go>

SineSeries<0,0,0,0>:
  1;
```

Where `go` is the result of `(K+1 != J)`. Here are the corresponding class implementations:

```
template<int N, int I>
class Sine {
public:
  static inline float sin()
  {
    return (I*2*M_PI/N) *
        SineSeries<N,I,10,0>::accumulate();
  }
};
// compute J terms in the series expansion.
// K is the loop variable.
template<int N, int I, int J, int K>
class SineSeries {
public:
  enum { go = (K+1 != J) };
  static inline float accumulate()

  {
    return 1-(I*2*M_PI/N)*(I*2*M_PI/N)/(2*K+2)/(2*K+3) *
      SineSeries<N*go,I*go,J*go,(K+1)*go>::accumulate();
  }
};
// Specialization to terminate loop class
SineSeries<0,0,0,0> {
public:
  static inline float accumulate()
  { return 1; }
};
```

The redeeming quality of that cryptic implementation is that a line of code such as:

```
float f = Sine<32,5>::sin();
```

gets compiled into this single 80486 assembly statement by Borland C++:

```
mov   dword ptr [bp-4],large 03F7A2DDEh
```

The literal `03F7A2DDEh` represents the floating point value 0.83147, which is the sine of `2*Pi*5/32`. The sine function is evaluated at compile time, and the result is stored as part of the processor instruction. This is very useful in applications where sine and cosine values are needed, such as computing a Fast Fourier Transform *(FFT)*.2 Rather than retrieving sine and cosine values from lookup tables, they can be evaluated using compile-time functions and stored in the instruction stream. Although the implementation of an inlined *FFT* server is too complex to describe in detail here, it serves as an illustration that template metaprograms are not limited to simple applications such as sorting. An *FFT* server implemented with template metaprograms does much of its work at compile time, such as computing sine and cosine values, and determining the reordering needed for the input array. It can use template specialization to squeeze out optimization for special cases, such as replacing:

```
y = a * cos(0) + b * sin(0);
```

with:

```
y = a;
```

The result is a massively inlined *FFT* server containing no loops or function calls, which runs at roughly three times the speed of an optimized nonspecialized routine.

References

1. Unruh, E. "Prime number computation," *ANSI* X3J16-94-0075/*ISO* WG21-462.
2. Press, W., *et al.*, *Numerical Recipes in C*, Cambridge University Press, 1992.

Expression Templates

Todd Veldhuizen
todd@cybervision.kwnet.on.ca

Passing an expression to a function is a common occurrence. In C, expressions are usually passed using a pointer to a callback function containing the expression. For example, the standard C library routines `qsort()`, `lsearch()`, and `bsearch()` accept an argument `int (*cmp)(void*, void*)` that points to a user-defined function to compare two elements.

Another common example is passing mathematical expressions to functions. The problem with callback functions is that repeated calls generate a lot of overhead, especially if the expression that the function evaluates is simple. Callback functions also slow pipelined machines, since the function calls force the processor to stall.

The technique of expression templates allows expressions to be passed to functions as an argument and inlined into the function body. Here are some examples:

```
// Integrate a function from 0 to 10
DoublePlaceholder x;
double result = integrate(x/(1.0+x), 0.0, 10.0);

// Count the elements between 0 and 100 in a collection of
// int
List<int> myCollection;
IntPlaceholder y;
int n = myCollection.count(y >= 0 && y <= 100);

// Fill a vector with a sampled sine function
Vector<double> myVec(100);
```

```
Vector<double>::placeholderType i;
myVec.fill(sin(2*M_PI*i/100)); // eqn in terms of element #
```

In each of these examples, the compiler produces a function instance that contains the expression inline. The technique has a similar effect to Jensen's Device in ALGOL 60.[1] Expression templates also solve an important problem in the design of vector and matrix class libraries. The technique allows developers to write code such as:

```
Vector<double> y(100), a(100), b(100), c(100), d(100);
 y = (a+b)/(c-d);
```

and have the compiler generate code to compute the result in a single pass, without using temporary vectors.

SO HOW DOES IT WORK?

The trick is that the expression is parsed at compile time, and stored as nested template arguments of an "expression type." Let's work through a simplified version of the first example, which passes a mathematical function to an integration routine. We'll invoke a function `evaluate()` that will evaluate a function `f(x)` at a range of points:

```
int main()
{
  DExpr<DExprIdentity> x;     // Placeholder
  evaluate(x/(1.0+x), 0.0, 10.0);
  return 0;
}
```

For this example, an expression is represented by an instance of the class `DExpr<A>` (short for double expression). This class is a wrapper that disguises more interesting expression types. `DExpr<A>` has a template parameter (`A`) representing the interesting expression, which can be of type `DBinExprOp` (a binary operation on two subexpressions), `DExprIdentity` (a placeholder for the variable `x`), or `DExprLiteral` (a constant or literal appearing in the expression). For example, the simple subexpression "`1.0+x`" would be represented by the expression type shown in Figure 1. These expression types are inferred by the compiler at compile time (described later).

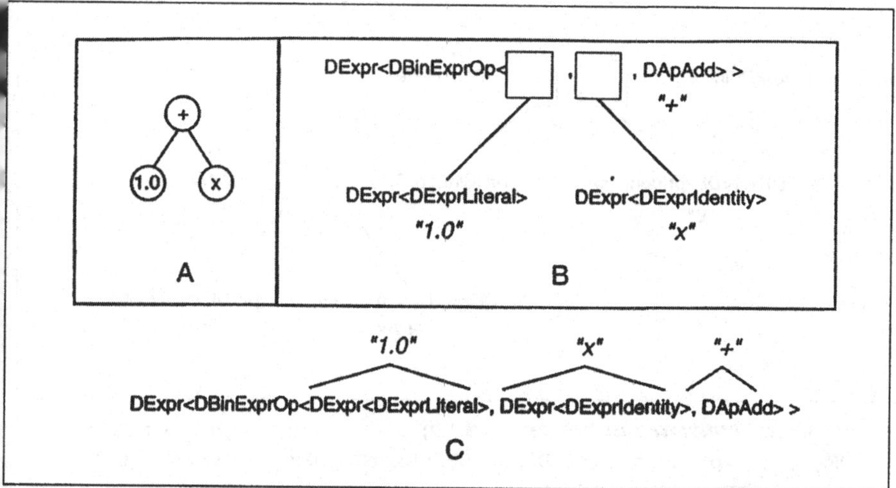

FIGURE 1. *Parse tree (A) of 1.0+x, showing the similarity to the expression type generated by the compiler (B). The type* `DApAdd` *is an applicative template class that represents an addition operation. The expression type (C) is similar to a postfix traversal of the expression tree.*

To write a function that accepts an expression as an argument, we include a template parameter for the expression type. Here is the code for the `evaluate()` routine. The parenthesis operator of `expr` is overloaded to evaluate the expression:

```
template<class Expr>
void evaluate(DExpr<Expr> expr, double start, double end)
{
  const double step = 1.0;
  for (double i=start; i < end; i += step)
    cout << expr(i) << endl;
}
```

When the previous example is compiled, an instance of `evaluate()` is generated that contains code equivalent to the line:

```
cout << i/(1.0+i) << endl;
```

This happens because when the compiler encounters: “x/(1.0+x)” in:

```
evaluate(x/(1.0+x), 0.0, 10.0);
```

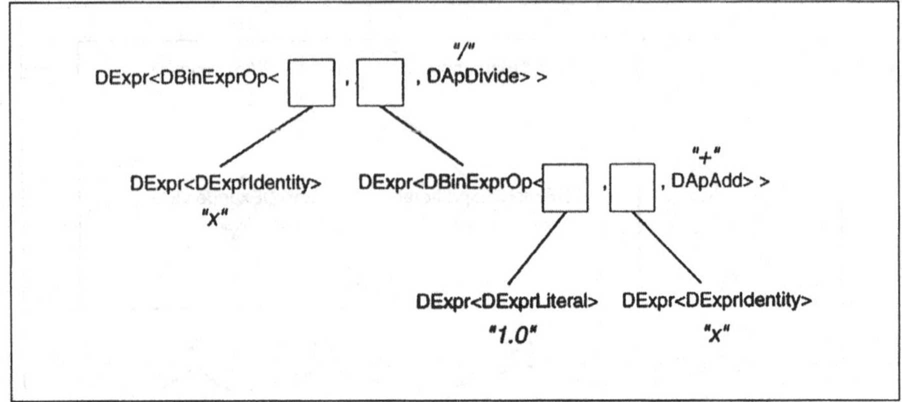

FIGURE 2. *Template instance generated by* `x/(1.0+x)`: `DExpr<DBinExprOp< DExpr <DExprIdentity>, DExpr<DBinExprOp<DExpr<DExprLiteral>, DExpr<DExprIdentity>, DApAdd>>, DApDivide>>`.

it uses the return types of overloaded `+` and `/` operators to infer an expression type that is a palsetree of `x/(1.0+x)`. This expression type is shown in Figure 2. An instance of this expression type is passed to the `evaluate()` function as the first argument. When the fragment `expr(i)` is encountered, the compiler builds the expression inline, substituting `i` for the placeholder `x`. The mechanics of this are explained further on.

As an example of how the return types of operators cause the compiler to infer expression types, here is an `operator/()` that produces a type representing the division of two subexpressions `DExpr<A>` and `DExpr<B>`:

```
template<class A, class B>
DExpr<DBinExprOp<DExpr<A>, DExpr<B>, DApDivide> >
operator/(const DExpr<A>& a, const DExpr<B>& b)
{
  typedef DBinExprOp<DExpr<A>, DExpr<B>, DApDivide>
      ExprT;
  return DExpr<ExprT>(ExprT(a,b));
}
```

The return type contains a `DBinExprOp`, which represents a binary operation, with template parameters `DExpr<A>` and `DExpr<B>` (the two subexpressions being added), and `DApDivide`, which is an applicative template class encapsulating the division operation. The return type is a `DBinExprOp<...>` disguised by wrapping it with a `DExpr<...>` class. If we didn't disguise everything as

`DExpr<>`, we would have to write eight different operators to handle the combinations of `DBinExprOp<>`, `DExprIdentity`, and `DExprLiteral` that can occur with `operator/()`. (More if we wanted unary operators!)

The `typedef ExprT` provides a short form for the type `DBinExprOp< ... , ... , DApDivide>` that is to be wrapped by a `DExpr<...>`. Expression classes take constructor arguments of the embedded types; for example, `DExpr<A>` takes a `const A&` as a constructor argument. So `DExpr<ExprT>` takes a constructor argument of type `const ExprT&`. These arguments are needed so that instance data (such as literals that appear in the expression) are preserved.

The idea of applicative template classes has been borrowed from the Standard Template Library developed by Alexander Stepanov and Meng Lee of Hewlett-Packard Laboratories.[2] The has been accepted as part of the Standard C++ Library. In the , an applicative template class provides an inline `operator()` that applies an operation to its arguments and returns the result. For expression templates, the application function can (and should) be a static member function. Since `operator()` cannot be declared static, an `apply()` member function is used instead:

```
// DApDivide—divide two doubles
class DApDivide {
public:
  static inline double apply(double a, double b)
  { return a/b; }
};
```

When a `DBinExprOp`'s `operator()` is invoked, it uses the applicative template class to evaluate the expression inline:

```
template<class A, class B, class Op>
class DBinExprOp {
  A a_;
  B b_;

public:
  DBinExprOp(const A& a, const B& b)
    : a_(a), b_(b)
  { }
  double operator()(double x) const
  { return Op::apply(a_(x), b_(x)); }
};
```

It is also possible to incorporate functions such as `exp()` and `log()` into expressions, by defining appropriate functions and applicative templates. For example, an expression object representing a normal distribution can be easily constructed:

```
double mean=5.0, sigma=2.0;  // mathematical constants
DExpr<DExprIdentity> x;
evaluate( 1.0/(sqrt(2*M_PI)*sigma) * exp(sqr(x-mean)/
   (-2*sigma*sigma)), 0.0, 10.0);
```

One of the neat things about expression templates is that mathematical constants are evaluated only once at runtime, and stored as literals in the expression object. The `evaluate()` line above is equivalent to:

```
double __t1 = 1.0/(sqrt(2*M_PI)*sigma);
double __t2 = (-2*sigma*sigma);
evaluate( __t1 * exp(sqr(x-mean)/__t2), 0.0, 10.0);
```

Another advantage is that it's very easy to pass parameters (such as the mean and standard deviation)—they're stored as variables inside the expression object. With pointers-to-functions, these would have to be stored as globals (messy), or passed as arguments in each call to the function (expensive).

Figure 3 shows a benchmark of a simple integration function, comparing callback functions and expression templates to manually inlined code. Expression template versions ran at 95% the efficiency of hand-coded C. With larger expressions, the advantage over pointers-to-functions shrinks. This advantage is also diminished if the function using the expression (in this example, `integrate()`) does significant computations other than evaluating the expression.

It is possible to generalize the classes presented here to expressions involving arbitrary types (instead of just doubles). Expression templates can also be used in situations in which multiple variables are needed—such as filling out a matrix according to an equation.

Optimizing Vector Expressions

C++ class libraries are wonderful for scientific and engineering applications, since operator overloading makes it possible to write algebraic expressions containing vectors and matrices:

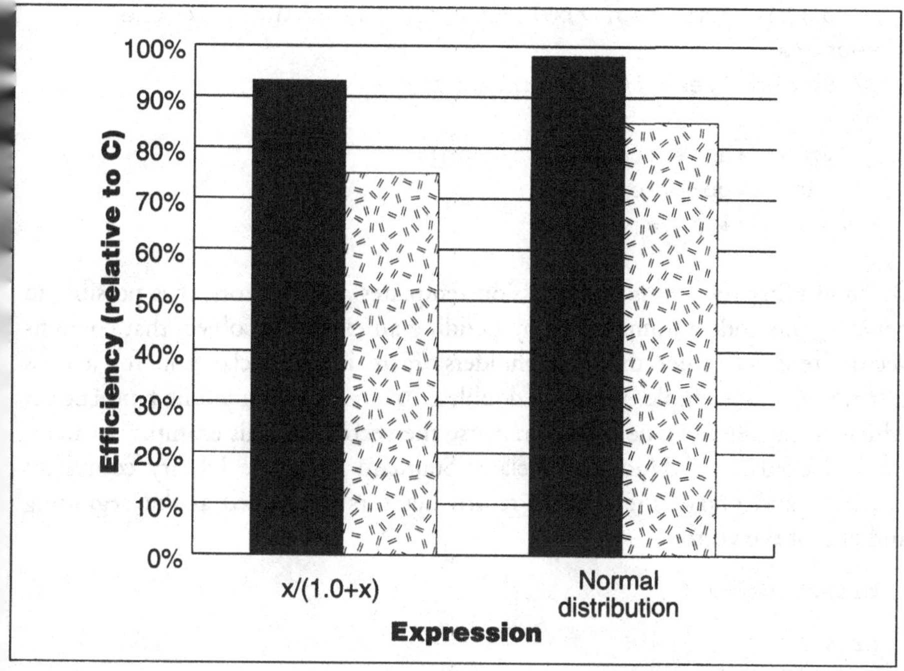

FIGURE 3. *Efficiency for* `integrate()` *as compared to handcoded C (1000 evaluations per call).*

```
DoubleVec y(1000), a(1000), b(1000), c(1000), d(1000);
y = (a+b)/(c-d);
```

Until now, this level of abstraction has come at a high cost, since vector and matrix operators are usually implemented using temporary vectors.[3] Evaluating the above expression using a conventional class library generates code equivalent to:

```
DoubleVec __t1 = a+b;
DoubleVec __t2 = c-d;
DoubleVec __t3 = __t1/__t2;
y = __t3;
```

Each line in the previous code is evaluated with a loop. Thus, four loops are needed to evaluate the expression `y=(a+b)/(c-d)`. The overhead of allocating storage for the temporary vectors (`__t1, __t2, __t3`) can also be significant, particularly for small vectors. What we would like to do is evaluate the expression in a single pass, by fusing the four loops into one:

```
// double *yp, *ap, *bp, *cp, *dp all point into the
vectors.
// double *yend is the end of the y vector.
do {
  *yp = (*ap + *bp)/(*cp - *dp);
  ++ap; ++bp; ++cp; ++dp;
} while (++yp != yend);
```

By combining the ideas of expression templates and iterators, it is possible to generate this code automatically, by building an expression object that contains vector iterators rather than placeholders. Here is the declaration for a class `DVec`, which is a simple "vector of doubles." `DVec` declares a public type `iterT`, which is the iterator type used to traverse the vector (for this example, an iterator is a `double*`). `DVec` also declares Standard Template Library compliant `begin()` and `end()` methods to return iterators positioned at the beginning and end of the vector:

```
class DVec {

private:
  double* data_;
  int length_;

public:
  typedef double* iterT;

  DVec(int n)
    : length_(n)
  { data_ = new double[n]; }

  ~DVec()
  { delete [] data_; }

  iterT begin() const
  { return data_; }

  iterT end() const
  { return data_ + length_; }

  template<class A>
  DVec& operator=(DVExpr<A>);
};
```

Expressions involving DVec objects are of type DVExpr<A>. An instance of DVExpr<A> contains iterators that are positioned in the vectors being combined. DVExpr<A> lets itself be treated as an iterator by providing two methods: double operator*() evaluates the expression using the current elements of all iterators, and operator++() increments all the iterators:

```
template<class A>
class DVExpr {

private:
  A iter_;

public:
  DVExpr(const A& a)
    : iter_(a)
  { }

  double operator*() const
  { return *iter_; }

  void operator++()
  { ++iter_; }
};
```

The constructor for DVExpr<A> requires a const A& argument, which contains all the vector iterators and other instance data (eg. constants) for the expression. This data is stored in the iter_ data member. When a DVExpr<A> is assigned to a Dvec, the Dvec::operator=() method uses the overloaded * and ++ operators of DVExpr<A> to store the result of the vector operation:

```
template<class A>
DVec& DVec::operator=(DVExpr<A> result)
{
  // Get a beginning and end iterator for the vector
  iterT iter = begin(), endIter = end();
  // Store the result in the vector
```

```
    do {
      *iter = *result; // Inlined expression
      ++result;
    } while (++iter != endIter);
    return *this;
  }
```

Binary operations on two subexpressions or iterators A and B are represented by a class DVBinExprOp<A,B,Op>. The operation itself (Op) is implemented by an applicative template class. The prefix ++ and unary * (dereferencing) operators of DVBinExprOp<A,B,Op> are overloaded to invoke the ++ and unary * operators of the A and B instances that it contains.

As before, operators build expression types using nested template arguments. Several versions of the each operator are required to handle the combinations in which DVec, DVExpr<A>, and numeric constants can appear in expressions.

For a simple example of how expressions are built, consider the code snippet:

```
DVec a(10), b(10);
y = a+b;
```

Since both a and b are of type DVec, the appropriate operator+() is:

```
DVExpr<DVBinExprOp<DVec::iterT,DVec::iterT,DApAdd> >

operator+(const DVec& a, const DVec& b)
{
  typedef DVBinExprOp<DVec::iterT,DVec::iterT,DApAdd>
      ExprT;
  return DVExpr<ExprT>(ExprT(a.begin(),b.begin()));
}
```

All the operators that handle DVec types invoke DVec::begin() to get iterators. These iterators are bundled as part of the returned expression object. As before, it's possible to add to this scheme so that literals can be used in expressions, as well as unary operators (such as x = -y), and functions (sin, exp). It's also not difficult to write a templatized version of DVec and the DVExpr classes, so that vectors of arbitrary types can be used. By using another template technique called "traits," it's even possible to implement standard type promotions for vector algebra, so that adding a Vec<int> to a Vec<double> produces a Vec<double>, etc.

Figure 4 shows the template instance inferred by the compiler for the expression `y = (a+b)/(c-d)`. Although long and ugly type names result, the vector expression is evaluated entirely inline in a single pass by the `assignResult()` routine.

To evaluate the efficiency of this approach, benchmarks were run comparing its performance to handcrafted C code, and that of a conventional vector class (i.e., one that evaluates expressions using temporaries). The performance was measured for the expression `y = a+b+c`.

Figure 5 shows the performance of the expression template technique, as compared to handcoded C, using the Borland C++ V4.0 compiler under MS-DOS. With a few adjustments of compiler options and tuning of the `assignResult()` routine, the same assembly code was generated by the expression template technique as hand coded C. The poorer performance for smaller vectors was due to the time spent in the expression object constructors. For longer vectors (e.g., length 100) the benchmark results were 95 to 99.5% the speed of hand-coded C.

Figure 6 compares the expression template technique to a conventional vector class that evaluates expressions using temporaries. For short vectors (up to a length of 20 or so), the overhead of setting up temporary vectors caused the conventional vector class to have very poor performance, and the expression template technique was 8 to 12 times faster. For long vectors, the performance of expression templates settles out to twice that of the conventional vector class.

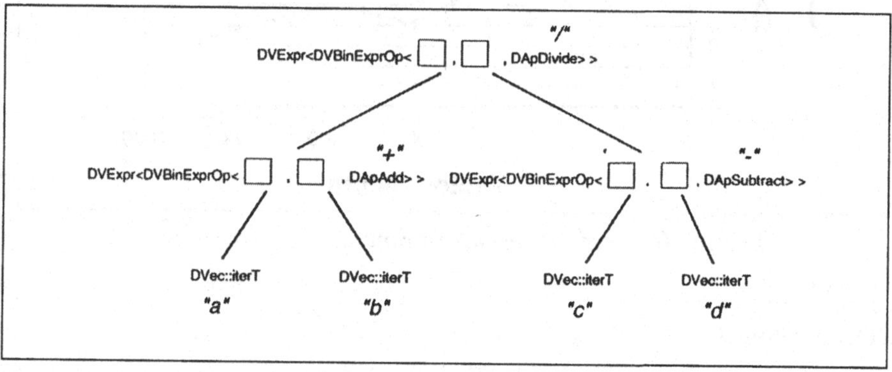

FIGURE 4. *Type name for the expression* `(a+b)/(c-d)`: `DVExpr<DVBinExprOp<DVExpr< DVBinExprOp<DVec::iterT, DVec::iterT, DApAdd>>, DVExpr<DVBinExprOp< DVec::iterT, DVec::iterT, DApSubtract>>, DApDivide>>`.

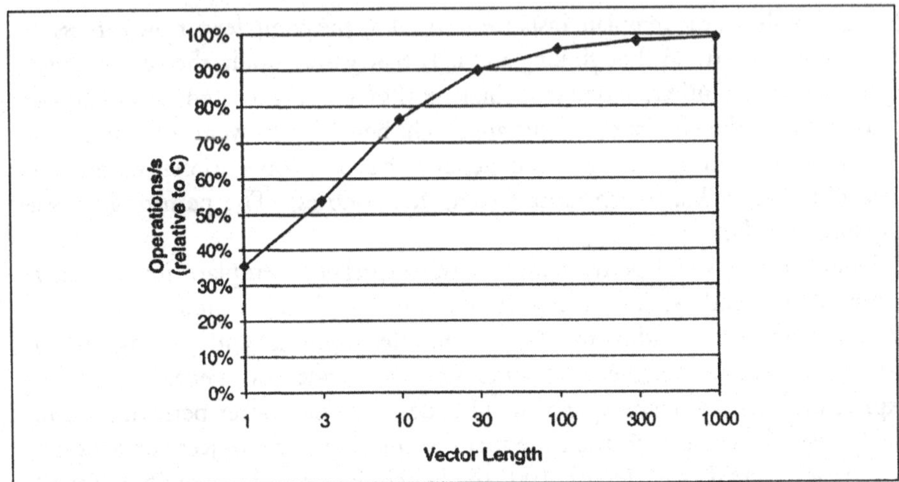

FIGURE 5. *Performance relative to hand coded C.*

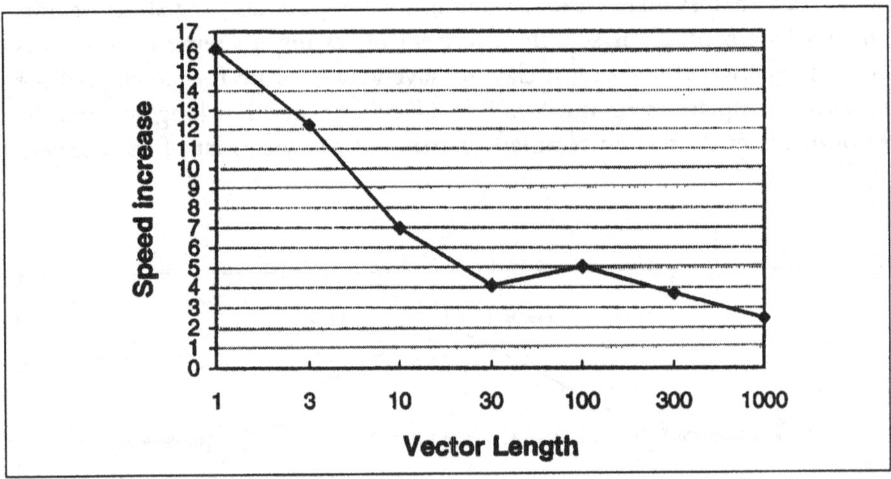

FIGURE 6. *Speed increase over a conventional vector class.*

CONCLUSION

The technique of expression templates is a powerful and convenient alternative to C-style callback functions. It allows logical and algebraic expressions to be passed to functions as arguments, and inlined directly into the function body. Expression templates also solve the problem of evaluating vector and matrix expressions in a single pass without temporaries.

References

1. Rutihauser, H. *Description of ALGOL 60*, Springer-Verlag, New York, 1967.
2. Stepanov, A. and M. Lee., The Standard Template Library, ISO Programming Language C++ Project, ANSI X3J16-94-0095/ISO WG21-NO482.
3. Budge, K. G. C++ Optimization and Excluding Middle-Level Code , 107–121, Sunriver, OR, Apr. 24–27, 1994.

What's that Template Argument About?

John J. Barton
jjb@watson.ibm.com

Lee R. Nackman
lrn@watson.ibm.com

Technical programmers often work with models of reality populated with many identical objects. Two tools important for their work are arrays and templates. Arrays store the many objects, and templates allow efficient, adaptable code to be written to manipulate the objects. In this issue we use templates to write array classes. The story is about arrays; the message is about templates.

In our preceding column (*C++ Report*, 5[9]), we argued that there is no kitchen-sink array class that can meet the spectrum of performance, compatibility, and flexibility requirements that arise in scientific and engineering computing. As we support more function in a general purpose array class, we lose performance.

Instead of loading all kinds of function into one array class, a coordinated system of array classes is needed. Even better would be a customizable system of array classes that was already coordinated. Then we could crank out the kinds we want today: Fortran-compatible and C++-compatible arrays, arrays with size fixed at creation time and arrays with arrays;see also multidimensional array variable size, arrays with and without virtual function interfaces, and so on. And later we could come back and get new custom arrays suited to new special purposes.

This column outlines a plan for building a coordinated family of multidimensional array class templates. Along the way, we study the plan itself.

Collection Parameterization

The archetypal use of templates is for *collection parameterization*, to allow reuse of one piece of source code to create multiple collections. For example, collection parameterization can be used to create new array classes like this:

```
template<class T>
class Array2d {
public:
  typedef T EltT;
  Array2d(int, int);
  int shape(int) const;
  EltT operator()(int, int) const;
  // ...
};
```

Then we can create an `Array2d<double>`, and, if we have a class called Spinor, we can create an `Array2d<Spinor>`.

Function templates can use collection parameterization to work on the elements of every collection generated from a template. Here is an example from our preceding column:

```
template<class T>
T runningSum(const Array2d<T>& a) {
  T sum(0);
  int m = a.shape(0);
  int n = a.shape(1);
  for (int i = 0; i < m; i++) {
    for (int j = 0; j < n; j++) {
      sum += a(i,j);
    }
  }
  return sum;
}
```

A function generated from this function template sums the elements of the array passed to it. Collection parameterization supports reuse: we can write one piece of source code, `Array2d<T>` or `runningSum()`, and use it for double objects or Spinor objects and so on.

SERVICE PARAMETERIZATION

Notice that the template `Array2d` will work for most template argument values: we can expect to make an array of `Spinor` objects even though we don't have a clue what they might represent. The preceding `runningSum()` function template makes more demands on the type parameter: the element type must support += for example. Another version of `runningSum()`, also from our last column, makes even more demands on the template parameter:

```
template<class AnArray2d>
AnArray2d::EltT runningSum(const AnArray2d& a) {
  AnArray2d::EltT sum(0);
  int m = a.shape(0);
  int n = a.shape(1);
  for (int i = 0; i < m; i++) {
    for (int j = 0; j < n; j++) {
      sum += a(i, j);
    }
  }
  return sum;
}
```

When this `runningSum()` is called, as in the code

```
Array2d<int> a(2, 3);
// ...
int sum = runningSum(a);
```

the compiler generates a function (assuming no nontemplate `runningSum()` function that exactly matches the argument type exists) from the template, substituting the argument's type for the type parameter `AnArray2d`.

Unlike the `T` template parameter in `Array2d<T>`, only certain array types will work as matches for `AnArray2d`. The array type must supply a nested type `EltT`, a member function named shape taking an int argument, and a function-call operator taking two int arguments. These are all used directly in the code for `runningSum()`. Also, the nested type must have a constructor that can accept the integer `0` as its argument, a copy constructor, and a += operator. Without these, the function generated from the template won't compile.

These requirements boil down to certain names being supplied like `EltT` or shape. Some of the names must have particular properties. For example, shape must be a function that can be called with an int argument. Let's call all these requirements services: function templates like the second version of `runningSum()` will only work if their template parameter provides these services. To emphasize the tighter coupling of such templates to their template argument, we'll call this service parameterization. Since `runningSum()` uses services supplied by the type substituted for `AnArray2d`, we can say that it is a client of the `AnArray2d` parameter.

Our focus on the names needed and supplied dominates when we begin to use templates to generate the requirements of service parameters. So `runningSum()` needs `shape()` for every `AnArray`? No problem: we'll supply a `shape()` in a system of array classes built with templates.

CLASS TEMPLATES AS CLIENTS

As we have discussed, many kinds of arrays are necessary for scientific and engineering programming. A large family of arrays can be built from a pointer to the first element plus a function of subscripts that gives the offset to other elements. For example, arrays stored with column-major layout, like Fortran arrays, arrays stored with row-major layout, like C++ arrays, packed symmetric triangular arrays, and reduced-dimension projections of these arrays can all be implemented this way. (See Figure 1.)

Our system combines collection parameterization for the element type with service parameterization for the computation of the offset, and the whole system is designed to supply the services needed by array-using clients like `runningSum()`. The central class template, `ConcreteArray2d`, provides the pointer to the first element, but it gets its offset computation from the template argument called `Subscriptor`:

```
template<class Subscriptor, class T>
class ConcreteArray2d :
    private Subscriptor {
public:
    typedef T EltT;
    // Expose Subscriptor's `shape' members
    Subscriptor::dim;
    Subscriptor::shape;
    Subscriptor::numElts;
    // Element access via subscripts
    const T& operator()(int s0, int s1) const;
   T& operator()(int s0, int s1);
protected:
    ConcreteArray2d(const Subscriptor& s, T* p) :
    Subscriptor(s), datap(p) {}
    ~ConcreteArray2d() { delete [] datap; }
    T* datap;
private:
    // Prohibit copy and assignment
```

```
    typedef ConcreteArray2d<Subscriptor, T> rhstype;
    ConcreteArray2d(const rhstype&);
    void operator=(const rhstype&);
};
```

The familiar parts are the parameterized pointer to the elements, `datap`, and the subscripting functions returning a reference to an element. We protect the constructor to require that specific kinds of arrays be defined by derivation from this template. The derived classes are responsible for allocating memory to hold the elements and for providing appropriate copy constructors and assignment operators. We shall come to an example shortly. First let's look at the unfamiliar part, the Subscriptor base class.

The Subscriptor template argument is a class that supplies members that know the shape of the array and one member, `offset()`, that provides an appropriate offset computation. The class `ConcreteArray2d<Subscriptor,T>` is derived from Subscriptor to inherit these members; the derivation is private because we are inheriting implementation and don't want to expose that fact. The three access declarations make the corresponding functions public in the derived class; `offset()` remains private.

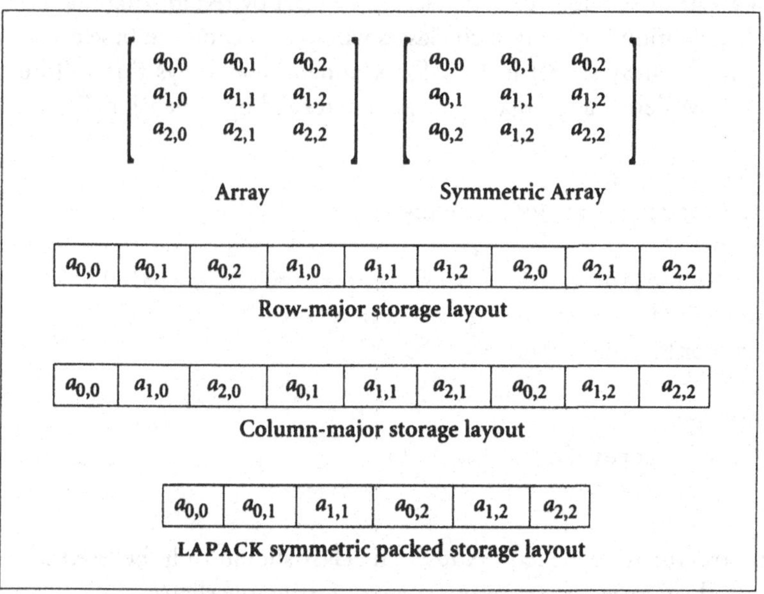

FIGURE 1. *Example array storage layouts. The array elements indicated in the top left array can be stored in continguous memory locations using, for example, either row-major or column-major formats. The symmetric array in the top right could be stored in the packed storage layout used by LAPACK1, storing only the upper triangle of a symmetric matrix.*

The element access functions can be written using the offset computation service provided by `Subscriptor`:

```
template<class Subscriptor, class T>
T& ConcreteArray2d<Subscriptor, T>::
operator()(int s0, int s1) {
  return datap[offset(s0, s1)];
}
template<class Subscriptor, class T>
const T& ConcreteArray2d<Subscriptor, T>::
operator()(int s0, int s1) const {
  return datap[offset(s0, s1)];
}
```

`Subscriptor` is not at all like `T`; it's a variable service on which `ConcreteArray2d` relies.

Services for Class Templates

To implement these `Subscriptor` classes, we start by recognizing that one simple implementation for many such classes will share a common base of two integers giving the array shape; in fact, for *n*-dimensional arrays this will be `ndim` integers, so we define a template class parameterized by dimensionality:

```
template<int ndim>
class ConcreteArrayShapeBase {
public:
  int shape(int dim)   const { return _shape[dim]; }
  int dim()       const { return ndim; }
  int numElts()  const;
protected:
  int _shape[ndim];
  ConcreteArrayShapeBase() {}
};
```

The constructor is protected because this class should only be used as a base class, with the derived classes responsible for setting the shape:

```
template<int ndim>
class ConcreteArrayShape {
```

```
    // Dummy definition: supply a specialization
    // for each value of ndim.
};

class ConcreteArrayShape<2> :
  public ConcreteArrayShapeBase<2> {
public:
  ConcreteArrayShape(int s0, int s1) {
    _shape[0] = s0;
    _shape[1] = s1;
  }
};

class ConcreteArrayShape<3> :
  public ConcreteArrayShapeBase<3> {
public:
  ConcreteArrayShape(int s0, int s1, int s2) {
    _shape[0] = s0;
    _shape[1] = s1;
    _shape[2] = s2;
  }
};
```

We supply a template specialization for each dimensionality, so that the constructor can be given the appropriate number of arguments. (There is no way to say that the constructor should take ndim int arguments.)

Our `Subscriptor` services can now build on this base. For example, Fortran-compatible arrays might use this class:

```
class ColumnMajorSubscriptor2d :
  public ConcreteArrayShape<2> {
public:
  ColumnMajorSubscriptor2d(int s0, int s1) :
    ConcreteArrayShape<2>(s0, s1) {
  }
protected:
  int offset(int i, int j) const {
     return i + j * shape(0);
  }
};
```

Then we can create a Fortran-compatible array by supplying this service to the core array class template:

```
template<class T>
class ConcreteFortranArray2d :
  public ConcreteArray2d<ColumnMajorSubscriptor2d, T> {
public:
  ConcreteFortranArray2d(int s0, int s1);
  // Copy constructors and assignment operators
  // ...
};
```

A `RowMajorSubscriptor2d` would have a different `offset()` calculation that arranges the elements in row-major order:

```
class RowMajorSubscriptor2d :
  public ConcreteArrayShape<2> {
public:
  RowMajorSubscriptor2d(int s0, int s1) :
    ConcreteArrayShape<2>(s0, s1) {
  }
protected:
  int offset(int i, int j) const {
     return j + i * shape(1);
  }
};
```

We can then supply it to the `ConcreteArray2d` template to obtain a two-dimensional array with C- and C++-compatible storage layout:

```
template<class T>
class ConcreteCArray2d : public
  ConcreteArray2d<RowMajorSubscriptor2d, T> {
public:
  ConcreteCArray2d(int s0, int s1);
  // Copy constructors and assignment operators
  // ...
};
```

This pattern is easily extended to various packed storage layouts. For example, the LAPACK Fortran subroutine library for linear algebra stores the upper triangle of a symmetric square matrix as shown in Figure 1. The corresponding `Subscriptor` can be written like this:

```
class SymPackedSubscriptor2d {
public:
  SymPackedSubscriptor2d(int s0) : n(s0) {}
  int shape(int) const { return n; }
  int dim()      const { return 2; }
  int numElts()  const { return (n * (n+1)) / 2; }
protected:
  int offset(int i, int j) const {
    if (i <= j)  return i + (j*(j+1)) / 2;
    else return j + (i*(i+1)) / 2;
  }
private:
  int n;   // n x n matrix
};
```

Unlike the previous two cases, this `Subscriptor` is not derived from `ConcreteArrayShape<2>`; the properties of symmetric matrices make a simpler representation desirable. Nevertheless, `SymPackedSubscriptor2d` supplies the same names and functions as the other subscriptor classes, and therefore meets the needs of a `FortranSymPackedArray2d` class template:

```
template<class T>
class FortranSymPackedArray2d : public
  ConcreteArray2d<SymPackedSubscriptor2d, T> {
public:
  FortranSymPackedArray2d(int s0);
  // Copy constructors and assignment operators
  // ...
};
```

We have omitted some of the details necessary for practical useful arrays, but every detail we add to `ConcreteArray2d` will apply to all of the arrays we derive from it. Moreover, the pattern is simple to extend to higher dimensions, to arrays with subscripts starting at one, as in Fortran, to arrays with subscript range determined when an array is created, and to other storage layouts.

CLASS TEMPLATE SERVERS

ConcreteArray2d<Subscriptor,T> is a client of the Subscriptor parameter and different Subscriptor types yield different arrays. But when we start using these arrays, they can become servers, providing just the names we need for function templates like our second runningSum(), the one that has a service parameter of AnArray. For example, if we create a ConcreteFortranArray2d<double>, we can apply runningSum() to it like this:

```
ConcreteFortranArray2d<int> a(2, 3);
// Set array elements ...
cout << runningSum(a) << endl;
```

We can do the same for FortranSymPackedArray2d<T> and so on because the whole group of arrays derive from our ConcreteArray2d-<Subscriptor,T> and that template supplies the services that runningSum() needs.

Can we put our finger on the exact difference between a collection parameter like T and a service parameter like Subscriptor? After all, the first version of runningSum() that we showed, the one parameterized by T, relies on services in T like +=. It's a matter of degree, but if we think about a template argument like a macro argument we call it a collection parameter; otherwise we call it a service parameter. The names aren't important, but getting beyond viewing templates as fancy macros is important.

Imagine trying to describe one of our array classes via macro expansion. When the ConcreteFortranArray2d<double> class is generated from the corresponding class template, it causes the ConcreteArray2d-<ColumnMajorSubscriptor2d,double> to be generated. This, in turn, causes the ColumnMajorSubscriptor2d class to be needed. It requires ConcreteArrayShape, which is supplied by template specialization instead of generation. Already we can see trouble: Adopting a macro-expansion view of templates leads to a complex view of this system, even before we imagine the expansion of the class member functions.

A view based on common names supplied by service classes and used by client classes or functions treats the relations between parts of a system of templates abstractly, avoiding the details that make the macro expansion view cumbersome. We view ConcreteFortranArray2d<double> as an array class that provides EltT, shape(), and operator()() to runningSum(). The array class happens to get these services from its base class, ConcreteArray2d-

<Subscriptor,T>. And, if we wish to look, the base class gets `shape()` from the `Subscriptor`. We can delve as shallow or as deep as we wish, relating each level to the next in the natural abstraction for that level.

Two major features are missing in our array implementation: projections and iterators that visit every element. As these are added, the client/server parameter view becomes more essential to understand how the system works. For example, how shall we express projections? The offset between elements of the rows of a column-major 2D array will differ from the offset between elements of the rows for a row-major 2D array. Selecting the offset computation for the projection of a 2D array must be a service provided by the Subscriptor. Thus the natural way to talk about the first parameter for the template `ConcreteArray2d` is as a class that will provide `offset()` service. We have used this approach in a previous work# to implement the features missing from the simplified example presented here. Stroustrup[3] has also used the same technique to supply a memory allocator to a container.

Static Polymorphism

We have argued that templates provide a means to supply services to a client by exploiting name commonality. How does this compare with using virtual functions? The big leverage in object-oriented programming comes from polymorphism: one piece of code being able to work with more than one type of object. Virtual functions—C++'s support for polymorphism—are very efficient compared to the support in other languages, but many scientific and engineering programs simply can't tolerate the space and time overheads of virtual functions, particularly since current compilers don't inline calls to virtual functions.

Templates do not have these overheads, and yet they offer some of the benefits of polymorphism. For example, the function template `runningSum()` is one piece of code that works with many types of arrays; the class template `ConcreteArray2d` has members that work with many different Subscriptors, each implementing a storage layout.

Of course, this polymorphism is different than polymorphism provided by virtual functions. But the differences are smaller than the templates-as-macros view leads you to believe. As we have discussed here, client/server templates work together by expecting and offering agreed-upon names for types and functions. Virtual function systems do the same, with client functions expecting the virtual functions in a base class and derived classes supplying these services.

The central difference between virtual function polymorphism and template polymorphism is time: the piece of code that exploits virtual function polymorphism is compiled and the binding to multiple objects happens at runtime, while the piece of code that exploits template polymorphism is source code and the binding happens at compile time. For this reason, we call the polymorphism captured by templates static *polymorphism*.

With this in mind, we can predict when template polymorphism will not work as well as virtual functions: whenever we try to mix a bunch of different object types at runtime. The classic example is a list of objects held by base class pointers: we can't do this with templates. But conventional science and engineering programs don't often mix a bunch of object types at runtime. Much more often we transform object values—add a scalar to a vector; or pass values on to other object types—factor a matrix. So we can get many of the advantages of polymorphism and still generate fast code by using static polymorphism in templates. The balancing cost is increased compile time, larger code size, and more frequent need to recompile as your program evolves.

References

1. Anderson, E., Z. Bai, C. Bischof, J. Demmel, J. Dongarra, J. Du Croz, A. Greenbaum, S. Hammarling, A. McKenney, S. Ostrouchov, and D. Sorensen, *LAPACK User's Guide.* Society for Industrial and Applied Mathematics, Philadelphia, PA, 1992.
2. Barton, J. J., and L. R. Nackman. *Scientific and Engineering C++: An Introduction with Advanced Techniques and Examples,* Addison-Wesley, Reading, MA, 1994.
3. B. Stroustrup. *The C++ Programming Language,* second edition, Addison-Wesley, Reading, MA, 1991, Section 8.7.1.

ALGEBRA FOR C++ OPERATORS

JOHN J. BARTON
jjb@watson.ibm.com

LEE R. NACKMAN
lrn@watson.ibm.com

SOME SCIENTISTS AND ENGINEERS "REGARD C++ AS ESSENTIALLY A metalanguage whose dialects can be tailored to a particular field of application."[1] The metalanguage idea means we write (or reuse) classes for vectors or currents or tensors or whatever, overload the arithmetic operators, and voilà, your code will look and read like mathematics. This comprehensive operator overloading approach gives clear code that is easy to read. It suffers from two problems: possible effciency loss and diffcult design. Many researchers, including Budge *et al.*[2] have discussed the effciency issues. This column attacks the design problem by introducing a system of class templates to help you define consistent and complete sets of arithmetic operators.

Along the way we will introduce two C++ programming techniques: templates to implement *function-structure categories* and *injected function declarations.* These techniques illustrate the power of C++ templates, and they are broadly applicable to global functions, not just to arithmetic operator overloading.

To create consistent arithmetic operators, we will consult with the experts. Mathematicians have explored operators and their interrelations in detail; this area of mathematics is called *abstract algebra.*[2] We capture some of the key ideas of abstract algebra for our programs by translating the mathematical ideas into C++ class and function templates. These templates will have a particular form—one might call it a design pattern[3,4]—that expresses the idea of "consistency" directly in our code.

The consistency is expressed by categorizing classes according to their arithmetic properties. We will create a template for each category and code the common arithmetic properties in the template. Since mathematicians call arithmetic properties *algebraic structure,* we will call the resulting templates *algebraic structure category templates;* since each template represents one category of classes, we will also call them *algebraic categories* for short.

Don't let words like *abstract* and *algebra* scare you off. Although the mathematical field of abstract algebra is, well, abstract, we need only to understand its most basic aspects, and we'll do this mostly by example. On the other hand, if you have not seen template base classes parameterized by derived classes or functions injected by template classes, you're in for a fun ride through some advanced features of C++.

Function-Structure Commonality

Let's begin with a trivial example to illustrate what we mean by complete and consistent operations. Suppose we are going to write a `ComplexFloat` class that represents complex numbers with float components. If `ComplexFloat` provides operator `==`, we expect it to compare its two operands and to return a `bool`, true or false:

```
bool operator==(const ComplexFloat& lhs,
                const ComplexFloat& rhs);
```

(If your compiler does not support `bool`, use

```
typedef int bool;
enum { false = 0, true = 1 };
```

instead.) Given an `operator ==`, we expect an `operator !=` that also compares its operands and returns a `bool`. And we expect these operators to be related so that for `ComplexFloat` objects `c1` and `c2`, `c1 == c2` and `!(c1 != c2)` give identical results.

This example illustrates three kinds of consistency: we expect operators `==` and `!=` to be binary, we expect them to appear in pairs, and we expect them to be related by the `!` operator. C++ enforces the first kind of consistency on all classes. The other kinds of consistency—completeness in the kinds of operators and their relationships to each other—are simple examples of what we call *function-structure commonality:* some functions in a group of classes that are related to each other in a logical way so that they work together. The `operators ==` and `!=` are written for class `ComplexFloat`, but our expectations for their consistency comes from experience with other types using these operators. In other words, these kinds of consistency are desirable *abstract* properties of the operators used in a group of classes. More generally, because operators are just a kind of function, we say that classes sharing a certain function structure are in a *function-structure category.*

The operators in this example happen to be comparison, but the same idea applies, in much richer form, to the arithmetic operators. But before moving on to arithmetic, let's see how we can implement this simple function-structure category in C++.

Function-Structure Category Templates

It's easy to obtain completeness and consistency for a single class:

```
bool operator!=(const ComplexFloat& lhs,
                const ComplexFloat& rhs) {
  return ! (lhs == rhs);
}
```

But we need to generalize in two ways: more operators and more classes. If we want to use, say, all of the relational operators, there are six functions to write; with arithmetic, there are at least eight. Using this one-class-at-a-time approach for numerical objects with both relational and arithmetic operators will be tedious if we intend to write more than one class. Worse, we have to be careful to do it completely and consistently each time. We seek a more compact and reliable method, one that will allow us to name the correctly related set of operators and reuse the relations.

For classes to be used in isolation (hint: there aren't many of these!), global function templates do the trick:

```
// Comparison
template<class T>
bool operator!=(const T& lhs, const T& rhs) {
  return ! (lhs == rhs);
}

// Arithmetic
template<class T>
T operator*(const T& lhs, const T& rhs) {
  T result = lhs;
  return result *= rhs;
}
```

```
template<class T>
T operator+(const T& lhs, const T& rhs) {
  T result = lhs;
  return result += rhs;
}

// ...
```

These establish the usual relationships between `==` and `!=`, `*` and `*=`, etc.

But these function templates are too powerful because they work for all possible classes `T`. Suppose you want to write a matrix class, parameterized by element type. You probably don't want to provide an `*=` operator, but you do want to provide `*` as matrix multiplication. So you write:

```
template<class T>
class Mat {
  // ...
};
template<class T>
Mat<T>
operator*(const Mat<T>& lhs, const Mat<T>& rhs) {
  // Code for Matrix multiplication ...
}
```

Everything is cool until you try your first matrix multiplication:

```
Mat<int> a;
Mat<int> b;
Mat<int> c = a * b;
```

The compiler complains that the call to `::operator*()` matches both `operator*(const T&, const T&)` and `operator*(const Mat<T>&, const Mat<T>&)`. Global function templates with simple template parameters as arguments are too strong.

We need some middle ground between implementing function structure manually for each class and blindly forcing the same function structure on all classes. We want to write the consistency rules as templates that can be reused, but control the reuse explicitly.

We can accomplish these goals by wrapping a class template around the necessary functions. For example:

```
template<class T>
class EquivalentCategory {
  friend bool operator!=(const T& lhs, const T& rhs) {
    return ! (lhs == rhs);
  }
};
```

Here's the technique (OK, it's a trick): since the declaration for the global function `!=` is part of a class template, it is effective only when a class is instantiated from the class template. To apply the consistency rule to a class `ComplexFloat` with an existing implementation for `==`, we need only instantiate the class `EquivalentCategory<ComplexFloat>`.

The ANSI/ISO C++ Standards Committee has introduced a statement that lets you explicitly instantiate a class.[5] With our example, you'd write:

```
template EquivalentCategory<ComplexFloat>;
```

Most compilers don't allow this yet. An alternative is to create a dummy object:

```
EquivalentCategory<ComplexFloat> dummy;
```

Either way, creating the class created a global function.

We wrote a `friend` declaration for the function `operator!=()` inside of class template `EquivalentCategory<T>`. When we wrote `EquivalentCategory<ComplexFloat>`, `T` became `ComplexFloat` and the friend became `operator!=()` taking two `ComplexFloat` objects as operands. This friend function is completely defined when the `EquivalenceCategory<ComplexFloat>` class is instantiated. Note that the friend itself is not a function template—`T` is fixed at `ComplexFloat`—it is just a plain function taking two `ComplexFloat` operands. We say that instantiating the class template *injects* the friend function declaration into global scope.

This *function injection* is a consequence of `friend` declarations and template expansion. A global `friend` function is a function that belongs logically in a class but that we want to call as a global function, not as a member function. Global friend functions are used routinely for operator functions so that conversion applies to both operands. Using global friend functions in class templates is a reasonable extension of using friends in classes. It is the "lazy-expansion" model of template expansion that yields injection: A class template is instantiated when the template is first used (exactly what this means is part of the standards committee's work[5]), and consequently the friend declaration appears when the first instance of the class appears.

Using dummy objects to force class template instantiation is, at best, clumsy. We prefer to use class derivation to instantiate function structure class templates:

```
class ComplexFloat :
  public EquivalentCategory<ComplexFloat> {
public:
  // ...
  friend bool operator==(const ComplexFloat& lhs,
                         const ComplexFloat& rhs) {
    return lhs._r == rhs._r && lhs._i == rhs._i;
  }
private:
  float _i;
  float _r;
};
```

Perhaps this looks a bit odd, too: we are deriving a class from a class template parameterized by the derived class. Again, this is a consequence of combining two independent C++ language features, class derivation and class templates. This approach to instantiating function-structure templates connects the point of function injection directly with the class: declaring `ComplexFloat` injects the operator `!=`.

Abstract Algebra

With C++ tools for function-structure categories in hand, we are ready to consult the mathematicians for the rules of consistency for arithmetic. We'll adopt the names of abstract algebra as the names of the class templates when we implement function-structure categories for arithmetic. After we outline the class templates, we will give a recipe for finding the right algebraic structure for a given class and show an example.

Algebraic structures deal with sets, composition laws (read operators), and a few properties of the composition laws. Some amazing and beautiful mathematics follows from relatively few definitions. We'll skip all that good stuff and just use the definitions. The important point is that the definitions capture, in an abstract setting, many of the arithmetic structures we commonly use.

To keep things simple, we'll focus on algebraic structures over one set with one or two composition laws. Table 1 lists the algebraic structures over a single

TABLE 1. *Algebraic structures over a single set.*

Algebraic Structure	Multiplicative Law			Additive Law		
	Operation	Identity	Inverse	Operation	Identity	Inverse
Semigroup	⋆					
Monoid	⋆	✓				
Group	⋆	✓	✓			
Abelian semigroup				+		
Abelian monoid				+	✓	
Abelian group				+	✓	✓
Ring	⋆			+	✓	✓
Ring with unit	⋆	✓		+	✓	✓
Field	⋆	✓	✓	+	✓	✓

set with one and two composition laws. The table calls the composition laws "multiplicative" and "additive," but they could be any kind of operation on two elements of a set that is associative (i.e., `a □ (b □ c) = (a □ b) □ c` for operation). The additive structures must also be commutative (`a □ b = b □ a`); commutative composition laws are called *Abelian* as shown in the table. An *identity* element (sometimes called a *unit*) is an element of the set, denoted `1`, having the property that `1 □ a = a □ 1 = a`. If, for an element `a`, there is an element `b` such that `a □ b = 1`, `b` is called the *inverse* of `a`. You can see from the table that there are three single-law additive structures and three single-law multiplicative structures. Successive structures each introduce one additional property (hmm, possible inheritance?). The two-law structures have one additive and one commutative law, related by two distributive laws: `a(b+c) = ab+ac` and `(a+b)c=ac+bc`.

In C++ code, the associativity is obtained by writing operators that are independent of calling order and commutativity is obtained by writing operators that are independent of argument order. Similarly, distributivity is obtained if the code from two operators does not depend on their calling order. The remaining algebraic properties will be defined in our algebraic structure category templates.

The simplest structure is a semigroup: a set and a multiplication operation. The corresponding template has only multiplication and repeated multiplication (`pow()`):

```
template<class T>
class SemiGroupCategory {
public:
   // User Must Define: T& operator*=(const T&);
```

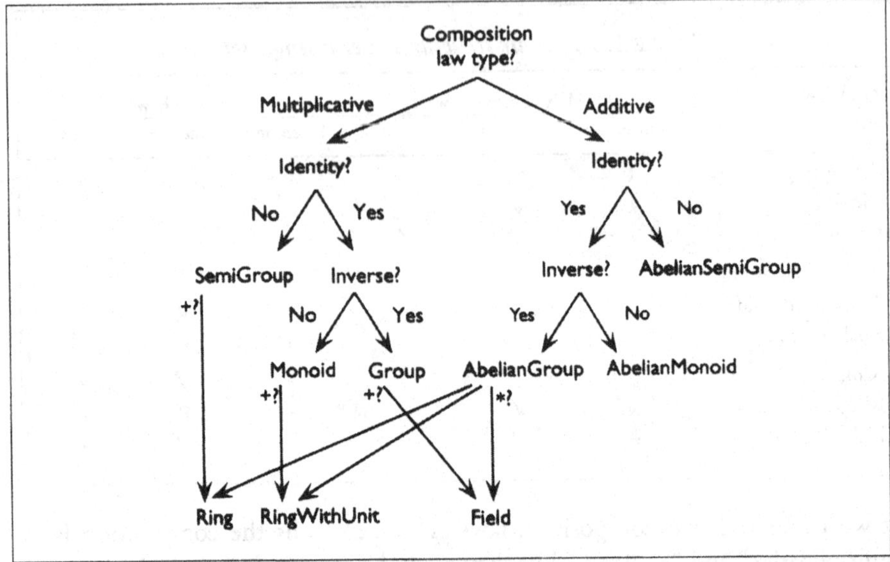

FIGURE 1. *Decision tree for choosing an algebraic structure category. The question +? means "also an addition?" while *? means "also a multiplier?"*

```
    friend T operator*(const T& lhs, const T& rhs) {
      T temp(lhs);
      return temp *= rhs;
    }

    friend T pow(const T& x, int n) {
      T temp(x);
      return temp.pow(n);
    }

    T& pow(Positive<int> n);    // update in-place
};
```

To see how this template works, it is helpful to imagine `T` as a specific target class that we want to put in the algebraic structure category. Let's use `ComplexFloat`. To join the `SemiGroupCategory`, `ComplexFloat` will derive from `SemiGroupCategory<ComplexFloat>`. This base class is given by the previous template with `T` set to `ComplexFloat`. The functions in this base class call the `*=` member of `ComplexFloat` (e.g., operator `*` above and `pow()` shown later). The `ComplexFloat` class must define this function. We call such functions required by the function-structure category templates ***user-must-define functions*** because this is what you need to supply to use the category templates. For semigroup, we chose `*=` since this function is intrinsically asymmetric and thus can be a member function without losing operand conversion.

The semigroup has no identity or inverse elements for multiplication, so only positive powers are allowed in pow(). We enforce this constraint with a simple and cheap runtime check using this helper class template:

```
template<class T>
class Positive {
public:
  Positive(T x)  : _x(x) {
    if (x <= 0) throw "not positive";
  }
  operator T() { return _x; }
private:
  int _x;
};
```

Repeated multiplication is implemented by the category member function template:

```
template<class T>
T& SemiGroupCategory<T>::pow(Positive<int> n) {
  T& x = (T&) *this;
  T t = x;
  int m = n;
  while (—m) x *= t;
  return x;
}
```

The type cast in the first statement is safe, because the category template is always parameterized by the derived target class. Therefore, we "know" that `*this` is really an instance of a `T`.

The next level of abstract algebra is a *monoid*, a semigroup with an identity element. In C++, we use derivation to implement this relation between the two algebra structures:

```
template<class T>
class MonoidCategory : public SemiGroupCategory<T> {
public:

  // User Must Define: T& setToOne();
  T& pow(NonNegative<int> n);
};
```

Typical string classes in C++ are monoids with string concatenation being the composition law and the null string being the identity.

A `Monoid<T>` class must supply a `setToOne()` member, which sets an object to the identity element. The presence of an identity allows raising to nonnegative powers, so the monoid category introduces a new `pow()` member function that hides the semigroup `pow()` and uses a helper class template NonNegative that we leave to your imagination. The implementation illustrates the use of `setToOne()`:

```
template<class T>
T& MonoidCategory<T>::pow(NonNegative<int> n) {
  // Algorithm A, Knuth, The Art of Computer
  // Programming: Seminumerical Algorithms,
  // volume 2, 2nd ed., p. 442.  The variables N,
  // Y, and Z correspond to Knuth's variable names.
  int N = n;
  T& Y = (T&) *this;
  T Z = Y;
  Y.setToOne();

  while (true) {
    int oldN = N;
    N /= 2;
    if (N + N != oldN) Y *= Z;
    if (N == 0 ) return Y;
    Z *= Z;
  }
}
```

The class templates for the other structures in Table 1 follow this same pattern we have sketched out. After monoid we come to a (multiplication) ***group***. It has both an identity and an inverse. The corresponding class template defines inversion and division. (Groups are fundamental to many physical problems.) Group finishes the "multiplication" branch of abstract algebra, so we move over to addition. The structure of addition is the same as multiplication: the same names are used but mathematicians prefix the names with *Abelian*; we follow suit to define `AbelianSemiGroup<T>`, `AbelianMonoid<T>`, and `AbelianGroup<T>`.

When we pair multiplicative and additive algebraic structures we get new structures, with two composition laws. For example, an Abelian group and a multiplicative group form a *field*. In C++, this combining is easy:

```
template<class T>
class FieldCategory :
  public AbelianGroupCategory<T>,
  public GroupCategory<T> {
public:
  T& operator++();
  T  operator++(int);
  T& operator--();
  T  operator--(int);
};
```

We have added C++ increment and decrement operators that correspond to `x+=1`, that is addition of the multiplicative identity.

Even these combinations are not the end of the story: there are structures that have two operations (`*` and `+`) between set elements and operations between two sets. For example, when we work with the vectors of analytic geometry, there are two sets: vectors and scalars. There is a composition law on vectors as well a composition law that combines a scalar and a vector, a so-called *external composition law*. We won't delve into these more complicated structures here; see Chapter 16 of our book.[6]

Example—`ComplexFloat`

The algebraic structure categories will give us consistency, but we need a way to select the appropriate structure without relearning all of the math for each application.

Figure 1 provides a way: apply the tests at each node to the class you are designing and follow the arrows to the structure. For example, consider `ComplexFloat`: it has both additive and multiplicative composition with identity and inverse for both. We follow the multiplicative branch to `Group` and the additive branch to `AbelianGroup`, then combine them to select `Field`.

To put `ComplexFloat` in the `Field` category we derive it from `FieldCategory<T>` with `T` set to `ComplexFloat`. Since `FieldCategory` is derived from many base classes, it has six user-must-define operations as shown here:

```
class ComplexFloat :
  public FieldCategory< ComplexFloat > {
public:
  ComplexFloat(float r, float i = 0.)
    : _r(r), _i(i) {}
  ComplexFloat() {}

  float  real()  const { return _r;}
  float& real()  { return _r;}
  float  imag()  const { return _i;}
  float& imag()  { return _i;}

  ComplexFloat& conj() {
    _i = -_i;
    return *this;
  }

  // Field "user must provide"
  ComplexFloat& operator*=(const ComplexFloat& rhs);
  ComplexFloat& operator/=(const ComplexFloat& rhs);
  ComplexFloat& setToOne();

  ComplexFloat& operator+=(const ComplexFloat& rhs);
  ComplexFloat& operator-=(const ComplexFloat& rhs);
  ComplexFloat& setToZero();
private:
  float _r;
  float _i;
};

extern ostream& operator<<(ostream&, ComplexFloat);
```

(We omit the comparison operators we used in the version of this class shown earlier to simplify it here.) `ComplexFloat` inherits the binary operators `+`, `-`, `*`, and `/`, the unary operators `-`, `++`, and `--`, and the functions `pow()`, `invert()`, `repeat()`, and `negate()`.

Given such a class we can write functions of complex numbers, like the linear fractional transform that transforms circles into scaled and shifted circles in the complex plane:

$$w(z) = \frac{\{az+b\}}{\{cz+d\}}$$

for complex *a, b, c, d* and *z*, and we can do with confidence that our complex numbers are consistently defined:

```
class LinearFractionalTrans {
public:
  LinearFractionalTrans(
    ComplexFloat a, ComplexFloat b,
    ComplexFloat c, ComplexFloat d) :
      _a(a), _b(b), _c(c), _d(d) {}
  ComplexFloat operator()(ComplexFloat z) const {
    return (_a * z + _b) / (_c * z + _d);
  }
private:
  const ComplexFloat _a, _b, _c, _d;
};
```

Summary

We started out in search of a way to express completeness of and consistency among operators defined for C++ classes. We applied a time-honored method: we stole the solution developed in an existing branch of mathematics and twisted it around until it solved our problem. The mathematics we used was abstract algebra; the twisting involved focusing on the operations that C++ allows us to redefine and ignoring any aspect of abstract algebra that did not help us to get a consistent set of operations for a class.

As important as the consistent operations, we also get well-defined names for categories of consistent operations: we can look at `ComplexFloat`, see that it is derived from `FieldCategory` and, with a little practice, know exactly what arithmetic operations it will have and how they are related. What's more, function code in the template base classes gets reused in any class derived from them.

Our expression of the abstract algebra used relatively new techniques in C++: function declaration injection and derived-class parameterized base classes. Two compilers we tried support these techniques, but some older compilers may choke. We did not discuss performance here, but we note that a good compiler will expand the simple inline functions we use in these templates.

References

1. Budge, K.G., J.S. Peery, and A.C. Robinson. High-performance scientific computing using C++, in *USENIX C++ Conference Proceedings*, USENIX Assoc., Aug. 1992, pp. 131–150.
2. Roman, P. *Some Modern Mathematics for Physicists and Other Outsiders, vol. 1.* Pergamon Press, New York, 1975.
3. Coplien, J. O. *Generative Pattern Languages: An Emerging Direction of Software Design. C++ Report*, 6(6):19–22, 66–67, July–August 1994.
4. Gamma, E., R. Helm, R. Johnson, and J. Vlissides. *Design Patterns: Elements of Reusable Object-Oriented Software.* Addison-Wesley, Reading, MA, 1995.
5. Lajoie, J. Standard C++: Templates:—New and improved, like your favorite detergent :-). *C++ Report*, 6(4):62–69, May 1994.
6. Barton, J. J. and L. R. Nackman. *Scientific and Engineering C++: An Introduction with Advanced Techniques and Examples*, Addison-Wesley, Reading, MA, 1994.

CALLBACKS IN C++ USING TEMPLATE FUNCTORS

RICH HICKEY
rich@rcs-hq.mhs.compuserve.com CIS 73567,3042

ONE OF THE MANY PROMISES OF OBJECT-ORIENTED PROGRAMMING IS that it will allow for plug-and-play software design with reusable components. Designers will pull objects from their library "shelves" and hook them together to make software. In C++, this hooking together of components can be tricky, particularly if they are separately designed. We are still a long way from interoperable libraries and application components. Callbacks provide a mechanism whereby independently developed objects may be connected together. They are vital for plug-and-play programming, since the likelihood of Vendor A implementing their library in terms of Vendor B's classes, or your home-brewed classes, is nil.

Callbacks are in wide use, but current implementations differ and most suffer from shortcomings, not the least of which is their lack of generality. This article describes what callbacks are, how they are used, and the criteria for a good callback mechanism. It summarizes current callback methods and their weaknesses. It then describes a flexible, powerful, and easy-to-use callback technique based on template functors—objects that behave like functions.

CALLBACK FUNDAMENTALS

What Are Callbacks?

When designing application or subsystem-specific components we often know all of the classes with which the component will interact and thus explicitly code interfaces in terms of those classes. When designing general purpose or library components, however, it is often necessary or desirable to put in hooks for calling unknown objects. What is required is a way for one component to call another without having been written in terms of, or with knowledge of, the other component's type. Such a "type-blind" call mechanism is often referred to as a *callback*.

A callback might be used for simple notification, two-way communication, or to distribute work in a process. For instance an application developer might want to have a `Button` component in a GUI library call an application-specific object when clicked upon. The designer of a data entry component might want to offer the capability to call application objects for input validation. Collection classes often offer an `apply()` function, which applies a member function of an application object to the items they contain.

A callback, then, is a way for a component designer to offer a generic connection point that developers can use to establish communication with application objects. At some subsequent point, the component calls back the application object. The communication takes the form of a function call, since this is the way objects interact in C++.

Callbacks are useful in many contexts. If you use any commercial class libraries you have probably seen at least one mechanism for providing callbacks. All callback implementations must address a fundamental problem posed by the C++ type system: How can you build a component such that it can call a member function of another object whose type is unknown at the time the component is designed? C++'s type system requires that we know something of the type of any object whose member functions we wish to call, and is often criticized by fans of other object-oriented languages as being too inflexible to support true component-based design, since all the components have to "know" about each other. C++'s strong typing has too many advantages to abandon, but addressing this apparent lack of flexibility may encourage the proliferation of robust and interoperable class libraries.

C++ is in fact quite flexible, and the mechanism presented here leverages its flexibility to provide this functionality without language extension. In particular, templates supply a powerful tool for solving problems such as this. If you thought templates were only for container classes, read on!

Callback Terminology

There are three elements in any callback mechanism—the caller, the callback function, and the callee.

The *caller* is usually an instance of some class, for instance a library component (although it could be a function, like `qsort()`), that provides or requires the callback (i.e., it can, or must, call some third party code to perform its work, and uses the callback mechanism to do so). As far as the designer of the caller is concerned, the callback is just a way to invoke a process, referred to here as the callback function. The caller determines the signature of the callback function i.e. its argument(s) and return types. This makes sense, because it is the caller that has the work to do, or the information to convey. For instance, in the examples above, the `Button` class may want a callback function with no arguments and no return. It is a simple notification function used by the `Button` to indicate it has been clicked upon. The `DataEntryField` component might want to pass a `String` to the callback function and get a Boolean return.

A caller may require the callback for just the duration of one function, as with ANSI C's `qsort()`, or may want to hold on to the callback in order to call back at some later time, as with the `Button` class.

The "callee" is usually a member function of an object of some class, but it can also be a standalone function or static member function, that the application designer wishes to be called by the caller component. Note that in the case of a nonstatic member function a particular object/member-function pair is the callee. The function to be called must be compatible with the signature of the callback function specified by the caller.

Criteria for a Good Callback Mechanism

A callback mechanism in the object oriented model should support both component and application design. Component designers should have a standard, oï-the-shelf way of providing callback services, requiring no invention on their part. Flexibility in specifying the number and types of argument and return values should be provided. Since the component may be designed for use in as-yet-unthought-of applications, the component designer should neither need to know, nor dictate, the types of the objects which may be "called back" by the component.

Application developers, given a component with this standard callback mechanism and some instance of a class with a member function compatible with the callback function signature, should have to do no custom "glue" coding to connect the two together. Nor should they have to modify the callee class or hand-derive a new class. If they want to have the callback invoke a standalone, nonmember function, that should be supported as well.

To support this behavior the callback mechanism should be

Object oriented. Our applications are built with objects. In a C++ application most functionality is contained in member functions, which cannot be invoked via normal ptr-to-functions. Nonstatic member functions operate upon objects, which have state. Calling such functions is more than just invoking a process; it is operating upon a particular object, thus an object-oriented callback must contain information about which object to call.

Type safe. Type safety is a fundamental feature and benefit of C++ and any robust C++ callback mechanism must be type safe. That means we must ensure that objects are used in compliance with their specified interfaces, and that type rules are enforced for arguments, return values, and conversions. The best way to ensure this is to have the compiler do the work at compile time.

Noncoupling. This is the fundamental goal of callbacks—to allow components designed in ignorance of each other to be connected together. If the mechanism somehow introduces a dependency between caller and callee it has failed in its basic mission.

Non–type-intrusive. Some mechanisms for doing callbacks require a modification to, or derivation of, the caller or callee types. The fact that an object is connected to another object in a particular application often has nothing to do with its type. As we'll see below, mechanisms that are type intrusive can reduce the flexibility and increase the complexity of application code.

Generic. The primary differences between different callback situations are the types involved. This suggests that the callback mechanism should be parameterized using templates. Templates insure consistent interfaces and names in all callback situations, and provide a way to have any necessary support code be generated by the compiler, not the user.

Flexible. Experience has shown that callback systems that require an exact match between callback function and callee function signatures are too rigid for real-world use. For instance you may encounter a callback that passes a `Derived *` that you want to connect to a callee function that takes a `Base *`.

CURRENT MECHANISMS

Function Model

The simplest callback mechanism is a pointer-to-function, à la ANSI C's `qsort()`. Getting a standalone function to act upon a particular object, however, usually involves kludges like using static or global pointers to indicate the target object, or having the callback function take an extra parameter (usually a pointer to the object to act upon). The static/global pointer method breaks down when the callback relationship exists across calls (i.e. "I want to connect this `Button` to this `X` and this other `Button` to this other `X`, for the duration of the app"). The extra parameter method, if done type-safely, introduces undesirable coupling between the caller and callee types.

`qsort()` achieves its genericity by foregoing type safety. i.e., in order for it to be ignorant of the types it is manipulating it takes untyped (`void *`) arguments. There is nothing to prevent someone from calling `qsort()` on an array of apples and passing a pointer to a function that compares oranges!

An example of this typeless mechanism you'll frequently see is the apply function in collections. The purpose of an apply function is to allow a developer to pass a callback to a collection and have it be "applied" to (called on) each item in the collection. Unfortunately it often looks like this:

```
void apply(void (*func)(T &theItem,void *extraStuff),void
*theStuff);
```

Chances are really good you don't have a function like `func` sitting around, so you'll have to write one (lots of casting required). And make sure you pass it the right stuff. Ugh.

Single-Rooted Hierarchy

Beware callback mechanisms that appear type safe but are in fact not. These mechanisms usually involve some base-of-all-classes like `Object` or `EventHandler`, and use casts from ptr-to-member-of-derived to ptr-to-member-of-base. Experience has indicated that single-rooted systems are unworkable if components are to come from multiple sources.

Parameterize the Caller

The component designer could parameterize the component on the type of the callee. Such parameterization is inappropriate in many situations and callbacks are one of them. Consider:

```
class Button{
public:
  virtual void click();
  //...
};
```

```
template <class T>
class ButtonThatCallsBack:public class Button{
public:
  ButtonThatCallsBack(T *who,void (T::*func)(void)):
    callee(who),callback(func){}
  void click()
    {
    (callee->*callback)();
    }
private:
  T *callee;
      void (T::*callback)(void);
};

class CDPlayer{
public:
  void play();
  //...
};

//Connect a CDPlayer and a Button
CDPlayer cd;
ButtonThatCallsBack<CDPlayer> button(&cd,&CDPlayer::play);
button.click(); //calls cd.play()
```

A `ButtonThatCallsBack<CDPlayer>` would thus know about `CDPlayer` and provides an interface explicitly based on it. The problem is that this introduces rigidity in the system in that the callee type becomes part of the caller type (i.e. it is type-intrusive). All code that creates `ButtonThatCallsBack` objects must be made aware of the callee relationship, increasing coupling in the system. A `ButtonThatCallsBack<X>` is of a different type than a `ButtonThatCallsBack<Y>`, thus preventing by-value manipulation.

If a component has many callback relationships it quickly becomes unworkable to parameterize them all. Consider a `Button` that wants to maintain a dynamic list of callees to be notified upon a click event. Since the callee type is built into the `Button` class type, this list must be either homogeneous or typeless.

Library code cannot even create `ButtonThatCallsBack` objects because their instantiation depends on application types. This is a severe constraint.

Consider GUI library code that reads a dialog description from a resource file and creates a `Dialog` object. How can it know that you want the `Buttons` in that `Dialog` to call back `CDPlayers`? It can't; therefore, it can't create the `Buttons` for you.

Callee Mix-In

The caller component designer can invent an abstract base class to be the target of the callback, and indicate to application developers that they mix-in this base to connect their class with the component. I call this the "callee mix-in."

Here the designer of the `Button` class wants to offer a click notification callback and so defines a nested class `Notifiable` with a pure virtual function `notify()` that has the desired signature. Clients of the `Button` class will have to pass to its constructor a pointer to a `Notifiable`, which the `Button` will use (at some point later on) for notification of clicks:

```
class Button{
public:
  class Notifiable{
  public:
    virtual void notify()=0;
  };
  Button(Notifiable *who):callee(who){}
  void click()
    {callee->notify();}
private:
  Notifiable *callee;
};
```

Given :

```
class CDPlayer{
public:
  void play();
  //...
};
```

an application developer wishing to have a `Button` call back a `CDPlayer` would have to derive a new class from both `CDPlayer` and `Button::Notifiable`, overriding the pure virtual function to do the desired work:

```
class MyCDPlayer:public CDPlayer,public
Button::Notifiable{
public:
  void notify()
    {play();}

};
```

and use this class rather than `CDPlayer` in the application:

```
MyCDPlayer cd;
Button button(&cd);
button.click(); //calls cd.play()
```

This mechanism is type safe, achieves the decoupling of `Button` and `CDPlayer`, and is good magazine article fodder. It is almost useless in practice, however.

The problem with the callee mix-in is that it, too, is type-intrusive (i.e., it impacts the type of the callee, in this case by forcing derivation). This has three major flaws. First, the use of multiple inheritance, particularly if the callee is a callee of multiple components, is problematic due to name clashes, etc. Second, derivation may be impossible; for instance, if the application designer gets `CDPlayers` from an unchangeable, untouchable API (library designers note: this is a big problem with mix-in based mechanisms in general). The third problem is best demonstrated. Consider this version of `CDPlayer`:

```
class CDPlayer{
public:
  void play();
  void stop();
  //...
};
```

It doesn't seem unreasonable to have an application where one `Button` calls `CDPlayer::play()` and another `CDPlayer::stop()`. The mix-in mechanism fails completely here, since it can only support a single mapping between caller/callee/member-function, i.e., `MyCDPlayer` can have only one `notify()`.

Callbacks Using Template Functors

When I first thought about the inter-component callback problem I decided that what was needed was a language extension to support "bound-pointers," special pointers representing information about an object and a member function of that object, storable and callable much like regular pointers to functions. ARM 5.5 commentary has a brief explanation of why bound pointers were left out.

How would bound pointers work? Ideally you would initialize them with either a regular pointer-to-function or a reference to an object and a pointer-to-member-function. Once initialized, they would behave like normal pointer-to-functions. You could apply the function call `operator ()` to them to invoke the function. In order to be suitable for a callback mechanism, the information about the type of the callee would not be part of the type of the bound-pointer. It might look something like this:

```
// Warning - NOT C++

class Fred{
public:
  void foo();
};

Fred fred;
void (* __bound fptr)() = &fred.foo;
```

Here `fptr` is a bound-pointer to a function that takes no arguments and returns void. Note that `Fred` is not part of `fptr`'s type. It is initialized with the object `fred` and a pointer-to-member-function-of-`Fred`, `foo`. Saying

```
fptr();
```

would invoke `foo` on `fred`.

Such bound-pointers would be ideal for callbacks:

```
// Warning - NOT C++

class Button{
public:
  Button(void (* __bound uponClickDoThis)() )
  _bound_notify(uponClickDoThis);
    {}
  void click()
    {
    notify();
```

```
    }
private:
  void (* __bound notify)();
};

class CDPlayer{
public:
  void play();
};

CDPlayer cd;
Button button(&cd.play);
button.click();          //calls cd.play()
```

Bound-pointers would require a nontrivial language extension and some tricky compiler support. Given the extreme undesirability of any new language features I'd hardly propose bound-pointers now. Nevertheless, I still consider the bound-pointer concept to be the correct solution for callbacks and set out to see how close I could get in the current and proposed language. The result is the Callback library described below. As it turns out, the library solution can not only deliver the functionality shown above (albeit with different syntax), it proved more flexible than the language extension would have been!

Returning from the fantasy world of language extension, the library must provide two things for the user. The first is some construct to play the role of the "bound-pointer." The second is some method for creating these "bound-pointers" from either a regular pointer-to-function or an object and a pointer-to-member-function.

In the "bound-pointer" role we need an object that behaves like a function. Coplien has used the term *functor* to describe such objects. For our purposes a functor is simply an object that behaves like a pointer-to-function. It has an `operator()` (the function call operator) which can be used to invoke the function to which it points. The library provides a set of template `Functor` classes. They hold any necessary callee data and provide pointer-to-function like behavior. Most important, their type has no connection whatsoever to the callee type. Components define their callback interface using the `Functor` classes.

The construct provided by the library for creating functors is an overloaded template function, `makeFunctor()`, which takes as arguments the callee information (either an object and a ptr-to-member-function, or a ptr-to-function) and returns something suitable for initializing a `Functor` object.

The resulting mechanism is very easy to use. A complete example:

```
//include the callback library header
#include <callback.h>
#include <iostream.h>

class Button{
public:
  Button(const Functor0 &uponClickDoThis)
    :notify(uponClickDoThis)
    {}
  void click()
    {
    notify(); //a call to operator()
    }
private:
  Functor0 notify; //note - held by value
};

//Some application stuff we'd like to connect to Button:

class CDPlayer{ public:
  void play(){cout<<"Playing"<<endl;}
  void stop(){cout<<"Stopped"<<endl;}
};

void wow()
  {cout<<"Wow!"<<endl;}

void main()
  {
  CDPlayer cd;

  //makeFunctor from object and ptr-to-member-function

  Button playButton(makeFunctor(cd,&CDPlayer::play));
  Button stopButton(makeFunctor(cd,&CDPlayer::stop));

  //makeFunctor from pointer-to-function
```

```
    Button wowButton(makeFunctor(&wow));

    playButton.click(); //calls cd.play()
    stopButton.click(); //calls cd.stop()
    wowButton.click(); //calls wow()
    }
```

Voilà! A component (`Button`) has been connected to application objects and functions it knows nothing about and that know nothing about `Button`, without any custom coding, derivation or modification of the objects involved. And it's type safe.

The `Button` class designer specifies the callback interface in terms of `Functor0`, a functor that takes no arguments and returns void. It stores the functor away in its member notify. When it comes time to call back, it simply calls `operator()` on the functor. This looks and feels just like a call via a pointer-to-function.

Connecting something to a component that uses callbacks is simple. You can just initialize a `Functor` with the result of an appropriate call to `makeFunctor()`. There are two flavors of `makeFunctor()`. You can call it with a ptr-to-stand-alone function:

```
makeFunctor(&wow)
```

or with an object and a pointer-to-member function:

```
makeFunctor(cd,&CDPlayer::play)
```

I must come clean at this point, and point out that the syntax above for `makeFunctor()` is possible only in the proposed language, because it requires template members (specifically, the `Functor` constructors would have to be templates). In the current language the same result can be achieved by passing to `makeFunctor()` a dummy parameter of type ptr-to-the-`Functor`-type-you-want-to-create. This iteration of the callback library requires you pass `makeFunctor()` the dummy as the first parameter. Simply cast `0` to provide this argument:

```
makeFunctor((Functor0 *)0,&wow)
makeFunctor((Functor0 *)0,cd,&CDPlayer::play);
```

I will use this current-language syntax from here on.

The `Button` class above only needs a callback function with no arguments that returns void. Other components may want to pass data to the callback or get a return back. The only things distinguishing one functor from another are the number and types of the arguments to `operator()` and its return type, if any. This indicates that functors can be represented in the library by (a set of) templates:

```
//Functor classes provided by the Callback library:

Functor0 //not a template - nothing to parameterize
Functor1<P1>
Functor2<P1,P2>
Functor3<P1,P2,P3>
Functor4<P1,P2,P3,P4>
Functor0wRet<RT>
Functor1wRet<P1,RT>
Functor2wRet<P1,P2,RT>
Functor3wRet<P1,P2,P3,RT>
Functor4wRet<P1,P2,P3,P4,RT>
```

These are parameterized by the types of their arguments (P1, etc.) and return value (RT) if any. The numbering is necessary because we can't overload template class names on number of parameters. "`wRet`" is appended to distinguish those with return values. Each has an `operator()` with the corresponding signature. For example:

```
template <class P1>
class Functor1{
public:
  void operator()(P1 p1)const;
  //...
};

template <class P1,class P2,class RT>
class Functor2wRet{
public:
  RT operator()(P1 p1,P2 p2)const;
  //...
};
```

These `Functor` classes are sufficient to meet the callback needs of component designers, as they offer a standard and consistent way to offer callback services, and a simple mechanism for invoking the callback function. Given these templates in the library, a component designer need only pick one with the correct number of arguments and specify the desired types as parameters. Here's the `DataEntryField` that wants a validation callback that takes a `const String&` and returns a `Boolean`:

```
#include <callback.h>

class DataEntryField{
public:
  DataEntryField(const Functor1wRet<const String
     &,Boolean> &v):
    validate(v){}
  void keyHit(const String & stringSoFar)
    {
    if(validate(stringSoFar))
      // process it etc...
    }
private:
  Functor1wRet<const String &,Boolean> validate;
  //validate has a
  //Boolean operator()(const String &)
};
```

These trivial examples just scratch the surface of what you can do given a general-purpose callback library such as this. Consider their application to state machines, dispatch tables, etc.

The callback library is 100% compile-time type safe. (Where compile time includes template-instantiation time). If you try to make a functor out of something that is not compatible with the functor type you will get a compiler error. All correct virtual function behavior is preserved.

The system is also type flexible. You'll note that throughout this article I have said "type compatible" rather than "exactly matching" when talking about the relationship between the callback function and the callee function. Experience has shown that requiring an exact match makes callbacks too rigid for practical use. If you have done much work with pointer-to-function based interfaces you've probably experienced the frustration of having a pointer to a function "that would work" yet was not of the exact type required for a match.

To provide flexibility the library supports building a functor out of a callee function that is type compatible with the target functor—it need not have an exactly matching signature. By type compatible I mean a function with the same number of arguments, of types reachable from the functor's argument types by implicit conversion. The return type of the function must be implicitly convertible to the return type of the functor. A functor with no return can be built from a function with a return—the return value is safely ignored.

```
//assumes Derived publicly derived from Base
void foo(Base &);
long bar(Derived &);

Functor1<Derived&> f1 =
  makeFunctor((Functor1<Derived&> *)0,&foo);
  //ok - will implicitly convert

f1 = makeFunctor((Functor1<Derived&> *)0,&bar);
  //ok - ignores return
```

Any necessary argument conversions or ignoring of returns is done by the compiler (i.e., there is no coercion done inside the mechanism or by the user). If the compiler can't get from the arguments passed to the functor to the arguments required by the callee function, the code is rejected at compile time. By allowing the compiler to do the work we get all of the normal conversions of arguments—derived to base, promotion and conversion of built-in types, and user-defined conversions.

The type-flexibility of the library is something that would not have been available in a language extension rendition of bound pointers.

Rounding out the functionality of the `Functor` classes are a default constructor that will also accept `0` as an initializer, which puts the `Functor` in a known "unset" state, and a conversion to `Boolean`, which can be used to test whether the `Functor` is "set." The `Functor` classes do not rely on any virtual function behavior to work, so they can be held and copied by-value. Thus a `Functor` has the same ease-of-use as a regular pointer-to-function.

At this point you know everything you need to use the callback library. All of the code is in one file, `callback.h`. To use a callback in a component class, simply instantiate a `Functor` with the desired argument types. To connect some stuff to a component that uses `Functors` for callbacks, simply call `makeFunctor()` on the stuff. Easy.

Power Templates

As usual, what is easy for the user is often tricky for the implementor. Given the black-box descriptions of the `Functor` classes and `makeFunctor()` it may be hard to swallow the claims of type-safety, transparent conversions, correct virtual function behavior, etc. A look behind the curtain reveals not only how it works, but also some neat template techniques. Warning: most people find the pointer-to-member and template syntax used in the implementation daunting at first.

Obviously, some sort of magic is going on. How can the `Functor` class, with no knowledge of the type or signature of the callee, ensure a type safe call to it, possibly with implicit conversions of the arguments? It can't, so it doesn't. The actual work must be performed by some code that knows both the functor callback signature and everything about the callee. The trick is to get the compiler to generate that code, and have the `Functor` point to it. Templates can help out all around.

The mechanism is spread over three components—the `Functor` class, a `Translator` class, and the `makeFunctor()` function. All are templates.

The `Functor` class is parameterized on the types of the callback function signature, holds the callee data in a typeless manner, and defines a typed `operator()` but doesn't actually perform the work of calling back. Instead it holds a pointer to the actual callback code. When it comes time to call back, it passes the typeless data (itself actually), as well as the callback arguments, to this pointed-to function.

The `Translator` class is derived from `Functor` but is parameterized on both the `Functor` type and the callee types. It knows about everything, and is thus able to define a fully type-safe static "thunk" function that takes the typeless `Functor` data and the callback arguments. It constructs its `Functor` base class with a pointer to this static function. The thunk function does the work of calling back, turning the typeless `Functor` data back into a typed callee and calling the callee. Since the `Translator` does the work of converting the callee data to and from untyped data the conversions are considered "safe." The `Translator` is a `Functor`, so it can be used to initialize a `Functor`.

The `makeFunctor()` function takes the callee data, creates a `Translator` out of it and returns the `Translator`. Thus the `Translator` object exists only briefly as the return value of `makeFunctor()`, but its creation is enough to cause the compiler to lay down the static thunk function, the address of which is carried in the `Functor` that has been initialized with the `Translator`.

All of this will become clearer with the details.

For each of the ten `Functor` classes there are two translator classes and three versions of `makeFunctor()`. We'll examine a slice of the library here, `Functor1` and its associated translators and `makeFunctors`. The other `Functors` differ only in the number of arguments and return value.

The Functors

Since the `Functor` objects are the only entities held by the caller, they must contain the data about the callee. With some care we can design a base class which can hold, in a typeless manner, the callee data, regardless of whether the callee is a ptr-to-function or object/`ptr-to-member-function` combo:

```
//typeless representation of a function
//or object/mem-func

class FunctorBase{
public:
   typedef void (FunctorBase::*_MemFunc)();
   FunctorBase():callee(0),func(0){}
   FunctorBase(const void *c,const void *f,size_t sz)
      {
      if(c) //must be callee/memfunc
         {
         callee = (void *)c;
         memcpy(memFunc,f,sz);
         }
      else //must be ptr-to-func
         {
         func = f;
         }
      }
   //for evaluation in conditions
   //will be changed to bool when bool exists
   operator int()const{return func||callee;}

   class DummyInit{
   };
   // Note: this code depends on all ptr-to-mem-funcs being
   // same size
```

```
    // If that is not the case then make memFunc as large as
    // largest
    union{
    const void *func;
    char memFunc[sizeof(_MemFunc)];
    };
    void *callee;
};
```

All `Functors` are derived (protected) from this base. `FunctorBase` provides a constructor from typeless `args`, where if `c` is `0` the callee is a pointer-to-function and `f` is that pointer, else `c` is pointer to the callee object and `f` is a pointer to a pointer-to-member function and `sz` is that ptr-to-member-function's size (in case an implementation has pointer-to-members of differing sizes). It has a default constructor which inits to an "unset" state, and an operator `int` to allow for testing the state (set or unset).

The `Functor` class is a template. It has a default constructor and the required `operator()` corresponding to its template parameters. It uses the generated copy constructor and assignment operators:

```
/************************** one arg - no return
*******************/
template <class P1>
class Functor1:protected FunctorBase{
public:
  Functor1(DummyInit * = 0){}
  void operator()(P1 p1)const
    {
    thunk(*this,p1);
    }
  FunctorBase::operator int;
  protected:
    typedef void (*Thunk)(const FunctorBase &,P1);
  Functor1 (Thunk+,const void*c, const void*f, size_t
      sz);
  FunctorBase(c,f,sz),thunk(t){}
  private:
  Thunk thunk;
};
```

The Functor class has a protected constructor that takes the same typeless args as `FunctorBase`, plus an additional first argument. This argument is a pointer to function (the thunk function) that takes the same arguments as the `operator()`, plus an additional first argument of type `const FunctorBase &`. The `Functor` stores this away (in thunk) and implements `operator()` by calling `thunk()`, passing itself and the other arguments. Thus it is this `thunk()` function that does the work of calling back.

A key issue at this point is whether `operator()` should be virtual. In the first iteration of my mechanism the `Functor` classes were abstract and the `operator()`s pure virtual. To use them for callbacks, a set of derived template classes parameterized on the callee type was provided. This required that functors always be passed and held by reference or pointer and never by value. It also required the caller component or the client code maintain the derived object for as long as the callback relationship existed. I found the maintenance and lifetime issues of these functor objects to be problematic, and desired by-value syntax.

In the current mechanism the `Functor` classes are concrete and the `operator()` is nonvirtual. They can be treated and used just like ptr-to-functions. In particular, they can be stored by value in the component classes.

The Translators

Where does the `thunk()` come from? It is generated by the compiler as a static member of a template translator class. For each `Functor` class there are two translator classes, one for standalone functions (`FunctionTranslator`) and one for member functions (`MemberTranslator`). The translator classes are parameterized by the type of the `Functor` as well as the type(s) of the callee. With this knowledge they can, in a fully type-safe manner, perform two important tasks.

First, they can initialize the `Functor` data. They do this by being publicly derived from the `Functor`. They are constructed with typed `Callee` information that they pass (untyped) to the functor's protected constructor.

```
template <class P1,class Func>
class FunctionTranslator1:public Functor1<P1>{
public:
  FunctionTranslator1(Func f):Functor1<P1>(thunk,0,f,0){}
  static void thunk(const FunctorBase &ftor,P1 p1)
    {
    (Func(ftor.func))(p1);
    }
};
```

`FunctionTranslator` is the simpler of the two. It is parameterized by the argument type of the Functor and some ptr-to-function type (`Func`). Its constructor takes an argument of type Func and passes it and a pointer to its static `thunk()` function to the base class constructor. The thunk function, given a `FunctorBase ftor`, casts `ftors func` member back to its correct type (`Func`) and calls it. There is an assumption here that the `FunctorBase` ftor is initialized by the constructor (or a copy). There is no danger of it being otherwise, since the functors are always initialized with matching callee data and thunk functions. This is what is called a "safe" cast, since the same entity that removed the type information also reinstates it, and can guarantee a match. If `Func`'s signature is incompatible with the call (i.e., if it cannot be called with a single argument of type `P1`), then `thunk()` will not compile.

If implicit conversions are required the compiler will perform them.

Note that if `func` has a return, it is safely ignored:

```
template <class P1,class Callee, class MemFunc>
class MemberTranslator1:public Functor1<P1>{
public:
  MemberTranslator1(Callee &c,const MemFunc &m):
 Functor1<P1>(thunk,&c,&m,sizeof(MemFunc)){}
  static void thunk(const FunctorBase &ftor,P1 p1)
    {
    Callee *callee = (Callee *)ftor.callee;
    MemFunc &memFunc(*(MemFunc*)(void *)(ftor.memFunc));
    (callee->*memFunc)(p1);
    }
};
```

`MemberTranslator` is parameterized by the argument type of the `Functor`, some class type (`Callee`), and some `ptr-to-member-function` type (`MemFunc`). Not surprisingly, its constructor is passed two arguments, a `Callee` object (by reference) and a `ptr-to-member-function`, both of which are passed, along with the thunk function, to the base class constructor. Once again, the thunk function casts the typeless info back to life, and then calls the member function on the object, with the passed parameter.

Since the Translator objects are `Functor` objects, and fully 'bound' ones at that, they are suitable initializers for their corresponding `Functor`, using the `Functor's` copy constructor. We needn't worry about the chopping effect since the data is all in the base class portion of the `Translator` class and there are no virtual functions involved. Thus they are perfect candidates for the return value of `makeFunctor()`!

The `makeFunctor` *Functions*

For each `Functor` class there are three versions of `makeFunctor()`, one for `ptr-to-function` and a const and non-`const` version for the `object/ptr-to-member-function` pair:

```
template <class P1,class TRT,class TP1>
inline FunctionTranslator1<P1,TRT (*)(TP1)>
makeFunctor(Functor1<P1>*,TRT (*f)(TP1))
  {
  return FunctionTranslator1<P1,TRT (*)(TP1)>(f);
  }
```

The function version is straightforward. It uses the dummy argument to tell it the type of the functor and merely returns a corresponding `FunctionTranslator`. I mentioned previously that the `Func` type parameter of `FunctionTranslator` was invariably a `ptr-to-function` type. This version of `makeFunctor()` ensures that by explicitly specifying it as such.

```
template <class P1,class Callee,class TRT,class
CallType,class TP1>
inline MemberTranslator1<P1,Callee,TRT (CallType::*)(TP1)>
makeFunctor(Functor1<P1>*,Callee &c,TRT (CallType::* const
&f)(TP1))
  {
  typedef TRT (CallType::*MemFunc)(TP1);
  return MemberTranslator1<P1,Callee,MemFunc>(c,f);
  }
```

This is the gnarliest bit. Here, `makeFunctor` is parameterized with the type of the argument to the `Functor`, the type of the `Callee`, the type of the class of which the member-function is a member, and the argument and return types of the member function. Whew! We're a long way from `Stack<T>` land! Like the `ptr-to-function` version, it uses the dummy first argument of the constructor to determine the type of the `Functor`. The second argument is a `Callee` object (by reference). The third argument is this thing:

```
TRT (CallType::* const &f)(TP1)
```

Here, f is a reference to a constant pointer to a member function of CallType taking TP1 and returning TRT. You might notice that pointer-to-member-functions are all handled by reference in the library. On some implementations, they can be expensive to pass by value and copy. The significant feature here is that the function need not be of type pointer-to-member-of-Callee. This allows makeFunctor to match on (and ultimately work with) a ptr-to-member-function of some base of Callee. It then typedefs that bit and returns an appropriate MemberTranslator.

```
template <class P1,class Callee,class TRT,class
CallType,class TP1>
inline MemberTranslator1<P1,const Callee,TRT
(CallType::*)(TP1)const>
makeFunctor(Functor1<P1>*,const Callee &c,TRT (CallType::*
const &f)(TP1)const)
  {
  typedef TRT (CallType::*MemFunc)(TP1)const;
  return MemberTranslator1<P1,const Callee,MemFunc>(c,f);
  }
```

This last variant just ensures that if the Callee is const, the member function is also (note the const at the end of the third argument to the constructor—that's where it goes!).

That, for each of ten Functors, is the whole implementation.

Can Your Compiler Do This?

The callback library has been successfully tested with IBM CSet++ 2.01, Borland C++ 4.02 (no, its not twice as good ;-) and Watcom C++32 10.0. It is ARM-compliant with the exception of expecting trivial conversions of template function arguments, which is the behavior of most compilers. I am interested in feedback on how well it works with other implementations.

Summary

Callbacks are a powerful and necessary tool for component-based object-oriented development in C++. They can be a tremendous aid to the interoperability of libraries. The template functor system presented here meets all the stated criteria for a good callback mechanism—it is object-oriented, compile-time type-safe, generic, non–type-intrusive, flexible, and easy to use. It is sufficiently general to be used in any situation calling for callbacks. It can be implemented in the current language and somewhat more elegantly in the proposed language.

This implementation of callbacks highlights the power of C++ templates—their type-safety, their code-generation ability, and the flexibility they offer by accepting ptr-to-function and ptr-to-member-function-type parameters.

Ultimately, the greatest benefit is gained when class libraries start using a standard callback system. If callbacks aren't in the components, they can't be retrofitted. On publication of this article, I am making this callback library freely available in the hope that it will be adopted by library authors and serve as a starting point for discussion of a standard callback system.

Acknowledgments

Thanks to my fellow developers at RCS and to Greg Comeau for reviewing and commenting on this article.

References

1. Coplien, J.O. *Advanced C++ Programming Styles And Idioms,* Addison-Wesley, Reading, MA, 1992.
2. Ellis, M.A. and B. Stroustrup. *The Annotated C++ Reference Manual,* Addison-Wesley, Reading, MA, 1990.
3. Lippman, S.B. *C++ Primer,* second ed., Addison-Wesley, Reading, MA, 1991.
4. Stroustrup, B. *The Design and Evolution of C++,* Addison-Wesley, Reading, MA, 1994.

Standard Template Library

Michael J. Vilot

THE WIDESPREAD ADOPTION OF OBJECT-ORIENTED DESIGN (OOD) and C++ is having a profound impact on software engineering. While others philosophize about the "right" methodology and debate about "pure" object-oriented languages, C++ developers are busily delivering solutions to their customers' needs. Increasingly, these solutions are exploiting a quiet revolution in the practice of software development—creating programs from reusable software components.

Why are C++ development projects so much more numerous and successful than their counterparts in C or even Smalltalk? At first glance, the odds seem against such results: C++ is a larger, more complex language than many of its rivals. But despite the esoteric language features, uneven quality of implementations, and long learning curves, C++ still offers advantages to those who use it. Perhaps the key advantage is access to an established—and growing—marketplace of well-crafted, high-quality C++ libraries. Reusing software components from these libraries offers C++ developers advantages in quality, reliability, efficiency, and time to market.

Of course, these advantages do not accrue from just any arbitrary collection of C++ classes and functions offered up as a "library." To be effective, a software component library must be clearly designed, soundly engineered, and carefully implemented. A successful library must also serve the needs of its intended users, or it will quickly find itself abandoned for one of the other library products available. Ideally, such a library will be easy to use, thus simplifying its application within a C++ project.

An example of a library meeting these criteria is the Standard Template Library (STL), developed at Hewlett-Packard by Alex Stepanov, Meng Lee, and their colleagues. STL contains general-purpose mechanisms,[1] using C++'s templates for component parameterization.[2] A notable aspect of this library is that it focuses primarily on algorithms—once thought to be the exclusive province of FORTRAN subroutine libraries.

This article focuses on using STL, rather than on presenting a comprehensive treatment of its internal technical details. The first section provides an overview of the library. The second section provides a series of C++ code examples that illustrate various aspects of using the library's "algorithm-oriented generic software" approach.[3] Finally, the last section concludes with a more detailed overview of the library. It can be used as a roadmap to the detailed reference material.

The Library

Like many of the most successful C++ component libraries, STL has been in development a long time, has a simple design at its core, and offers significant advantages to its users. In the case of STL, these advantages are flexibility, efficiency, and theoretical soundness.

Unlike GUI components or application frameworks, STL provides general-purpose components for common programming tasks. Its main value is in providing efficient and reliable implementations that eliminate the need to handcraft low-level algorithms and data structures. As such, it can be used as the foundation for more ambitious libraries.

Background

The present library is the result of iterative development. STL evolved from several earlier libraries, developed in Scheme, Ada, and C++. Dave Musser and Alex Stepanov designed the earlier versions of the library. The key aspects of the design that emerged from these iterations included the overall structure, semantic requirements, algorithm design, complexity analysis, and performance tuning.

In November 1993, Alex Stepanov and Meng Lee approached the *ANSI/ISO* C++ Standards Committee and suggested a small subset of STL might be appropriate for the Standard C++ Library. Because its size rivals that of standard iostreams, the STL proposal to X3J16 has itself been through several iterations.[4–6] It was accepted as part of the C++ Standard Library in July 1994.

Quick Overview

The essential structure of STL can be represented by the OOD class category diagram[7] of Figure 1.

The primary focus of the library is on the components in the Algorithms category. They use Iterators (a generalization of pointers) and Function

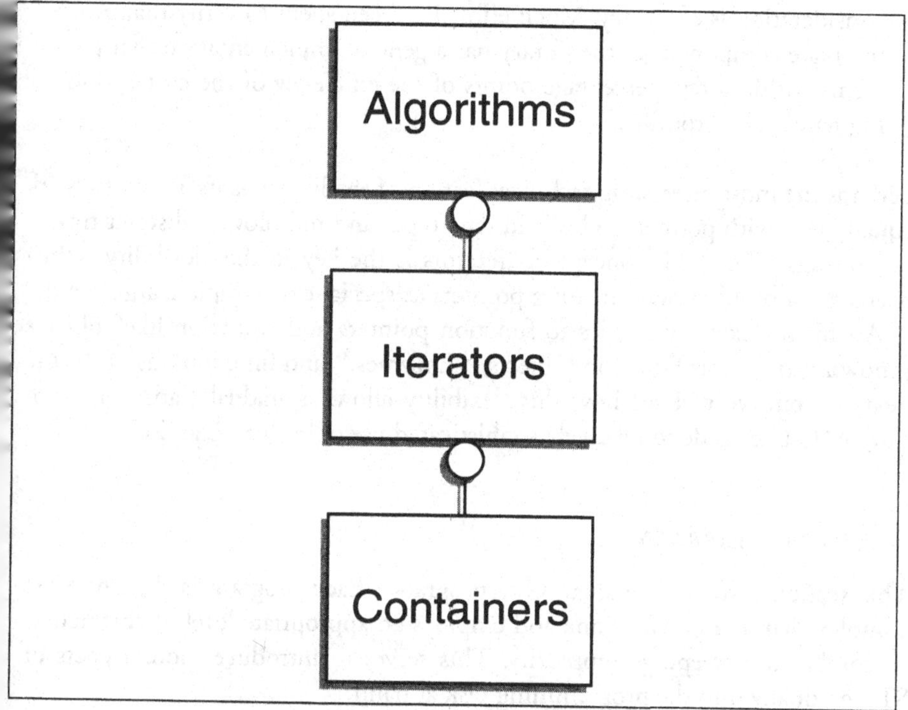

FIGURE 1. *Key abstractions in the STL Library.*

Objects (a generalization of functions) to operate upon components in the Containers category.

An important result of this design is that new algorithms and containers can be added independently, and the existing components will adapt to them unchanged. This kind of extensibility and adaptability is essential for any such library of general-purpose mechanisms.

Key Features

The essential design criteria are stated clearly in the STL proposal to X3J16:

> The Standard Template Library provides a set of well structured generic C++ components that work together in a seamless way. Special care has been taken to ensure that all the template algorithms work not only on the data structures in the library, but also on built-in C++ data [types]. For example, all the algorithms work on regular pointers.... Another important

> consideration is efficiency. Much effort has been spent to verify that every template component in the library has a generic implementation that performs within a few percentage points of the efficiency of the corresponding hand coded routine.[5]

Perhaps the most interesting technical feature of the library is its ability to work equally well with pointers to built-in data types and full-blown "abstract traversal" objects.[8] The STL concept of Iterators is the key to this flexibility—they overcome a problem with treating pointers as special case template arguments.[9]

A similar flexibility applies to function pointers and "function-like" objects (known variously as Function Objects,[10] Enzymes,[11] and functionoids[12]). In the next section, we will see how this flexibility allows a gradual transition from simple "C-like" code to relatively sophisticated use of both STL and C++.

USING THE LIBRARY

This section contains ten small C++ programs. Each program is slightly more complex than the previous one and employs an appropriate level of abstraction to combat the creeping complexity. This serves to introduce more aspects of STL gradually into the programming task at hand.

A Simple Example

The first example is very simple. It searches a character string for the first occurrence of a particular character. This task is so trivial, the program provides three solutions to it (*Editor's Note:* The absence of `.h` on an include file is deliberate and reflects the *ANSI/ISO* inclusion of namespaces):

```
#include "stl"
#include <iostream>
#include <string.h>

int main() // Example 1: finding a character
{
  const char data[] = "Bjarne Stroustrup";
  const char* end = data + sizeof data;
  const char c = 'u';

  for (const char* p = data; p != end; ++p)
    if (*p == c) break;
```

```
    cout << "Found at " << (p-data) << endl;

    p = strchr(data, c);
    cout << "Found at " << (p-data) << endl;

    p = find(data, end, c);
    cout << "Found at " << (p-data) << endl;

    return 0;
}
```

The declarations establish a null-terminated character sequence to search. The `for` loop searches from the beginning to the end of the sequence, looking for an exact match on the target character. The second solution is a call to the standard `strchr()` function, which searches through the pointer. `strchr()` advances the pointer until the character is found or the pointer value becomes null. The third solution is to use the STL `find()` function. All three locate the character at index 11.

Note that `strchr()` may well be optimized to work particularly well on character sequences for the current platform. This makes it potentially more efficient than the equivalent for loop. It also depends critically on the null terminator convention used throughout much of the Standard C Library.

Being a function template, `find()` may also be specialized for the `char` data type. However, because it does not depend on null termination, `find()` will not wander all over memory looking for one if the string fails to contain one. This means that `find()` is not only as efficient as `strchr()`, but also more reliable.

The next example illustrates that `find()` is also more flexible. Consider using some representation for strings other than hopefully null-terminated char arrays:

```
#include "stl"
#include <iostream>
#include <string.h>

int main() // Example 2: adding a new data structure
{
    const char data[] = "Bjarne Stroustrup";
    const char* end = data + sizeof data;
    const char c = 'u';
    vector<char> name(data, end);
```

```
    for (const char* p = data; p != end; ++p)
      if (*p == c) break;
    cout << "Found at " << (p-data) << endl;

    p = strchr(data, c);
    cout << "Found at " << (p-data) << endl;

    p = find(data, end, c);
    cout << "Found at " << (p-data) << endl;

    p = find(name.begin(), name.end(), c);
    cout << "Found at " << (p-name.begin())
        << endl;
    return 0;
}
```

This second program introduces the use of the STL `vector` data structure component, whose constructor initializes it to the same characters. Even though we are still using `char` sequences, we cannot reuse the `strchr()` library function—there is no guarantee that vectors null-terminate their contents. Indeed, because vectors are parameterized by the type of item they contain, they cannot assume that a null value even exists for arbitrary types.

On the other hand, the `find()` function continues to work, unchanged. In fact, since the `begin()` and `end()` member functions return char pointers for `vector<char>`, the same efficient specialization of `find<char>` can be called.

Note that `find()` is not restricted to using pointers: any class with `operator*()` and `operator++()` meets the requirements of an STL-compatible iterator type.

Using Strings

Of course, arrays of chars represent a rather low level of abstraction. They are, however, quite pervasive—they form the backbone of many C and C++ programs. The reason is simple: `char` sequences are a useful representation of a fundamental abstraction, the string.

The next two example programs move away from the low-level array of `chars` representation. The string class used for these programs illustrates that requirements for an STL-compatible "sequence" are quite simple, as shown here:

```
class string {
  char* _rep;
  void assign(const char*);
public:
  string();
  string(const char*);
  string(const string&);
  ~string();

  string& operator=(const string&);
  string& operator=(const char*);

  const int size() const;
  const char* data() const;
};

int operator==(const string&, const string&);
int operator!=(const string&, const string&);
int operator <(const string&, const string&);

class istream;
istream& operator>>(istream&, string&);

class ostream;
ostream& operator<<(ostream&, const string&);
```

The main responsibility of this class is to encapsulate the details of storage management, so that callers can concentrate on more abstract operations. In particular, this `string` component provides few operations: equality, simple comparison, and iostreams extraction and insertion. Of course, in a production system, we would use a standard string.

First, we'll exercise the default constructor and iostreams operations:

```
#include <fstream>
#include "string.h"

int main() // Example 3: using arrays
{
  string a[16]; // hopefully large enough
```

```
// input:
  ifstream in("meeting.members");
  for (int i =0; in; ++i) {
    in >> a[i];
  }

// output:
  for (int j =0; j<i; ++j) {
    cout << a[j] << endl;
  }
  return 0;
}
```

This example uses a fixed-size array to hold some strings and uses a file stream to fill the array. This program is adequate for the following small file used for input.

```
The meeting.members file:

Tom
Bjarne
Nathan
Alex
Mike
Larry
Meng
```

However, note that this program has a fatal flaw: if given more than 16 names, it merrily writes over memory past the end of the array! This is almost certainly going to cause unpleasant behavior at run-time. The next step is to replace the low-level array with a more flexible data structure:

```
#include "stl"
#include <fstream>
#include "string.h"

int main() // Example 4: vectors encapsulate
{          // memory management
  vector<string> v;
```

```
// input:
   ifstream in("meeting.members");
   while (in) {
     string s;
     in >> s;
     v.insert(v.end(),s); // append
   }

// output:
   for (size_t i =0; i<v.size(); ++i) {
     cout << v[i] << endl;
   }
   return 0;
}
```

This fourth example program simply reads in the strings from the file and appends them to the end of the `vector`. It is functionally equivalent to the previous example, but is not limited to a fixed number of names (it is limited only by the amount of dynamic memory available on the system). It is also more reliable—it doesn't scribble all over memory if we happen to read a larger file.

The `string` and `vector` components encapsulate the memory management details of character and array storage. If we replace the string component with a sophisticated copy-on-write implementation,[13] these programs do not have to change. We can also tune the vector component, overriding its default allocator template argument with a class that does special-purpose memory allocation (for example, one that uses DOS extended memory).

As it turns out, the minimal facilities defined for strings are all that we need to use this type with the rest of the STL library. The next example illustrates that even such a simple type is usable as the argument type of a `sort()`:

```
#include "stl"
#include <fstream>
#include "string.h"

int main() // Example 5: sorting strings
{
  vector<string> v;

// input:
  ifstream in("meeting.members");
```

```
    while (in) {
      string s;
      in >> s;
      v.insert(v.end(),s); // append
    }

  // process:
    sort(v.begin(),v.end());

  // output:
    for (size_t i =0; i<v.size(); ++i) {
      cout << v[i] << endl;
    }

    return 0;
  }
```

As noted earlier, the `begin()` and `end()` members provide pointers to the elements stored in the vector. `sort()` then uses these to iterate through the strings to order them, using the `operator<()` defined in the first example.

Notice how easily this program combined components from two substantial C++ libraries: iostreams and STL. Given the same `meeting.members` file, this fifth example program produces the output:

```
Alex
Bjarne
Larry
Meng
Mike
Nathan
Tom
```

Recall the original example of finding a character in a sequence. A similar problem is finding a string in a list. This next example illustrates that the STL `find()` component is just as effective at this new task. Note that this is exactly the same `find()` used in Examples 1 and 2:

```
#include "stl"
#include <fstream>
#include "string.h"
```

```
int main() // Example 6: finding Alex in a
 // lineup
{
  Vector<string> lineup;

// input:
  ifstream in("meeting.members");
  while (in) {
    string s;
    in >> s;
    lineup.insert(lineup.end(),s); // append
  }

// process:
  const string data = "Alex";
  const string* p =
    find(lineup.begin(), lineup.end(), data);
  if (p != lineup.end()) {   // sentinel
    cout << "Found at " << (p-lineup.begin())
      << endl;
  }

// output:
  for (size_t i =0; i<lineup.size(); ++i) {
    cout << i << ' ' << lineup[i] << endl;
  }

  return 0;
}
```

Given the same `meeting.members` input file, this sixth example program produces:

```
Found at 3
0 Tom
1 Bjarne
2 Nathan
3 Alex
4 Mike
5 Larry
6 Meng
```

Note that the STL components make minimal assumptions about the types they handle through the iterators. `find()` only requires equality comparison, and `sort()` only requires a less-than ordering relation. In fact, we are not restricted to providing `operator==()` and `operator<()` for these operations. Overloaded versions of `find()` and `sort()` take a template argument that let us use any name for the requisite operations. As we'll see, these need not even be functions.

Handling Address Lists

Although computers were invented as number crunchers, a more common task today is manipulating structured information. This is often more string-oriented than number-oriented. A typical activity, and one often performed on PC-class machines, is address list processing. The next few examples illustrate how STL can be used in this domain of "business" programming.

For example, suppose we have files containing the names, addresses, and phone numbers of people belonging to some organization. These plain-text files have a regular, if not quite convenient, organization, such as the following the `address.list` file:

```
Name :Alex Stepanov
Address    :      HP Labs
      1501 Page Mill Rd.
      Palo Alto, CA 94304
      USA
Tel  :(999) 111-2222

Name :Bjarne Stroustrup
Address    :      AT&T Bell Labs
      600 Mountain Ave
...
```

We could use our existing `string` component to read and write the individual lines in this file. However, that would not help much: for example, sorting the lines in the file would yield meaningless data.

The files contain just the text representation of the important information. Using only strings, we would still be left with the relatively low-level task of figuring out what they mean.

Of course, object-oriented design helps us approach this task from another direction. Another way to think about the text files is that they are simply the persistent form of a collection of objects. As Figure 2 illustrates, we can identify the abstractions that describe the objects in this collection.

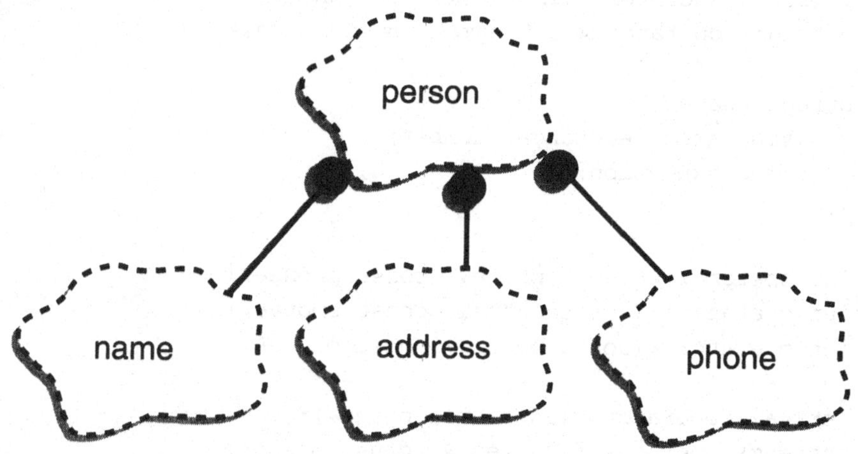

FIGURE 2. *OOD class diagram for person.*

One of the important benefits of using C++ is that it lets us represent these design ideas directly in a program's source text.The following code illustrates how we might build on the string component to represent the key abstractions of this problem.

```
struct name {
  string first, middle, last;
};

int operator==(const name&, const name&);
int operator!=(const name&, const name&);
int operator <(const name&, const name&);
istream& operator>>(istream&, name&);
ostream& operator<<(ostream&, const name&);

struct address {
  string line1, line2;
  string city, state, zip;
  string country;
};

int operator==(const address&, const address&);
int operator!=(const address&, const address&);
int operator <(const address&, const address&);
```

```
istream& operator>>(istream&, address&);
ostream& operator<<(ostream&, const address&);

struct phone {
  string area, exchange, number;
  string extension;
};

int operator==(const phone&, const phone&);
int operator!=(const phone&, const phone&);
int operator <(const phone&, const phone&);

istream& operator>>(istream&, phone&);
ostream& operator<<(ostream&, const phone&);

struct person {
  name n;
  address a;
  phone p;
};

int operator==(const person&, const person&);
int operator!=(const person&, const person&);
int operator <(const person&, const person&);

istream& operator>>(istream&, person&);
ostream& operator<<(ostream&, const person&);
```

As with the string component, these classes encapsulate the necessary details of input/output and storage management. They are straightforward, given the supporting abstractions. Indeed, many of the operations are defined trivially in terms of their string counterparts. The name, address, and phone extractors also encapsulate the formatting of address list entries in the file. Following the usual iostreams conventions, the `operator>>()` functions manipulate the stream state if things should go awry.[14] The example programs (and the STL components) can then rely on the usual iostreams semantics.

The next example program is much the same as the previous one. It deals with persons instead of strings, and it uses istream iterators to obtain its input:

```
#include "stl"
#include <fstream>
#include "names.h"

int main() // Example 7: input iterators
{
  vector<person> list;

// input:
  ifstream in("address.list");
  istream_iterator<person> input(in), eof(0);
  vector<person>::iterator put(list, list.end());
  copy(input, eof, put);
// process:
  sort(list.begin(), list.end());

// output:
  for (size_t i =0; i<list.size(); ++i) {
    cout << list[i].n << endl;
  }

  return 0;
}
```

Iostream iterators are the result of generalizing the notion of a "sequence." The first and second example programs used a char array to store a sequence of characters in memory. The subsequent example programs used a vector to store various sequences of things in memory. Why not treat a file as a sequence of things on secondary storage? Applying this concept, the seventh example program copies the sequence of persons from the file-based sequence to the vector, sorts them, then displays each person's name:

```
Bruce Eckel
Thomas Keffer
Andrew Koenig
Alex Stepanov
Bjarne Stroustrup
Mike Vilot
```

Note that the STL components `copy()` and `sort()` work exactly as before. They are not affected by the changes in the type of information the programs are manipulating, nor how they obtain their information. The next example shows that ostream iterators provide the complementary facility for output. It uses one to write the sorted address list back out to a file:

```
#include "stl"
#include <fstream>
#include "names.h"

int main() // Example 8: output iterators
{
  vector<person> list;

// input:
  ifstream in("address.list");
  istream_iterator<person> input(in), eof(0);
  vector<person>::iterator put(list, list.end());
  copy(input, eof, put);

// process:
  sort(list.begin(), list.end());

// output:
  ostream_iterator<person> out("\n\n");
   // argument is the record separator
  copy(list.begin(), list.end(), out);
  return 0;
}
```

At this point, we can see the value of STL's design using algorithms, iterators, and containers. Programs can manipulate arbitrary kinds of information, including built-in types. They can store sequences, iterating over them as necessary to use various algorithms. The sequences can be either in memory or in files on secondary store. Obviously, we can generalize this further. For example, we could use kinds of streams that are connected to mainframe-based databases, and extractors and inserters that use remote transactions instead of local file access.

Some Advanced Uses

Note that the previous example program has an important change over the seventh example: it outputs the full name, address, and phone number of each person. Suppose we still wanted just their names? STL supports this kind of customization. The next example program uses the `for_each()` component to iterate through the sorted list and print only the names:

```
#include "stl"
#include <fstream>
#include "names.h"

static void print_name(const person& p);

int main() // Example 9: transforming the output
{
  vector<person> list;

// input:
  ifstream in("address.list");
  vector<person>::iterator put(list, list.end());
  istream_iterator<person> input(in), eof (0);
  copy(input, eof, put);

// process:
  sort(list.begin(), list.end());

// output:
  for_each(list.begin(), list.end(), print_name);

  return 0;
}
```

In this case, `for_each()` takes a pointer to the `print_name()` function and calls it once for each person on the list. The `print_name()` function is straightforward:

```
static void print_name(const person& p)
{
  cout << p.n << endl;
}
```

However, notice that this function is rather inflexible: it relies on global data (cout), and thus hard-codes the destination output stream into the program. Removing this restriction illustrates another kind of flexibility in STL. Just as iterators do not have to be pointers, operations do not have to be functions. Specifically, the for_each() component can be instantiated with any class that has an operator()() defined.

For example, instead of defining a print_name() function, we can use a printer class:

```
// printer.h
#include "names.h"
#include <fstream>

class printer {          // functional object
  unsigned count;
  ostream& out;
public:
  printer(ostream& o);
  void operator()(const person& p);
};

printer::printer(ostream& o)
  : out(o), count(0) {}

void printer::operator()(const person& p)
{
  out.width(2);
  out << count << ' ' << p.n << endl;
  ++count;
}
```

This class encapsulates not only the output destination, but also some additional formatting state: it provides a sequence number next to each person's name. Obviously, we could define other semantics. But we have avoided tying the program to an inflexible design through global data. The final example program uses an instance of the printer class to effect output. It also uses a second address list file for input:

```
#include "stl"
#include "printer.h"
```

```
int main() // Example 10: merge 2 address lists
{
  vector<person> list;

// input:
  ifstream in("address.list");
  vector<person>::iterator put(list, list.end());
  istream_iterator<person> input(in), eof(0)
  copy(input, eof, put);

  ifstream in2("other.list");
  istream_iterator<person> input2(in2);
  copy(input2, eof, put);

// process:
  sort(list.begin(), list.end());
  unique(list.begin(),list.end());
// output:
  printer p = cout;
  for_each(list.begin(), list.end(), p);

  return 0;
}
```

This program performs a classic "merge/purge" operation, combining mailing lists and eliminating duplicates. Once the sequence is sorted, `unique()` removes all but the first in any run of duplicated items, using == to compare for equality. Together with the `printer` object's formatting, it uses the equality defined for persons to produce output such as:

```
0 Mike Ball
1 Peter Becker
2 Greg Comeau
3 Bruce Eckel
4 Thomas Keffer
5 Andrew Koenig
6 Josee Lajoie
7 J. Lawrence Podmolik
8 Jerry Schwarz
```

```
 9 Alex Stepanov
10 Bjarne Stroustrup
11 Mike Vilot
```

With this final example, we can see how the simple ideas of searching and sorting can be important in useful programs. An obvious generalization would be processing a list of files given as command line arguments. Other STL components provide the extensibility for even more ambitious uses.

Other Library Elements

The STL library is comprehensive and contains many more components than these example programs have used. Tables 1–3 indicate some of the other components contained in the library.

The container components implement a minimal set of data structures commonly found in many general-purpose foundation class libraries is shown in Table 1. The predefined iterators provide support for all the algorithm components is shown in Table 2. The most extensive category includes the algorithmic components is shown in Table 3.

Because the STL components are designed as an extensible foundation, the list of useful components is open-ended.

Conclusion

The HP Standard Template Library provides a collection of general-purpose software components. Like many successful C++ libraries, it provides reliable, efficient, and flexible components. Unlike most similar libraries, however, STL focuses primarily on algorithmic abstractions. The library's implementation relies heavily on the C++ template mechanism for parameterization. It uses very little inheritance and does not rely on dynamic binding through virtual functions. As a result, the performance of STL components is at least as good as the equivalent C or C++ code. In many cases, it is better—using an inlined operation on a functional object is usually less expensive than calling a function through a pointer.

The components are reliable, having been designed with a firm theoretical foundation. A notable aspect of each component's interface is a statement of its time and space complexity requirements and guarantees. Perhaps the most important aspect of STL is the flexibility of using the components with built-in

TABLE 1. *Containters*

Sequences	Associative	
vector	set	multiset
list	map	multimap
deque		
queue		
priority_queue		
stack		

TABLE 2. *Iterators*

input_iterator	output_iterator
forward_iterator	
bidirectional_iterator	
random_access_iterator	
istream_iterator	ostream_iterator

types and pointers as easily as with arbitrary classes. As the example programs in this article have illustrated, this flexibility supports the evolutionary process that is characteristic of *object-oriented design.*

Developers of C++ software component libraries will gain some valuable insights from STL's design. Its decomposition illustrates how effective parameterization can dramatically reduce the size of a library (for example, instead of providing a search member function for every kind of container, STL provides generic algorithms that work with all of them):

> If software components are tabulated as a three-dimensional array, where one dimension represents different data types (e.g., `int`, `double`), the second dimension represents different containers (e.g., vector, linked-list, file), and the third dimension represents different algorithms on the containers (e.g., searching, sorting, rotation), if `i`, `j`, and `k` are the size of the dimensions, then `i * j * k` different versions of code have to be designed. By using template functions that are parameterized by a data type, we need only `j * k` versions. Further, by making our algorithms work on different containers, we need merely `j + k` versions.

Table 3. *Algorithms*	
for_each	
find	find_if
adjacent_find	
count	count_if
mismatch	
equal	
search	
copy	copy_backward
swap	swap_ranges
transform	
replace	replace_if
replace_copy	replace_copy_if
rill	fill_n
generate	generate_n
remove	remove_if
remove_copy	remove_copy_if
unique	unique_copy
reverse	reverse_copy
rotate	rotate_copy
random_shuffle	
partition	stable_partition
sort	stable_sort
partial_sort	partial_sort_copy
nth_element	
lower_bound	upper_bound
equal_range	
binary_search	
merge	inplace_merge
accumulate	inner-product
partial_sum	adjacent_difference

This significantly simplifies the library's design. It also makes it possible to use components in the library together with user defined components in a very flexible way.

C++ developers who use STL components will gain some valuable assistance through advantages in quality, reliability, efficiency, and time to market.

References

1. Vilot, M., and G. Booch. Component library design considerations, *C++ Report,* 4(5):18.
2. Vilot, M., and G. Booch, Component design considerations, *C++ Report,* 4(7):18.
3. Stepanov, A., and D. R. Musser. Algorithm-oriented generic software library development, HPL-92-65 (R.1), Hewlett-Packard Company, Palo Alto CA, Nov. 1993.
4. Stepanov, A., and M. Lee. The standard template library, Doc. No. X3J16/94-0030 WG21/N0417, 25 Jan. 1994.
5. Stepanov, A., and M. Lee. The standard template library, Doc. No. X3J16/94-0030R1 WG21/N0417, 7 Mar. 1994.
6. Stepanov, and Lee. The Standard template library, Doc. No. X3J16/94-0095 WG21/N0482, 31 May 1994.
7. Booch, G., *Object-Oriented Analysis and Design,* Benjamin/Cummings, Redwood City CA, 1994.
8. Dewhurst, S. Control abstraction, *C++ Journal,* Fall 1990: 23.
9. Davidson, A. More on the USENIX C++ Advanced topics workshop, *C++ Report,* 3(9):1.
10. Koenig, A. Applicators, manipulators, and function objects, *C++ Journal,* Summer 1990: 21.
11. Coggins, J. Design criteria for C++ libraries, USENIX C++ Conference, San Francisco CA, 9–11 Apr. 1990: 25.
12. Jossman, P., E. Scheibel, and J. Shank. Climbing the C++ learning tree, USENIX C++ Conference, San Francisco CA, 9–11 Apr. 1990: 11.
13. Keffer, T. The design and architecture of Tools.h++, *C++ Report,* 5(5): 28.
14. Horstmann, C. Understanding the iostream library, *C++ Report,* 6(4): 23.

Making a Vector Fit for a Standard

Bjarne Stroustrup

An important detail of the design of a vector template class is discussed: how to generalize a vector in such a way that it can be used conveniently with a variety of memory models. The presentation progresses through a series of versions of the vector class from the most obvious to the vector from Alex Stepanov's STL library, which is part of the C++ standard. Each example presents a problem, a solution to that problem, and notes that the simplest and most common uses of vector remain unchanged under the various generalizations.

The STL Library

By now, we know what a `vector` looks like—it is a class template taking the element type as a template argument and the size as a constructor argument:

```
template<class T> class vector {
    // ...
};

vector<int> v(10);
```

The generic algorithm library by Stepanov and Musser,[1] the direct ancestor of Stepanov's STL library, had one of those; its other details were what you would expect from a good foundation library: convenient, efficient, not bloated, etc. These details are not relevant to the points I want to make here, so I will not discuss them here.

What makes this particular `vector` worth discussing is that it is part of a large, systematic, clean, formally sound, comprehensible, elegant, and efficient framework of containers, iterators, and algorithms. In addition, it has been accepted as part of the library of the upcoming ANSI/ISO C++ standard.

Let me present a brief example to give a hint why the STL[2] is simple, flexible, and powerful enough to be part of the standard. If you use STL containers directly, you write code exactly as usual:

```
vector<complex> vc(10);

void h()
{
  // ...
  vc[3] = complex(7,3);
  vc[5] = vc[7];
  // ...
}

void print_complex_vec(const vector<complex>& v)
{
  for (complex* p=v.begin(); p!=v.end(); p++) cout<<*p;
}
```

That's very similar to C++ code or even to plain C code. The member functions `begin()` and `end()` yield pointers to the first element and to the one-beyond-the-last element of the `vector`, respectively. This is exactly the way `&a[0]` and `&a[sizeof(a)/sizeof(*a)]` can be used for an ordinary C++ array:

```
complex a[100];

for (complex* p=&a[0]; p!=&a[100]; p++) cout<<*p;
```

Only if you want to write generic code do you need to use fancier stuff and even that's pretty easy. For example:

```
template<class C> void print_all(const C& c)
{
  for (C::const_iterator p=c.begin(); p!=c.end(); p++)
      cout<<*p;
}
```

Here, `C::const_iterator` is an appropriate iterator type for the container `C`.

Typically `C::const_iterator` is `const T*` where `T` is the element type of the container `C`. The `print_all()` function can now be called for a variety of containers. For example:

```
void gg(const vector<complex>& vc, const list<dude>& dl)
{
  print_all(vc); // print the members of vector<complex>
                 // vc
  print_all(dl); // print the members of list<dude> dl
}
```

where `list` is another STL container. However, this article isn't a tutorial on STL use, but a discussion of a design detail, so I'll not pursue this line of thought further here. STL tutorial material is available.[3–5]

The Problem

At first glance, the original `vector` looked good enough for a standard and we knew that it had been extensively tested and used. However, we wanted to specify the STL with greater precision and formality and ensure that its parts didn't have unnecessary restrictions and limitations, so we started asking formal and practical questions:

- In which way is the specification of `vector` overconstrained?
- What assumptions have been made in the STL that will prevent users from applying `vector` in ways we haven't anticipated?
- What assumptions are not really necessary?
- What uses have people had for other vector-like classes that hasn't been tried for `vector`?

In this context, *we* refers to a loosely organized group of people who have worked to polish the original STL into a library suitable for a standard. This group included Tom Keffer, Andrew Koenig, Meng Lee, David Musser, Nathan Myers, Larry Podmolik, Alex Stepanov, Bjarne Stroustrup, and Mike Vilot. In fact, we never met around a table as a complete group; in addition to face-to-face meetings, e-mail was essential. Throughout, Alex Stepanov was the driving force, though, the one who together with Meng Lee tested out the ideas by implementation, who discovered the problems with the intermediate versions, and had the final say in the design decisions. This was an example of a group contributing to a design, rather than design by committee. Many algorithms rely on iterators pointing to elements of a vector. The simplest example of an iterator is a pointer, and the simplest example of an algorithm relying on iterators is a distance function returning the number of elements between pointers:

```
template<class T> ptrdiff_t distance(const T* p1, const T*
p2)
{
  return p2-p1;
}
```

Many sorting and searching algorithms rely on constructs similar to this.

The type `ptrdiff_t` was chosen as the return type because that is the standard (C and C++) type of the result of a pointer subtraction. However, using `ptrdiff_t` prevents us from having truly large vectors. Using `ptrdiff_t` means that the size of a vector must—in a portable program—be limited to the largest `ptrdiff_t` on the smallest conforming C++ implementation. This seems unreasonable for a standard—though it would be acceptable for a foundation library intended for a single platform and for a limited range of applications.

In particular, I have multigigabyte files that I would like to poke around in and I have an iterator type that allows me to address them. In general, I would like my algorithms to work on all `vectors` and for any iterator type. For example, I want `distance()` to be a standard library template function (as it is in STL) rather than having to write my own for each iterator type as I would have to if the return type was an unacceptably small `ptrdiff_t`. But how?

Extra Template Parameters

We must somehow make the type used to represent the distance between two elements a parameter. For example:

```
template<class T, class Dist> class vector {
  // ...
};
```

Now I can write:

```
template<class Iter, class Dist> void distance(Iter i1,
Iter i2, Dist& d)
{
  d = i2-i1;
}
```

However, declaring vectors like this:

```
vector<int, ptrdiff_t> vi(10);
vector<complex, ptrdiff_t> vc(20);
```

seems awkward, and the second template argument will be redundant for most people most of the time. To be acceptable, the Dist argument must be optional with a good default. In other words:

```
template<class T, class Dist = ptrdiff_t> class vector {
  // ...
};
vector<int> vi(10);               // that is, vector<int,
                                  // ptrdiff_t> vi(10);
vector<complex> vc(20);           // that is, vector<complex,
                                  // ptrdiff_t> vc(20);
```

So far, so good. However, ptrdiff_t was only the tip of the iceberg.

An Aside: Dodging a type deduction problem

The distance function is used like this:

```
void f(int* p1, int* p2, Iter<int> i1, Iter<int> i2)
{
  ptrdiff_t d1;
  distance(p1,p2,d1);

  IterDiff d2;
  distance(i1,i2,d2);
}
```

I consider this pretty ugly. I'd prefer to write:

```
void f(int* p1, int* p2, Iter<int> i1, Iter<int> i2)
{
  ptrdiff_t d1 = distance(p1,p2);
  IterDiff d2 = distance(i1,i2);
}
```

However, I don't know how to write a sufficiently general `distance()` function to do that. I can think of two ways of doing this, but neither is allowed in C++.

The first way would be to select a `distance()` function based on both its argument types and its return type. For several reasons, I'm reluctant to extend C++ in that direction.

The second is somehow to deduce the difference type from the type of the iterator. In principle, that is possible. Consider:

```
template<class Iter> Iter::diff_t distance(Iter i1, Iter i2)
{
  return i2-i1;
}
```

This works if the iterator type `Iter` has a member type `Iter::diff_t`. However, this technique doesn't extend to the most common iterator types: built-in pointers. For example, an attempt to call this last version of `distance` with an ordinary pointer would lead to a type error:

```
void g(int* p1, int* p2)
{
  int d = distance(p1,p2); // error: int*::diff_t
        // int* has no member diff_t
}
```

To avoid having to face such language-technical problems and design extensions to solve them, we chose to define the STL `distance()` to take three parameters:

```
template<class Iter, class Dist> void distance(Iter i1,
Iter i2, Dist& d)
  // place the distance between i1 and i2 in d
{
  d = i2-i1;
}
```

It isn't as pretty as I'd like, but it is simple and it works.

Dealing with too Many Template Parameters

When Alex Stepanov revised the STL to introduce a template parameter to represent the iterator difference type, he found several other items that by the same logic ought to be template parameters. This led to this bloated definition:

```
template <class T,
      class PrimaryIterator = T*,
      class ConstIterator = const T*,
      class Size = size_t,
      class Allocator = vector_allocator<T>,
      Size initial_vector_size = 16U>
class vector {
  // ...
};
```

My comment was along the lines "Yuck! It is legal, but is it right? There must be a way of bundling those parameters. How about making all the default arguments members of a class?" A couple of days later, Alex came back with a new `vector`:

```
template<class T, class Alloc = allocator<T> > class
vector {
  // ...
};
```

An allocator defines the memory model for a `vector` type. Here is the default allocator:

```
template <class T> class allocator {
public:
  typedef T* pointer;
  typedef const T* const_pointer;
  typedef T value_type;

  typedef size_t size_type;
  typedef ptrdiff_t difference_type;

  allocator();
  ~allocator();
```

```
    pointer allocate(size_type);      // get array of Ts

    void deallocate(pointer);         // free array of Ts
    size_type init_page_size();       // optimal size of
                                      // initial buffer

    size_type max_size();             // the largest possible
                                      // size of buffer

};
```

The member functions of `allocator` provide a means for the `vector` to allocate and free storage. The definition of `vector` relies on the types and functions specified by its allocator. For example:

```
template<class T, class Alloc = allocator<T> > class
vector {
public:
  typedef Alloc::pointer iterator;

  typedef Alloc::const_pointer const_iterator;
  typedef T value_type;
  typedef Alloc::size_type size_type;
  typedef Alloc::difference_type difference_type;

  // ...

  iterator elems; // start of elements

  // ...
};
```

The implementation of `vector` operations can now use the `Alloc` parameter and the `typedef`s to avoid having to make assumptions about pointers and sizes. For example, this function makes room for more elements in a vector by moving all current elements to newly allocated space:

```
template<class T, class Alloc = allocator<T> >
  T& vector<T,Alloc>::reserve(size_type n)
  {
    iterator p = Alloc::allocate(n);
    // copy elements elems to p
```

```
        iterator old_elems = elems;
        elems = p;
        // adjust size
        Alloc::deallocate(old_elems);
    }
```

Naturally, users can ignore the `Alloc` parameter when they don't need it:

```
vector<int> v(10);
```

If you want to supply your own allocator, you can do it like this:

```
vector< int, your_allocator<int> > v2(10);
```

The `typedef`s can be used to write code that makes only a few assumptions about the types involved:

```
template<class C> void print_all(const C& c)
{
    for (C::const_iterator p=c.begin(); p!=c.end(); p++)
    cout<<*p;
}
```

Had `C::const_iterator` not been used, the user would have had to pass a value type along. For example:

```
template<class C, class T> void print_all2(const C& c)
{
    for (T* p=c.begin(); p!=c.end(); p++) cout<<*p;
}
```

This is both less convenient and more error-prone. For example, `print_all2()` would not work for a `vector` keeping its elements in secondary storage and relying on a clever iterator type for access rather than ordinary pointers (see the section "An example.").

The original `print_all()` handles this correctly by default.

Note that `allocate()` returns uninitialized storage. This is unfortunate because it allows raw memory to masquerade as objects of type `T`. However, this helps to prevent inefficiencies that might arise from default initialization followed by copy construction. Alternative solutions appear to require too much additional work from users of allocators and are hard to express in the presence of multiple memory models. In particular, systems with more than one kind of pointer to data becomes hard to deal with unless an allocator returns an iterator. Fortunately, the potential problems need to be dealt with only by container implementors; this implementation detail is below the level where most users operate.

Generalizing the Allocator

As defined previously, an `allocator` is a template of `T`. However, the implementation of a `vector` doesn't usually just allocate objects of type `T`. A realistic implementation allocates large chunks of memory, will often need to manipulate raw memory directly, defer initialization of members until actual use, allocate objects of other types for housekeeping, etc. These are not services one would expect from an `allocator<T>` but for a more general allocator.

This point becomes more obvious when you consider `vector` as part of a framework of container classes that behave similarly wherever possible. In particular, container classes should be parameterized with information about their memory model in a uniform manner. For example, a `list` should be parameterized by an `allocator` in the same way as a `vector`. Many implementations of a list of `T` allocate link objects rather than `T`s. This is not what one would expect an `allocator<T>` to handle.

Consequently, we decided that the parameter describing allocation should be a template:

```
template<
  class T,
  template<class U> class Alloc = allocator
  > class vector {
public:
  typedef Alloc<T>::pointer iterator;
  typedef Alloc<T>::const_pointer const_iterator;
  typedef T value_type;

  typedef Alloc<T>::size_type size_type;
  typedef Alloc<T>::difference_type difference_type;

  // ...
};
```

Again, the default and typical usage is unchanged:

```
vector<int> v(10);
```

Supplying your own allocator actually becomes marginally simpler:

```
vector<int,your_allocator> v2(10);
```

Except for such cosmetic details, code implementing and using `vectors` remain unaffected by this generalization of the `Alloc` template parameter. The generalization is more important for containers such as `lists`, `deques`, `sets`, and `maps` where the implementation tends to manipulate several different types. For example:

```
template <class T, template <class U>
class Alloc = allocator>
class list {
  // ...
  struct list_node { /* ... */ };
  // ...
  typedef Alloc<list_node>::pointer link_type;
  // ...
};

template<class T, template<class U>
class Alloc = allocator>
void list<T,Alloc>::push_front(const T& x)
{
  link_type p = Alloc<list_node>::allocate(1);
  // use p to link x onto the list
}
```

The reason we don't want to use `new` directly here is that secondary data structures, such as `list_nodes`, should go in the same kind of storage as the container itself and its elements. Passing the `allocator` along in this way solves a serious problem for database users. Without this ability (or an equivalent) a container class cannot be written to work with and without a database and with more than one database. Knowledge of the database would have to be built into the container. For me, this was an unanticipated benefit of parameterization by allocator and a strong indication that the design was on the right track. I had experienced the problem with databases and libraries, but knew of no general solution.

An Aside

When dealing with databases one often wants to allocate both a `vector` and its elements in the same arena. The most obvious way to do that is to use the placement syntax to specify the arena for the `vector` and then to give the `vector` a suitable allocator to use for the allocations it performs. For example:

```
new(myalloc) vector<mytype,myalloc>(100);
```

The repetition of `myalloc` isn't going to be popular. One solution is to define a template to avoid that:

```
template <class T, template <class U> Alloc = allocator>
  Alloc<T>::pointer newT(Alloc<T>::size_type s)
  {
    return myalloc<T,Alloc>::allocate(s);
  }
```

This allows us to write

```
newT<mytype,myalloc>(100);
```

The default case can be written as either

```
newT<mytype>(100);
```

or

```
new mytype(100);
```

The template notation approximates the built-in notation for allocation in both terseness and clarity.

An Example

Consider how to provide a `vector` with an `allocator` that makes it possible to work with gigantic sets of elements located on secondary storage and accessed through pointer-like objects that manage transfer of data to and from main memory.

First, we must define iterators to allow convenient access:

```
template<class T> class Iter {
  // usual operators (++, *, etc.)
  // doing buffered access to disk
};

template<class T> class cIter {
  // usual operators (++, *, etc.)
```

```
    // doing buffered access to disk (no writes allowed)
};
```

Next, we can define an allocator that can be used to manage memory for elements:

```
template<class T>
class giant_alloc {
public:
  typedef Iter<T> pointer;
  typedef cIter<T> const_pointer;
  typedef T value_type;

  typedef unsigned long size_type;
  typedef long difference_type;

  giant_alloc();
  ~giant_alloc();

  pointer allocate(size_type);          // get array of Ts
  void deallocate(pointer);             // free array of Ts

  size_type init_page_size();           // optimal size of
                                        // initial buffer
  size_type max_size();                 // the largest possible
                                        // size of buffer
};
```

Functions written in terms of iterators will now work with these "giant" vectors. For example:

```
void f(vector<rec,giant_alloc>& giant)
{
  // ...
  print_all(giant);
}

vector<rec,giant_alloc> v(100000000);

void g()
```

```
{
  f(v);
}
```

One might question the wisdom of writing a multigigabyte file to cout like this, though.

Compiler Problems

What can I do if my compiler doesn't yet support new language features such as default template arguments? The original STL used a very conservative set of language features. It was tested with Borland, Cfront, Lucid, Watcom, and—I suspect—other compilers. Until your compiler supplier catches up, use a version of STL without the newer features. That was the way the revised STL was tested.

For example, if default template arguments are a problem, you might use a version that doesn't use the extra template parameters. For example:

```
template<class T> class vector {
  // ...
};

vector<int> vi(10);
```

instead of

```
template<class T, template<class U>
class Alloc = allocator> class vector {
  // ...
};

vector<int> vi(10);
```

For the majority of uses, the default is sufficient, and removing the Alloc argument restricts the uses of the library but doesn't change the meaning of the uses that remain.

Alternatively, you can use macro trickery to temporarily circumvent the limitation. During testing, it was determined that for every C++ compiler supporting templates, every such problem has a similarly simple temporary workaround.

Conclusion

Adding a template argument describing a memory model to a container template adds an important degree of flexibility. In particular, a single template parameter can describe a memory model so that both the implementor of the container and its users can write code independently of any particular model. Default template arguments make this generality invisible to users who don't care to know about it.

Acknowledgments

Brian Kernighan, Nathan Myers, and Alex Stepanov made many constructive comments on previous versions of this article.

References

1. Stepanov, A., and Musser, D. R. Algorithm-oriented generic software library development, HP Laboratories Technical Report HPL-92-66 (R.1). Nov. 1993.
2. Stepanov, A., and M. Lee, The standard template library, ISO Programming language C++ project. Doc No: X3J16/94-0095, WG21/N0482, May 1994.
3. Koenig, A. Templates and generic algorithms, *Journal of Object-Oriented Programming,* 7(3).
4. Koenig, A. Generic iterators, *Journal of Object-Oriented Programming,* 7(4).
5. Vilot, M. J. An Introduction to the STL library, *C++ Report,* 6(8).

Last Thoughts

A PERSPECTIVE ON ISO C++

BJARNE STROUSTRUP
bs@research.att.com

AS C++ PROGRAMMERS, WE ALREADY FEEL THE IMPACT OF THE WORK of the ANSI/ISO C++ standards committee. Yet the ink is hardly dry on the first official draft of the standard. Already, we can use language features only hinted at in the ARM[1] and *The C++ Programming Language* (second edition), compilers are beginning to show improved compatibility, implementations of the new standard library are appearing, and the recent relative stability of the language definition is allowing extra effort to be spent on implementation quality and tools. This is only the beginning.

We can now with some confidence imagine the poststandard C++ world. To me, it looks good and exciting. I am confident that it will give me something I have been working toward for about 16 years: a language in which I can express my ideas directly; a language suitable for building large, demanding, efficient, real-world systems; a language supported by a great standard library and effective tools. I am confident because most of the parts of the puzzle are already commercially available and tested in real use. The standard will help us to make all of those parts available to hundreds of thousands or maybe even millions of programmers. Conversely, those programmers provide the community necessary to support further advances in quality, programming and design techniques, tools, libraries, and environments. What has been achieved using C++ so far has exceeded my wildest dreams and we must realistically expect that the best is yet to come.

THE LANGUAGE

C++ supports a variety of styles—it is a multiparadigm programming language. The standards process strengthened that aspect of C++ by providing extensions that didn't just support one narrow view of programming but made several styles easier and safer to use in C++. Importantly, these advances have not been bought at the expense of run-time efficiency.

At the beginning of the standards process templates were considered experimental; now they are an integral part of the language, more flexible than originally specified, and an essential foundation for standard library. Generic programming based on templates is now a major tool for C++ programmers.

The support for object-oriented programming (programming using class hierarchies) was strengthened by the provision for run-time type identification, the relaxation of the overriding rules, and the ability to forward declare nested classes.

Large-scale programming—in any style—received major new support from the exception and namespace mechanisms. Like templates, exceptions were considered experimental at the beginning of the standards process. Namespaces evolved from the efforts of many people to find a solution to the problems with name clashes and from efforts to find a way to express logical groupings to complement or replace the facilities for physical grouping provided by the extralinguistic notion of source and header files.

Several minor features were added to make general programming safer and more convenient by allowing the programmer to state more precisely the purpose of some code. The most visible of those are the `bool` type, the explicit type conversion operators, the ability to declare variables in conditions, and the ability to restrict user-defined conversions to explicit construction.

A description of the new features and some of the reasoning that led to their adoption can be found in *The Design and Evolution of C++* (D&E).[6] So can discussions of older features and of features that were considered but didn't make it into C++.

The new features are the most visible changes to the language. However, the cumulative effect of minute changes to more obscure corners of the language and thousands of clarifications of its specification is greater than the effect of any extension. These improvements are essentially invisible to the programmer writing ordinary production code, but their importance to libraries, portability, and compatibility of implementations cannot be overestimated. The minute changes and clarifications also consumed a large majority of the committee's efforts. That is, I believe, also the way things ought to be.

For better or worse, the principle of C++ being "as close to C as possible—and no closer"[3] was repeatedly reaffirmed. C compatibility has been slightly strengthened, and the remaining incompatibilities documented in detail. Basically, if you are a practical programmer rather than a conformance tester, and if you use function prototypes consistently, C appears to be a subset of C++. The fact that every example in *K&R*[2] is (also) a C++ program is no fluke.

Coherence

ISO C++ is not just a more powerful language than the C++ presented in *The C++ Programming Language* (second edition)5; it is also more coherent and a better approximation of my original view of what C++ should be.

The fundamental concept of a statically typed language relying on classes and virtual functions to support object-oriented programming, templates to support generic programming, and providing low-level facilities to support detailed systems programming is sound. I don't think this statement can be proven in any strict sense, but I have seen enough great C++ code and enough successful large-scale projects using C++ for it to satisfy me of its validity.

You can also write ghastly code in C++, but so what? We can do that in any language. In the hands of people who have bothered learning its fairly simple key concepts, C++ is helpful in guiding program organization and in detecting errors.

C++ is not a "kitchen sink language" as evil tongues are fond of claiming. Its features are mutually reinforcing and all have a place in supporting C++'s intended range of design and programming styles. Everyone agrees that C++ could be improved by removing features. However, there is absolutely no agreement which features could be removed. In this, C++ resembles C.

During standardization, only one feature that I don't like was added. We can now initialize a static constant of integral type with a constant expression within a class definition. For example:

```
class X {          // in .h file
    static const int c = 42;
    char v[c];
    // ...
};

int X::c = 42;     // in .c file
```

I consider this half-baked and prefer:

```
class X {
    enum { c = 42 };
    char v[c];
    // ...
};
```

I also oppose a generalization of in-class initialization as an undesirable complication for both implementors and users. However, this is an example where reasonable people can agree to disagree. Standardization is a democratic process, and I certainly don't get my way all the time—nor should any person or group.

AN EXAMPLE

Enough talk! Here is an example that illustrates many of the new language features.* It is one answer to the common question "how can I read objects from a stream, determine that they are of acceptable types, and then use them?" For example:

```
void user(istream& ss)
{
  io_obj* p = get_obj(ss);   // read object from stream

  if (Shape* sp = dynamic_cast<Shape*>(p)) { // is it a
                                             // Shape?
    sp->draw();          // use the Shape
                         // ...
  }
  else// oops: non-shape in Shape file
          throw unexpected_shape();
}
```

The function `user()` deals with shapes exclusively through the abstract class `Shape` and can therefore use every kind of shape. The construct

```
dynamic_cast<Shape*>(p)
```

performs a run-time check to see whether `p` really points to an object of class `Shape` or a class derived from `Shape`. If so, it returns a pointer to the `Shape` part of that object. If not, it returns the null pointer. Unsurprisingly, this is called a dynamic cast. It is the primary facility provided to allow users to take advantage of run-time type information (RTTI). The `dynamic_cast` allows convenient use of RTTI where necessary without encouraging switching on type fields.

---

*Borrowed with minor changes (and with permission from the author :-) from D&E.[6]

The use of `dynamic_cast` here is essential because the object I/O system can deal with many other kinds of objects and the user may accidentally have opened a file containing perfectly good objects of classes that this user has never heard of.

Note the declaration in the condition of the if-statement:

```
if (Shape* sp = dynamic_cast<Shape*>(p)) { ... }
```

The variable `sp` is declared within the condition, initialized, and its value checked to determine which branch of the if-statement is executed. A variable declared in a condition must be initialized and is in scope in the statements controlled by the condition (only). This is both more concise and less error-prone than separating the declaration, the initialization, or the test from each other and leaving the variable around after the end of its intended use the way it is traditionally done:

```
Shape* sp = dynamic_cast<Shape*>(p);
if (sp) { ... }
// sp in scope here
```

This "miniature object I/O system" assumes that every object read or written is of a class derived from `io_obj`. Class `io_obj` must be a polymorphic type to allow us to use `dynamic_cast`. For example:

```
class io_obj {   // polymorphic
public:
  virtual io_obj* clone();
  virtual ~io_obj() { }
};
```

The critical function in the object I/O system is `get_obj()` that reads data from an `istream` and creates class objects based on that data. Let me assume that the data representing an object on an input stream is prefixed by a string identifying the object's class. The job of `get_obj()` is to read that string prefix and call a function capable of creating and initializing an object of the right class. For example:

```
typedef io_obj* (*PF)(istream&);
```

```
// maps strings to creation functions
map<string,PF> io_map;

io_obj* get_obj(istream& s)
{
  string str;
// read initial word into str
  if (get_word(s,str) == false)
    throw no_class();

  PF f = io_map[str];  // lookup `str' to get function
// no match for `str'
  if (f == 0) throw unknown_class();
  return f(s);         // construct object from stream
}
```

The map called io_map is an associative array that holds pairs of name strings and functions that can construct objects of the class with that name. The associate array is one of the most useful and efficient data structures in any language. This particular map type is taken from the C++ standard library. So is the string class.

The get_obj() function throws exceptions to signal errors. An exception thrown by get_obj() can be caught be a direct or indirect caller like this:

```
try {
     // ...
     io_obj* p = get_obj(cin);
     // ...
}
catch (no_class) {
     cerr << "format error on input";
     // ...
}
catch (unknown_class) {
     cerr << "unknown class on input";
     // ...
}
```

A catch clause is entered if (and only if) an exception of its specified type is thrown by code in or invoked from the try block.

We could, of course, define class `Shape` the usual way by deriving it from `io_obj` as required by `user()`:

```
class Shape : public io_obj {
  // ...
  virtual void draw() = 0;    // pure virtual function
  // ...
};
```

However, it would be more interesting (and also more realistic) to use some previously defined `Shape` class hierarchy unchanged by incorporating it into a hierarchy that adds the information needed by our I/O system:

```
class iocircle : public Circle, public io_obj {
public:
  io_obj* clone()       // override io_obj::clone()
    { return new iocircle(*this); }

  iocircle(istream&);  // initialize from input stream

  static iocircle* new_circle(istream& s)
  {
    return new iocircle(s);
  }
  // ...
};
```

The `iocircle(istream&)` constructor initializes an object with data from its `istream` argument. The `new_circle` function is the one put into the `io_map` to make the class known to the object I/O system. For example:

```
io_map["iocircle"]=&iocircle::new_circle;
```

Other shapes are constructed in the same way:

```
class iotriangle : public Triangle, public io_obj {
  // ...
};
```

If the provision of the object I/O scaffolding becomes tedious, a template might be used:

```
template<class T>
class io : public T, public io_obj {
public:
  io_obj* clone() { return new io(*this); }

  io(istream&); // initialize from input stream

  static io* new_io(istream& s)
  {
    return new io(s);
  }
};
```

Given this, we could define `iocircle` like this:

```
typedef io<Circle> iocircle;
```

We would still have to define `io<Circle>::io(istream&)` explicitly, though, because it needs to know about the details of `Circle`.

This simple object I/O system may not do everything anyone ever wanted, but it almost fits on a single page, is general and extensible, is potentially efficient, and the key mechanisms have many uses. Undoubtedly, you would have designed and implemented an object I/O system somewhat differently. Please take a few minutes to consider how this general design strategy compares to your favorite scheme, and also think about what it would take to implement this scheme in pre-*ISO* C++ or some other language.

THE LIBRARY

I have long regretted that I was not initially able to provide C++ with a good enough standard library. In particular, I would have liked to provide a string class and a set of container classes (such as lists, vectors, and maps). However, I did not know how to design containers that were elegant enough, general enough, and efficient enough to serve the varied needs of the C++ community. Also, until I found the time to design the template mechanism, I had no good way of specifying type-safe containers.

Naturally, most programmers want essentially everything useful included in the standard library. That way, they assume, all that they need will be supplied elegantly, efficiently, and free of charge. Unfortunately, that is just a dream. Facilities will be designed by people with different views of how to do things, limited time, and limited foresight. Also, implementors will find some way of getting paid for their efforts. As the library grows, so does the chances of mistakes, controversy, inefficiencies, and cost.

Consequently, the scope of the standard library had to be restricted to something a relatively small group of volunteers could handle, something that most people would agree to be important, something most people could easily learn to use, something that would be efficient enough for essentially all people to use, and something C++ implementors could ship without exorbitant cost. In addition, the standard library must be a help, rather then a hindrance, to the C++ library industry.

The facilities provided by the standard library can be classified like this:

1. Basic run-time language support (for allocation, *RTTI*, etc.).

2. The standard C library (with very minor modifications to minimize violations of the type system).

3. Strings and I/O streams (with support for international character sets and localization).

4. A framework of containers (such as, `vector`, `list`, `set`, and `map`) and algorithms using containers (such as general traversals, sorts, and merges).

5. Support for numeric computation (complex numbers plus vectors with arithmetic operations, *BLAS*-like and generalized slices, and semantics designed to ease optimization).

This is quite a considerable set of facilities. The description of the standard library takes up about two thirds of the space in the standards document. Outside the standard C library, the standard C++ library consists mainly of templates. There are dozens of template classes and hundreds of template functions.

The main criteria for including a class in the library was that it would somehow be used by almost every C++ programmer (both novices and experts), that it could be provided in a general form that did not add significant overheads compared to a simpler version of the same facility, and that simple uses should be easy to learn. Essentially, the C++ standard library provides the most common fundamental data structures together with the fundamental algorithms used on them.

The standard library is described in Stepanov[7] and Vilot,[8] so let me just give a short—but complete—example of its use:

```
#include <string>      // get the string facilities
#include <fstream>     // get the I/O facilities
#include <vector>      // get the vector
#include <algorithms>  // get the operations on containers

int main()
{
  string from, to;     // standard string of char
  cin >> from >> to;   // get source and target file names

  istream_iterator<string> ii
    = ifstream(from.c_str());        // input iterator
  istream_iterator<string> eos;      // input sentinel

  ostream_iterator<string> oo
    = ofstream(to.c_str());          // output iterator

  vector<string> buf(ii,eos);// standard vector class
                             // initialized from input

  sort(buf.begin(),buf.end());       // sort the buffer
  unique_copy(buf.begin(),buf.end(),oo); // copy buffer to
                   // output discarding
                   // replicated values

  return ii && oo;             // return error state
}
```

As with any other library, parts will look strange at first glance. However, experience shows that most people get used to it fast.

I/O is done using streams. To avoid overflow problems, the standard library `string` class is used.

The standard container `vector` is used for buffering; its constructor reads input; the standard functions `sort()` and `unique_copy()` sort and output the strings.

Iterators are used to make the input and output streams look like containers that you can read from and write to, respectively. The standard library's notion of a container is built on the notion of "something you can get a series of values from or write a series of values to." To read something you need the place to begin reading from and the place to end; to write simply a place to start writing to. The word used for "place" in this context is *iterator.*

The standard library's notion of containers, iterators, and algorithms is based on work by Alex Stepanov and others.[7]

The Standards Process

Initially, I feared that the standardization effort would lead to confusion and instability. People would clamor for all kinds of changes and improvements, and a large committee was unlikely to have a firm and consistent view of what aspects of programming and design ought to be directly supported by C++ and how. However, I judged the risks worth the potential benefits. By now, I am sure that I underestimated both the risks and the benefits. I am also confident that we have surmounted most of the technical challenges and will cope with the remaining technical and political problems; they are not as daunting as the many already handled by the committee. I expect that we will have a formally approved standard in a year plus or minus a few months. Essentially all of that time will be spent finding precise wording for resolutions we already agree on and ferreting out further obscure details to nail down.

The *ISO* (international) and *ANSI* (*USA* national) standards groups for C++ meet three times a year. The first technical meeting was in 1990, and I have attended every meeting so far. Meetings are hard work; dawn to midnight. I find most committee members great people to work with, but I need a week's vacation to recover from a meeting—which of course I never get.

In addition to coming up with technically sound solutions, the committees are chartered to seek consensus. In this context, consensus means a large majority plus an honest attempt to settle remaining differences. There will be "remaining differences" because there are many things that reasonable people can disagree about.

Anyone willing and able to pay the ANSI membership fee and attend two meetings can vote (unless they work for a company who already has a representative). In addition, members of the committee bring in opinions from a wide variety of sources. Importantly, the national delegations from several countries conduct their own additional meetings and bring what they find to the joint ANSI/ISO meetings.

All in all, this is an open and democratic process. The number of people representing organizations with millions of lines of C++ precludes radical changes. For example, a significant increase or decrease in C compatibility would have been politically infeasible. Explaining anything significant to a large diverse group—such as 80 people at a C++ standards meeting—takes time, and once a problem is understood, building a consensus around a particular solution takes even longer. It seems that for a major change, the time from the initial presentation of an idea until its acceptance was usually a minimum of three meetings; that is, a year.

Fortunately, the aim of the standards process isn't to create the perfect programming language. It was hard at times, but the committee consistently decided to respect real-world constraints—including compatibility with C and older variants of C++. The result was a language with most of its warts intact. However, its run-time efficiency, space efficiency, and flexibility were also preserved, and the integration between features were significantly improved. In addition to showing necessary restraint and respect for existing code, the committee showed commendable courage in addressing the needs for extensions and library facilities.

Curiously enough, the most significant aspect of the committee's work may not be the standard itself. The committee provided a forum where issues could be discussed, proposals could be presented, and where implementors could benefit from the experience of people outside their usual circle. Without this, I suspect C++ would have fractured into competing dialects by now.

Challenges

Anyone who thinks the major software development problems are solved by simply using a better programming language is dangerously naive. We need all the help we can get and a programming language is only part of the picture. A better programming language, such as C++, does help, though. However, like any other tool it must be used in a sensible and competent manner without disregarding other important components of the larger software development process.

I hope that the standard will lead to an increased emphasis on design and programming styles that takes advantage of C++. The weaknesses in the compatibility of current compilers encourage people to use only a subset of the language and provides an excuse for people who for various reasons prefer to use styles from other languages that are sub-optimal for C++. I hope to see such native C++ styles supported by significant new libraries.

I expect the standard to lead to significant improvements in the quality of all kinds of tools and environments. A stable language provides a good target for such work and frees energy that so far has been absorbed tracking an evolving language and incompatible implementations.

C++ and its standard library are better than many considered possible and better than many are willing to believe. Now we "just" have to use it and support it better. This is going to be challenging, interesting, productive, profitable, and fun!

Acknowledgments

The first draft of this paper was written at 37,000 feet en route home from the Monterey standards meeting. Had the designer of my laptop provided a longer battery life, this paper would have been longer, though presumably also more thoughtful.

The standard is the work of literally hundreds of volunteers. Many have devoted hundreds of hours of their precious time to the effort. I'm especially grateful to the hard-working practical programmers who have done this in their scant spare time and often at their own expense. I'm also grateful to the thousands of people who—through many channels—have made constructive comments on C++ and its emerging standard.

References

1. Ellis, M.A. and B. Stroustrup. *The Annotated C++ Reference Manual.* Addison-Wesley, Reading, MA. 1990.
2. Kernighan, B.W., and D.M. Ritchie. *The C Programming Language,* second ed. Prentice-Hall, Englewood Cliffs, NJ, 1988.
3. Koenig, A., and B. Stroustrup. As close as possible to C—But no closer, *C++ Report,* 1(7), 1989.
4. Koenig, A., Ed. *The Working Papers for the ANSI-X3J16 /ISO-SC22-WG21 C++ Standards Committee.*
5. Stroustrup, B. *The C++ Programming Language,* second ed. Addison-Wesley, Reading, MA, 1991.
6. Stroustrup, B. *The Design and Evolution of C++.* Addison-Wesley, Reading, MA, 1994.
7. Stepanov, A., and M. Lee. *The Standard Template Library,* ISO Programming language C++ project, Doc No: X3J16/94-0095, WG21/N0482, May 1994.
8. Vilot, M.J. An introduction to the STL Library, *C++ Report,* 6(8), 1994.

Index

A

B

C

D

E

V

W

Printed in the United States
By Bookmasters